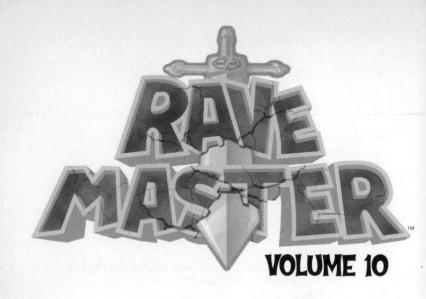

VOLUME 10

Story and Art by
HIRO MASHIMA

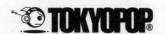

HAMBURG // LONDON // LOS ANGELES // TOKYO

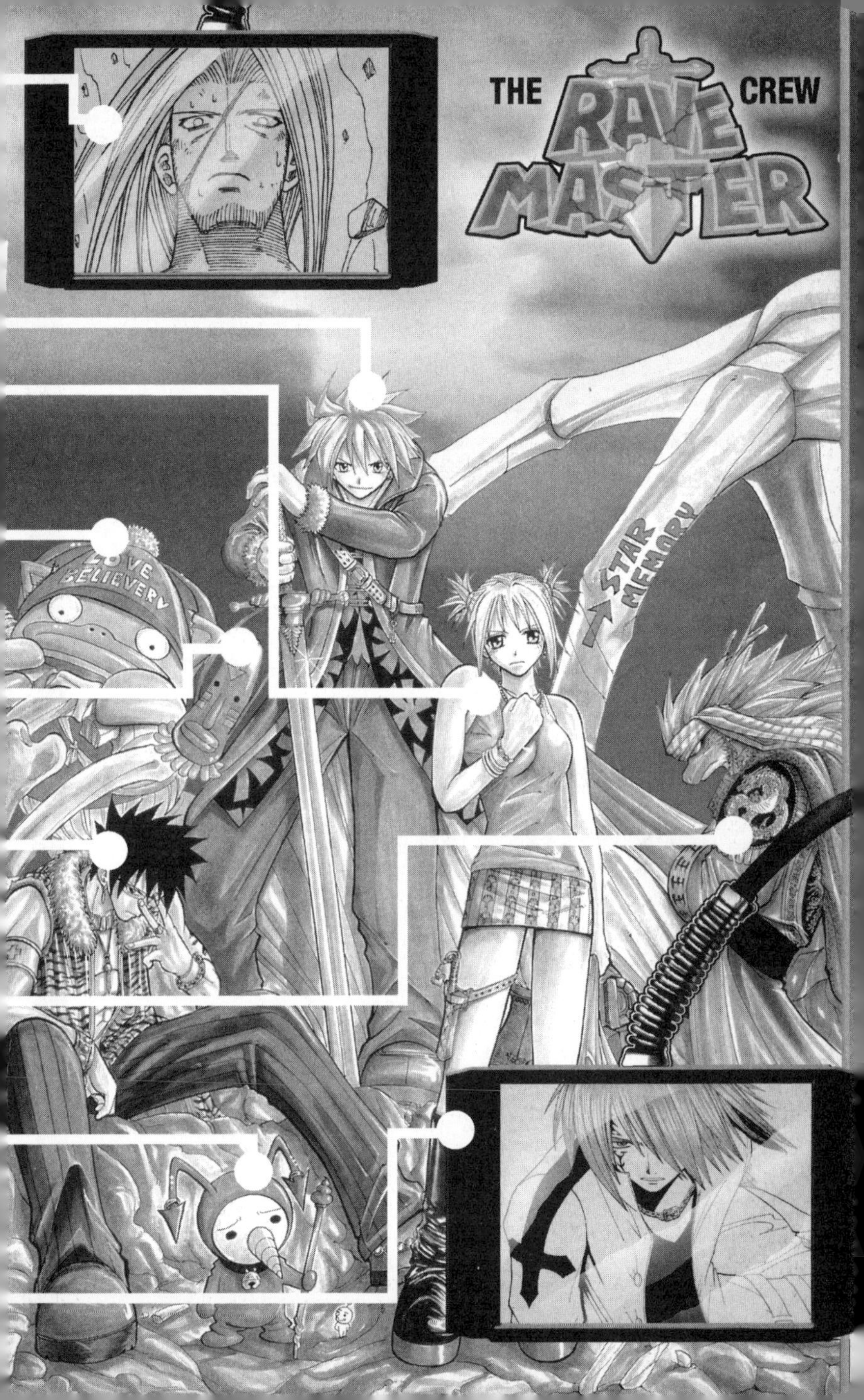
THE RAVE MASTER CREW
LOVE BELIEVER
STAR MEMORY

GALE GLORY

Haru's father and heir to the royal **Symphonia** bloodline. He gave his life to save his son. Before he died, he told Haru about **Star Memory**, a place that holds the collective memories of the universe.

HARU GLORY

A small-town boy turned savior of the world. As the **Rave Master** (the only one capable of using the holy weapon RAVE), Haru set forth to find the missing Rave Stones and defeat Demon Card. He fights with the **Ten Powers Sword,** a weapon that takes on different forms at his command. Now that Demon Card is destroyed, where will his adventures lead him next?

ELIE

The girl without memories. Elie joined Haru on his quest when he promised to help her find out about her past. She's cute, spunky and loves gambling and shopping in equal measures. Locked inside of her is the power of **Etherion.**

RUBY

You'll find out soon enough…

GRIFFON KATO (GRIFF)

Haru and Elie hired Griff and his "horse" Tanchimo to transport them across the Song Continent. Ever since, Griff just decided to tag along.

MUSICA

A **"Silverclaimer"** (an alchemist who can shape silver at will) and a former street punk who made good. He joined Haru for the adventure, but now that Demon Card is defeated, does he have any reason to stick around?

LET

A member of the Dragon race, he was formerly a member of the Demon Card's Five Palace Guardians. He was so impressed by Haru's fighting skills and pureness of heart that he made a truce with the Rave Master.

PLUE

The **Rave Bearer**, Plue is the faithful companion to the Rave Master. In addition to being Haru's guide, Plue also has powers of his own. When he's not getting Haru into or out of trouble, Plue can be found enjoying a sucker, his favorite treat.

SEIG HART

An **Element Master**, Seig Hart once worked with **Demon Card** to try and stop the Rave Master, but only while it suited his own agenda. In order to protect the **Timestream**, Seig Hart is trying to get to the bottom of Elie's origin and her connection to Etherion.

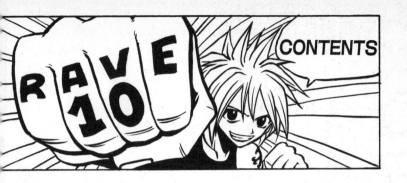

CONTENTS

RAVE0015 KNIGHTS OF KINGDOM PART 1 ▶▶ 7

RAVE0015 KNIGHTS OF KINGDOM PART 2 ▶▶ 42

RAVE:74 ✚ A BRAND NEW START! ▶▶ 72

RAVE:75 ✚ THE SIDE ROADS ARE FULL OF DANGER?!
▶▶ 91

RAVE:76 ✚ THE DARK'S OPPRESSIVE REGIME ▶▶ 111

RAVE:77 ✚ BAD PEOPLE ▶▶ 132

RAVE:78 ✚ THE COMING OF THE "STORM" ▶▶ 151

RAVE:79 ✚ BUSTING THROUGH!! ▶▶ 171

EXTRA COMIC
RAVE0077 ▶▶ 40

RAVE0015 KNIGHTS OF KINGDOM PART 1

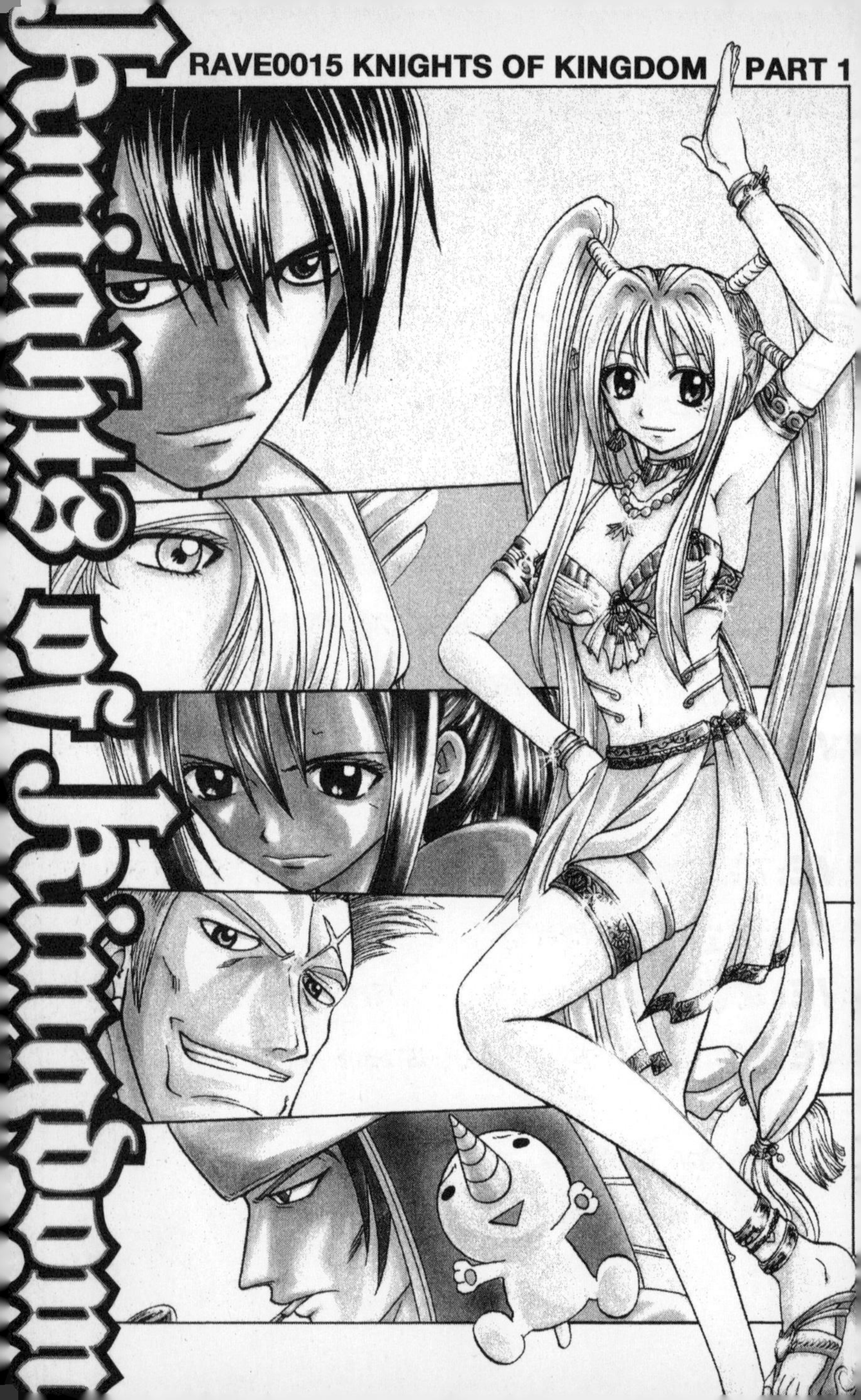
knights of kingdom

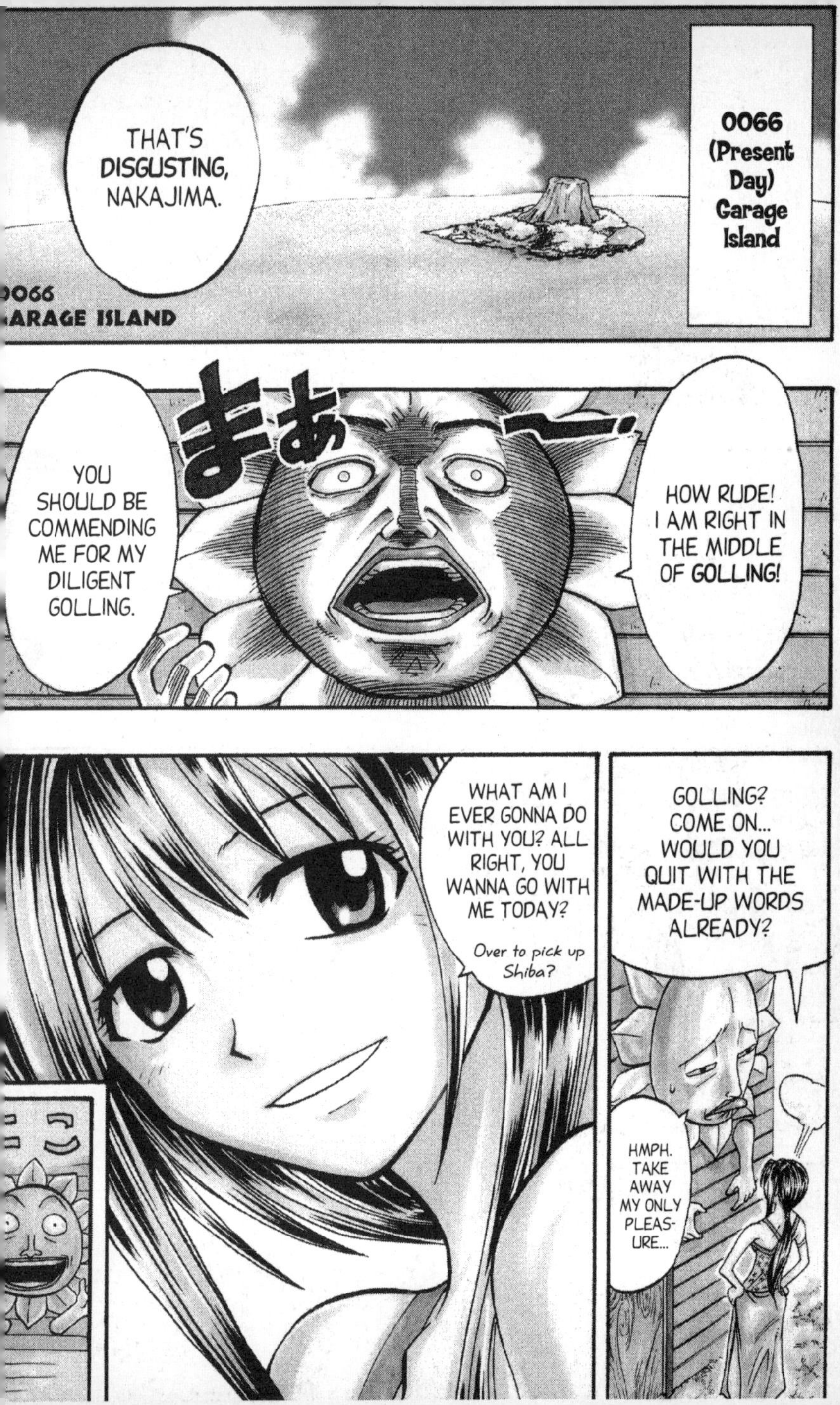

0066
(Present
Day)
Garage
Island
THAT'S DISGUSTING, NAKAJIMA.
0066
ARAGE ISLAND
まぁー
HOW RUDE! I AM RIGHT IN THE MIDDLE OF GOLLING!
YOU SHOULD BE COMMENDING ME FOR MY DILIGENT GOLLING.
GOLLING? COME ON... WOULD YOU QUIT WITH THE MADE-UP WORDS ALREADY?
HMPH. TAKE AWAY MY ONLY PLEAS-URE...
WHAT AM I EVER GONNA DO WITH YOU? ALL RIGHT, YOU WANNA GO WITH ME TODAY?
Over to pick up Shiba?

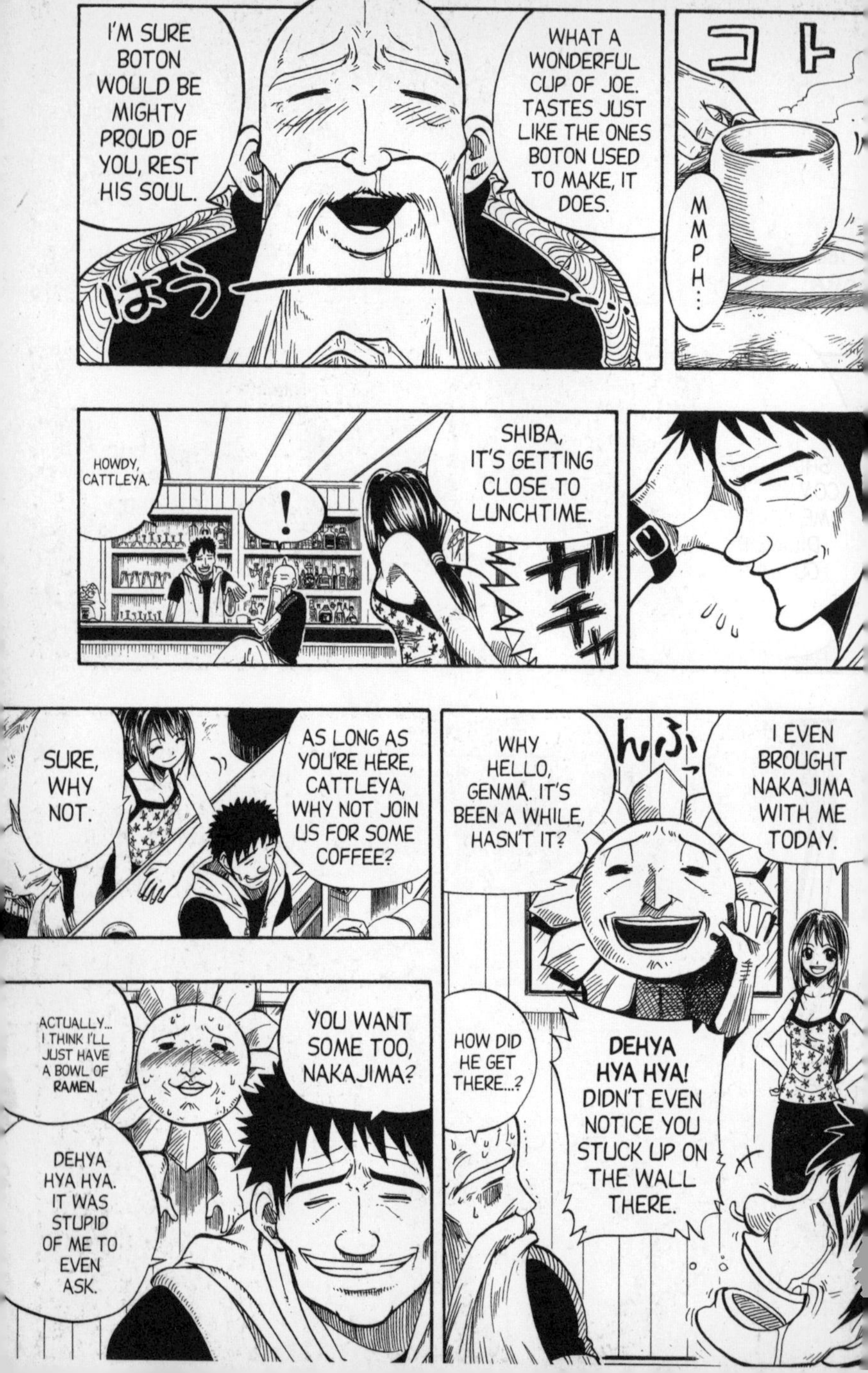
コト
MMPH...
WHAT A WONDERFUL CUP OF JOE. TASTES JUST LIKE THE ONES BOTON USED TO MAKE, IT DOES.
I'M SURE BOTON WOULD BE MIGHTY PROUD OF YOU, REST HIS SOUL.
はう
SHIBA, IT'S GETTING CLOSE TO LUNCHTIME.
ガチャ
!
HOWDY, CATTLEYA.
I EVEN BROUGHT NAKAJIMA WITH ME TODAY.
んふ
WHY HELLO, GENMA. IT'S BEEN A WHILE, HASN'T IT?
DEHYA HYA HYA! DIDN'T EVEN NOTICE YOU STUCK UP ON THE WALL THERE.
HOW DID HE GET THERE...?
AS LONG AS YOU'RE HERE, CATTLEYA, WHY NOT JOIN US FOR SOME COFFEE?
SURE, WHY NOT.
YOU WANT SOME TOO, NAKAJIMA?
ACTUALLY... I THINK I'LL JUST HAVE A BOWL OF RAMEN.
DEHYA HYA HYA. IT WAS STUPID OF ME TO EVEN ASK.

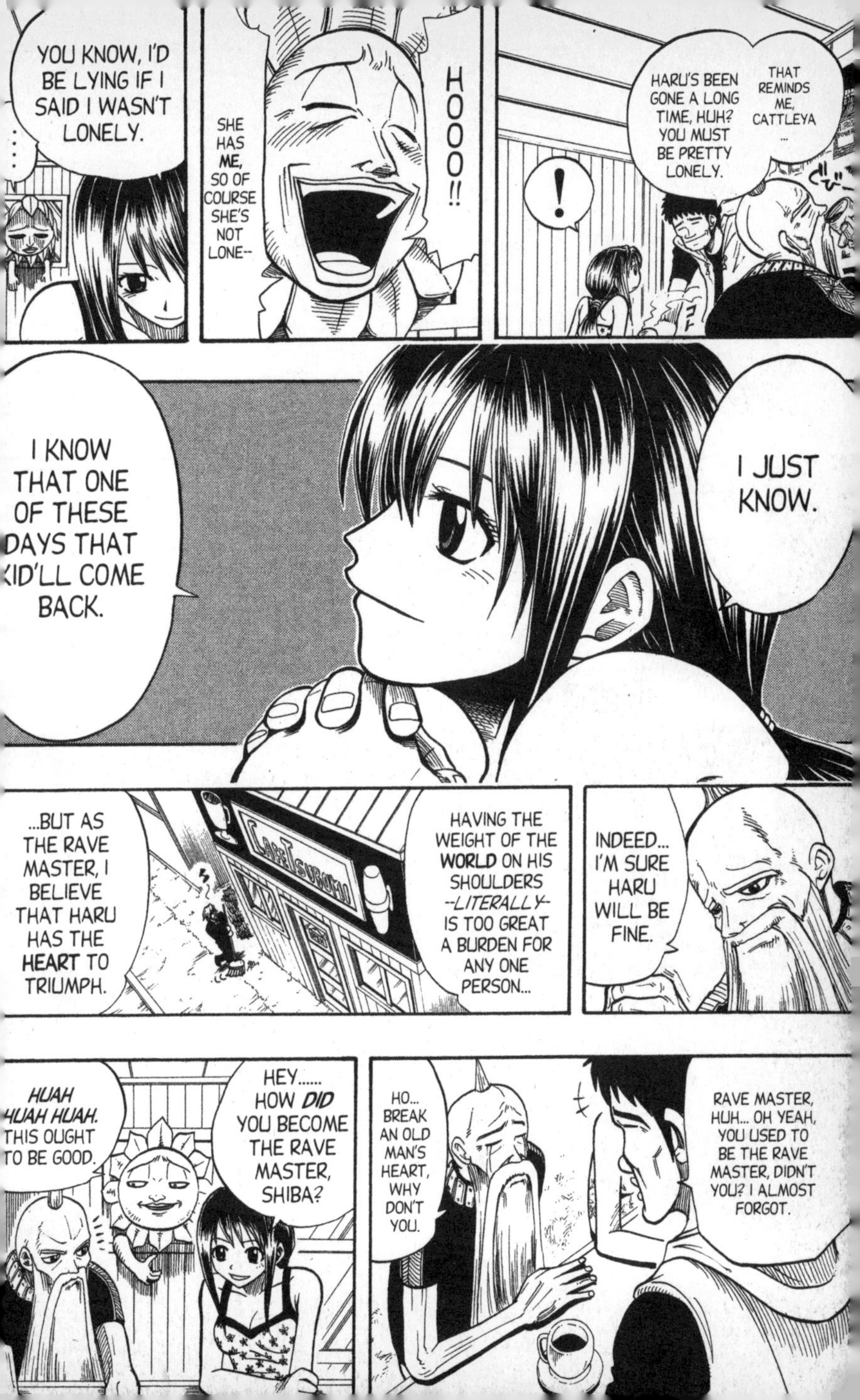

THAT REMINDS ME, CATTLEYA ...
HARU'S BEEN GONE A LONG TIME, HUH? YOU MUST BE PRETTY LONELY.
!
HOOOO!!
SHE HAS **ME**, SO OF COURSE SHE'S NOT LONE--
......
YOU KNOW, I'D BE LYING IF I SAID I WASN'T LONELY.
I JUST KNOW.
I KNOW THAT ONE OF THESE DAYS THAT KID'LL COME BACK.
INDEED... I'M SURE HARU WILL BE FINE.
HAVING THE WEIGHT OF THE **WORLD** ON HIS SHOULDERS *--LITERALLY--* IS TOO GREAT A BURDEN FOR ANY ONE PERSON...
CAFE TSUBOMI
...BUT AS THE RAVE MASTER, I BELIEVE THAT HARU HAS THE **HEART** TO TRIUMPH.
RAVE MASTER, HUH... OH YEAH, YOU USED TO BE THE RAVE MASTER, DIDN'T YOU? I ALMOST FORGOT.
HO... BREAK AN OLD MAN'S HEART, WHY DON'T YOU.
HEY...... HOW ***DID*** YOU BECOME THE RAVE MASTER, SHIBA?
HUAH HUAH HUAH. THIS OUGHT TO BE GOOD.

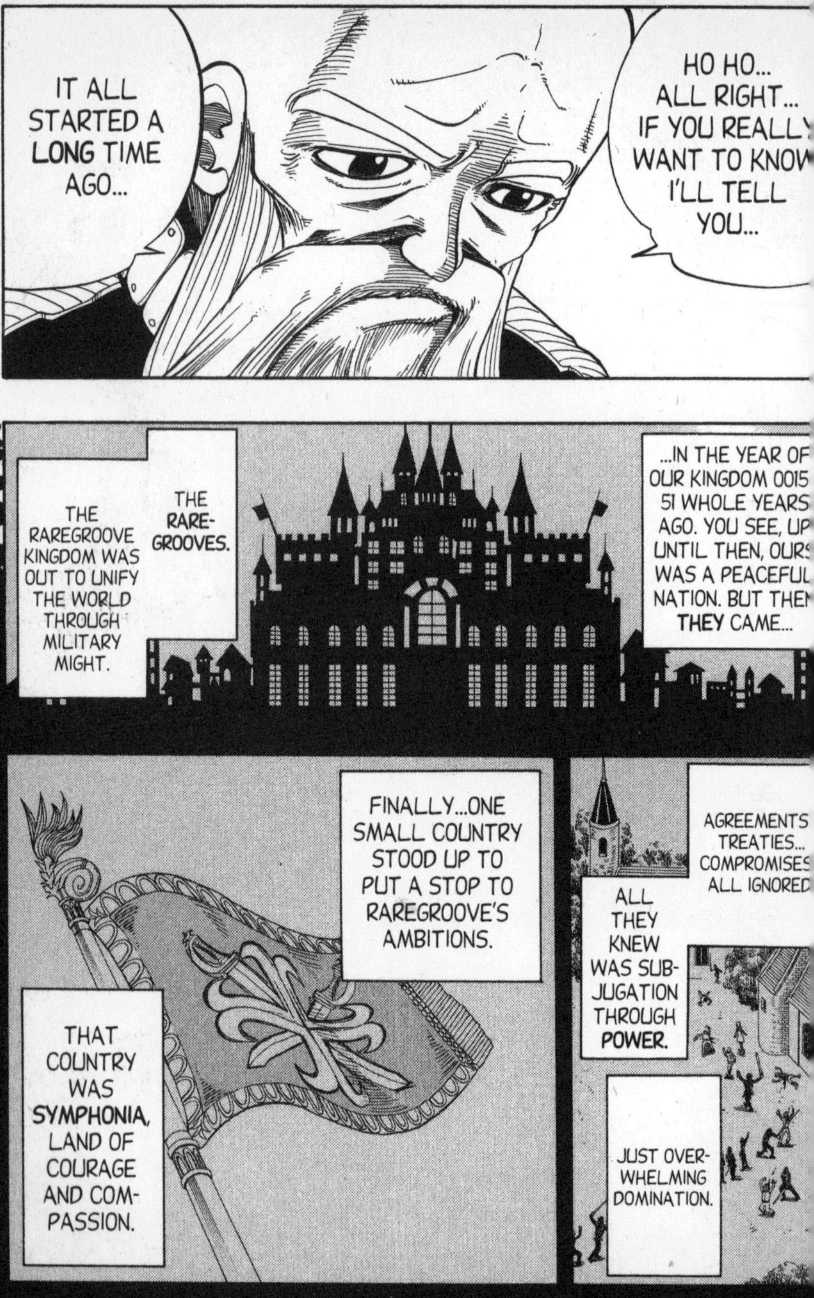
HO HO... ALL RIGHT... IF YOU REALLY WANT TO KNOW I'LL TELL YOU...
IT ALL STARTED A LONG TIME AGO...
...IN THE YEAR OF OUR KINGDOM 0015 51 WHOLE YEARS AGO. YOU SEE, UP UNTIL THEN, OURS WAS A PEACEFUL NATION. BUT THEN THEY CAME...
THE RAREGROOVES.
THE RAREGROOVE KINGDOM WAS OUT TO UNIFY THE WORLD THROUGH MILITARY MIGHT.
AGREEMENTS TREATIES... COMPROMISES ALL IGNORED
ALL THEY KNEW WAS SUBJUGATION THROUGH POWER.
JUST OVERWHELMING DOMINATION.
FINALLY...ONE SMALL COUNTRY STOOD UP TO PUT A STOP TO RAREGROOVE'S AMBITIONS.
THAT COUNTRY WAS SYMPHONIA, LAND OF COURAGE AND COMPASSION.

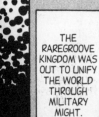

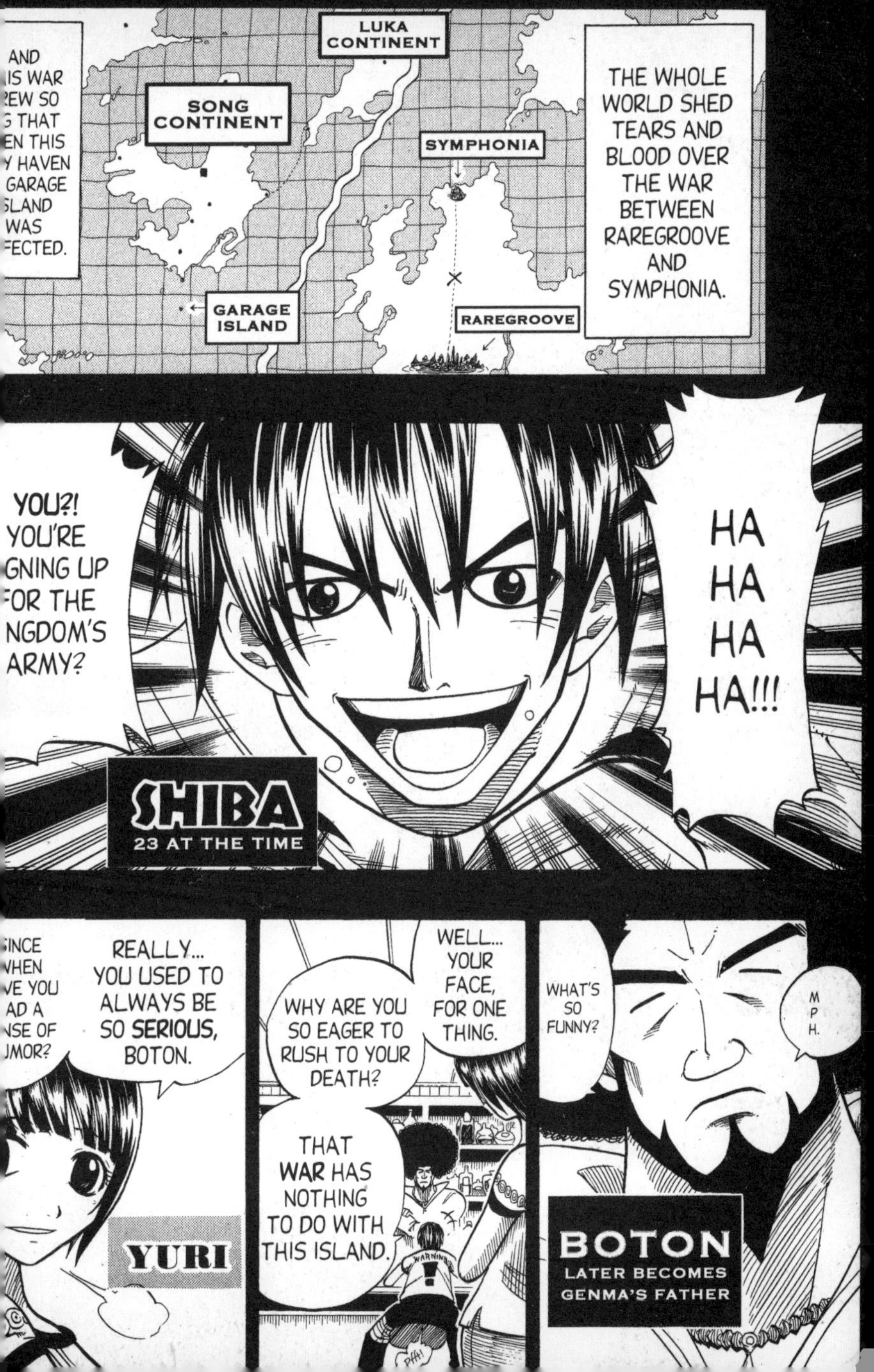
THE WHOLE WORLD SHED TEARS AND BLOOD OVER THE WAR BETWEEN RAREGROOVE AND SYMPHONIA.
LUKA CONTINENT
SYMPHONIA
RAREGROOVE
SONG CONTINENT
GARAGE ISLAND
AND IS WAR EW SO G THAT EN THIS Y HAVEN GARAGE LAND WAS FECTED.
HA HA HA HA!!!
SHIBA
23 AT THE TIME
YOU?! YOU'RE GNING UP FOR THE NGDOM'S ARMY?
MPH.
WHAT'S SO FUNNY?
BOTON
LATER BECOMES GENMA'S FATHER
WELL... YOUR FACE, FOR ONE THING.
WHY ARE YOU SO EAGER TO RUSH TO YOUR DEATH?
THAT WAR HAS NOTHING TO DO WITH THIS ISLAND.
REALLY... YOU USED TO ALWAYS BE SO SERIOUS, BOTON.
INCE VHEN VE YOU AD A NSE OF JMOR?
YURI

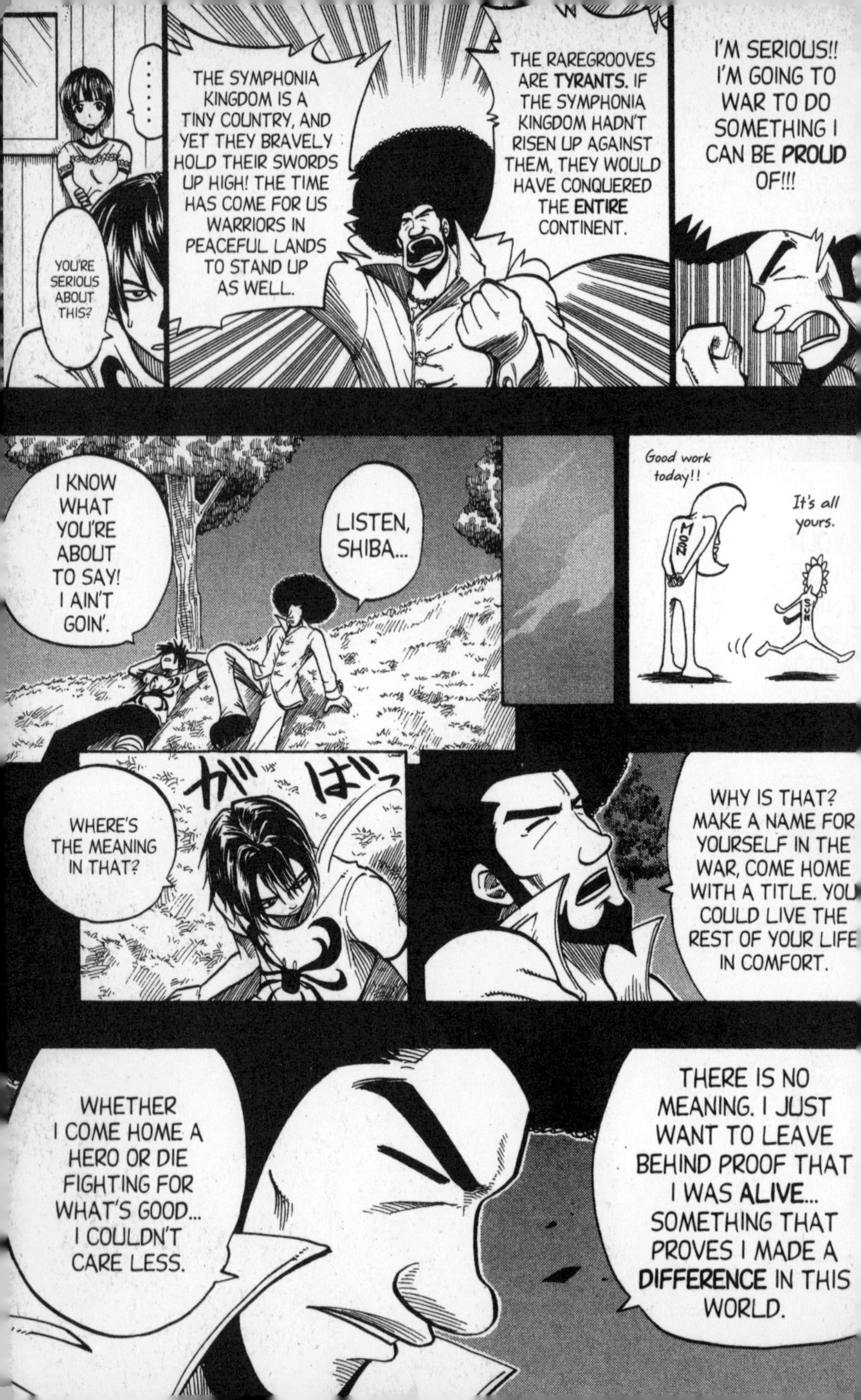
I'M SERIOUS!! I'M GOING TO WAR TO DO SOMETHING I CAN BE PROUD OF!!!
THE RAREGROOVES ARE TYRANTS. IF THE SYMPHONIA KINGDOM HADN'T RISEN UP AGAINST THEM, THEY WOULD HAVE CONQUERED THE ENTIRE CONTINENT.
THE SYMPHONIA KINGDOM IS A TINY COUNTRY, AND YET THEY BRAVELY HOLD THEIR SWORDS UP HIGH! THE TIME HAS COME FOR US WARRIORS IN PEACEFUL LANDS TO STAND UP AS WELL.
......
YOU'RE SERIOUS ABOUT THIS?
It's all yours.
Good work today!!
MOON
SUN
LISTEN, SHIBA...
I KNOW WHAT YOU'RE ABOUT TO SAY! I AIN'T GOIN'.
WHY IS THAT? MAKE A NAME FOR YOURSELF IN THE WAR, COME HOME WITH A TITLE. YOU COULD LIVE THE REST OF YOUR LIFE IN COMFORT.
がばっ
WHERE'S THE MEANING IN THAT?
THERE IS NO MEANING. I JUST WANT TO LEAVE BEHIND PROOF THAT I WAS ALIVE... SOMETHING THAT PROVES I MADE A DIFFERENCE IN THIS WORLD.
WHETHER I COME HOME A HERO OR DIE FIGHTING FOR WHAT'S GOOD... I COULDN'T CARE LESS.

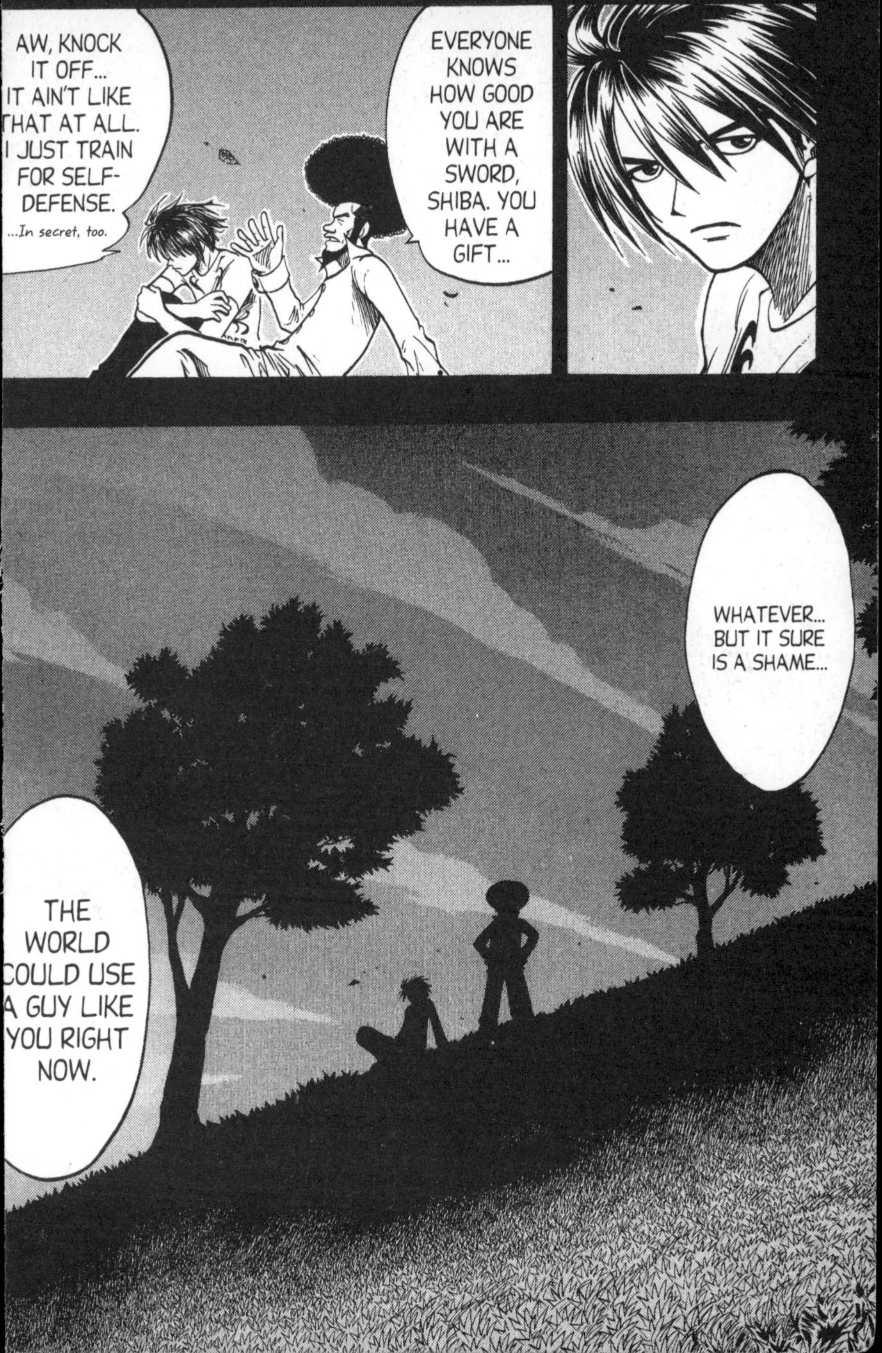
EVERYONE KNOWS HOW GOOD YOU ARE WITH A SWORD, SHIBA. YOU HAVE A GIFT...
AW, KNOCK IT OFF... IT AIN'T LIKE THAT AT ALL. I JUST TRAIN FOR SELF-DEFENSE.
...In secret, too.
WHATEVER... BUT IT SURE IS A SHAME...
THE WORLD COULD USE A GUY LIKE YOU RIGHT NOW.

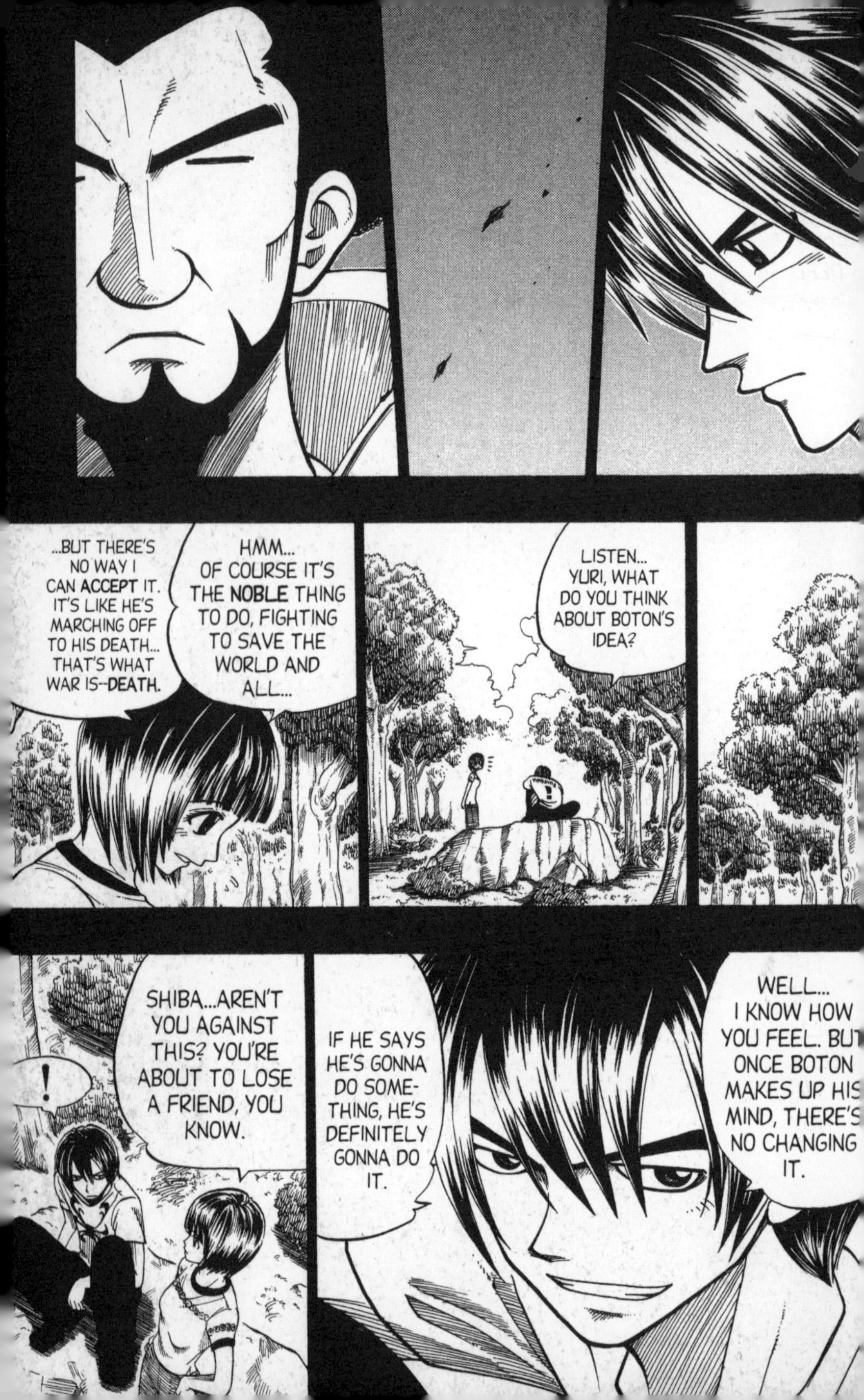

LISTEN... YURI, WHAT DO YOU THINK ABOUT BOTON'S IDEA?
HMM... OF COURSE IT'S THE NOBLE THING TO DO, FIGHTING TO SAVE THE WORLD AND ALL...
...BUT THERE'S NO WAY I CAN ACCEPT IT. IT'S LIKE HE'S MARCHING OFF TO HIS DEATH... THAT'S WHAT WAR IS--DEATH.
WELL... I KNOW HOW YOU FEEL. BUT ONCE BOTON MAKES UP HIS MIND, THERE'S NO CHANGING IT.
IF HE SAYS HE'S GONNA DO SOME-THING, HE'S DEFINITELY GONNA DO IT.
SHIBA...AREN'T YOU AGAINST THIS? YOU'RE ABOUT TO LOSE A FRIEND, YOU KNOW.
!

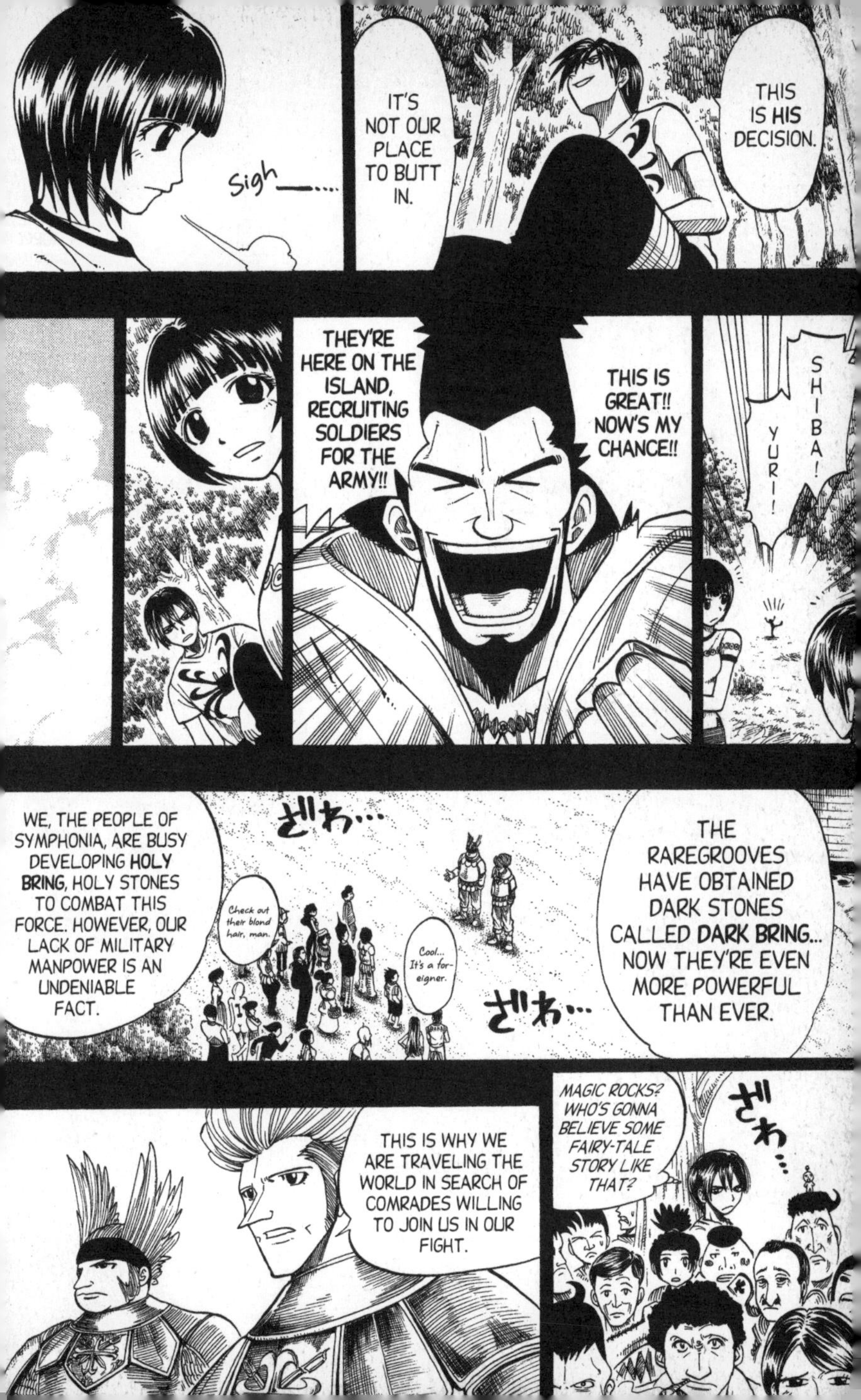
THIS IS HIS DECISION.
IT'S NOT OUR PLACE TO BUTT IN.
Sigh—....
SHIBA!
YURI!
THIS IS GREAT!! NOW'S MY CHANCE!!
THEY'RE HERE ON THE ISLAND, RECRUITING SOLDIERS FOR THE ARMY!!
THE RAREGROOVES HAVE OBTAINED DARK STONES CALLED DARK BRING... NOW THEY'RE EVEN MORE POWERFUL THAN EVER.
ざわ…
Cool... It's a foreigner.
ざわ…
Check out their blond hair, man.
WE, THE PEOPLE OF SYMPHONIA, ARE BUSY DEVELOPING HOLY BRING, HOLY STONES TO COMBAT THIS FORCE. HOWEVER, OUR LACK OF MILITARY MANPOWER IS AN UNDENIABLE FACT.
ざわ…
MAGIC ROCKS? WHO'S GONNA BELIEVE SOME FAIRY-TALE STORY LIKE THAT?
THIS IS WHY WE ARE TRAVELING THE WORLD IN SEARCH OF COMRADES WILLING TO JOIN US IN OUR FIGHT.

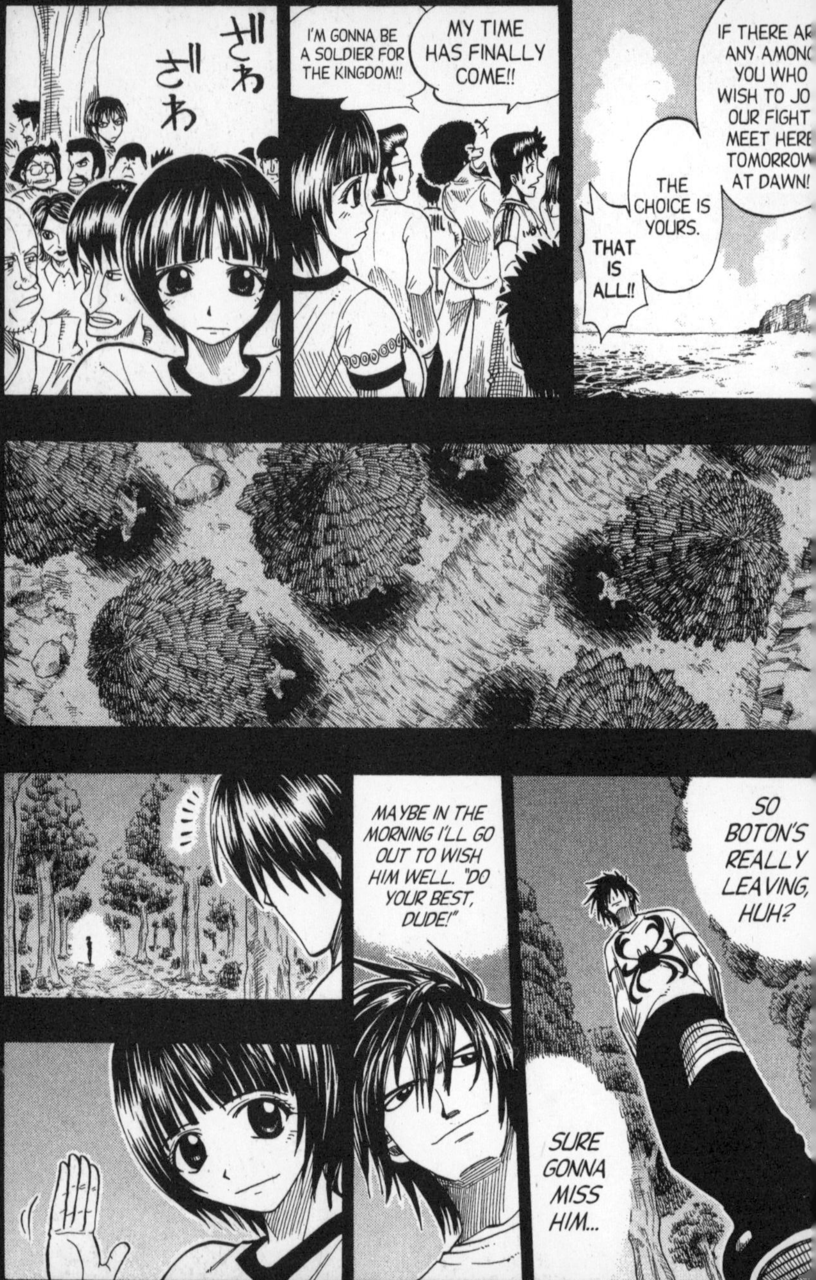
IF THERE AR ANY AMONG YOU WHO WISH TO JO OUR FIGHT MEET HERE TOMORROW AT DAWN!
THE CHOICE IS YOURS.
THAT IS ALL!!
MY TIME HAS FINALLY COME!!
I'M GONNA BE A SOLDIER FOR THE KINGDOM!!
ざわ ざわ
SO BOTON'S REALLY LEAVING, HUH?
SURE GONNA MISS HIM...
MAYBE IN THE MORNING I'LL GO OUT TO WISH HIM WELL. "DO YOUR BEST, DUDE!"
...

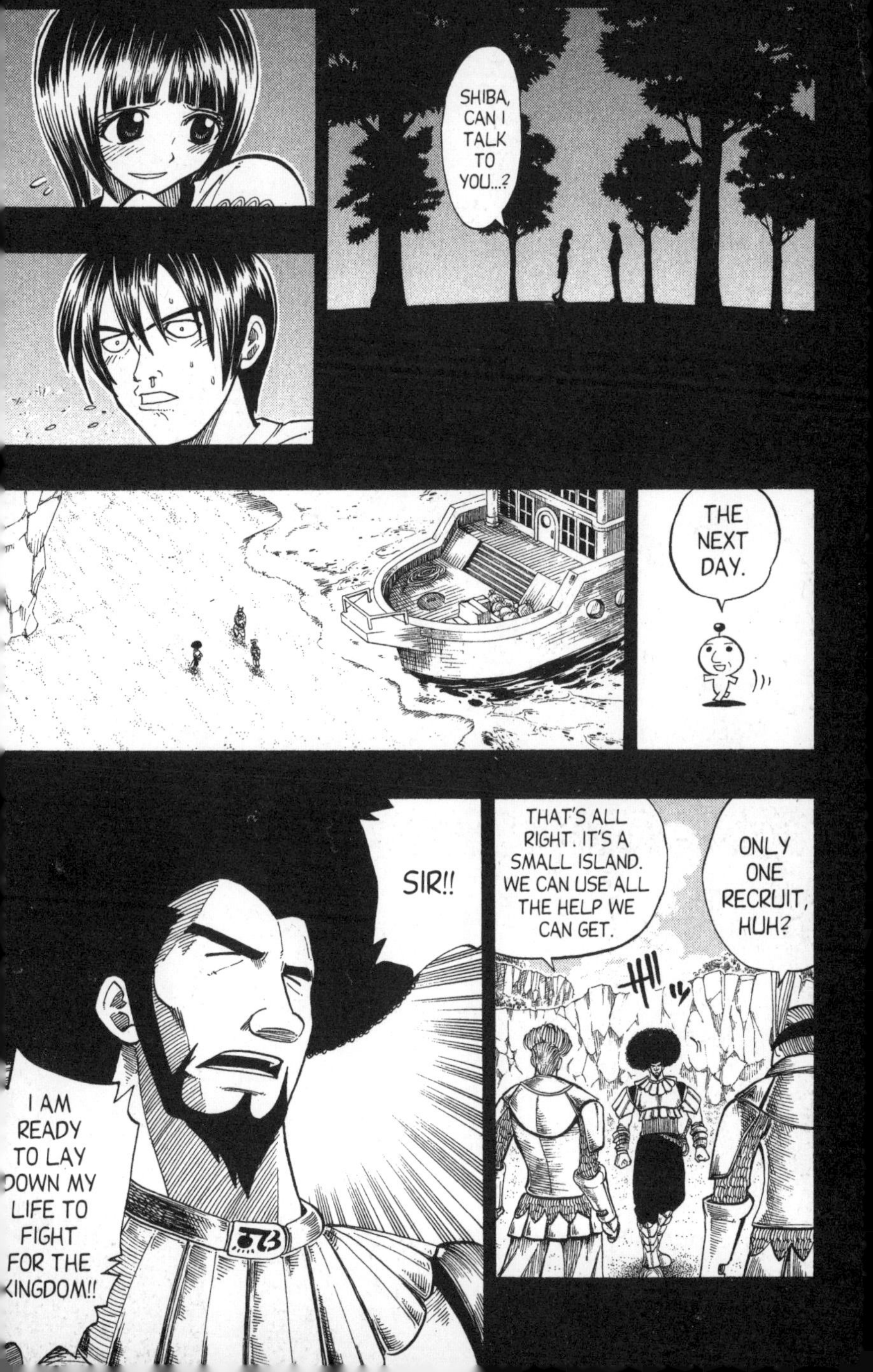
SHIBA, CAN I TALK TO YOU...?
THE NEXT DAY.
ONLY ONE RECRUIT, HUH?
THAT'S ALL RIGHT. IT'S A SMALL ISLAND. WE CAN USE ALL THE HELP WE CAN GET.
SIR!!
I AM READY TO LAY DOWN MY LIFE TO FIGHT FOR THE KINGDOM!!

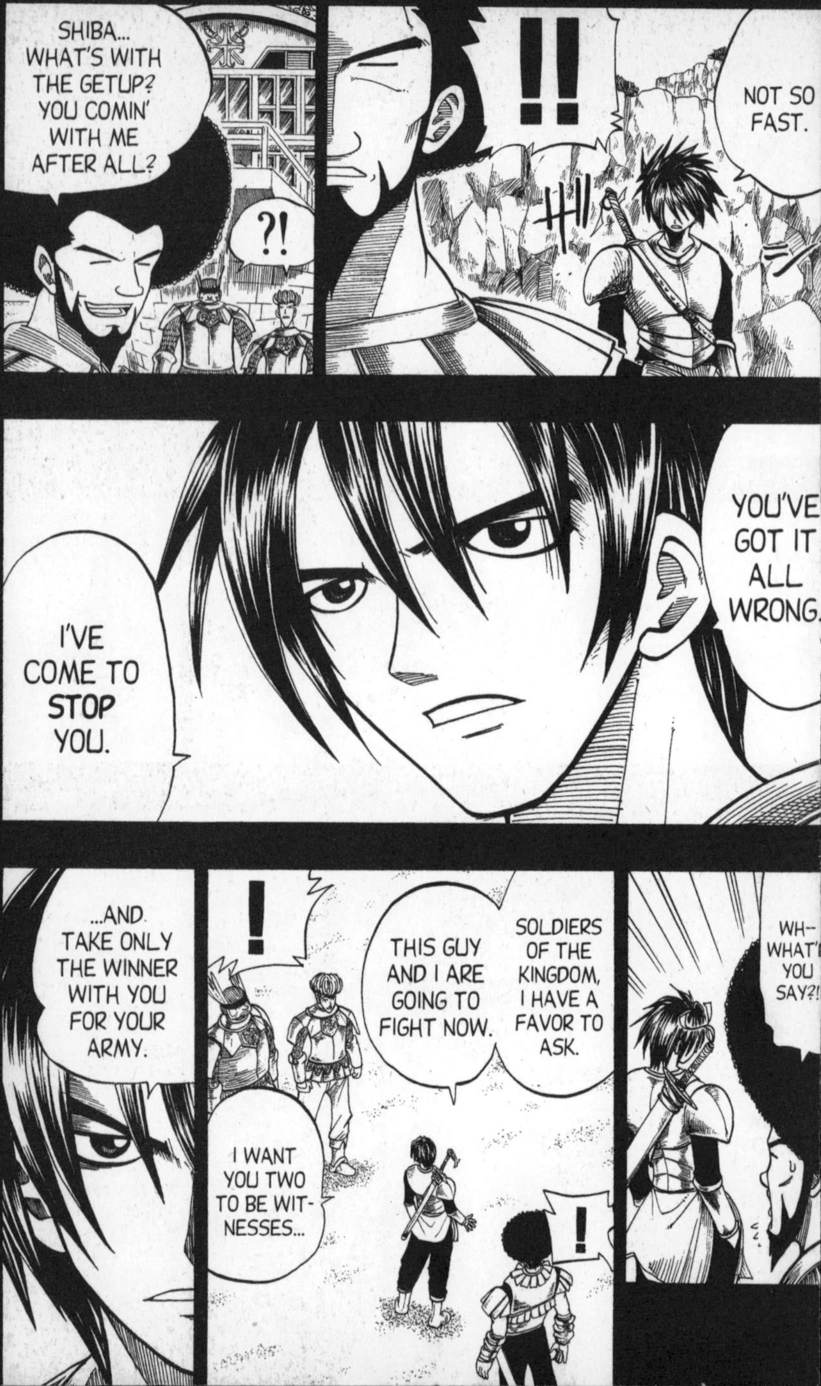
NOT SO FAST.
!!
SHIBA... WHAT'S WITH THE GETUP? YOU COMIN' WITH ME AFTER ALL?
?!
YOU'VE GOT IT ALL WRONG.
I'VE COME TO STOP YOU.
WH-- WHAT' YOU SAY?!
!
SOLDIERS OF THE KINGDOM, I HAVE A FAVOR TO ASK.
THIS GUY AND I ARE GOING TO FIGHT NOW.
I WANT YOU TWO TO BE WIT-NESSES...
!
...AND. TAKE ONLY THE WINNER WITH YOU FOR YOUR ARMY.

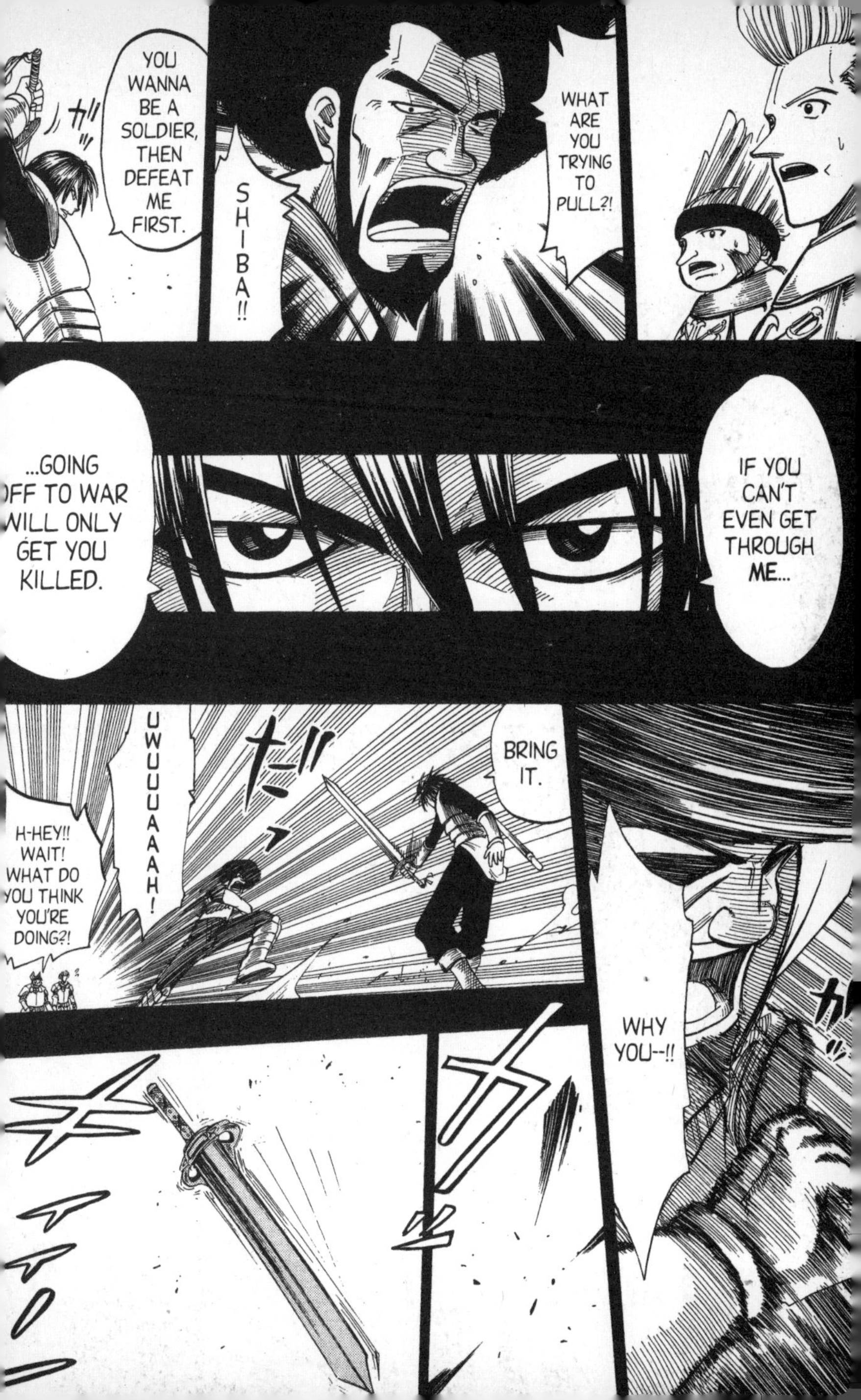
WHAT ARE YOU TRYING TO PULL?!
SHIBA!!
YOU WANNA BE A SOLDIER, THEN DEFEAT ME FIRST.
IF YOU CAN'T EVEN GET THROUGH ME...
...GOING OFF TO WAR WILL ONLY GET YOU KILLED.
WHY YOU--!!
BRING IT.
UWUUUAAAAH!
H-HEY!! WAIT! WHAT DO YOU THINK YOU'RE DOING?!

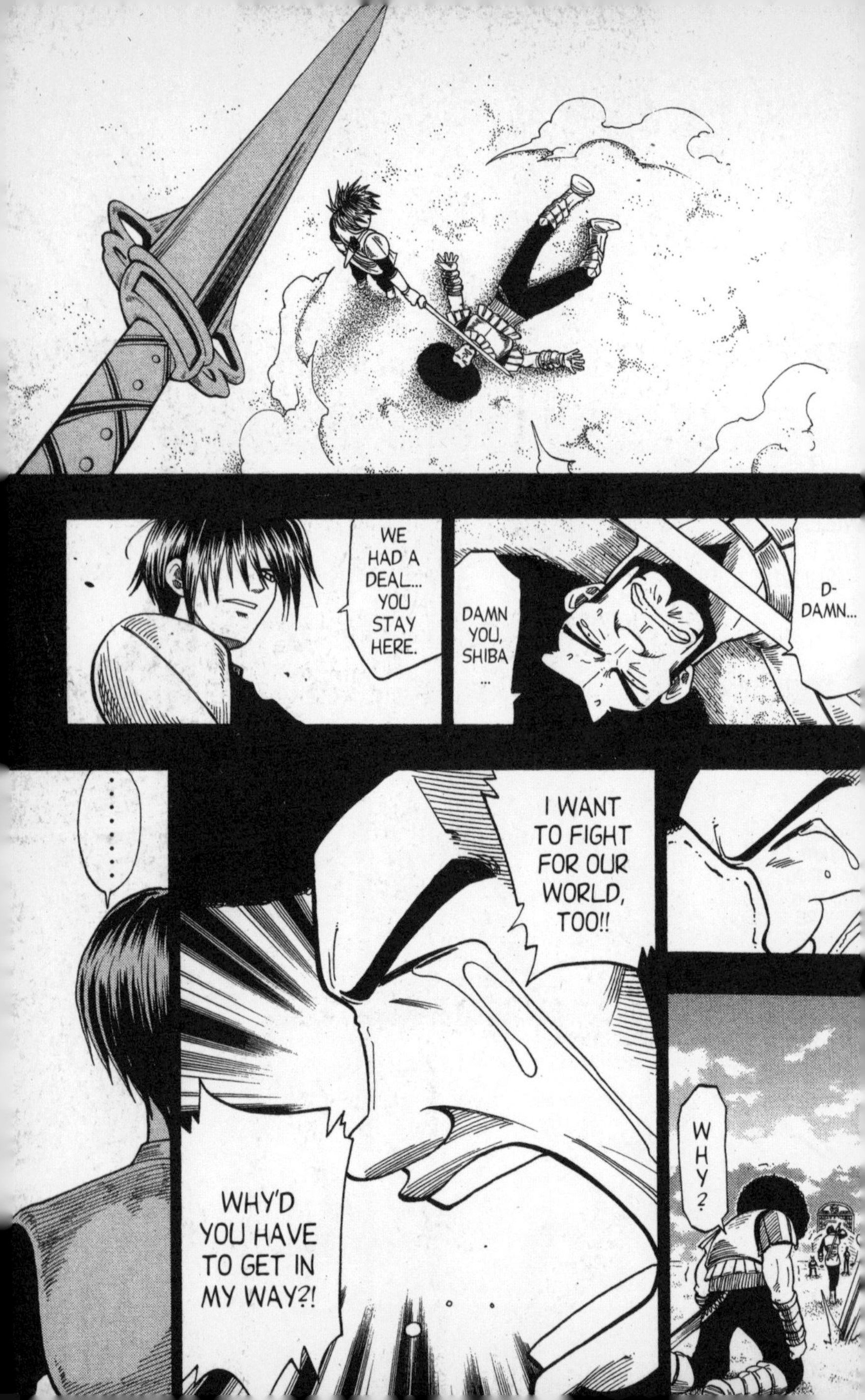
D-
DAMN...
DAMN YOU, SHIBA ...
WE HAD A DEAL... YOU STAY HERE.
WHY?
I WANT TO FIGHT FOR OUR WORLD, TOO!!
WHY'D YOU HAVE TO GET IN MY WAY?!
......

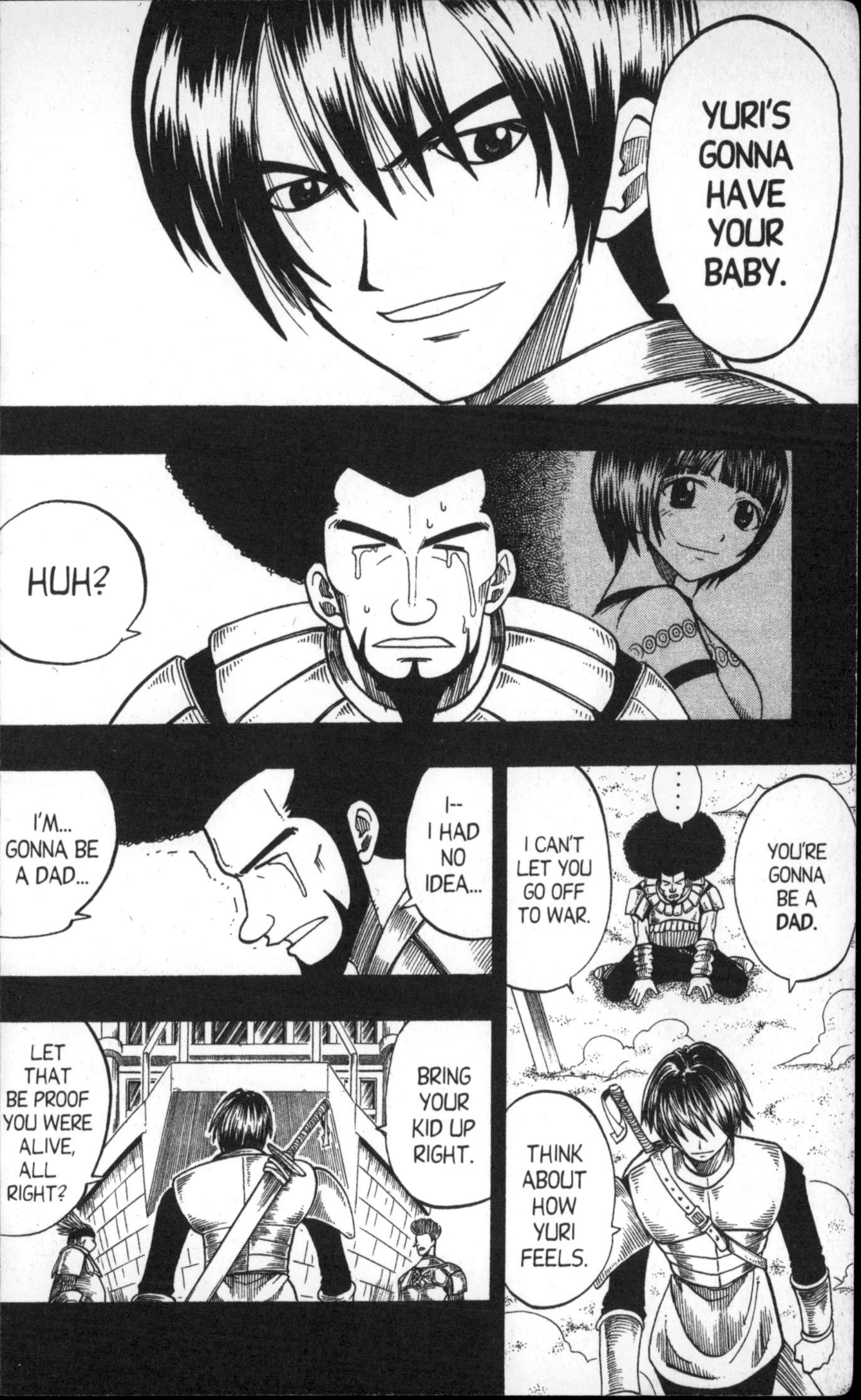
YURI'S GONNA HAVE YOUR BABY.
HUH?
...
YOU'RE GONNA BE A DAD.
I CAN'T LET YOU GO OFF TO WAR.
THINK ABOUT HOW YURI FEELS.
I-- I HAD NO IDEA...
I'M... GONNA BE A DAD...
BRING YOUR KID UP RIGHT.
LET THAT BE PROOF YOU WERE ALIVE, ALL RIGHT?

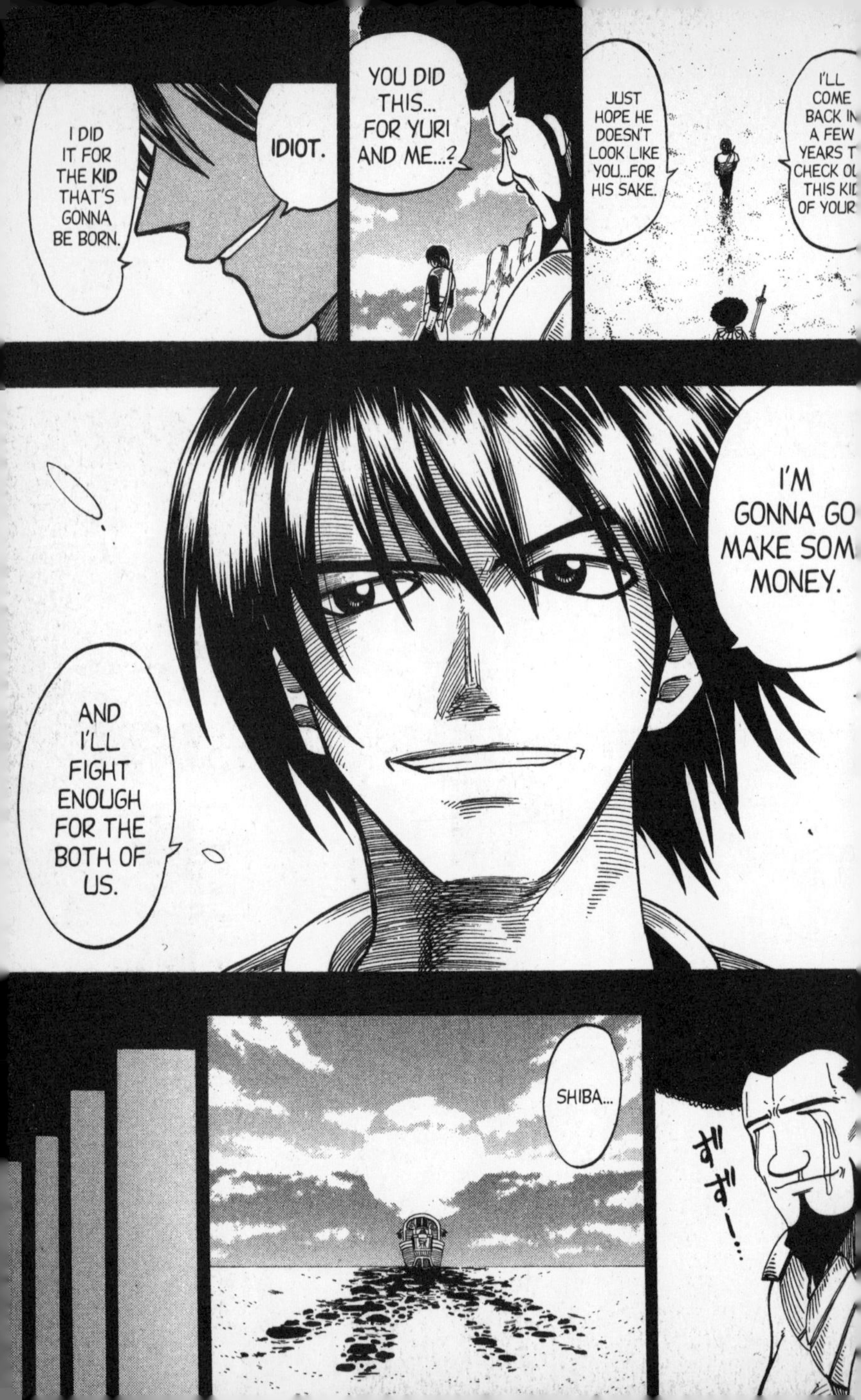
I'LL COME BACK IN A FEW YEARS T CHECK OU THIS KID OF YOUR
JUST HOPE HE DOESN'T LOOK LIKE YOU...FOR HIS SAKE.
YOU DID THIS... FOR YURI AND ME...?
IDIOT.
I DID IT FOR THE KID THAT'S GONNA BE BORN.
I'M GONNA GO MAKE SOM MONEY.
AND I'LL FIGHT ENOUGH FOR THE BOTH OF US.
ずずー...
SHIBA...

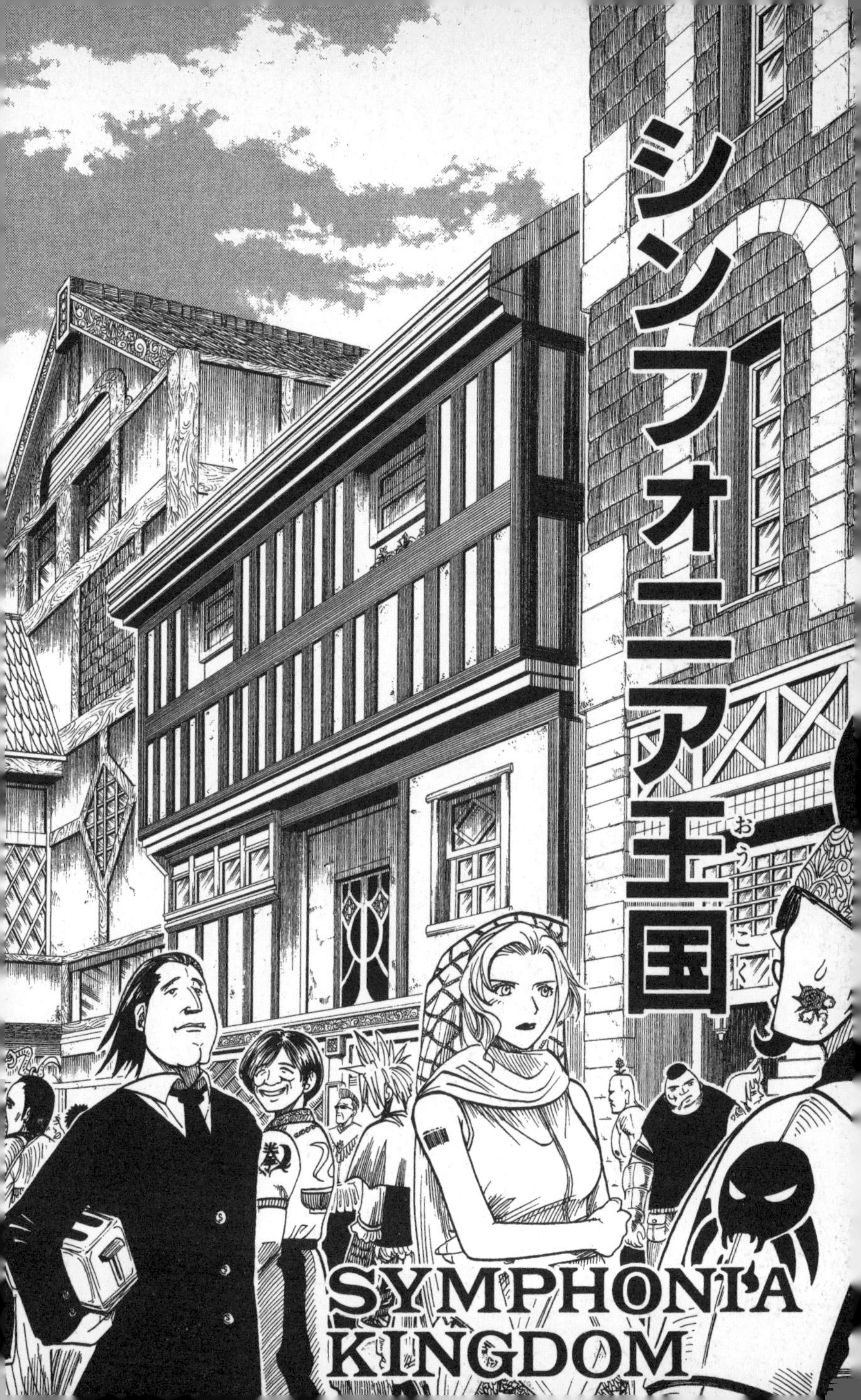

シンフォニア王国(おうこく)
SYMPHONIA KINGDOM

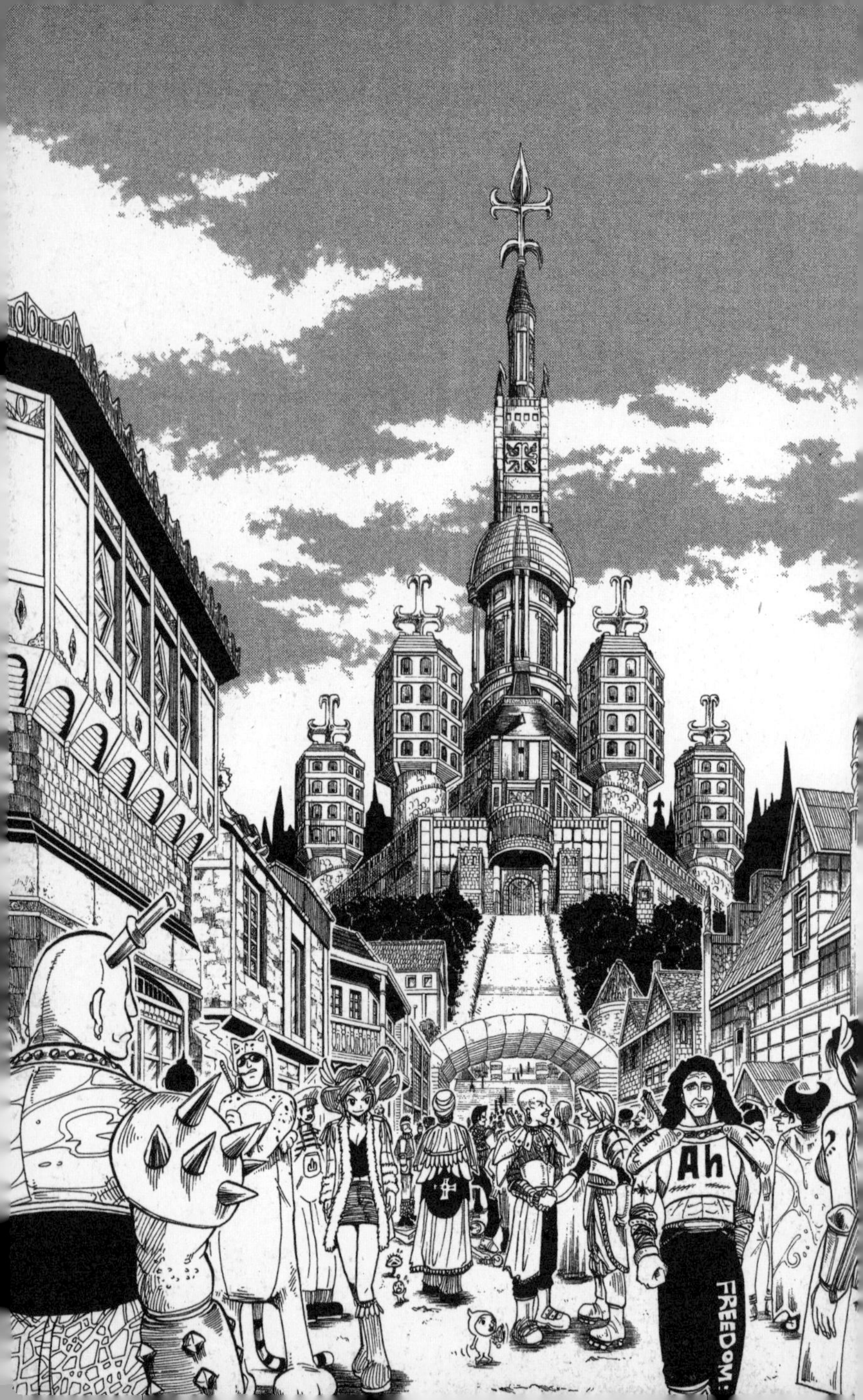
Ah
FREEDOM

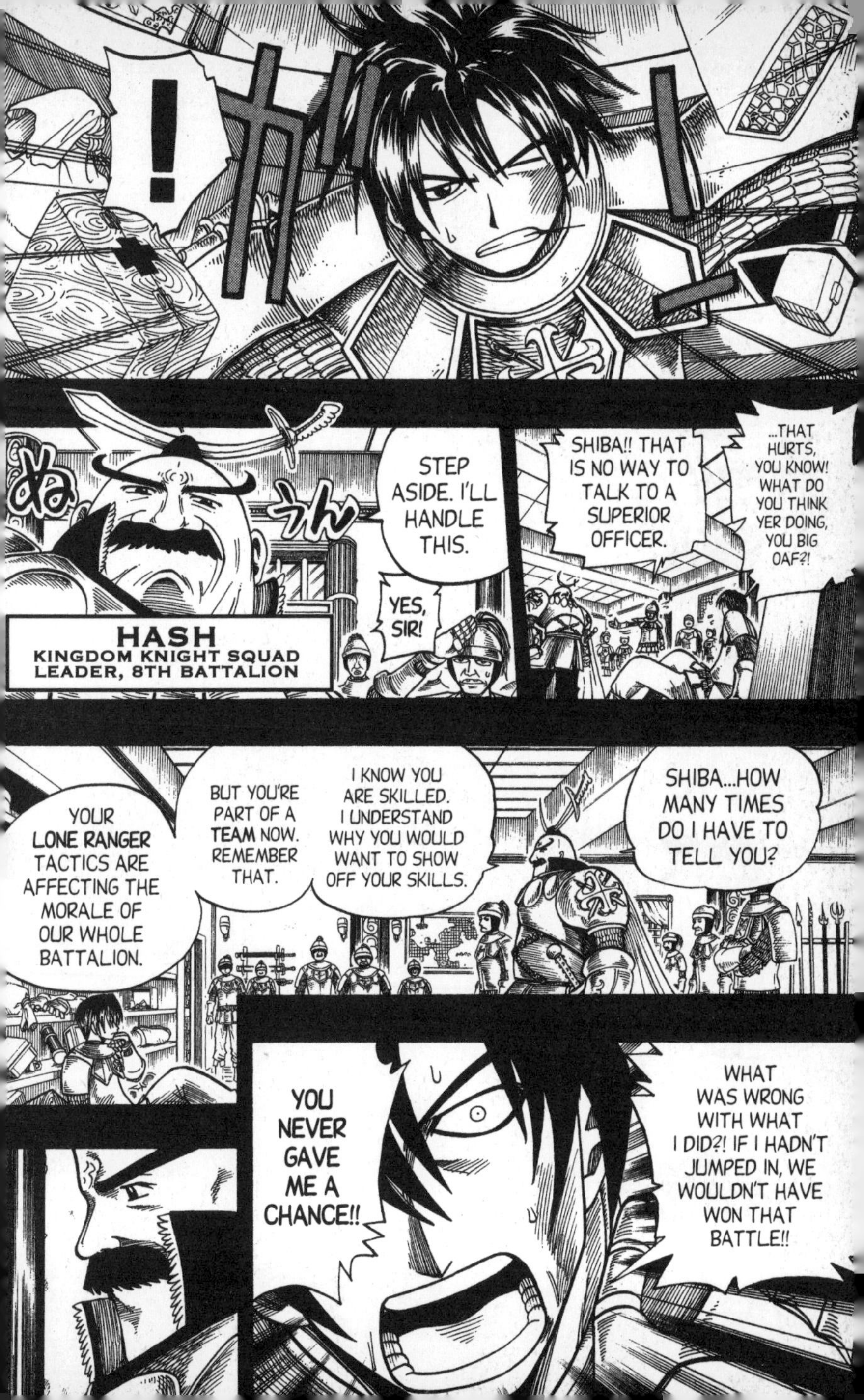
!
...THAT HURTS, YOU KNOW! WHAT DO YOU THINK YER DOING, YOU BIG OAF?!
SHIBA!! THAT IS NO WAY TO TALK TO A SUPERIOR OFFICER.
STEP ASIDE. I'LL HANDLE THIS.
ぬ
うん
YES, SIR!
HASH
KINGDOM KNIGHT SQUAD LEADER, 8TH BATTALION
SHIBA...HOW MANY TIMES DO I HAVE TO TELL YOU?
I KNOW YOU ARE SKILLED. I UNDERSTAND WHY YOU WOULD WANT TO SHOW OFF YOUR SKILLS.
BUT YOU'RE PART OF A TEAM NOW. REMEMBER THAT.
YOUR LONE RANGER TACTICS ARE AFFECTING THE MORALE OF OUR WHOLE BATTALION.
WHAT WAS WRONG WITH WHAT I DID?! IF I HADN'T JUMPED IN, WE WOULDN'T HAVE WON THAT BATTLE!!
YOU NEVER GAVE ME A CHANCE!!

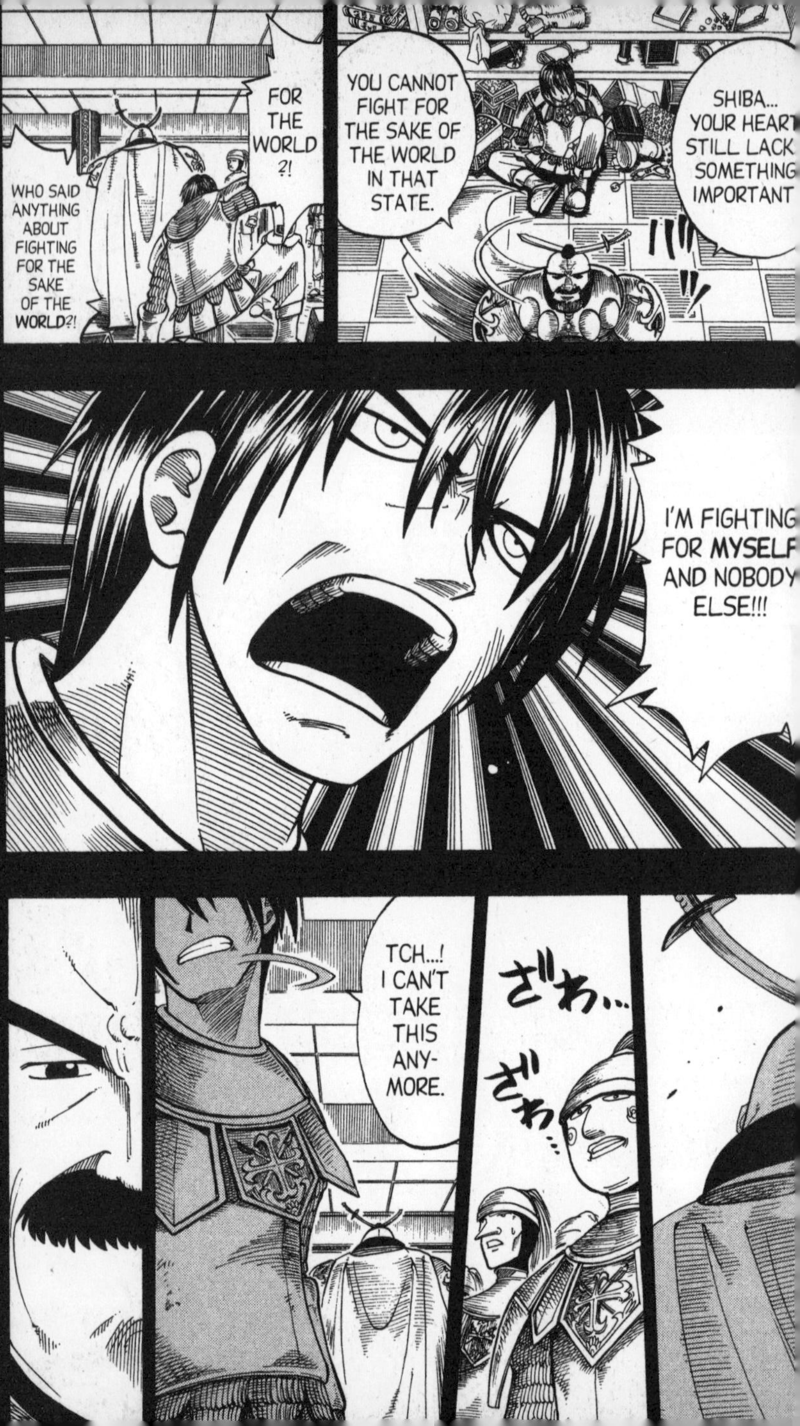
SHIBA... YOUR HEART STILL LACK SOMETHING IMPORTANT
YOU CANNOT FIGHT FOR THE SAKE OF THE WORLD IN THAT STATE.
FOR THE WORLD ?!
WHO SAID ANYTHING ABOUT FIGHTING FOR THE SAKE OF THE WORLD?!
I'M FIGHTING FOR MYSELF AND NOBODY ELSE!!!
ざわ...
ざわ...
TCH...! I CAN'T TAKE THIS ANY- MORE.

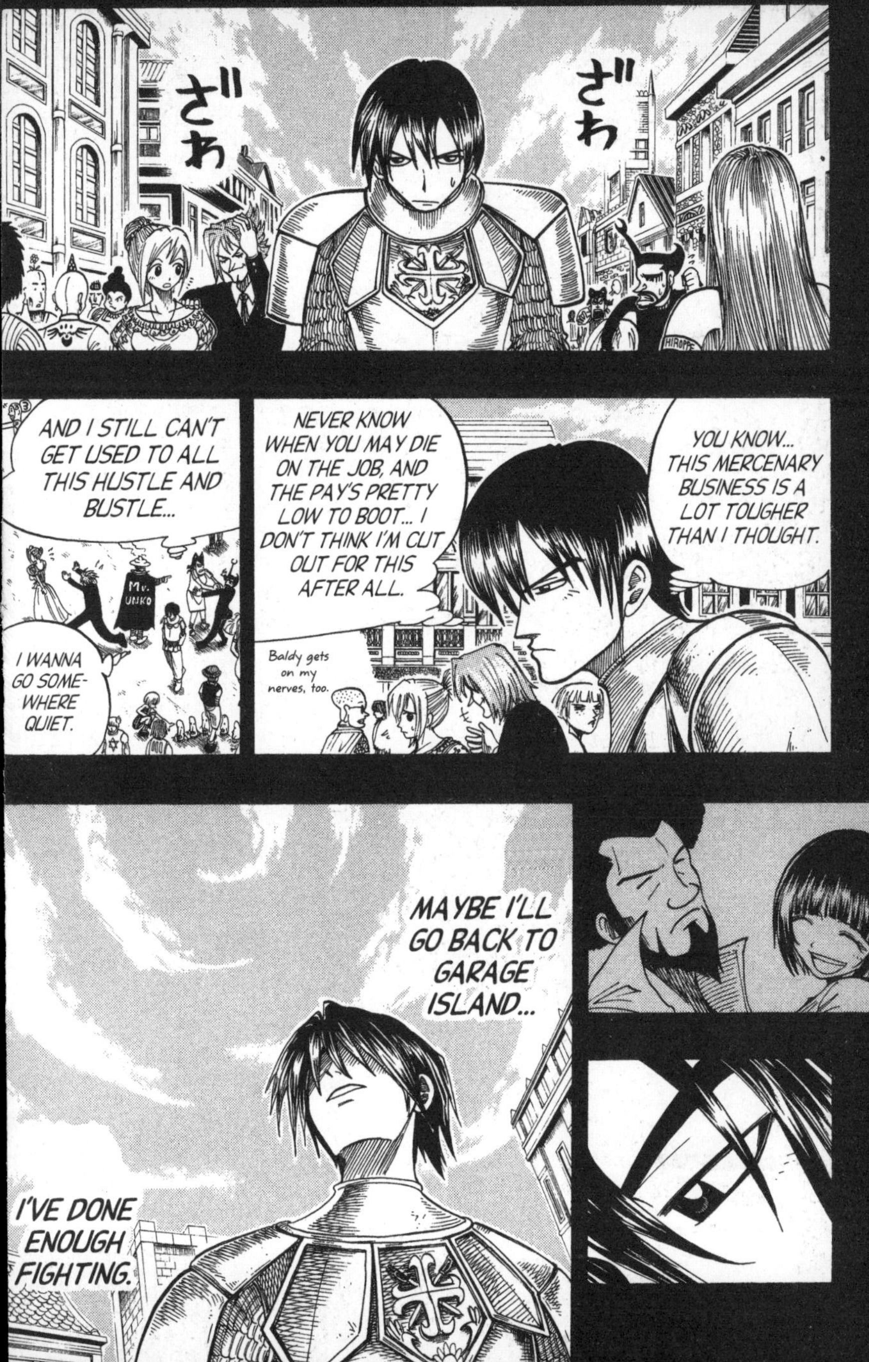
ざわ
ざわ
HIROPPE
YOU KNOW... THIS MERCENARY BUSINESS IS A LOT TOUGHER THAN I THOUGHT.
NEVER KNOW WHEN YOU MAY DIE ON THE JOB, AND THE PAY'S PRETTY LOW TO BOOT... I DON'T THINK I'M CUT OUT FOR THIS AFTER ALL.
Baldy gets on my nerves, too.
AND I STILL CAN'T GET USED TO ALL THIS HUSTLE AND BUSTLE...
Mr. UNKO
I WANNA GO SOME-WHERE QUIET.
MAYBE I'LL GO BACK TO GARAGE ISLAND...
I'VE DONE ENOUGH FIGHTING.

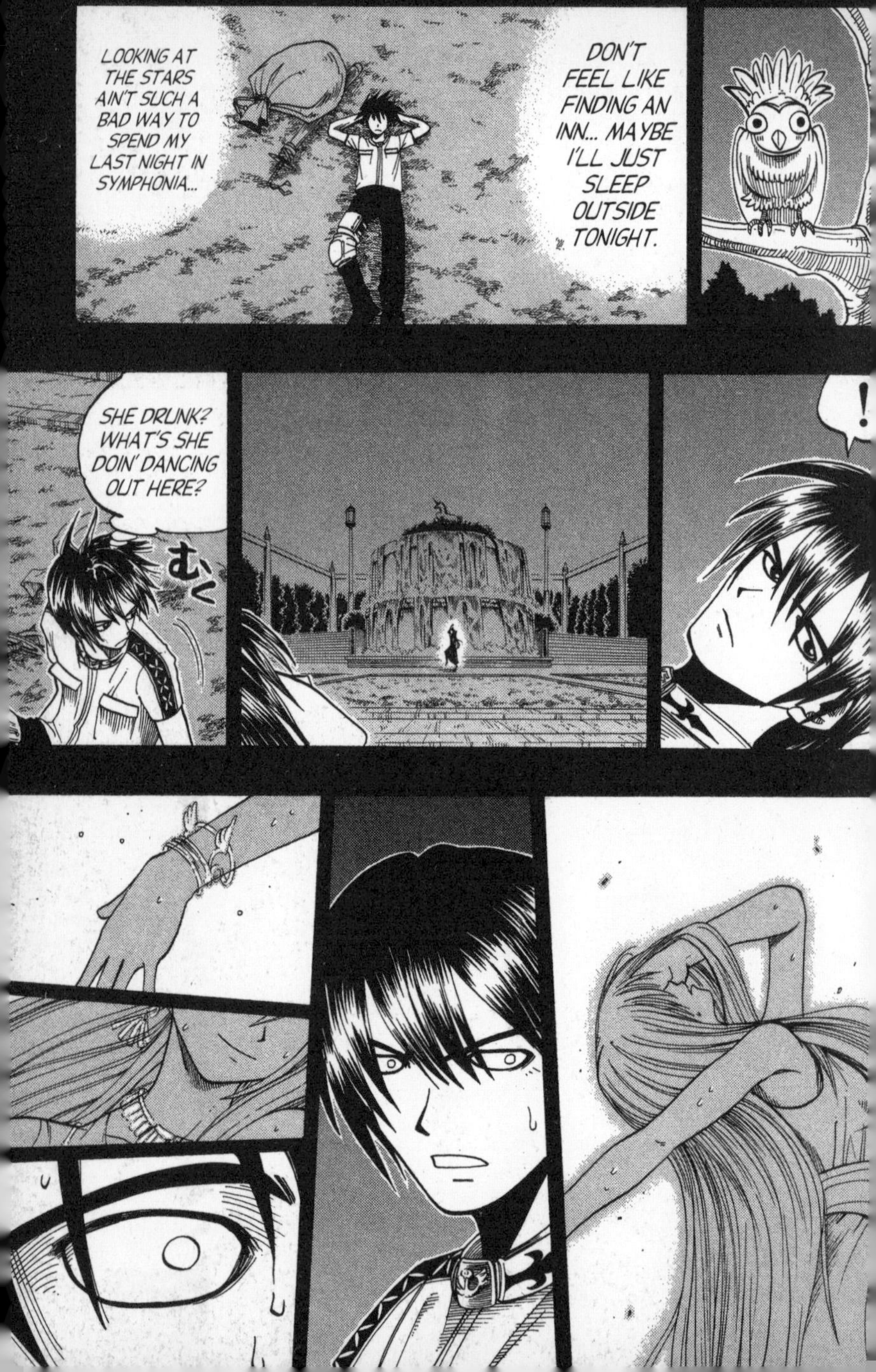
DON'T FEEL LIKE FINDING AN INN... MAYBE I'LL JUST SLEEP OUTSIDE TONIGHT.
LOOKING AT THE STARS AIN'T SUCH A BAD WAY TO SPEND MY LAST NIGHT IN SYMPHONIA...
!
SHE DRUNK? WHAT'S SHE DOIN' DANCING OUT HERE?
むく

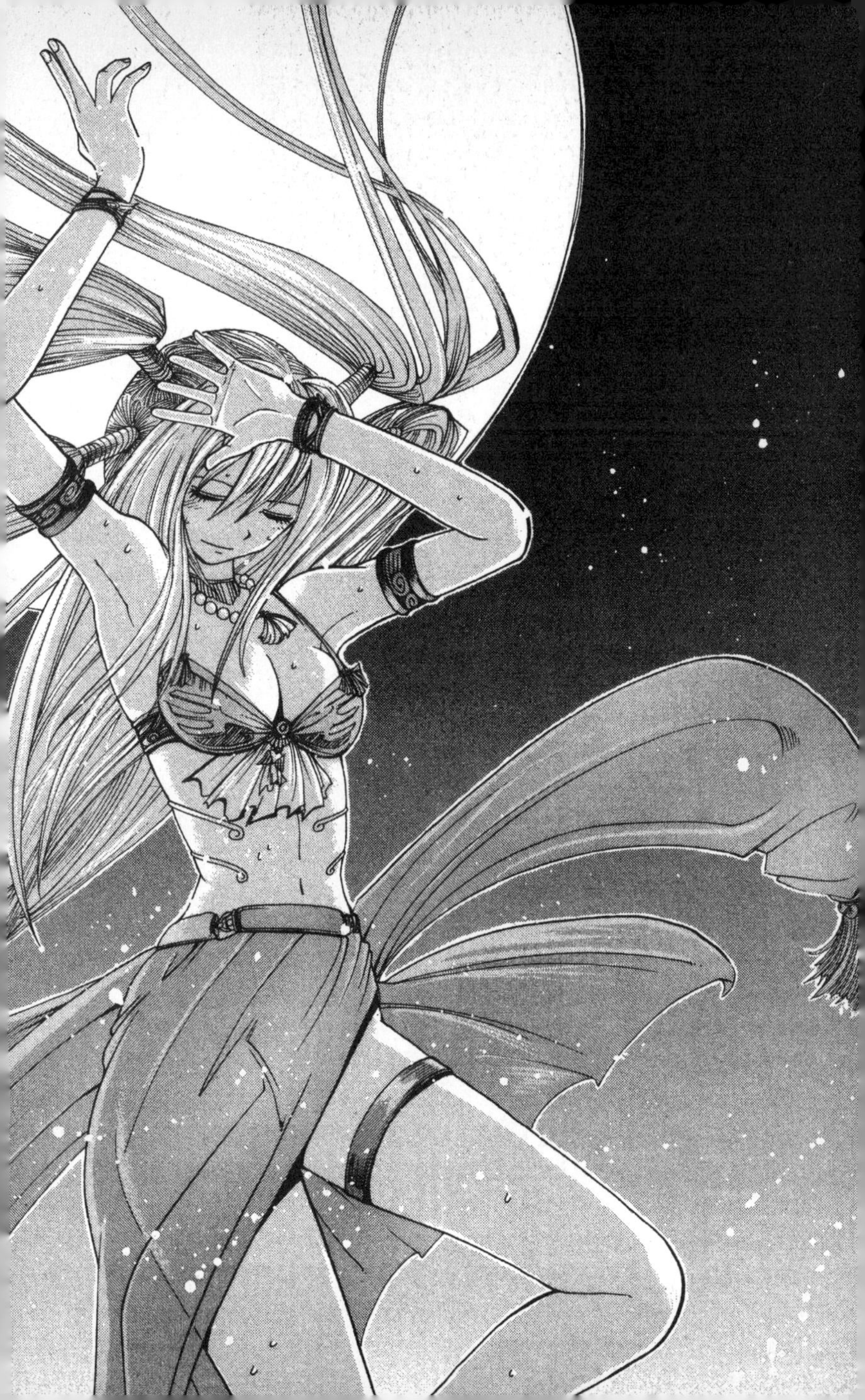

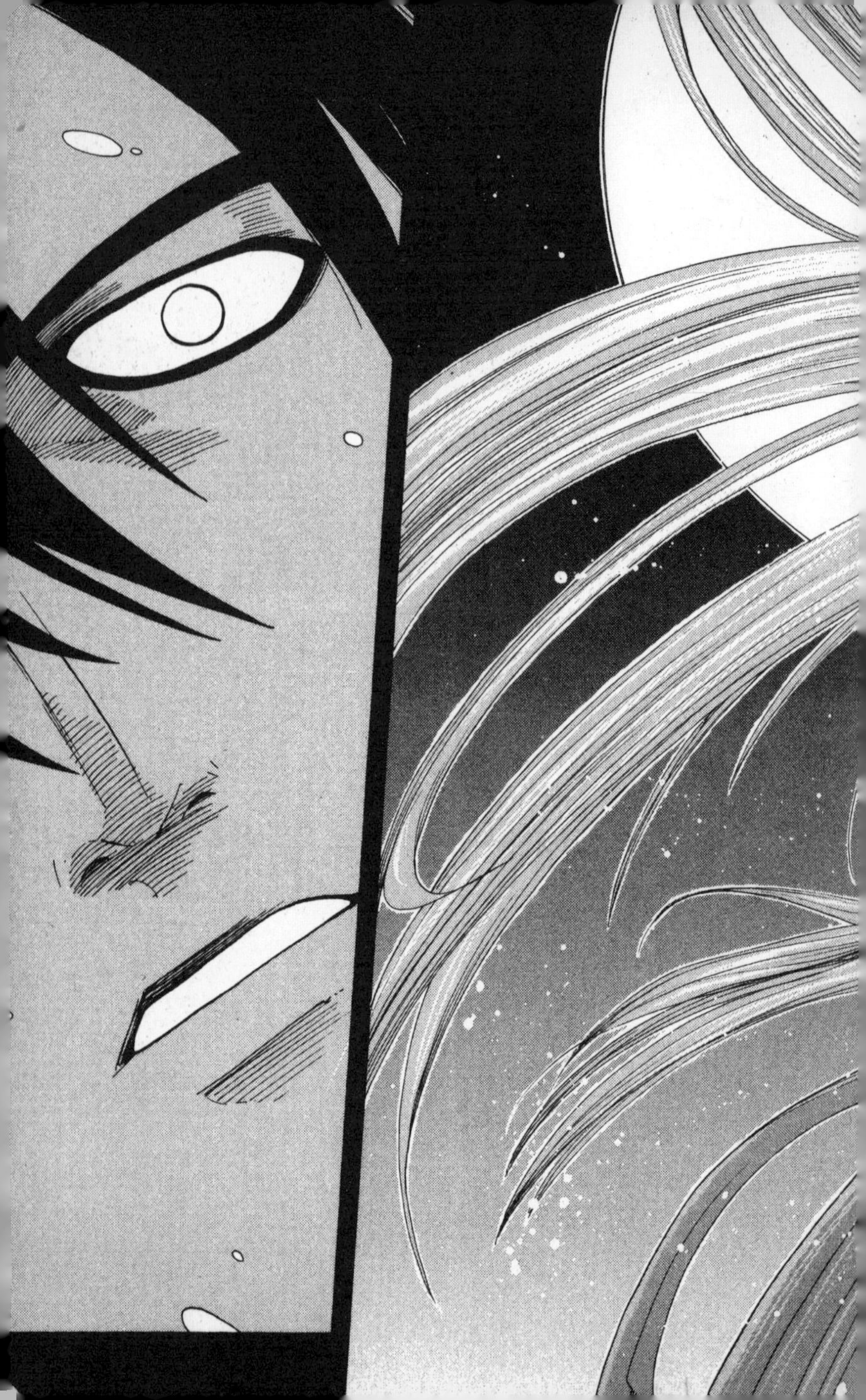

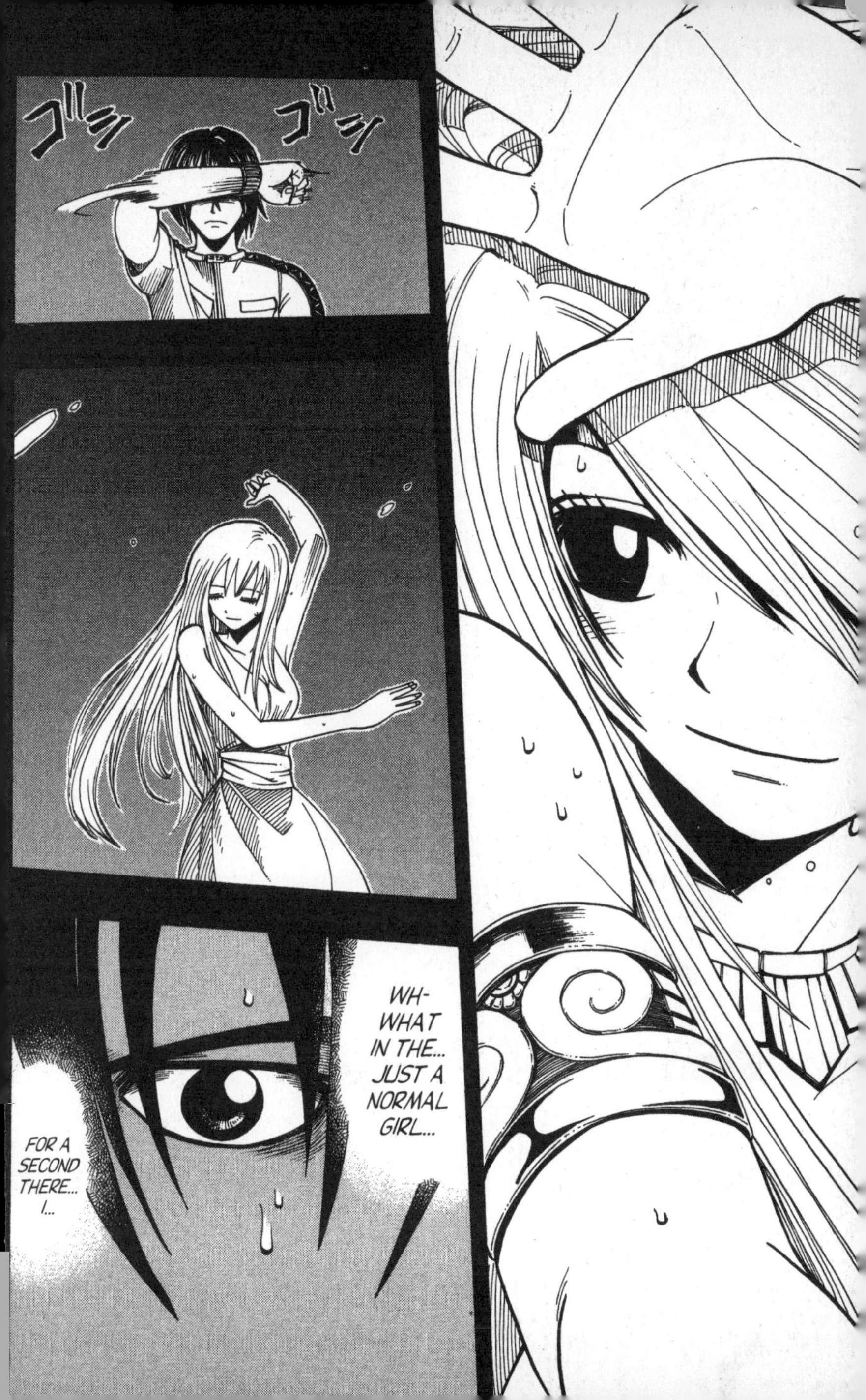
ゴシ
ゴシ
WH- WHAT IN THE... JUST A NORMAL GIRL...
FOR A SECOND THERE... I...

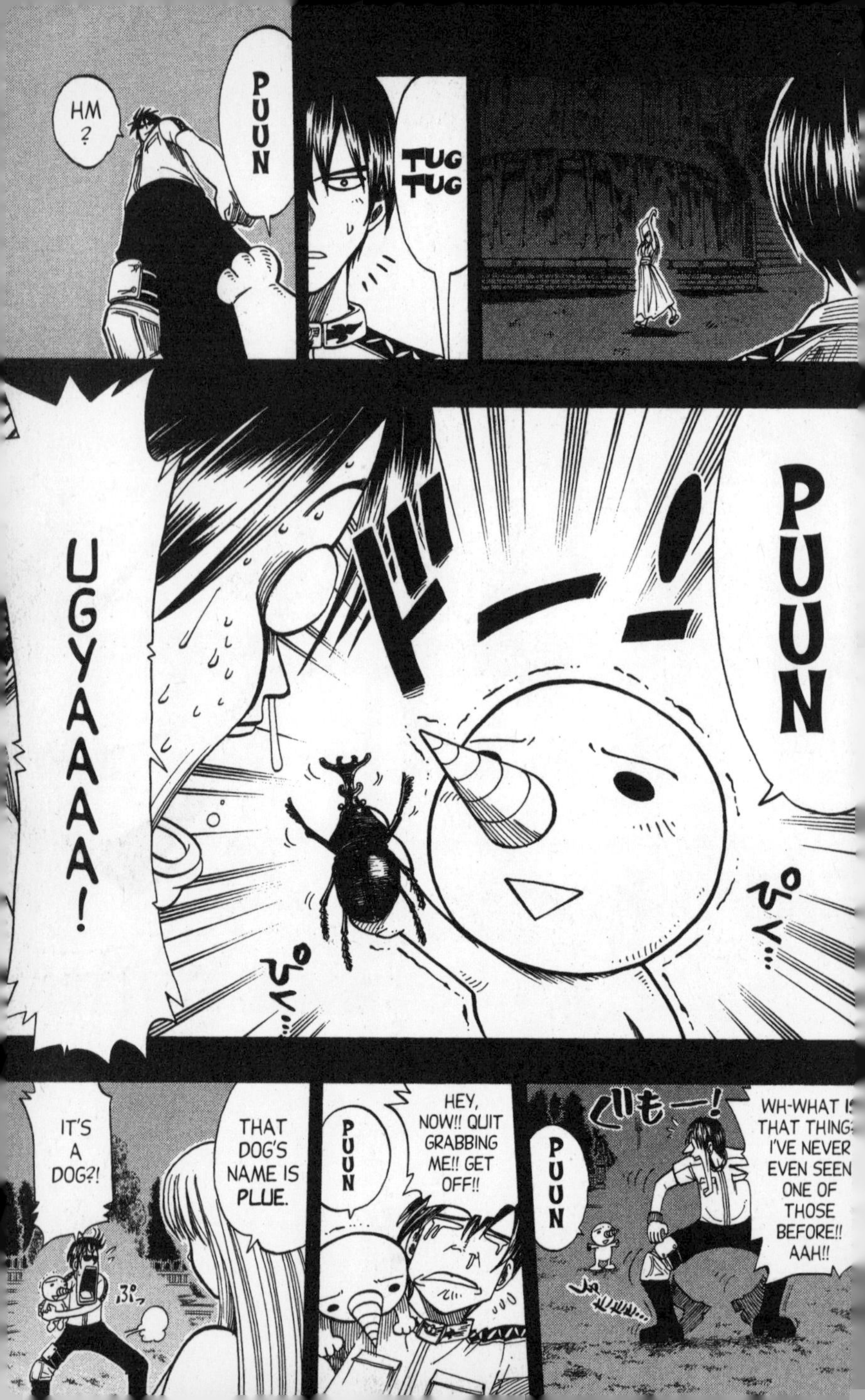

TUG TUG
PUUN
HM?
PUUN
ぴく…
ぴく…
UGYAAAA!
WH-WHAT IS THAT THING? I'VE NEVER EVEN SEEN ONE OF THOSE BEFORE!! AAH!!
PUUN
HEY, NOW!! QUIT GRABBING ME!! GET OFF!!
PUUN
THAT DOG'S NAME IS PLUE.
IT'S A DOG?!

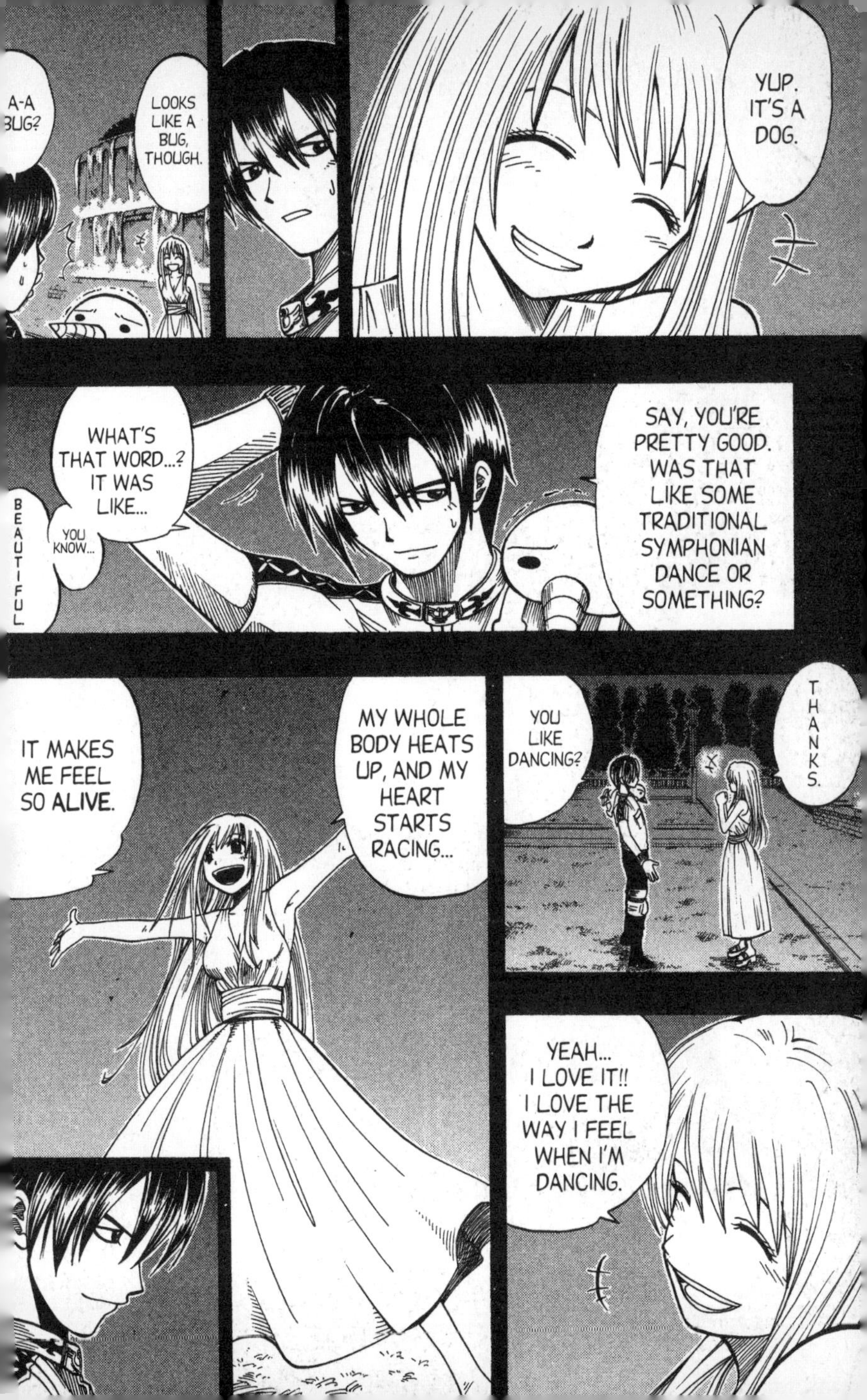
YUP. IT'S A DOG.
LOOKS LIKE A BUG, THOUGH.
A-A BUG?
SAY, YOU'RE PRETTY GOOD. WAS THAT LIKE SOME TRADITIONAL SYMPHONIAN DANCE OR SOMETHING?
WHAT'S THAT WORD...? IT WAS LIKE...
YOU KNOW...
BEAUTIFUL.
THANKS.
YOU LIKE DANCING?
YEAH... I LOVE IT!! I LOVE THE WAY I FEEL WHEN I'M DANCING.
MY WHOLE BODY HEATS UP, AND MY HEART STARTS RACING...
IT MAKES ME FEEL SO ALIVE.

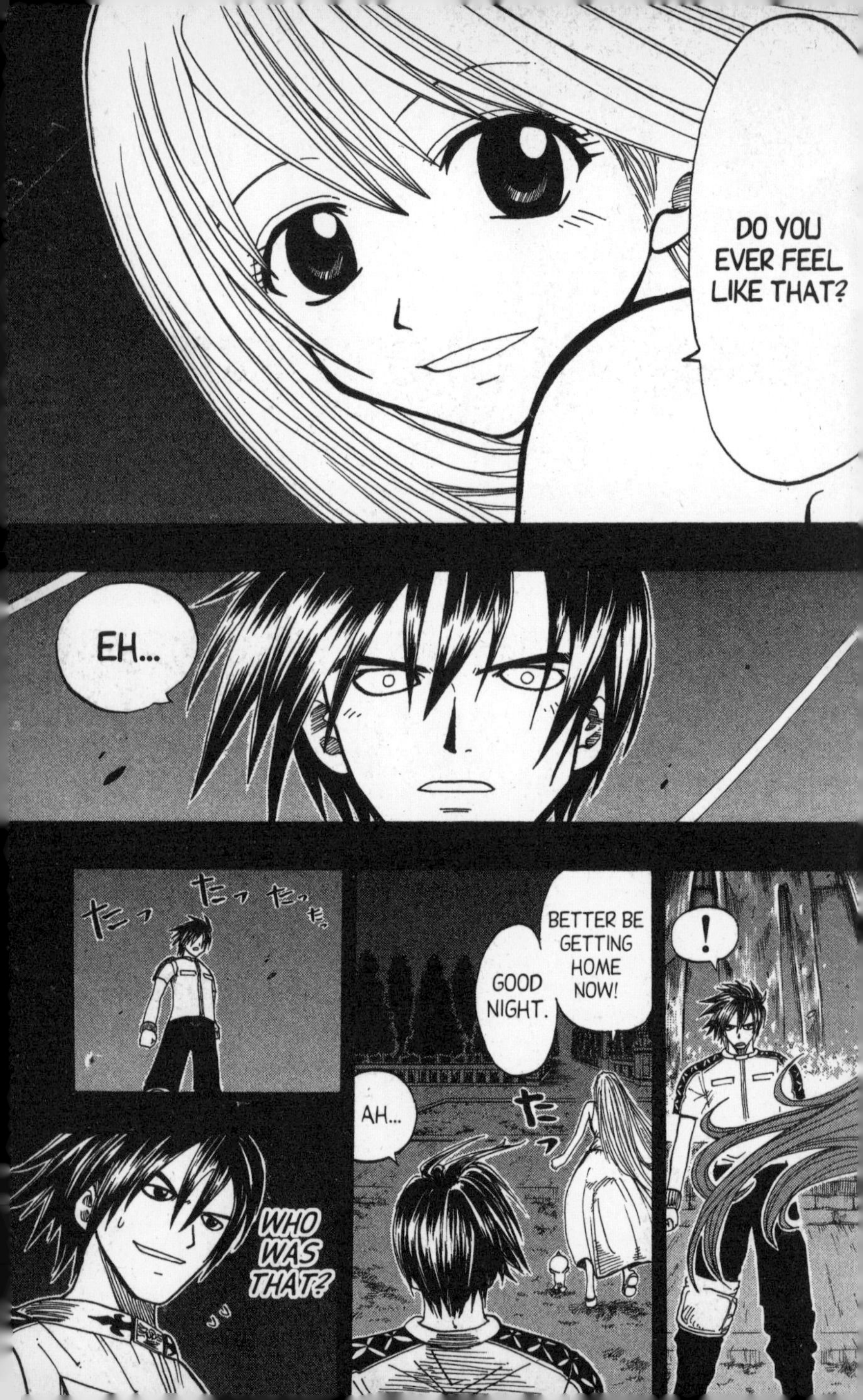
DO YOU EVER FEEL LIKE THAT?
EH...
!
BETTER BE GETTING HOME NOW!
GOOD NIGHT.
AH...
WHO WAS THAT?

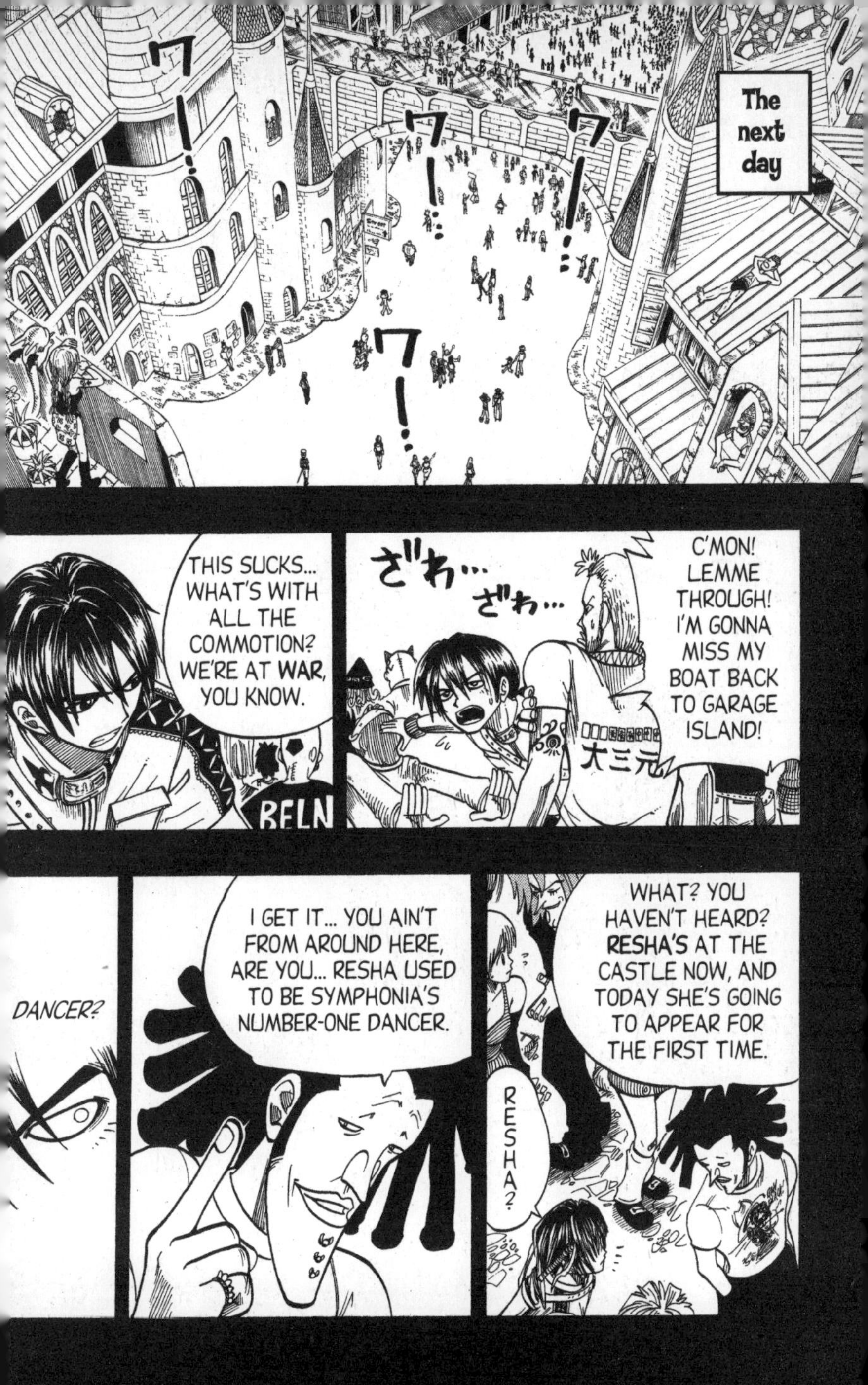

The next day
ワー!!
ワー!!
ワー!!
ワー!!
ざわ… ざわ…
C'MON! LEMME THROUGH! I'M GONNA MISS MY BOAT BACK TO GARAGE ISLAND!
大三元
THIS SUCKS... WHAT'S WITH ALL THE COMMOTION? WE'RE AT **WAR**, YOU KNOW.
WHAT? YOU HAVEN'T HEARD? **RESHA'S** AT THE CASTLE NOW, AND TODAY SHE'S GOING TO APPEAR FOR THE FIRST TIME.
RESHA?
I GET IT... YOU AIN'T FROM AROUND HERE, ARE YOU... RESHA USED TO BE SYMPHONIA'S NUMBER-ONE DANCER.
DANCER?

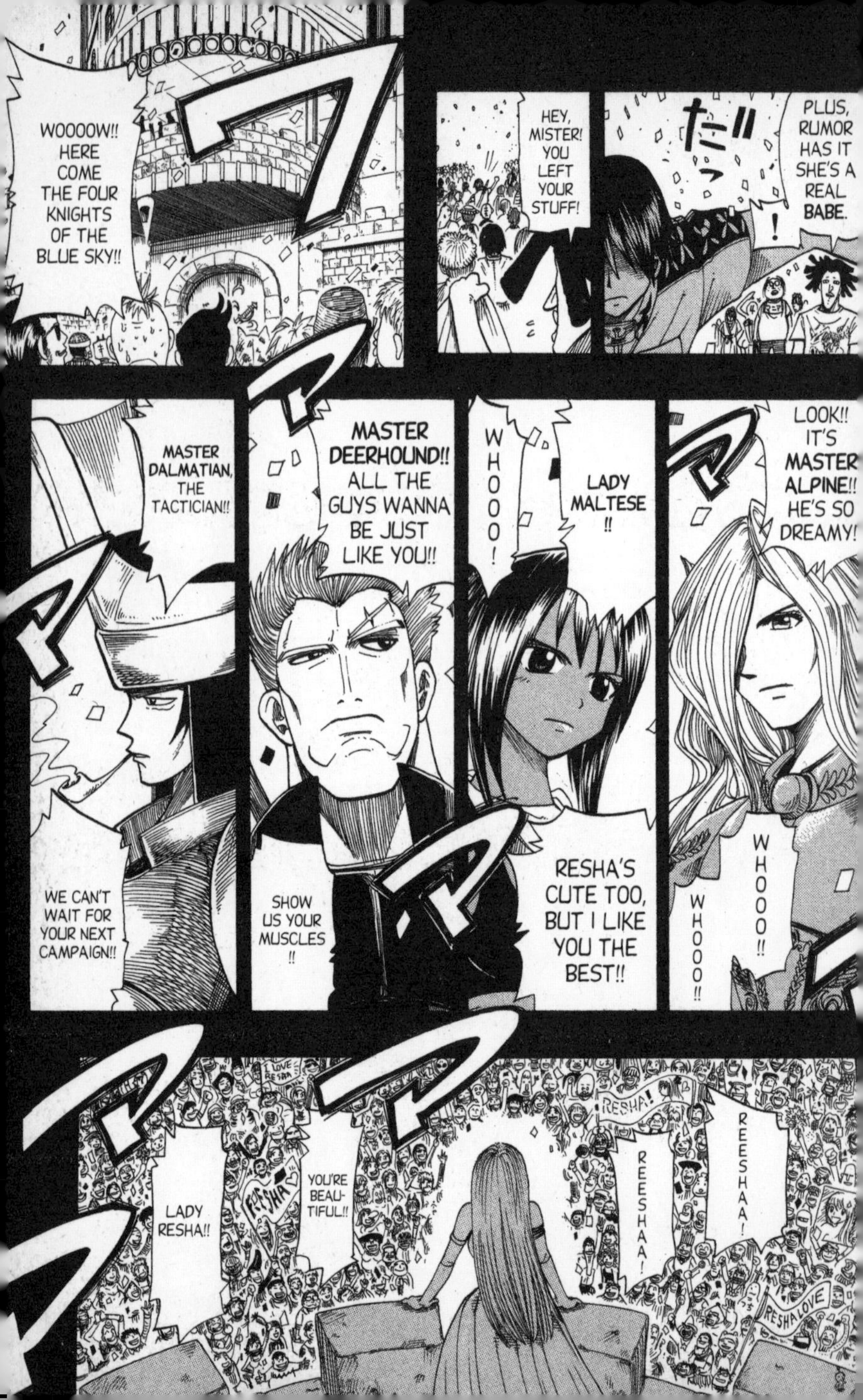

PLUS, RUMOR HAS IT SHE'S A REAL BABE.
!
HEY, MISTER! YOU LEFT YOUR STUFF!
WOOOOW!! HERE COME THE FOUR KNIGHTS OF THE BLUE SKY!!
LOOK!! IT'S MASTER ALPINE!! HE'S SO DREAMY!
WHOOOO!!
WHOOOO!!
LADY MALTESE!!
WHOOOO!
RESHA'S CUTE TOO, BUT I LIKE YOU THE BEST!!
MASTER DEERHOUND!! ALL THE GUYS WANNA BE JUST LIKE YOU!!
SHOW US YOUR MUSCLES!!
MASTER DALMATIAN, THE TACTICIAN!!
WE CAN'T WAIT FOR YOUR NEXT CAMPAIGN!!
REESHAA!
REESHAA!
RESHA!
RESHA LOVE
YOU'RE BEAUTIFUL!!
RESHA
LADY RESHA!!
I LOVE RESHA

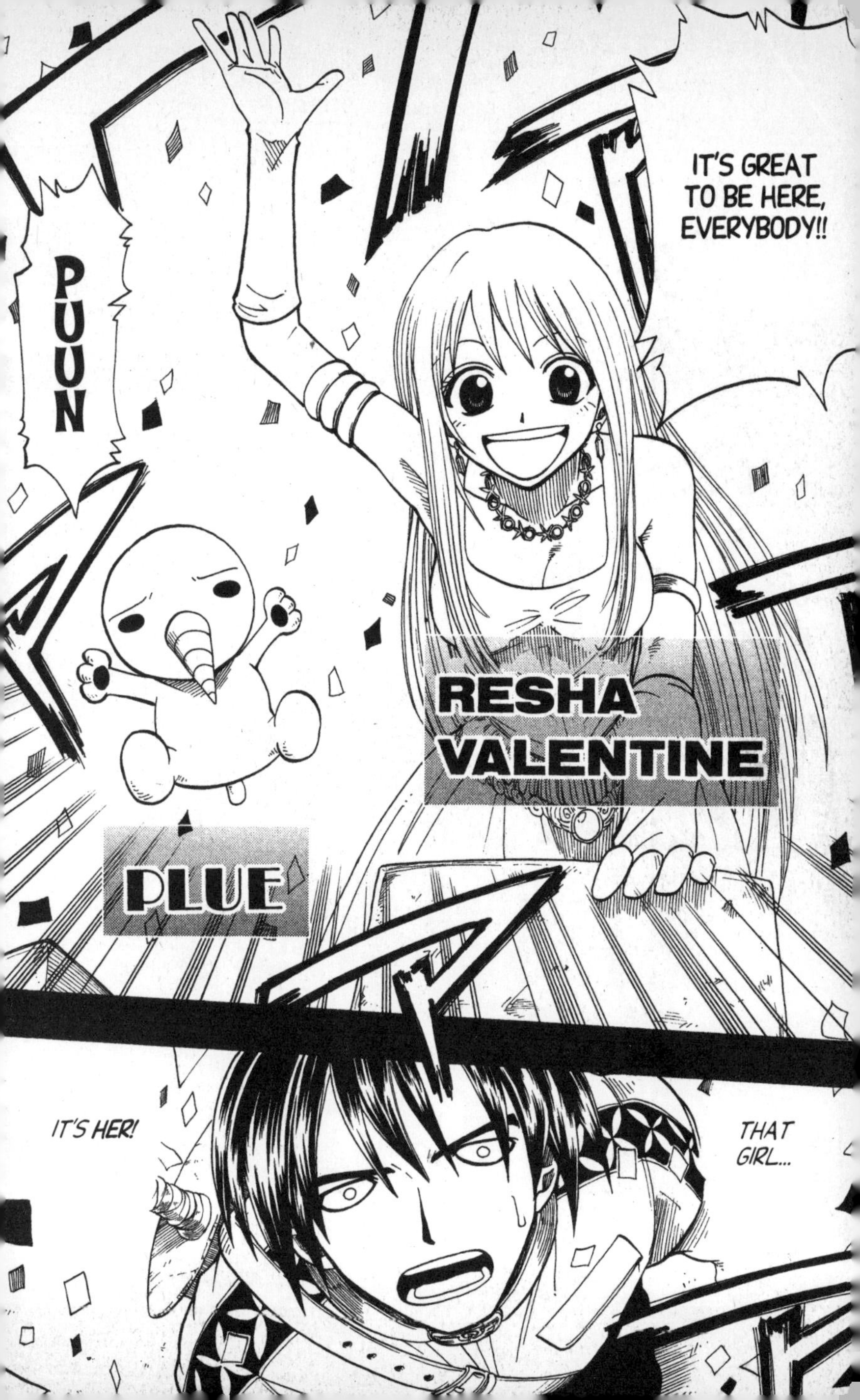
IT'S GREAT TO BE HERE, EVERYBODY!!
RESHA VALENTINE
PUUN
PLUE
THAT GIRL...
IT'S HER!

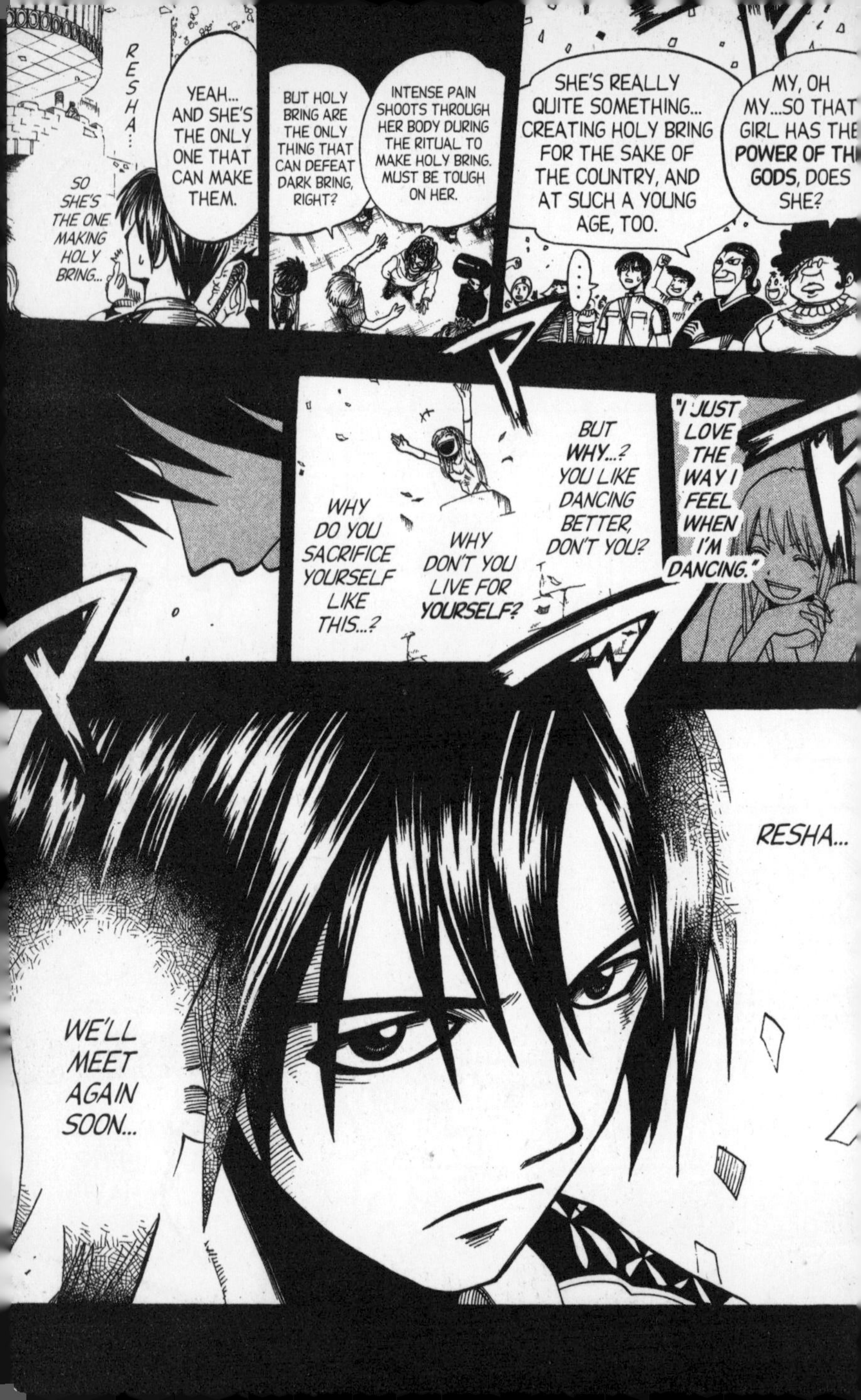
MY, OH MY...SO THAT GIRL HAS THE POWER OF TH GODS, DOES SHE?
SHE'S REALLY QUITE SOMETHING... CREATING HOLY BRING FOR THE SAKE OF THE COUNTRY, AND AT SUCH A YOUNG AGE, TOO.
...
INTENSE PAIN SHOOTS THROUGH HER BODY DURING THE RITUAL TO MAKE HOLY BRING. MUST BE TOUGH ON HER.
BUT HOLY BRING ARE THE ONLY THING THAT CAN DEFEAT DARK BRING, RIGHT?
YEAH... AND SHE'S THE ONLY ONE THAT CAN MAKE THEM.
RESHA...
SO SHE'S THE ONE MAKING HOLY BRING...
"I JUST LOVE THE WAY I FEEL WHEN I'M DANCING."
BUT WHY...? YOU LIKE DANCING BETTER, DON'T YOU?
WHY DON'T YOU LIVE FOR YOURSELF?
WHY DO YOU SACRIFICE YOURSELF LIKE THIS...?
RESHA...
WE'LL MEET AGAIN SOON...

RAVE0077
Levin Watches the House, Part 9: Feelin' Gollish!

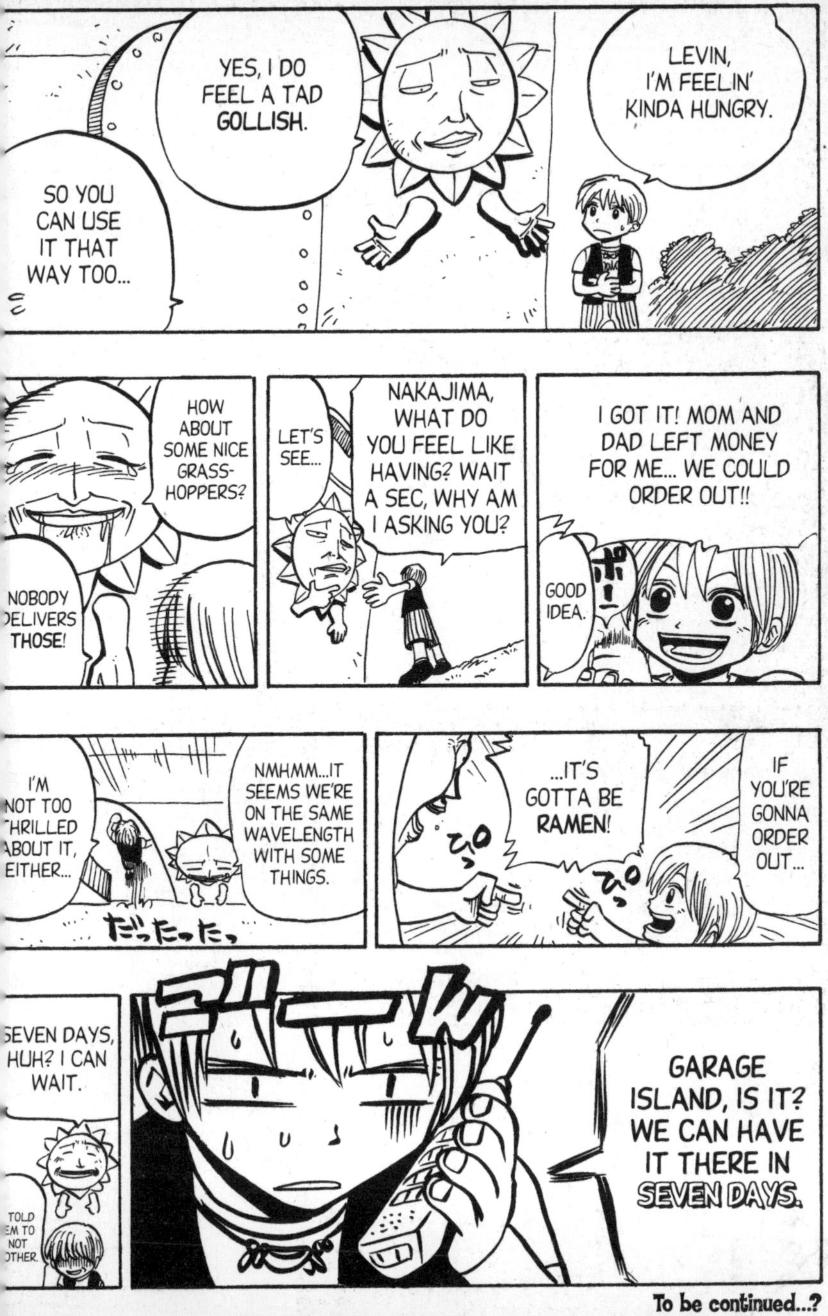
LEVIN, I'M FEELIN' KINDA HUNGRY.
YES, I DO FEEL A TAD GOLLISH.
SO YOU CAN USE IT THAT WAY TOO...
I GOT IT! MOM AND DAD LEFT MONEY FOR ME... WE COULD ORDER OUT!!
GOOD IDEA.
NAKAJIMA, WHAT DO YOU FEEL LIKE HAVING? WAIT A SEC, WHY AM I ASKING YOU?
LET'S SEE...
HOW ABOUT SOME NICE GRASS-HOPPERS?
NOBODY DELIVERS THOSE!
IF YOU'RE GONNA ORDER OUT...
...IT'S GOTTA BE RAMEN!
NMHMM...IT SEEMS WE'RE ON THE SAME WAVELENGTH WITH SOME THINGS.
I'M NOT TOO THRILLED ABOUT IT, EITHER...
だったたっ
GARAGE ISLAND, IS IT? WE CAN HAVE IT THERE IN SEVEN DAYS.
SEVEN DAYS, HUH? I CAN WAIT.
TOLD 'EM TO NOT BOTHER.

To be continued..?

Knights of Kingdom

RAVE0015 KNIGHTS OF KINGDOM PART 2

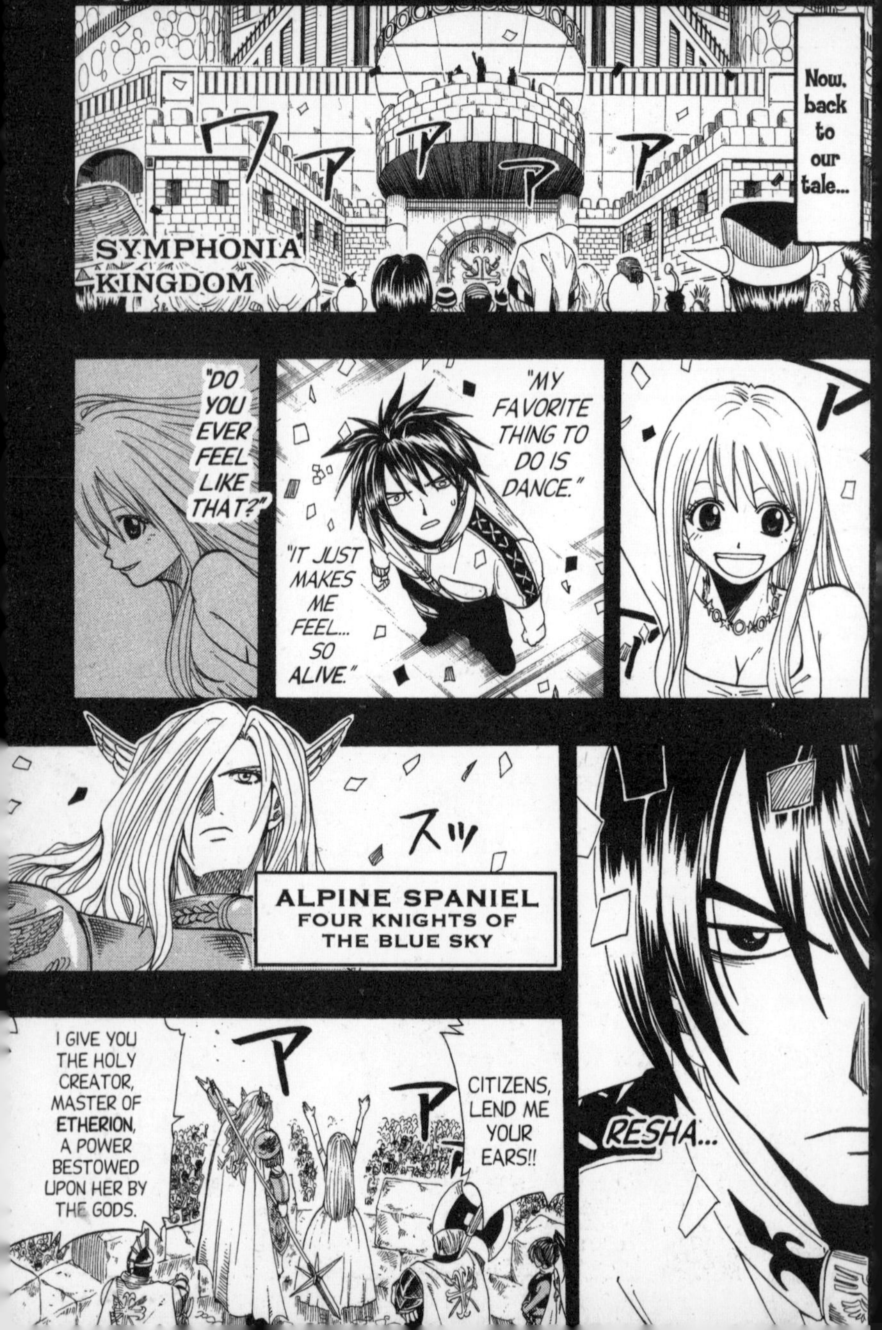
Now, back to our tale...
ワァァァ
SYMPHONIA KINGDOM
ア
"MY FAVORITE THING TO DO IS DANCE."
"IT JUST MAKES ME FEEL... SO ALIVE."
"DO YOU EVER FEEL LIKE THAT?"
RESHA...
スッ
ALPINE SPANIEL
FOUR KNIGHTS OF THE BLUE SKY
ア
ア
CITIZENS, LEND ME YOUR EARS!!
I GIVE YOU THE HOLY CREATOR, MASTER OF ETHERION, A POWER BESTOWED UPON HER BY THE GODS.

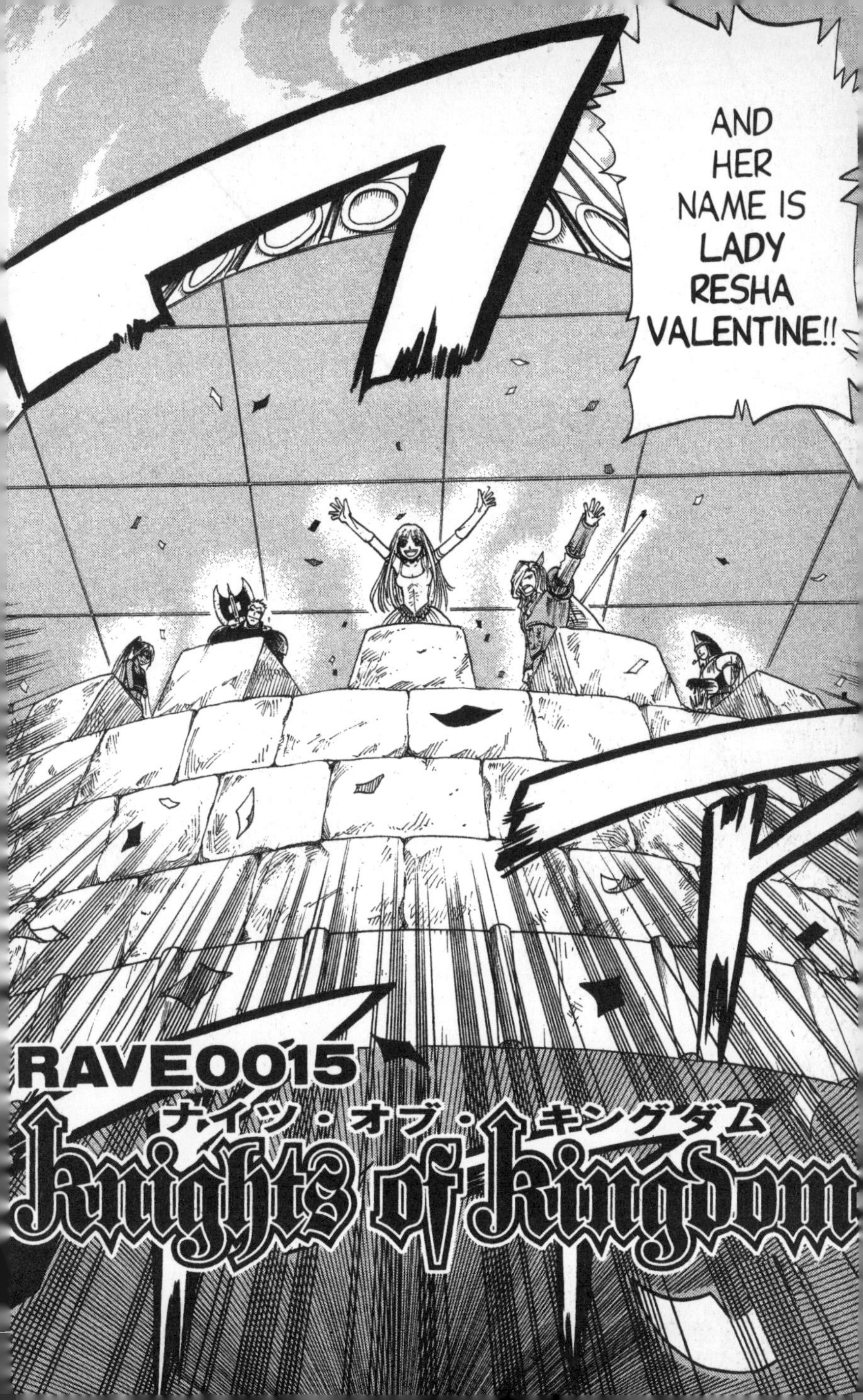
AND HER NAME IS LADY RESHA VALENTINE!!
RAVE0015
ナイツ・オブ・キングダム
Knights of Kingdom

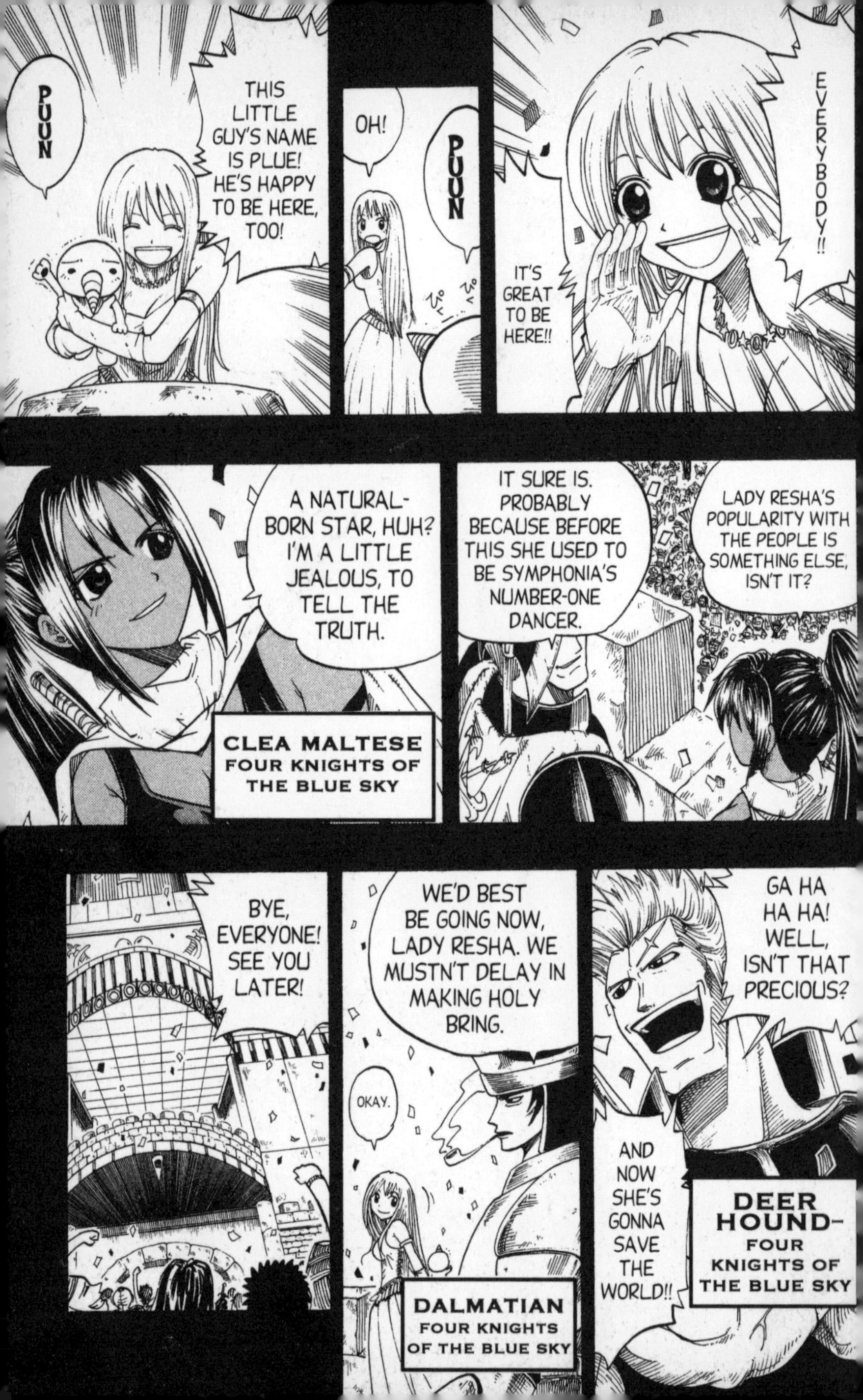
EVERYBODY!!
IT'S GREAT TO BE HERE!!
OH!
PUUN
THIS LITTLE GUY'S NAME IS PLUE! HE'S HAPPY TO BE HERE, TOO!
PUUN
LADY RESHA'S POPULARITY WITH THE PEOPLE IS SOMETHING ELSE, ISN'T IT?
IT SURE IS. PROBABLY BECAUSE BEFORE THIS SHE USED TO BE SYMPHONIA'S NUMBER-ONE DANCER.
A NATURAL-BORN STAR, HUH? I'M A LITTLE JEALOUS, TO TELL THE TRUTH.
CLEA MALTESE FOUR KNIGHTS OF THE BLUE SKY
GA HA HA HA! WELL, ISN'T THAT PRECIOUS?
AND NOW SHE'S GONNA SAVE THE WORLD!!
DEER HOUND– FOUR KNIGHTS OF THE BLUE SKY
WE'D BEST BE GOING NOW, LADY RESHA. WE MUSTN'T DELAY IN MAKING HOLY BRING.
OKAY.
DALMATIAN FOUR KNIGHTS OF THE BLUE SKY
BYE, EVERYONE! SEE YOU LATER!

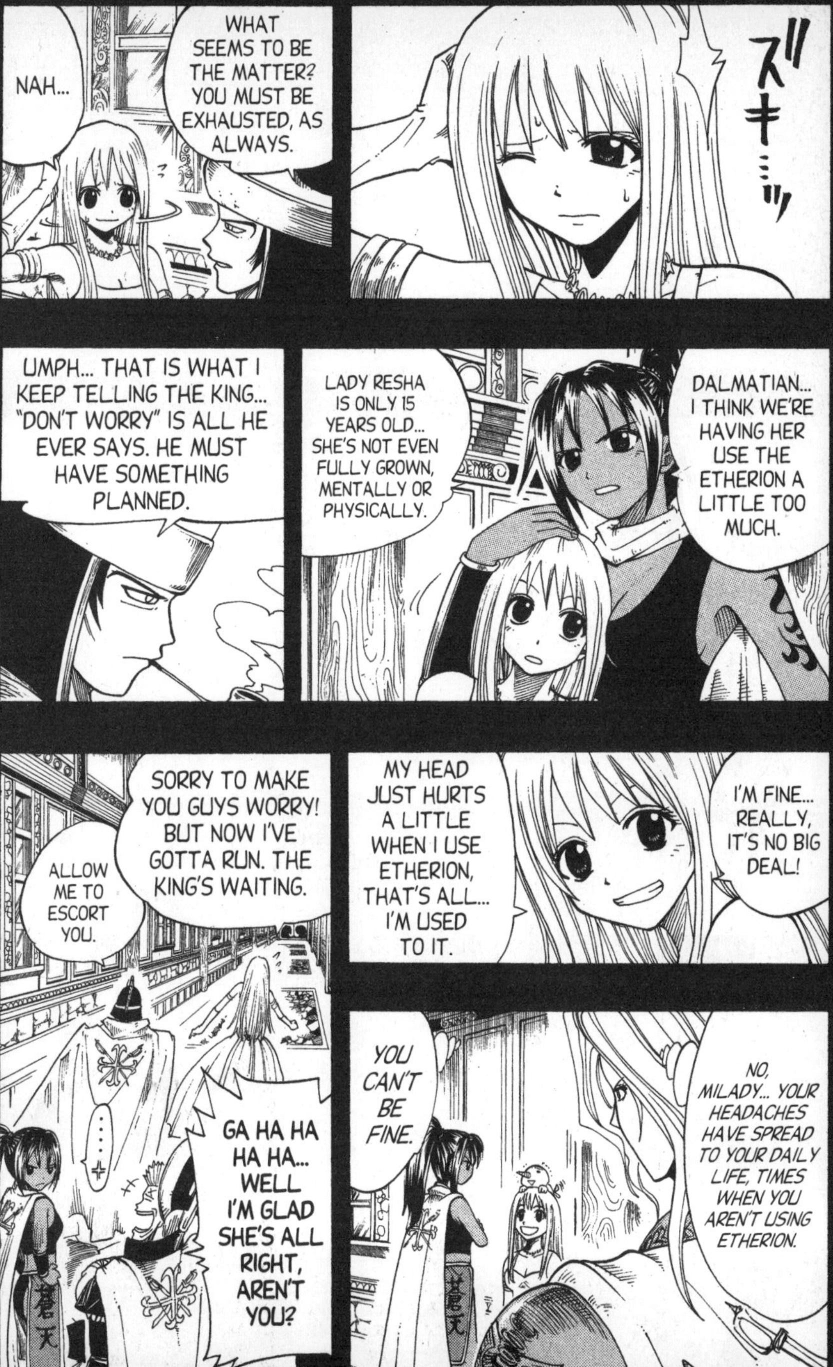
ズキミッ
WHAT SEEMS TO BE THE MATTER? YOU MUST BE EXHAUSTED, AS ALWAYS.
NAH...
DALMATIAN... I THINK WE'RE HAVING HER USE THE ETHERION A LITTLE TOO MUCH.
LADY RESHA IS ONLY 15 YEARS OLD... SHE'S NOT EVEN FULLY GROWN, MENTALLY OR PHYSICALLY.
UMPH... THAT IS WHAT I KEEP TELLING THE KING... "DON'T WORRY" IS ALL HE EVER SAYS. HE MUST HAVE SOMETHING PLANNED.
I'M FINE... REALLY, IT'S NO BIG DEAL!
MY HEAD JUST HURTS A LITTLE WHEN I USE ETHERION, THAT'S ALL... I'M USED TO IT.
NO, MILADY... YOUR HEADACHES HAVE SPREAD TO YOUR DAILY LIFE, TIMES WHEN YOU AREN'T USING ETHERION.
YOU CAN'T BE FINE.
SORRY TO MAKE YOU GUYS WORRY! BUT NOW I'VE GOTTA RUN. THE KING'S WAITING.
ALLOW ME TO ESCORT YOU.
GA HA HA HA HA... WELL I'M GLAD SHE'S ALL RIGHT, AREN'T YOU?
......

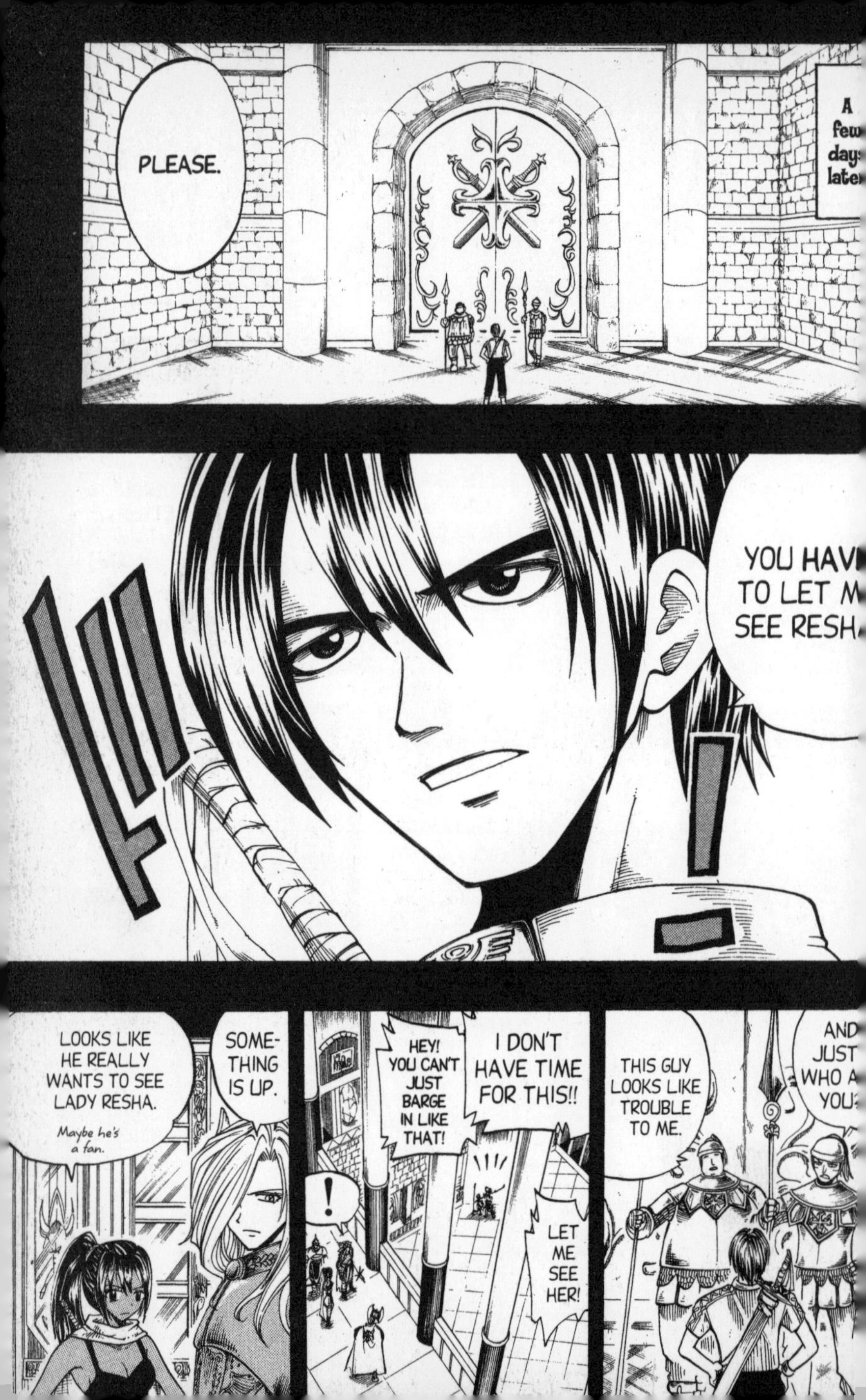

A few days later
PLEASE.
YOU HAVE TO LET ME SEE RESHA
AND JUST WHO ARE YOU?
THIS GUY LOOKS LIKE TROUBLE TO ME.
I DON'T HAVE TIME FOR THIS!!
HEY! YOU CAN'T JUST BARGE IN LIKE THAT!
LET ME SEE HER!
SOME-THING IS UP.
LOOKS LIKE HE REALLY WANTS TO SEE LADY RESHA.
Maybe he's a fan.

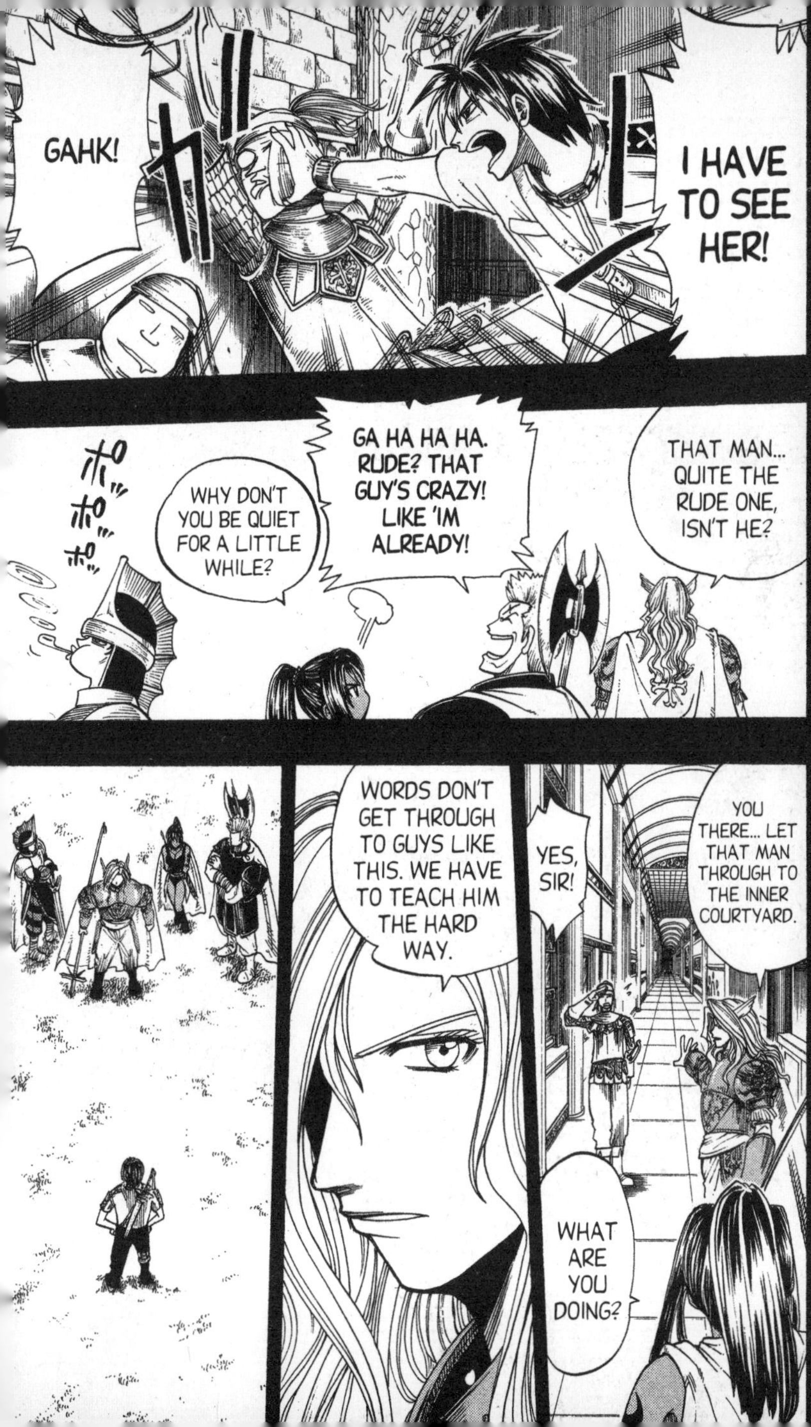
I HAVE TO SEE HER!
GAHK!
THAT MAN... QUITE THE RUDE ONE, ISN'T HE?
GA HA HA HA. RUDE? THAT GUY'S CRAZY! LIKE 'IM ALREADY!
WHY DON'T YOU BE QUIET FOR A LITTLE WHILE?
ポ ポ ポ
YOU THERE... LET THAT MAN THROUGH TO THE INNER COURTYARD.
YES, SIR!
WHAT ARE YOU DOING?
WORDS DON'T GET THROUGH TO GUYS LIKE THIS. WE HAVE TO TEACH HIM THE HARD WAY.

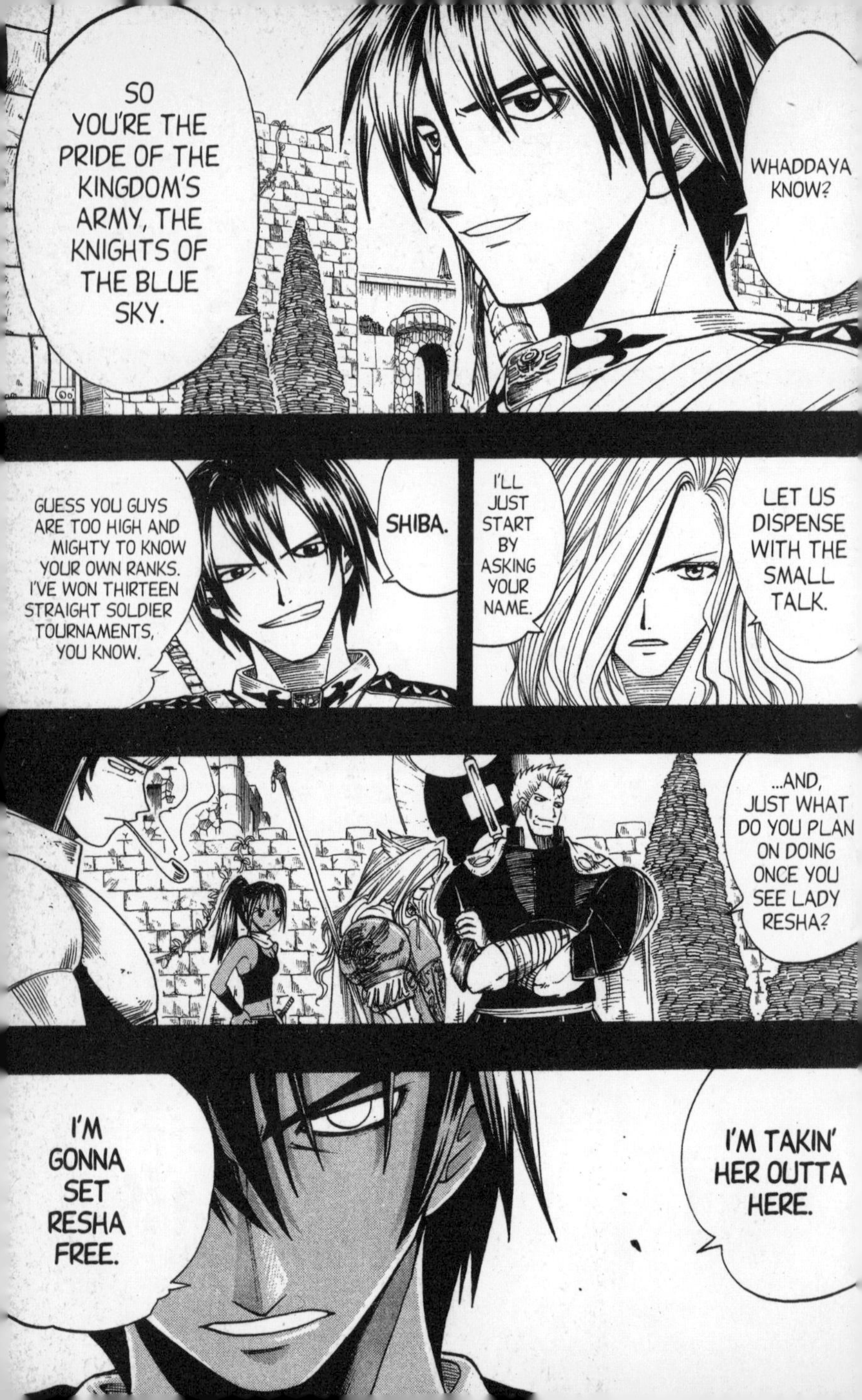
WHADDAYA KNOW?
SO YOU'RE THE PRIDE OF THE KINGDOM'S ARMY, THE KNIGHTS OF THE BLUE SKY.
LET US DISPENSE WITH THE SMALL TALK.
I'LL JUST START BY ASKING YOUR NAME.
SHIBA.
GUESS YOU GUYS ARE TOO HIGH AND MIGHTY TO KNOW YOUR OWN RANKS. I'VE WON THIRTEEN STRAIGHT SOLDIER TOURNAMENTS, YOU KNOW.
...AND, JUST WHAT DO YOU PLAN ON DOING ONCE YOU SEE LADY RESHA?
I'M TAKIN' HER OUTTA HERE.
I'M GONNA SET RESHA FREE.

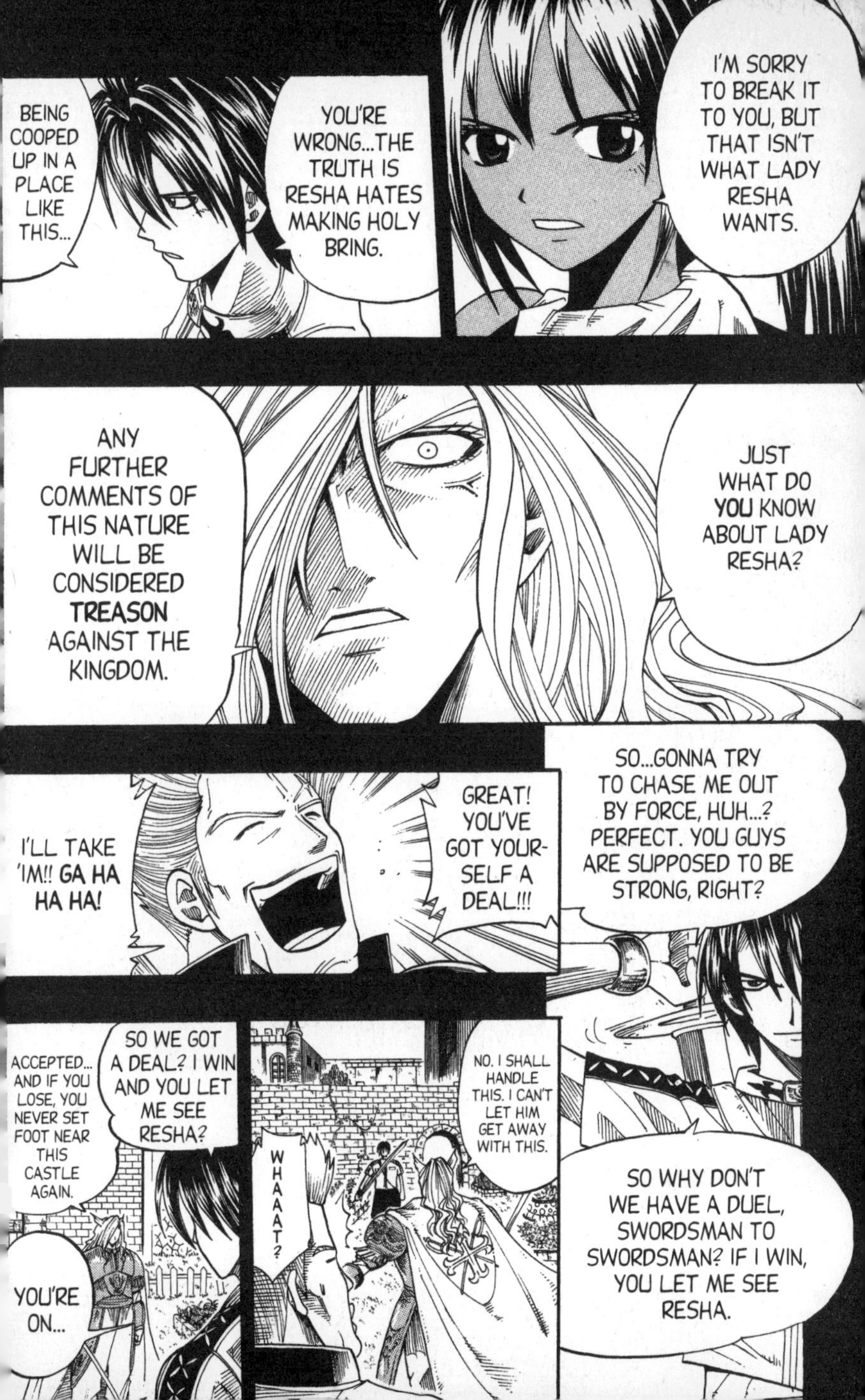
I'M SORRY TO BREAK IT TO YOU, BUT THAT ISN'T WHAT LADY RESHA WANTS.
YOU'RE WRONG...THE TRUTH IS RESHA HATES MAKING HOLY BRING.
BEING COOPED UP IN A PLACE LIKE THIS...
JUST WHAT DO **YOU** KNOW ABOUT LADY RESHA?
ANY FURTHER COMMENTS OF THIS NATURE WILL BE CONSIDERED **TREASON** AGAINST THE KINGDOM.
SO...GONNA TRY TO CHASE ME OUT BY FORCE, HUH...? PERFECT. YOU GUYS ARE SUPPOSED TO BE STRONG, RIGHT?
SO WHY DON'T WE HAVE A DUEL, SWORDSMAN TO SWORDSMAN? IF I WIN, YOU LET ME SEE RESHA.
GREAT! YOU'VE GOT YOURSELF A DEAL!!!
I'LL TAKE 'IM!! **GA HA HA HA!**
NO. I SHALL HANDLE THIS. I CAN'T LET HIM GET AWAY WITH THIS.
WHAAAT?
SO WE GOT A DEAL? I WIN AND YOU LET ME SEE RESHA?
ACCEPTED... AND IF YOU LOSE, YOU NEVER SET FOOT NEAR THIS CASTLE AGAIN.
YOU'RE ON...

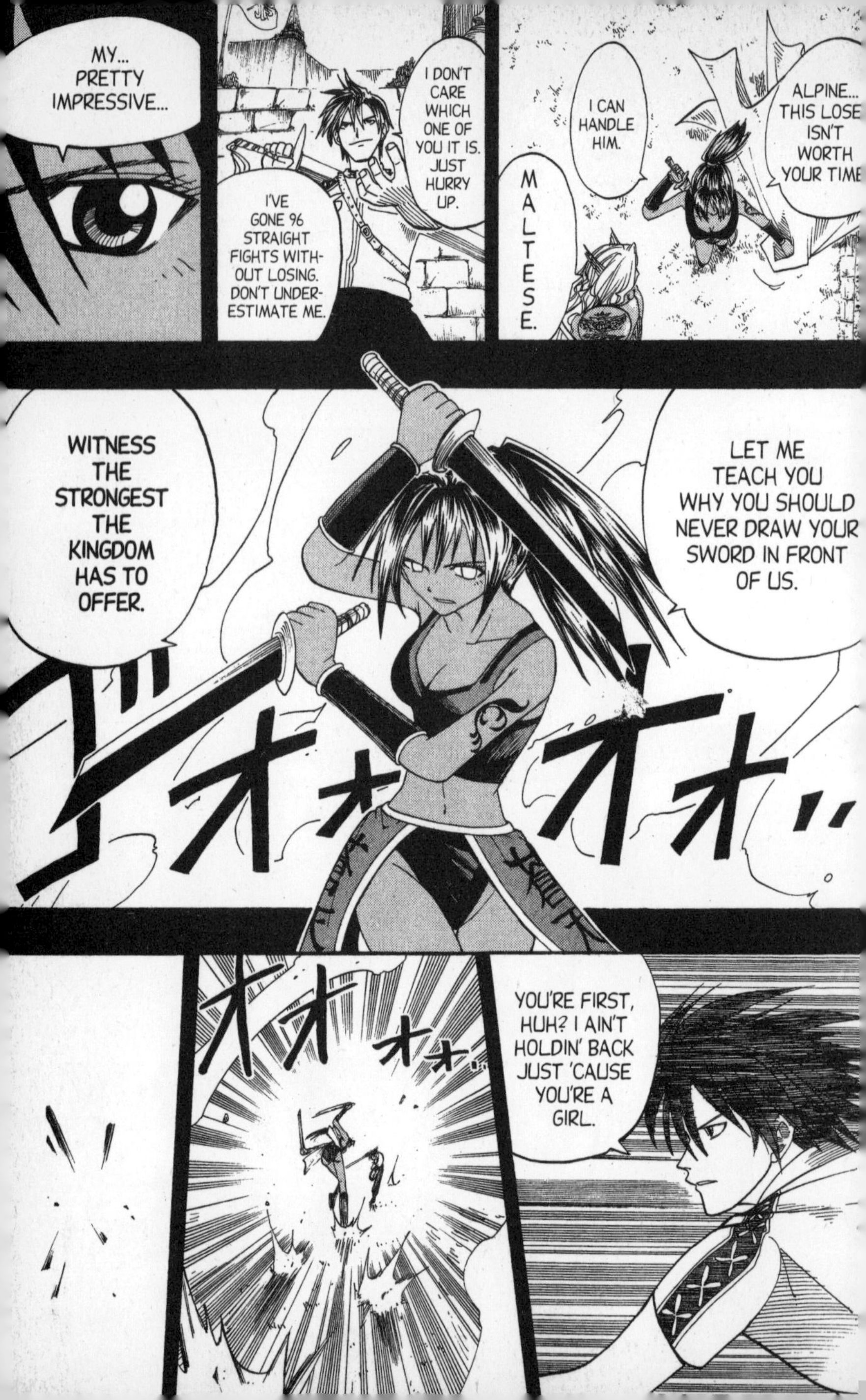
ALPINE... THIS LOSE ISN'T WORTH YOUR TIME
I CAN HANDLE HIM.
MALTESE.
I DON'T CARE WHICH ONE OF YOU IT IS. JUST HURRY UP.
I'VE GONE 96 STRAIGHT FIGHTS WITH-OUT LOSING. DON'T UNDER-ESTIMATE ME.
MY... PRETTY IMPRESSIVE...
LET ME TEACH YOU WHY YOU SHOULD NEVER DRAW YOUR SWORD IN FRONT OF US.
WITNESS THE STRONGEST THE KINGDOM HAS TO OFFER.
ゴオォオ
YOU'RE FIRST, HUH? I AIN'T HOLDIN' BACK JUST 'CAUSE YOU'RE A GIRL.
オオォォ

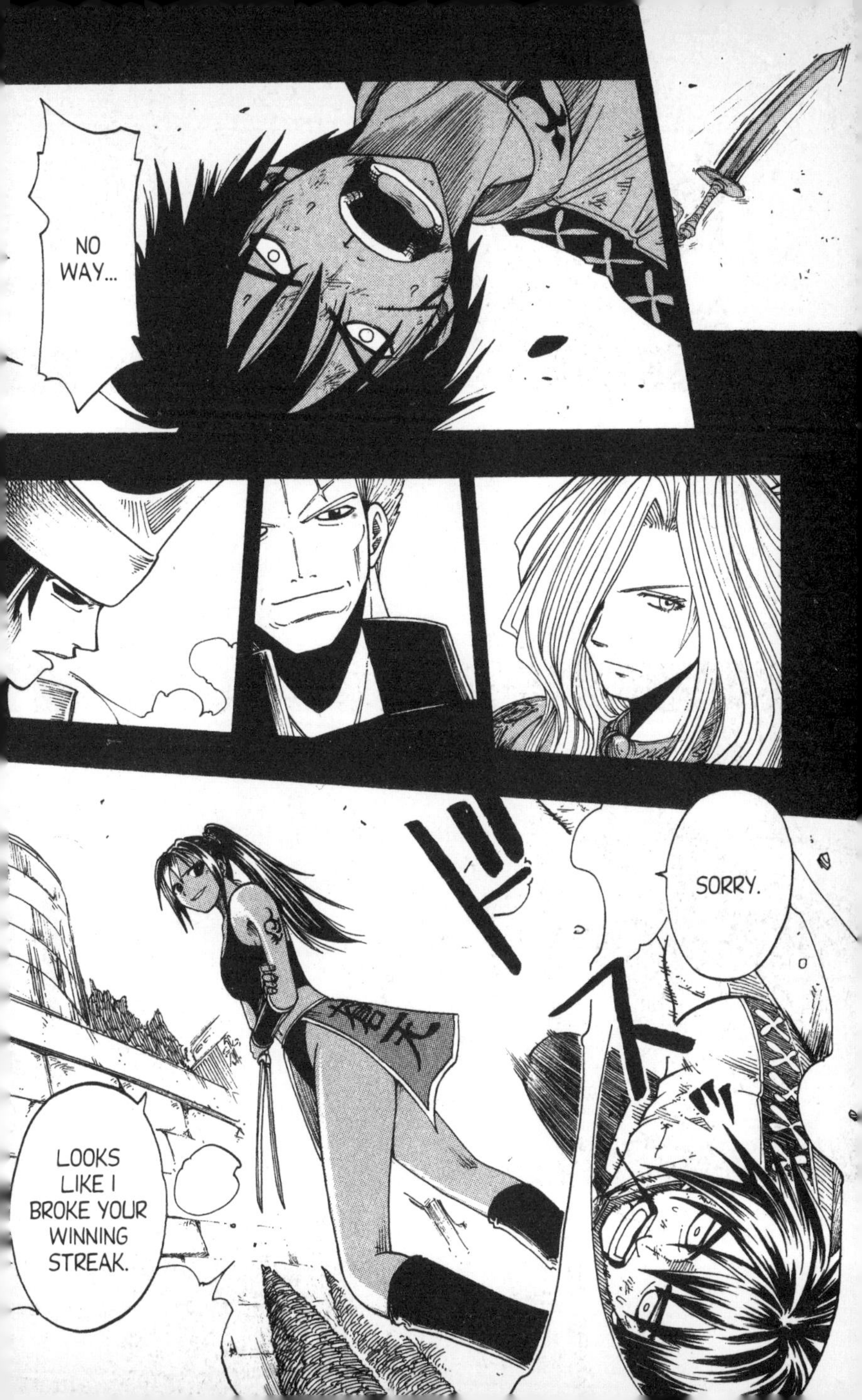
NO WAY...
SORRY.
LOOKS LIKE I BROKE YOUR WINNING STREAK.

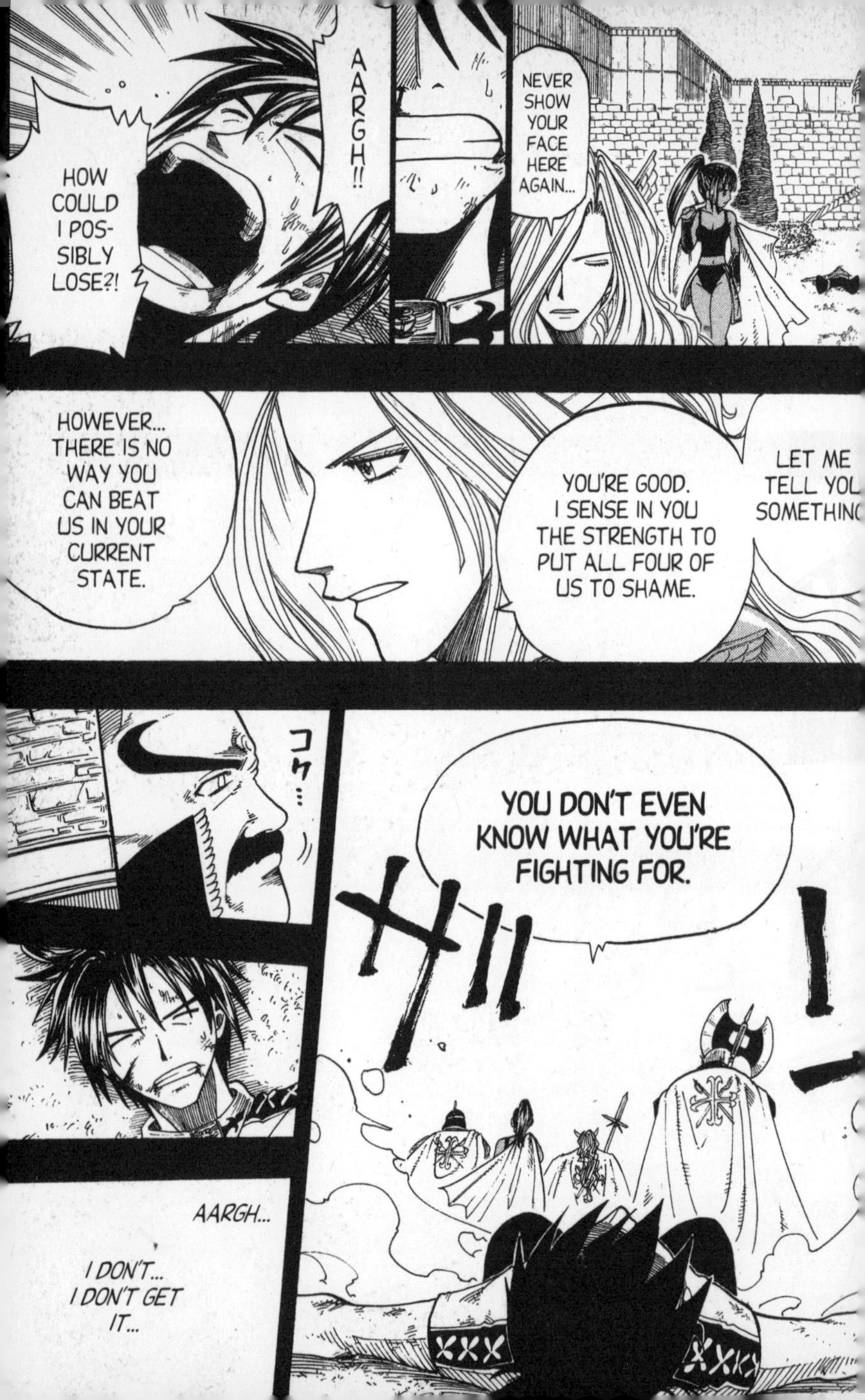
NEVER SHOW YOUR FACE HERE AGAIN...
AARGH!!
HOW COULD I POS-SIBLY LOSE?!
LET ME TELL YO SOMETHIN
YOU'RE GOOD. I SENSE IN YOU THE STRENGTH TO PUT ALL FOUR OF US TO SHAME.
HOWEVER... THERE IS NO WAY YOU CAN BEAT US IN YOUR CURRENT STATE.
YOU DON'T EVEN KNOW WHAT YOU'RE FIGHTING FOR.
コケ…
AARGH...
I DON'T... I DON'T GET IT...

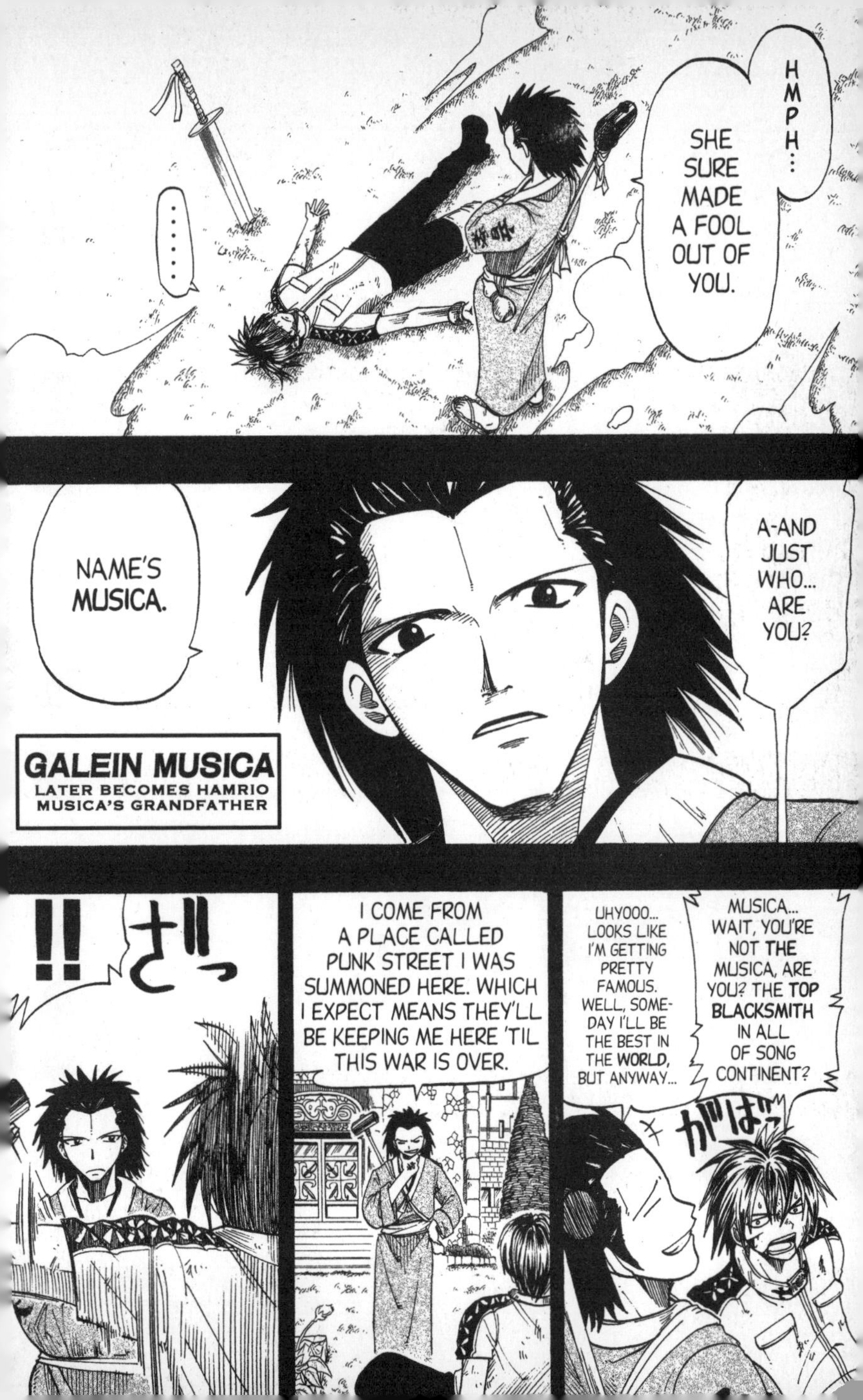

HMPH...
SHE SURE MADE A FOOL OUT OF YOU.
......
A-AND JUST WHO... ARE YOU?
NAME'S MUSICA.
GALEIN MUSICA
LATER BECOMES HAMRIO MUSICA'S GRANDFATHER
MUSICA... WAIT, YOU'RE NOT THE MUSICA, ARE YOU? THE TOP BLACKSMITH IN ALL OF SONG CONTINENT?
UHYOOO... LOOKS LIKE I'M GETTING PRETTY FAMOUS. WELL, SOME-DAY I'LL BE THE BEST IN THE WORLD, BUT ANYWAY...
がばっ
I COME FROM A PLACE CALLED PUNK STREET I WAS SUMMONED HERE. WHICH I EXPECT MEANS THEY'LL BE KEEPING ME HERE 'TIL THIS WAR IS OVER.
!!
ざっ

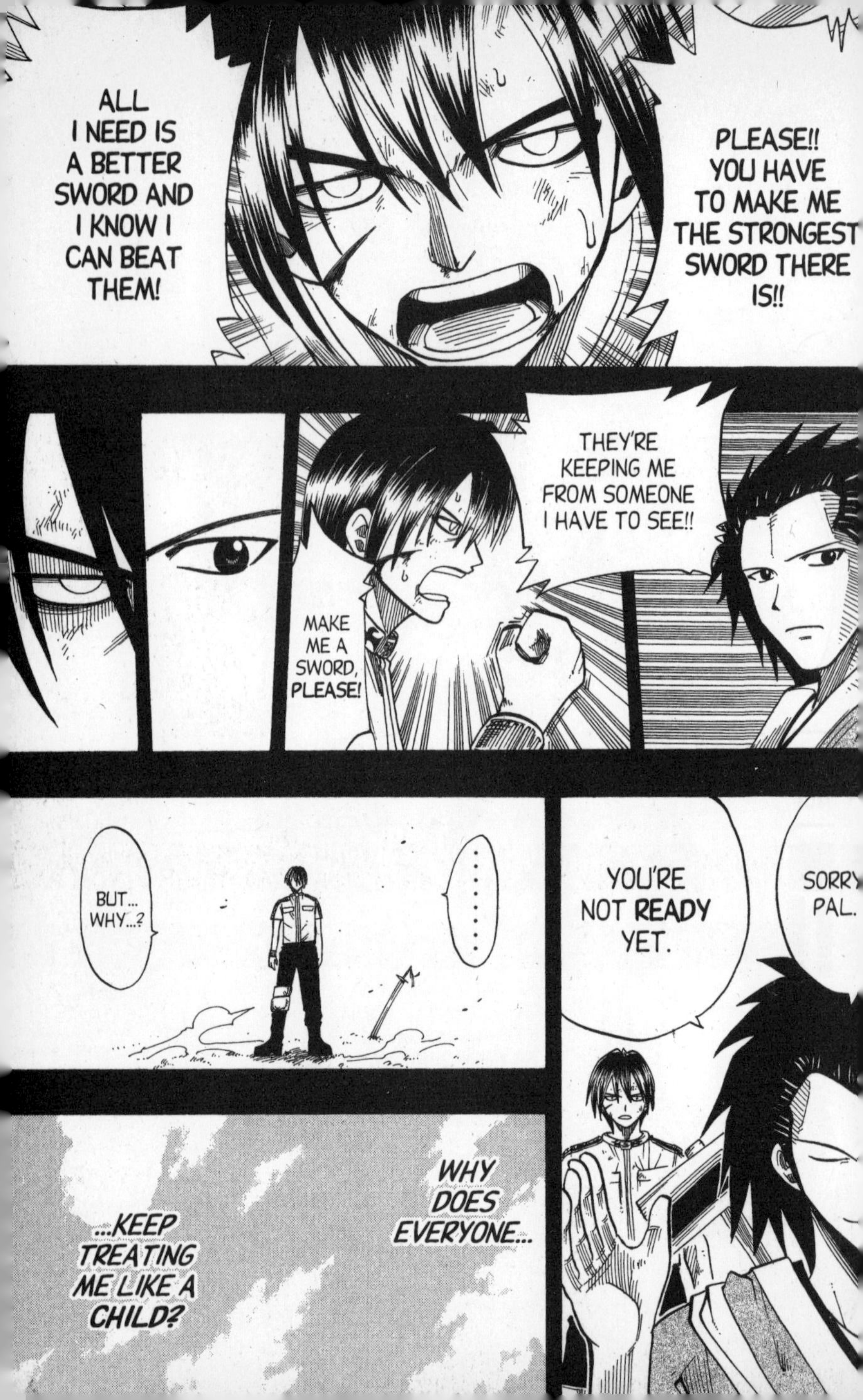
PLEASE!! YOU HAVE TO MAKE ME THE STRONGEST SWORD THERE IS!!
ALL I NEED IS A BETTER SWORD AND I KNOW I CAN BEAT THEM!
THEY'RE KEEPING ME FROM SOMEONE I HAVE TO SEE!!
MAKE ME A SWORD, PLEASE!
SORRY PAL.
YOU'RE NOT READY YET.
......
BUT... WHY...?
WHY DOES EVERYONE...
...KEEP TREATING ME LIKE A CHILD?

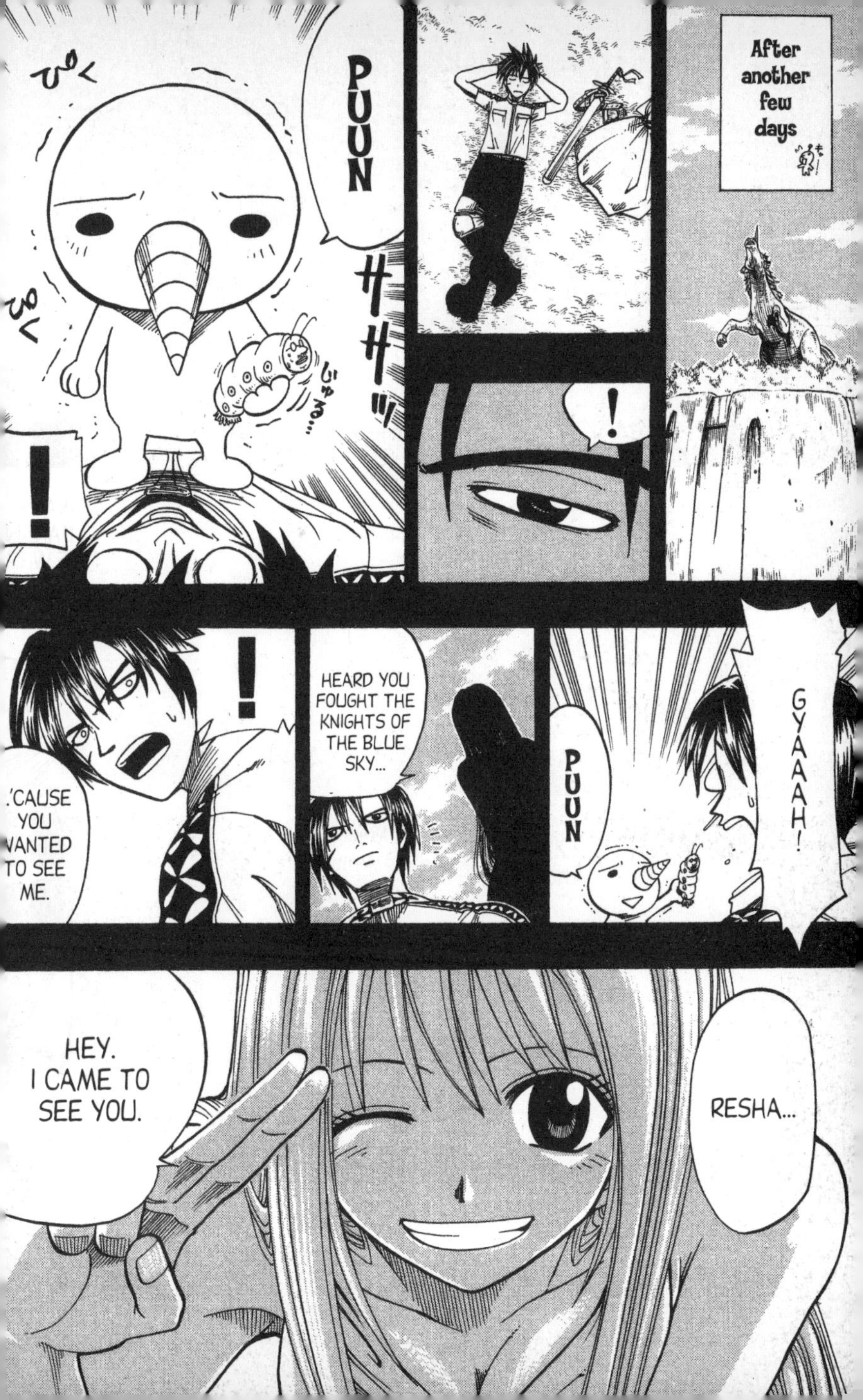
After another few days
!
PUUN
!
GYAAAH!
PUUN
HEARD YOU FOUGHT THE KNIGHTS OF THE BLUE SKY...
!
'CAUSE YOU WANTED TO SEE ME.
RESHA...
HEY. I CAME TO SEE YOU.

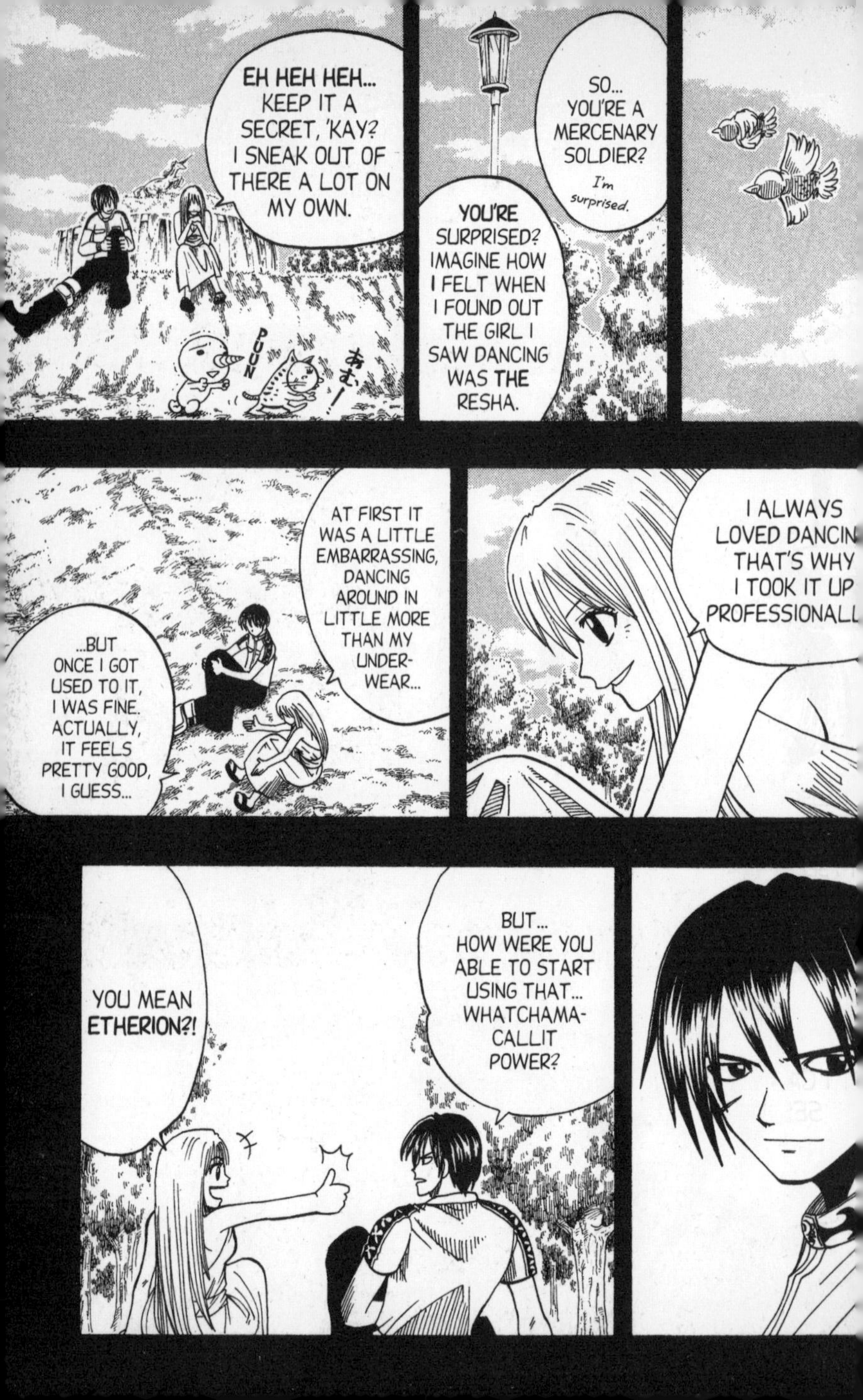
SO... YOU'RE A MERCENARY SOLDIER?
I'm surprised.
YOU'RE SURPRISED? IMAGINE HOW I FELT WHEN I FOUND OUT THE GIRL I SAW DANCING WAS THE RESHA.
EH HEH HEH... KEEP IT A SECRET, 'KAY? I SNEAK OUT OF THERE A LOT ON MY OWN.
PUUN
あむ!
I ALWAYS LOVED DANCIN THAT'S WHY I TOOK IT UP PROFESSIONALL
AT FIRST IT WAS A LITTLE EMBARRASSING, DANCING AROUND IN LITTLE MORE THAN MY UNDER-WEAR...
...BUT ONCE I GOT USED TO IT, I WAS FINE. ACTUALLY, IT FEELS PRETTY GOOD, I GUESS...
BUT... HOW WERE YOU ABLE TO START USING THAT... WHATCHAMA-CALLIT POWER?
YOU MEAN ETHERION?!

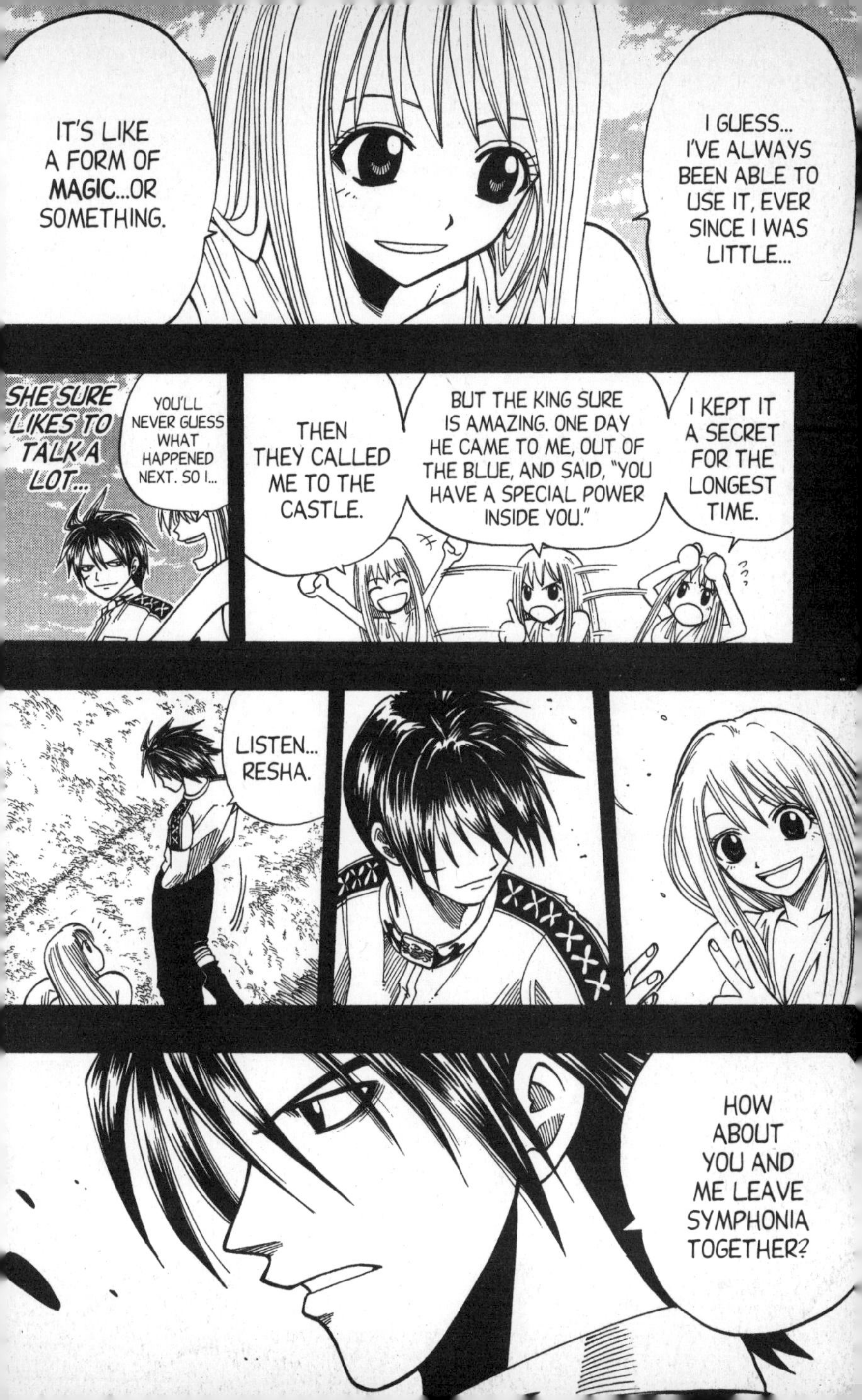
I GUESS... I'VE ALWAYS BEEN ABLE TO USE IT, EVER SINCE I WAS LITTLE...
IT'S LIKE A FORM OF MAGIC...OR SOMETHING.
I KEPT IT A SECRET FOR THE LONGEST TIME.
BUT THE KING SURE IS AMAZING. ONE DAY HE CAME TO ME, OUT OF THE BLUE, AND SAID, "YOU HAVE A SPECIAL POWER INSIDE YOU."
THEN THEY CALLED ME TO THE CASTLE.
YOU'LL NEVER GUESS WHAT HAPPENED NEXT. SO I...
SHE SURE LIKES TO TALK A LOT...
LISTEN... RESHA.
HOW ABOUT YOU AND ME LEAVE SYMPHONIA TOGETHER?

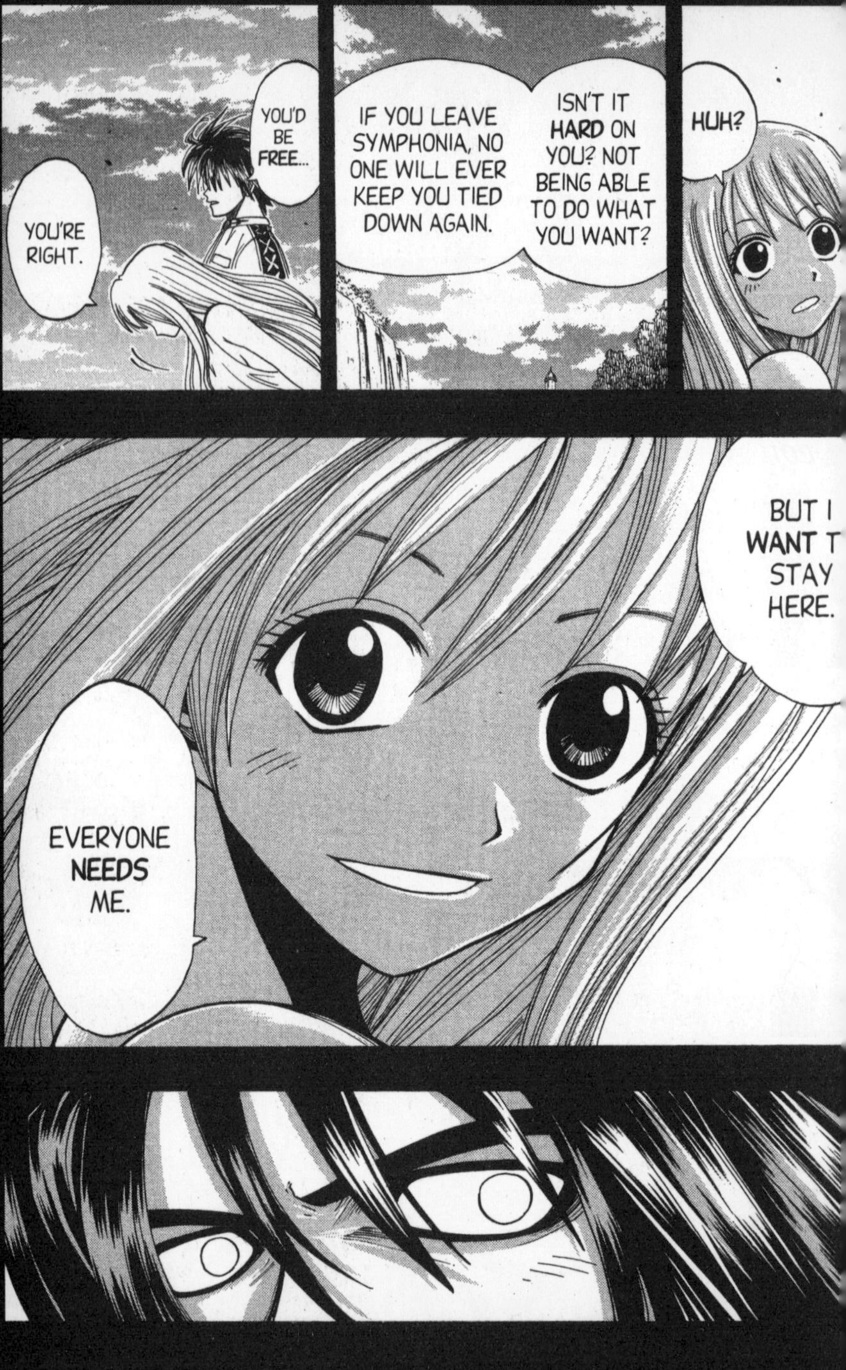
HUH?
ISN'T IT **HARD** ON YOU? NOT BEING ABLE TO DO WHAT YOU WANT?
IF YOU LEAVE SYMPHONIA, NO ONE WILL EVER KEEP YOU TIED DOWN AGAIN.
YOU'D BE FREE...
YOU'RE RIGHT.
BUT I **WANT** T STAY HERE.
EVERYONE **NEEDS** ME.

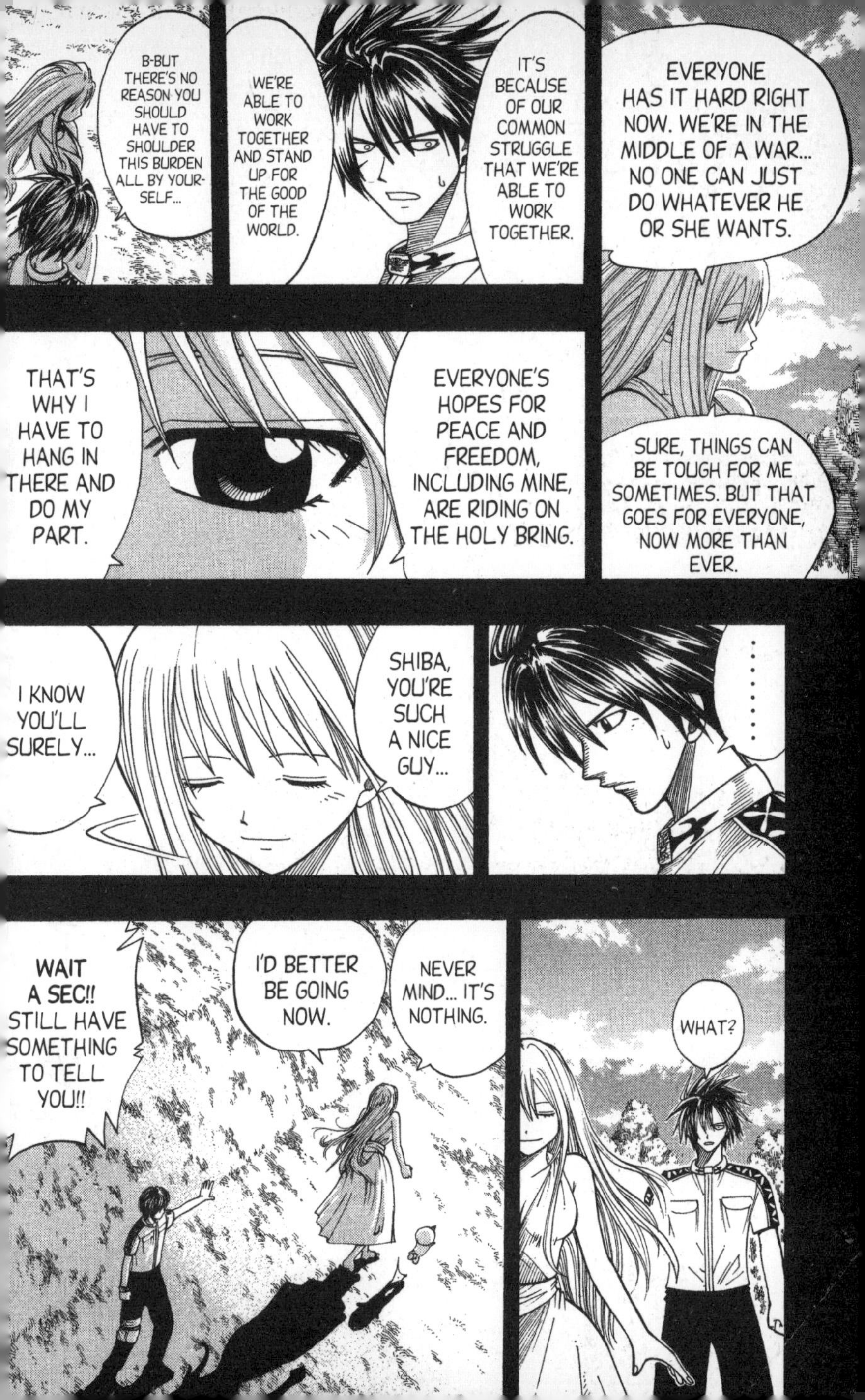
EVERYONE HAS IT HARD RIGHT NOW. WE'RE IN THE MIDDLE OF A WAR... NO ONE CAN JUST DO WHATEVER HE OR SHE WANTS.
SURE, THINGS CAN BE TOUGH FOR ME SOMETIMES. BUT THAT GOES FOR EVERYONE, NOW MORE THAN EVER.
IT'S BECAUSE OF OUR COMMON STRUGGLE THAT WE'RE ABLE TO WORK TOGETHER.
WE'RE ABLE TO WORK TOGETHER AND STAND UP FOR THE GOOD OF THE WORLD.
B-BUT THERE'S NO REASON YOU SHOULD HAVE TO SHOULDER THIS BURDEN ALL BY YOUR-SELF...
EVERYONE'S HOPES FOR PEACE AND FREEDOM, INCLUDING MINE, ARE RIDING ON THE HOLY BRING.
THAT'S WHY I HAVE TO HANG IN THERE AND DO MY PART.
......
SHIBA, YOU'RE SUCH A NICE GUY...
I KNOW YOU'LL SURELY...
WHAT?
NEVER MIND... IT'S NOTHING.
I'D BETTER BE GOING NOW.
WAIT A SEC!! STILL HAVE SOMETHING TO TELL YOU!!

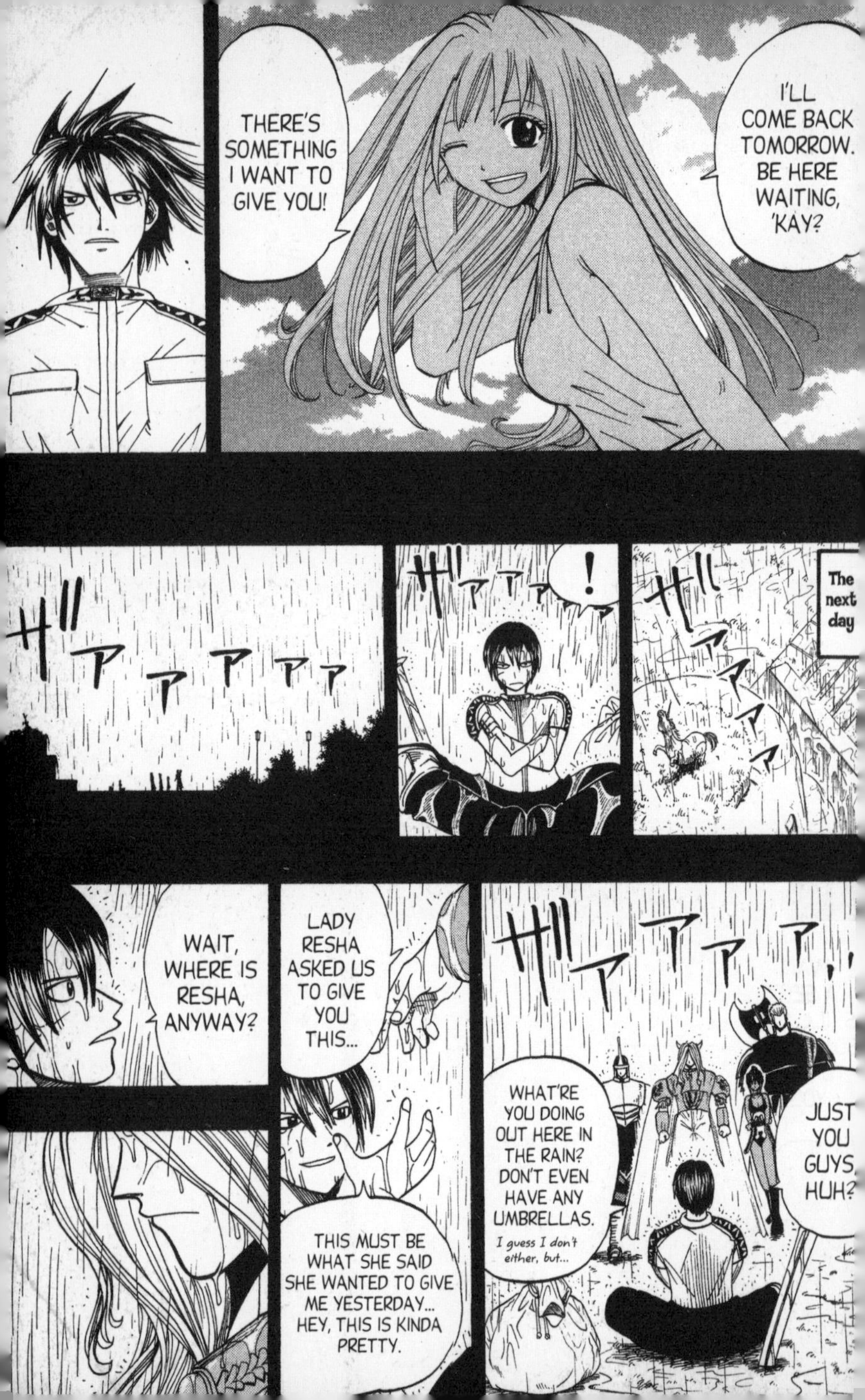
I'LL COME BACK TOMORROW. BE HERE WAITING, 'KAY?
THERE'S SOMETHING I WANT TO GIVE YOU!
The next day
ザアアアア
ザアアア
!
ザアアアア
ザアアアア
JUST YOU GUYS, HUH?
WHAT'RE YOU DOING OUT HERE IN THE RAIN? DON'T EVEN HAVE ANY UMBRELLAS.
I guess I don't either, but...
LADY RESHA ASKED US TO GIVE YOU THIS...
WAIT, WHERE IS RESHA, ANYWAY?
THIS MUST BE WHAT SHE SAID SHE WANTED TO GIVE ME YESTERDAY... HEY, THIS IS KINDA PRETTY.

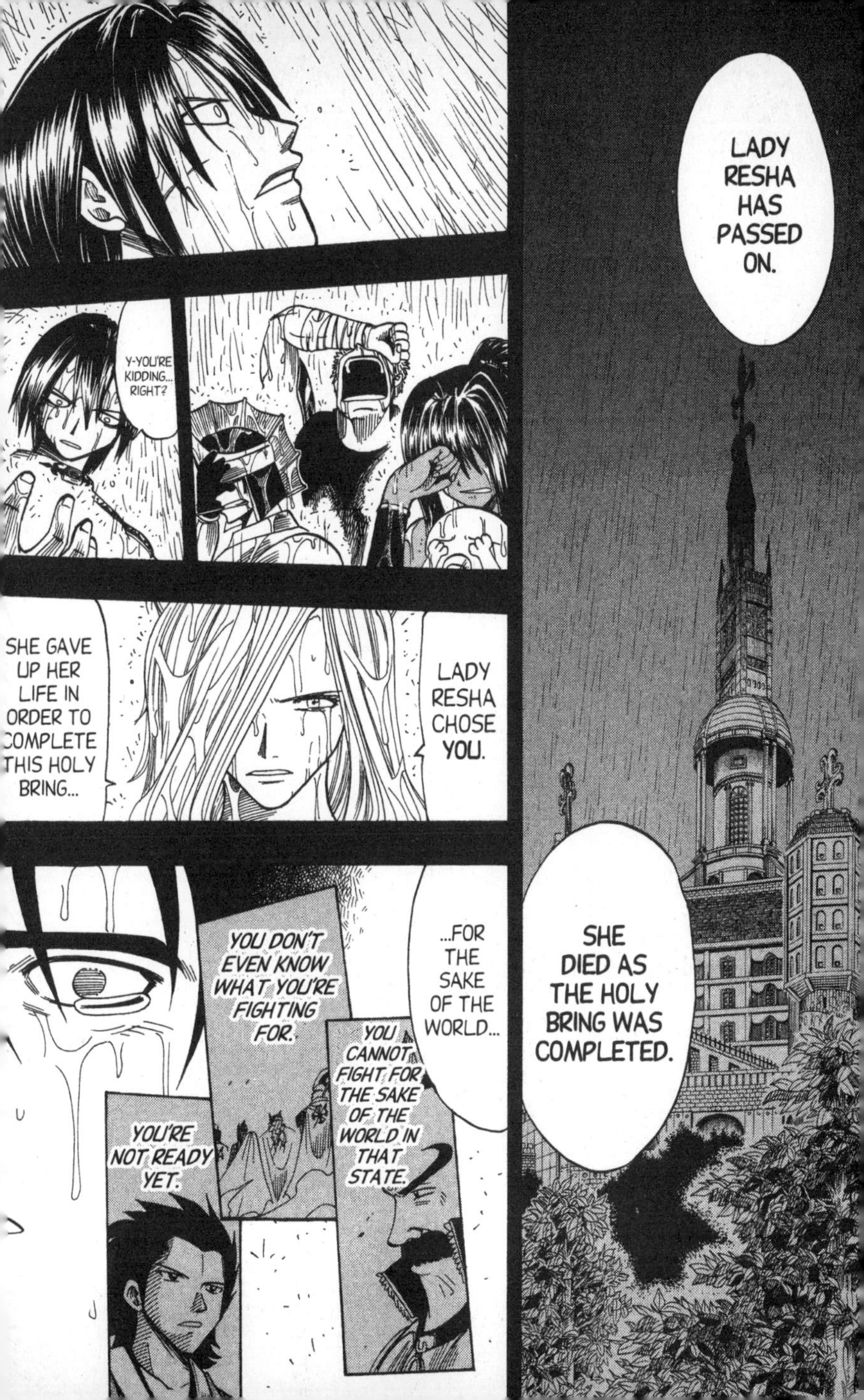
LADY RESHA HAS PASSED ON.
SHE DIED AS THE HOLY BRING WAS COMPLETED.
Y-YOU'RE KIDDING... RIGHT?
LADY RESHA CHOSE YOU.
SHE GAVE UP HER LIFE IN ORDER TO COMPLETE THIS HOLY BRING...
...FOR THE SAKE OF THE WORLD...
YOU DON'T EVEN KNOW WHAT YOU'RE FIGHTING FOR.
YOU CANNOT FIGHT FOR THE SAKE OF THE WORLD IN THAT STATE.
YOU'RE NOT READY YET.

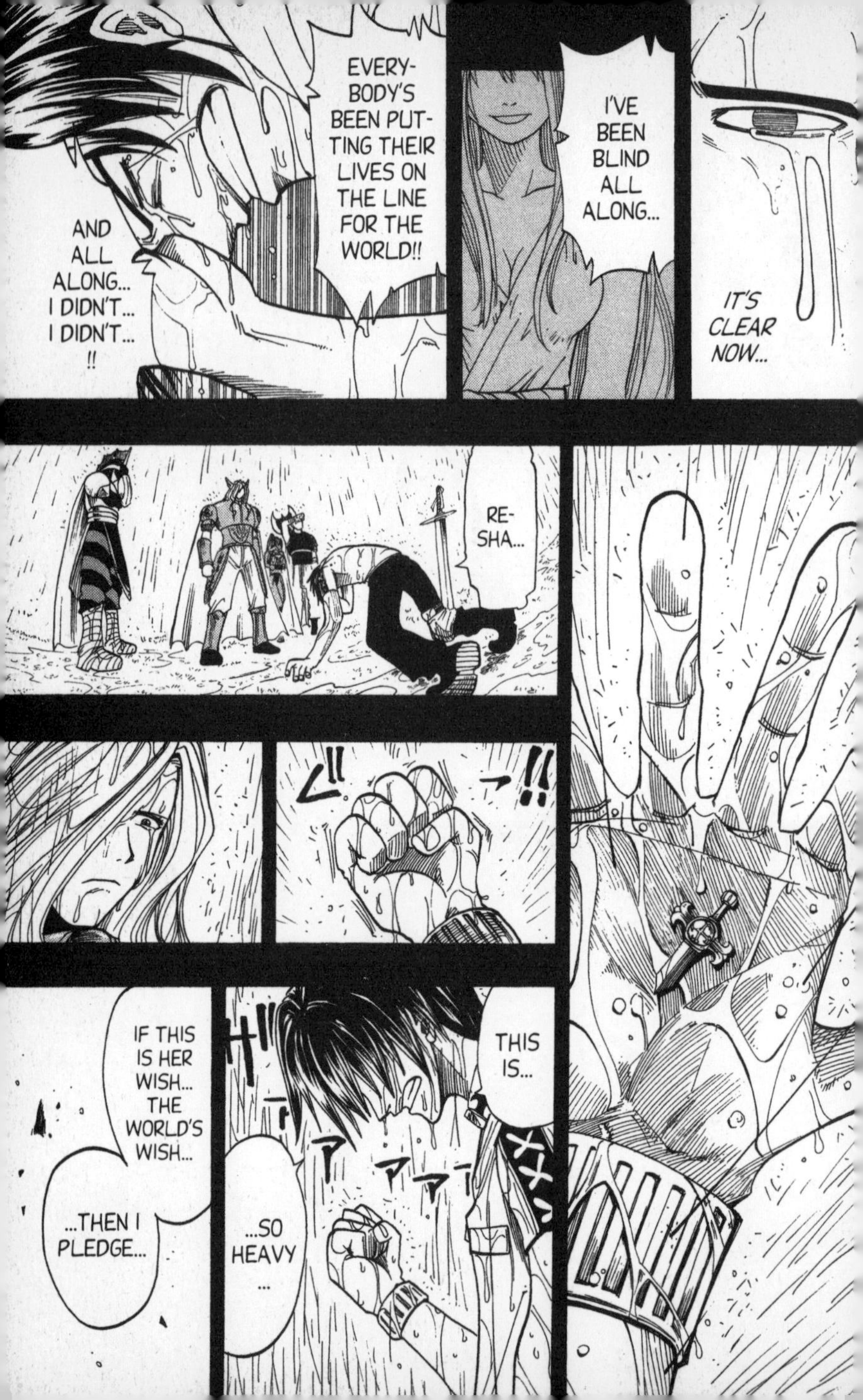
IT'S CLEAR NOW...
I'VE BEEN BLIND ALL ALONG...
EVERYBODY'S BEEN PUTTING THEIR LIVES ON THE LINE FOR THE WORLD!!
AND ALL ALONG... I DIDN'T... I DIDN'T... !!
RE-SHA...
THIS IS...
...SO HEAVY ...
IF THIS IS HER WISH... THE WORLD'S WISH...
...THEN I PLEDGE...

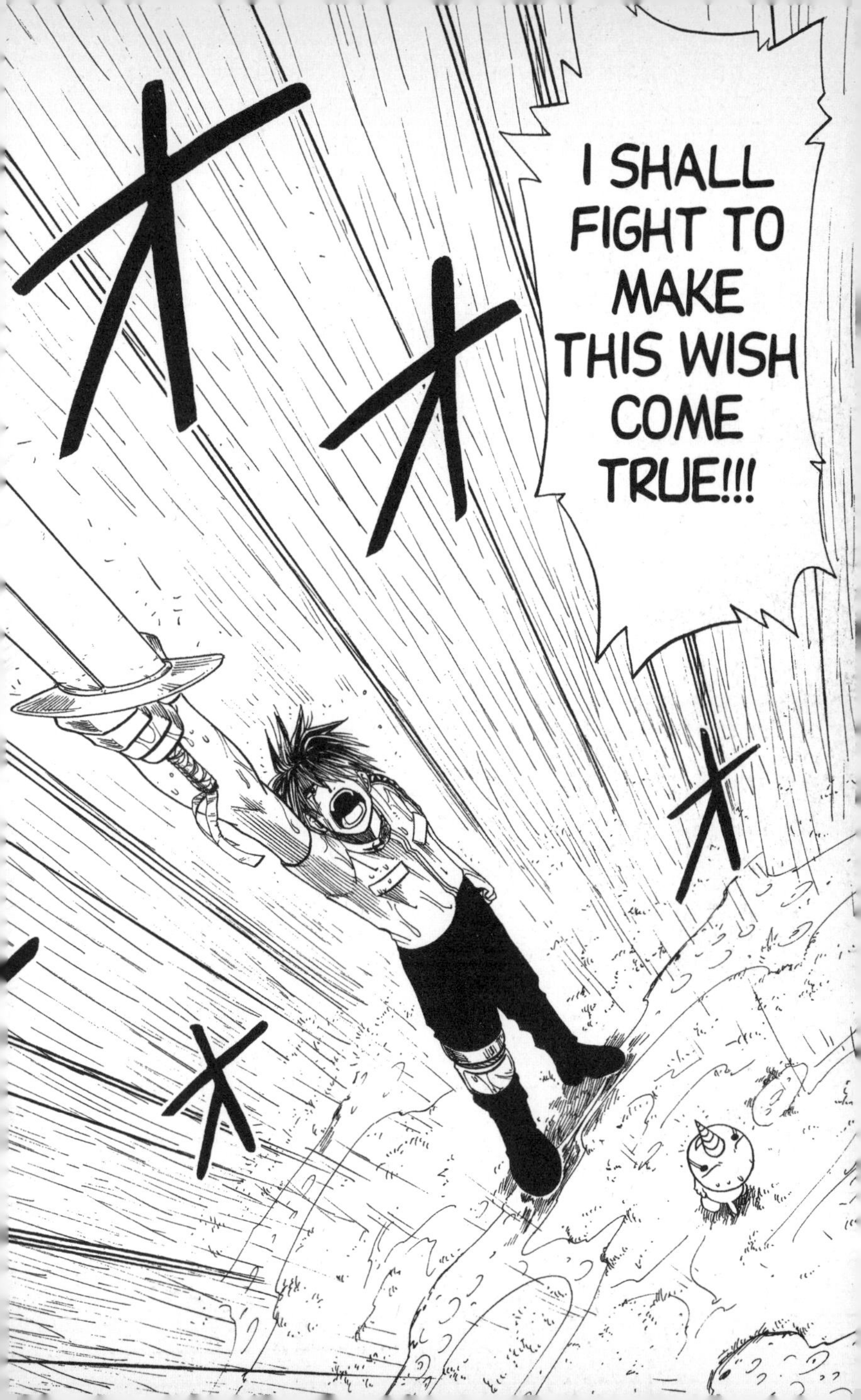
I SHALL FIGHT TO MAKE THIS WISH COME TRUE!!!

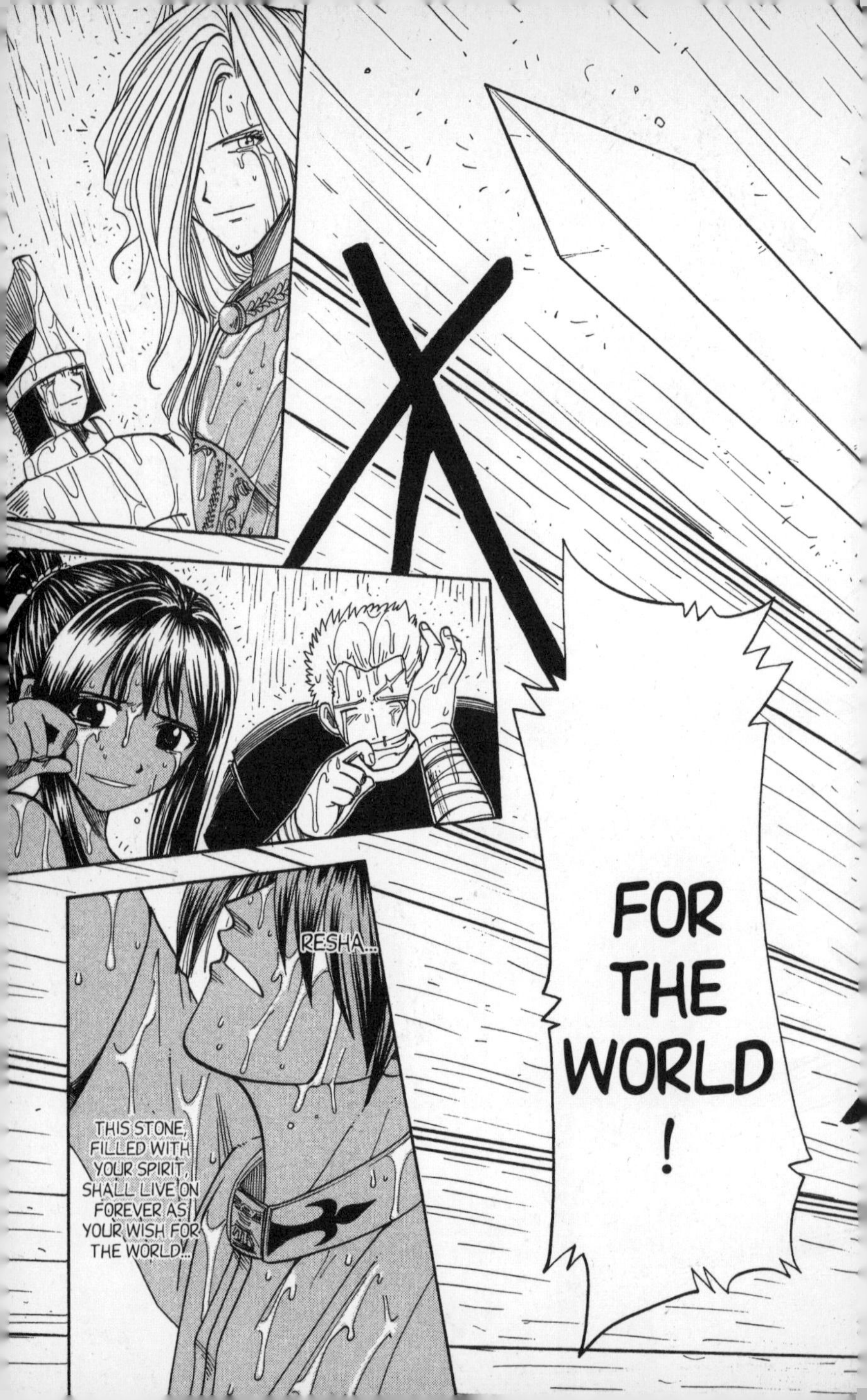

FOR THE WORLD!
RESHA...
THIS STONE, FILLED WITH YOUR SPIRIT, SHALL LIVE ON FOREVER AS YOUR WISH FOR THE WORLD...

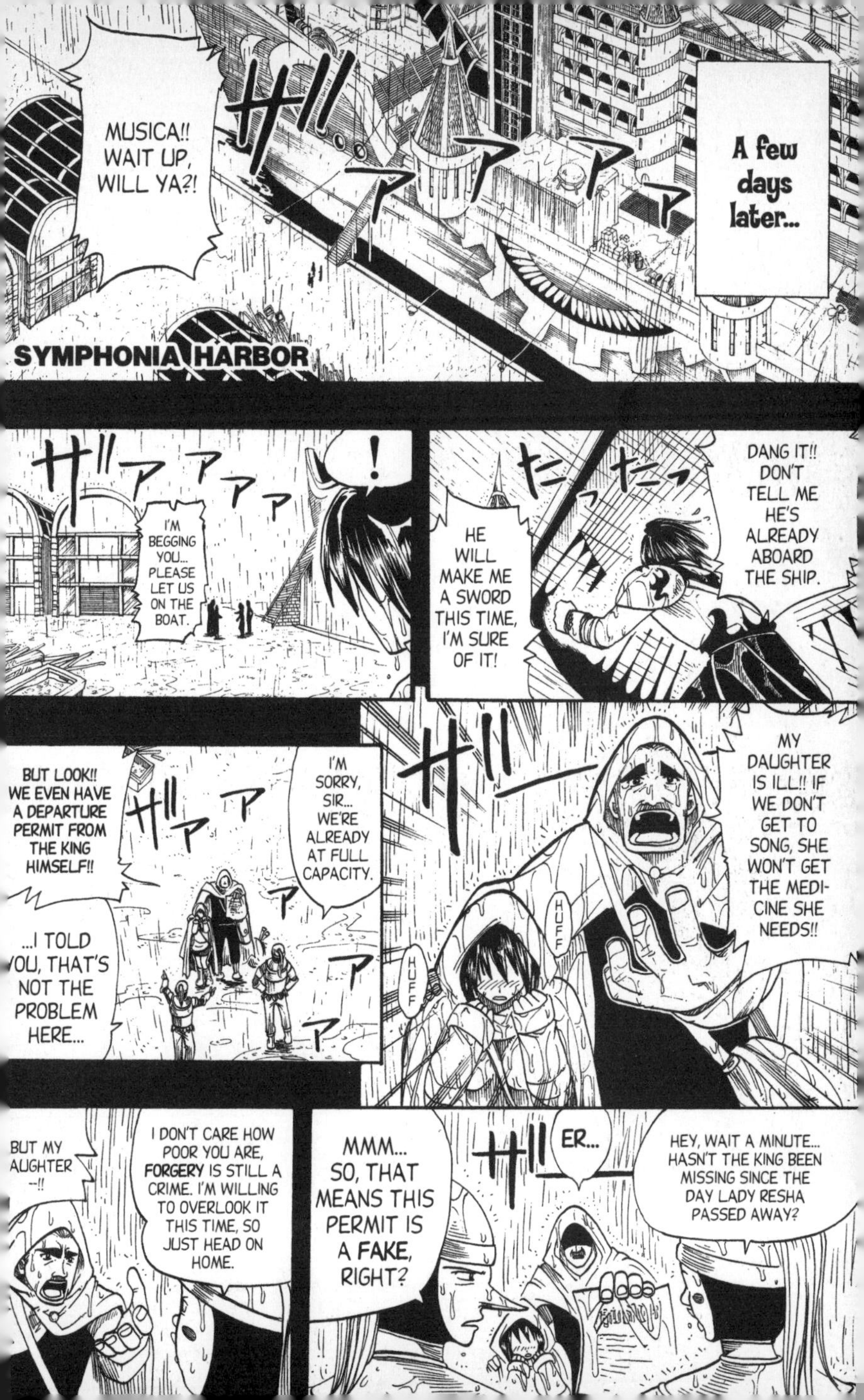
A few days later...
MUSICA!! WAIT UP, WILL YA?!
SYMPHONIA HARBOR
DANG IT!! DON'T TELL ME HE'S ALREADY ABOARD THE SHIP.
HE WILL MAKE ME A SWORD THIS TIME, I'M SURE OF IT!
!
I'M BEGGING YOU... PLEASE LET US ON THE BOAT.
MY DAUGHTER IS ILL!! IF WE DON'T GET TO SONG, SHE WON'T GET THE MEDI- CINE SHE NEEDS!!
HUFF
HUFF
I'M SORRY, SIR... WE'RE ALREADY AT FULL CAPACITY.
BUT LOOK!! WE EVEN HAVE A DEPARTURE PERMIT FROM THE KING HIMSELF!!
...I TOLD YOU, THAT'S NOT THE PROBLEM HERE...
HEY, WAIT A MINUTE... HASN'T THE KING BEEN MISSING SINCE THE DAY LADY RESHA PASSED AWAY?
ER...
MMM... SO, THAT MEANS THIS PERMIT IS A FAKE, RIGHT?
I DON'T CARE HOW POOR YOU ARE, FORGERY IS STILL A CRIME. I'M WILLING TO OVERLOOK IT THIS TIME, SO JUST HEAD ON HOME.
BUT MY AUGHTER --!!

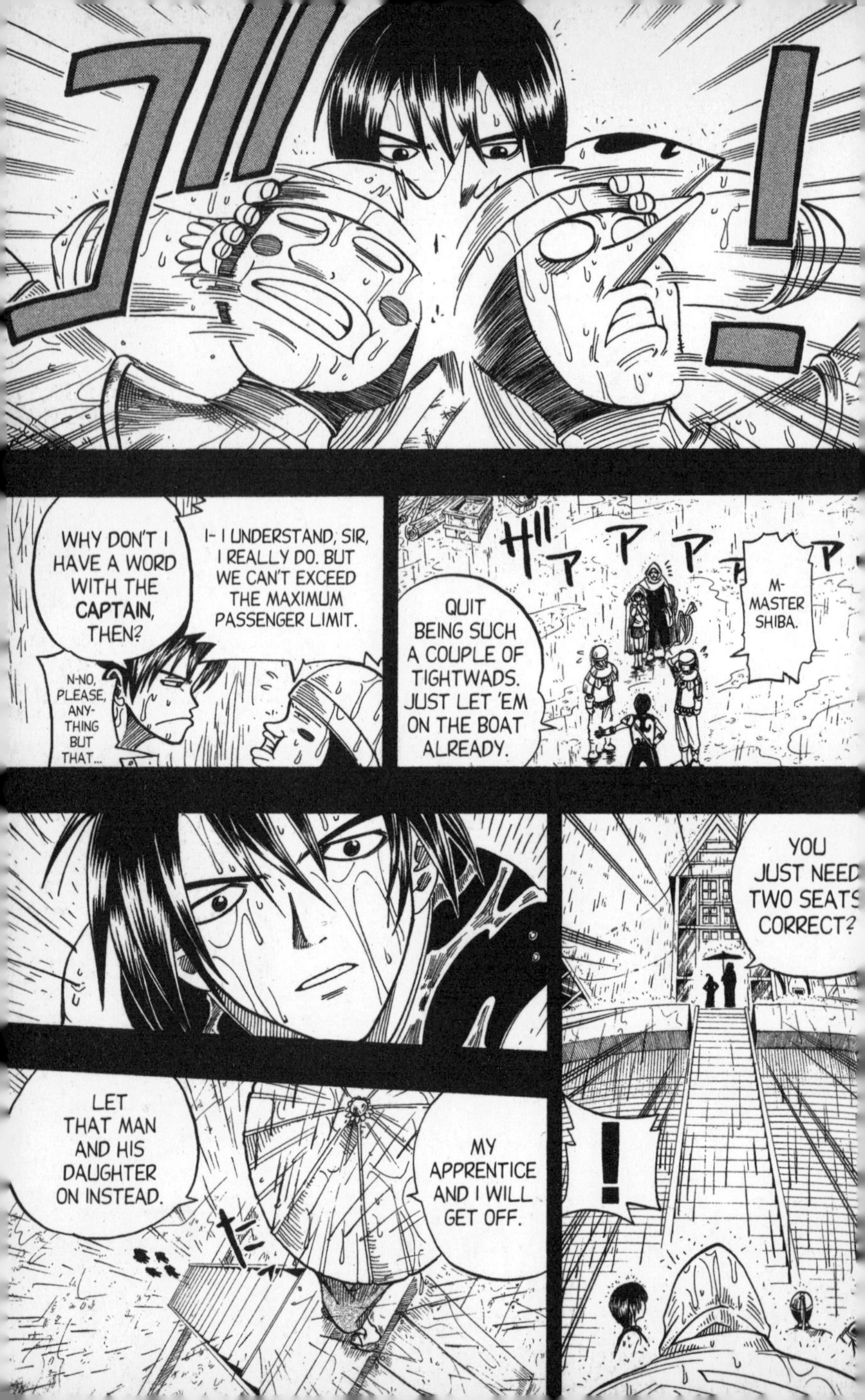

M-MASTER SHIBA.
QUIT BEING SUCH A COUPLE OF TIGHTWADS. JUST LET 'EM ON THE BOAT ALREADY.
I- I UNDERSTAND, SIR, I REALLY DO. BUT WE CAN'T EXCEED THE MAXIMUM PASSENGER LIMIT.
WHY DON'T I HAVE A WORD WITH THE **CAPTAIN**, THEN?
N-NO, PLEASE, ANYTHING BUT THAT...
YOU JUST NEED TWO SEATS, CORRECT?
!
MY APPRENTICE AND I WILL GET OFF.
LET THAT MAN AND HIS DAUGHTER ON INSTEAD.

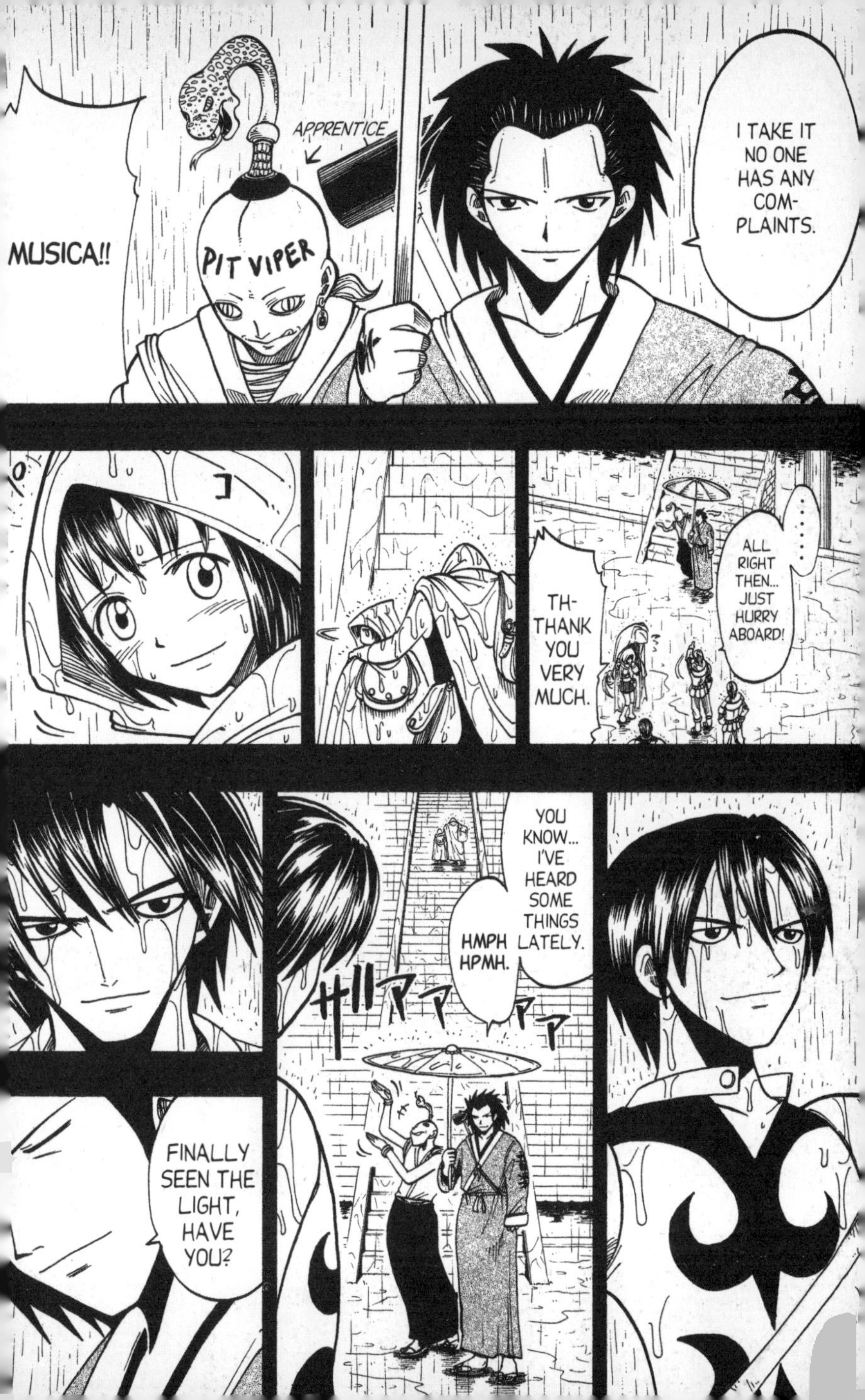
I TAKE IT NO ONE HAS ANY COM- PLAINTS.
APPRENTICE
PIT VIPER
MUSICA!!
......
ALL RIGHT THEN... JUST HURRY ABOARD!
TH- THANK YOU VERY MUCH.
YOU KNOW... I'VE HEARD SOME THINGS LATELY.
HMPH HPMH.
FINALLY SEEN THE LIGHT, HAVE YOU?

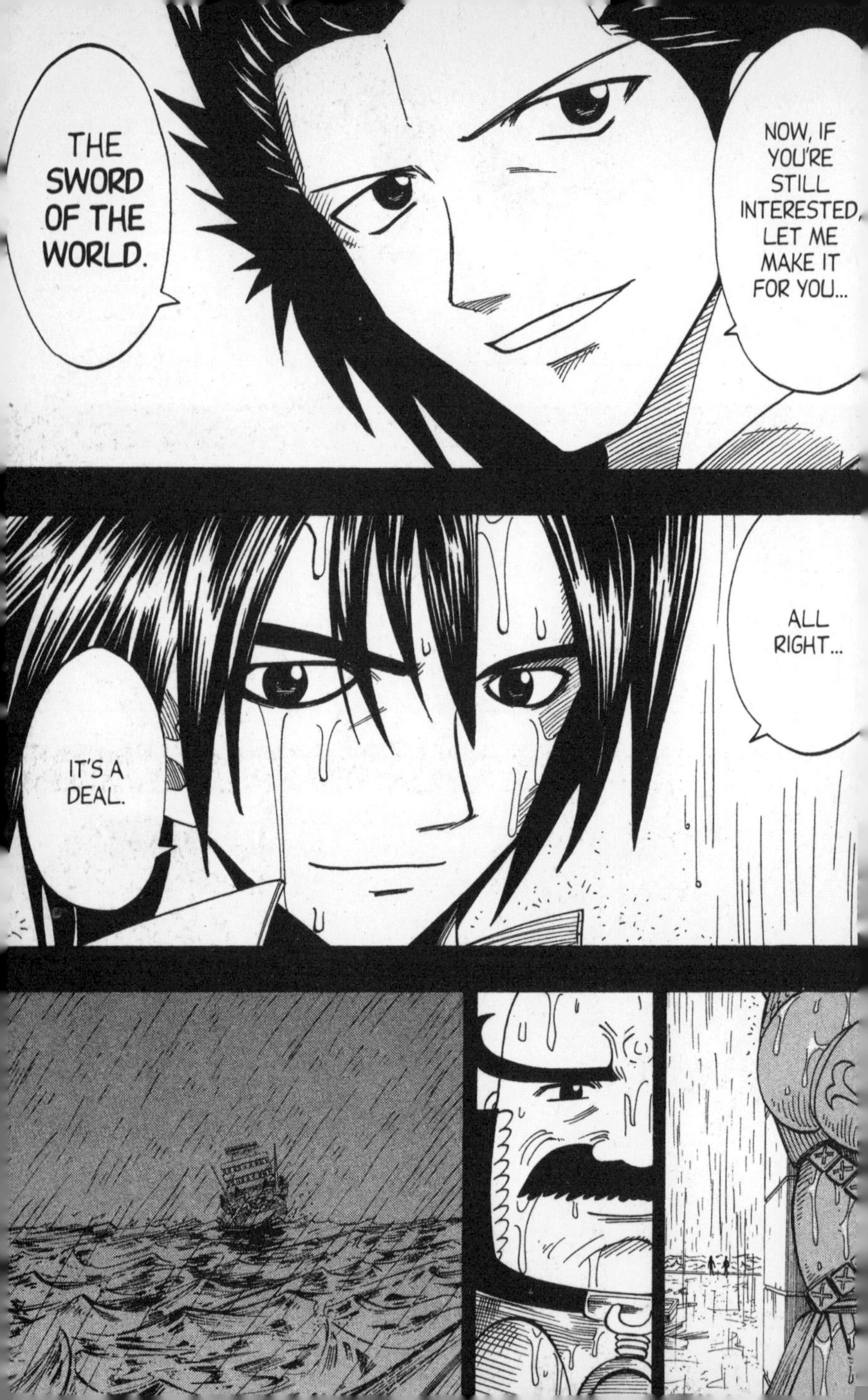
NOW, IF YOU'RE STILL INTERESTED, LET ME MAKE IT FOR YOU...
THE SWORD OF THE WORLD.
ALL RIGHT...
IT'S A DEAL.

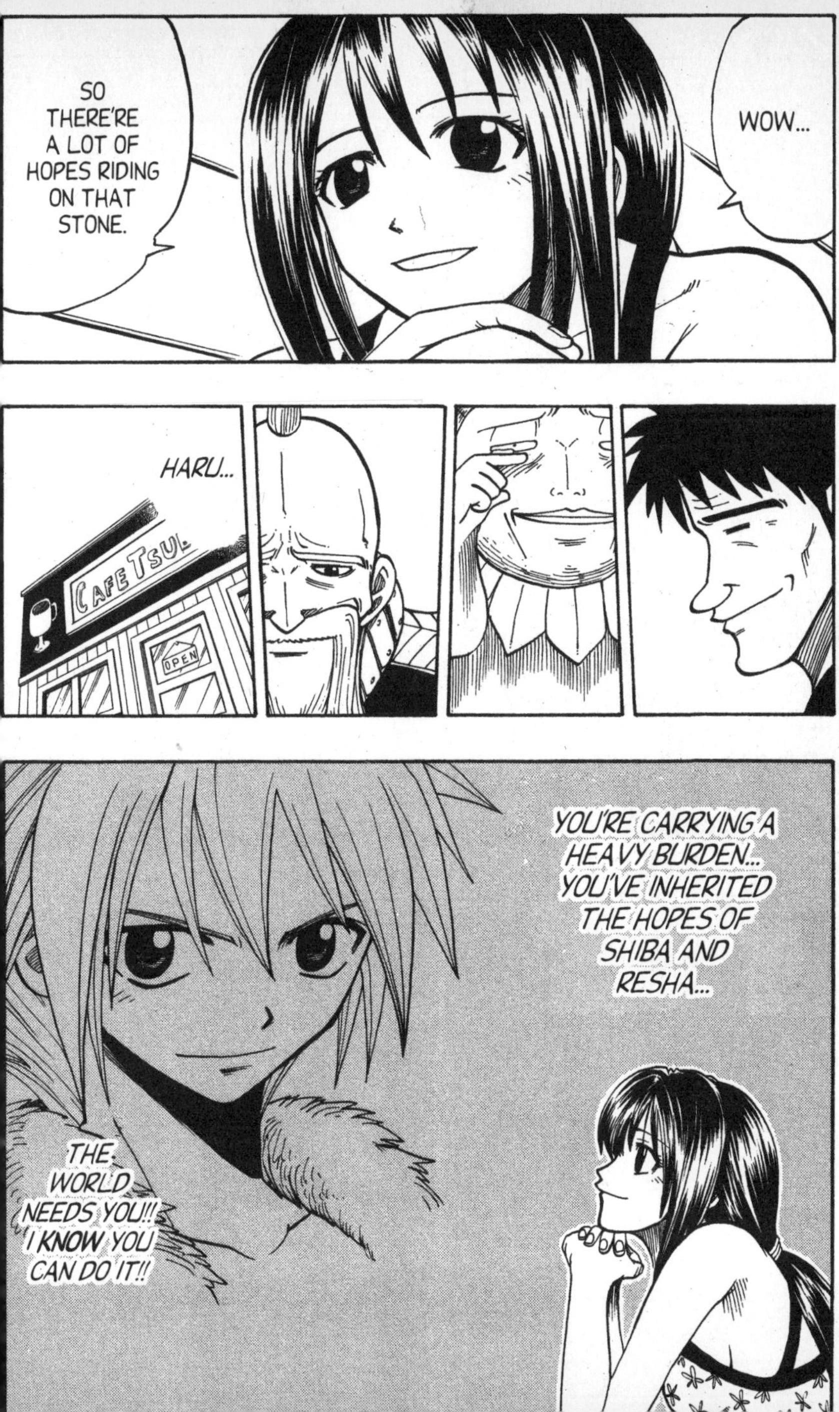
WOW...
SO THERE'RE A LOT OF HOPES RIDING ON THAT STONE.
HARU...
YOU'RE CARRYING A HEAVY BURDEN... YOU'VE INHERITED THE HOPES OF SHIBA AND RESHA...
THE WORLD NEEDS YOU!! I KNOW YOU CAN DO IT!!

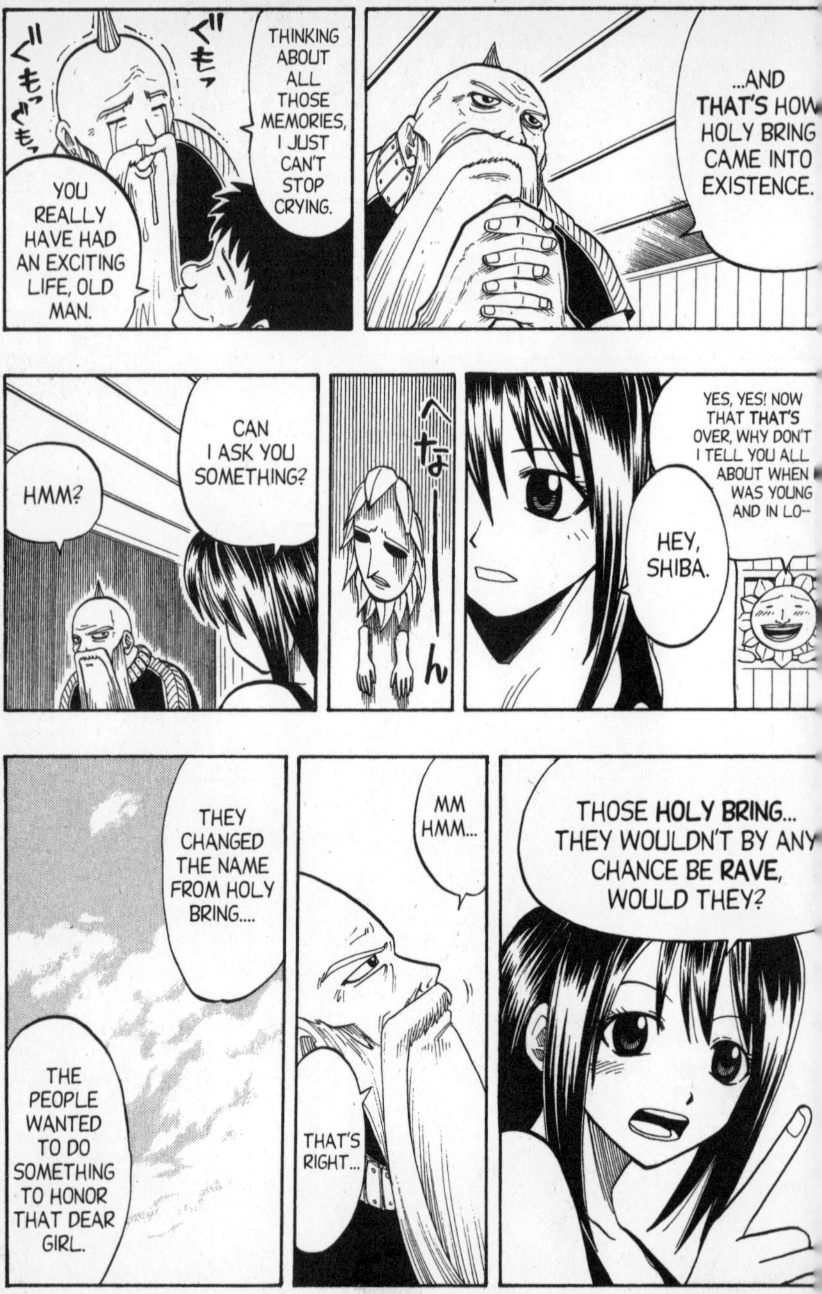
...AND THAT'S HOW HOLY BRING CAME INTO EXISTENCE.
ぐもっ
ぐもっぐもっ
THINKING ABOUT ALL THOSE MEMORIES, I JUST CAN'T STOP CRYING.
YOU REALLY HAVE HAD AN EXCITING LIFE, OLD MAN.
YES, YES! NOW THAT THAT'S OVER, WHY DON'T I TELL YOU ALL ABOUT WHEN I WAS YOUNG AND IN LO--
HEY, SHIBA.
へなーん
CAN I ASK YOU SOMETHING?
HMM?
THOSE HOLY BRING... THEY WOULDN'T BY ANY CHANCE BE RAVE, WOULD THEY?
MM HMM...
THAT'S RIGHT...
THEY CHANGED THE NAME FROM HOLY BRING....
THE PEOPLE WANTED TO DO SOMETHING TO HONOR THAT DEAR GIRL.

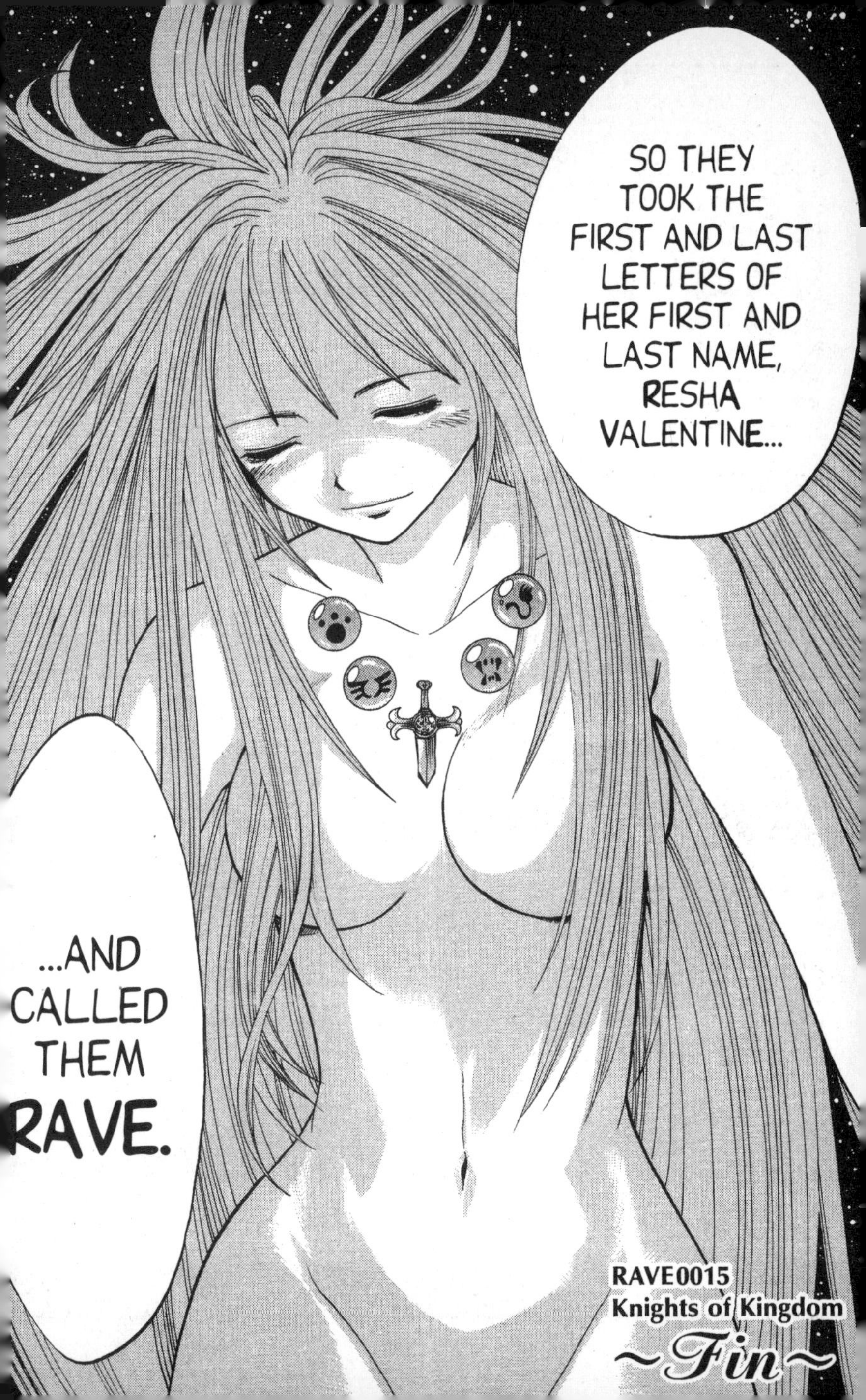
SO THEY TOOK THE FIRST AND LAST LETTERS OF HER FIRST AND LAST NAME, RESHA VALENTINE...
...AND CALLED THEM RAVE.
RAVE0015
Knights of Kingdom
~Fin~

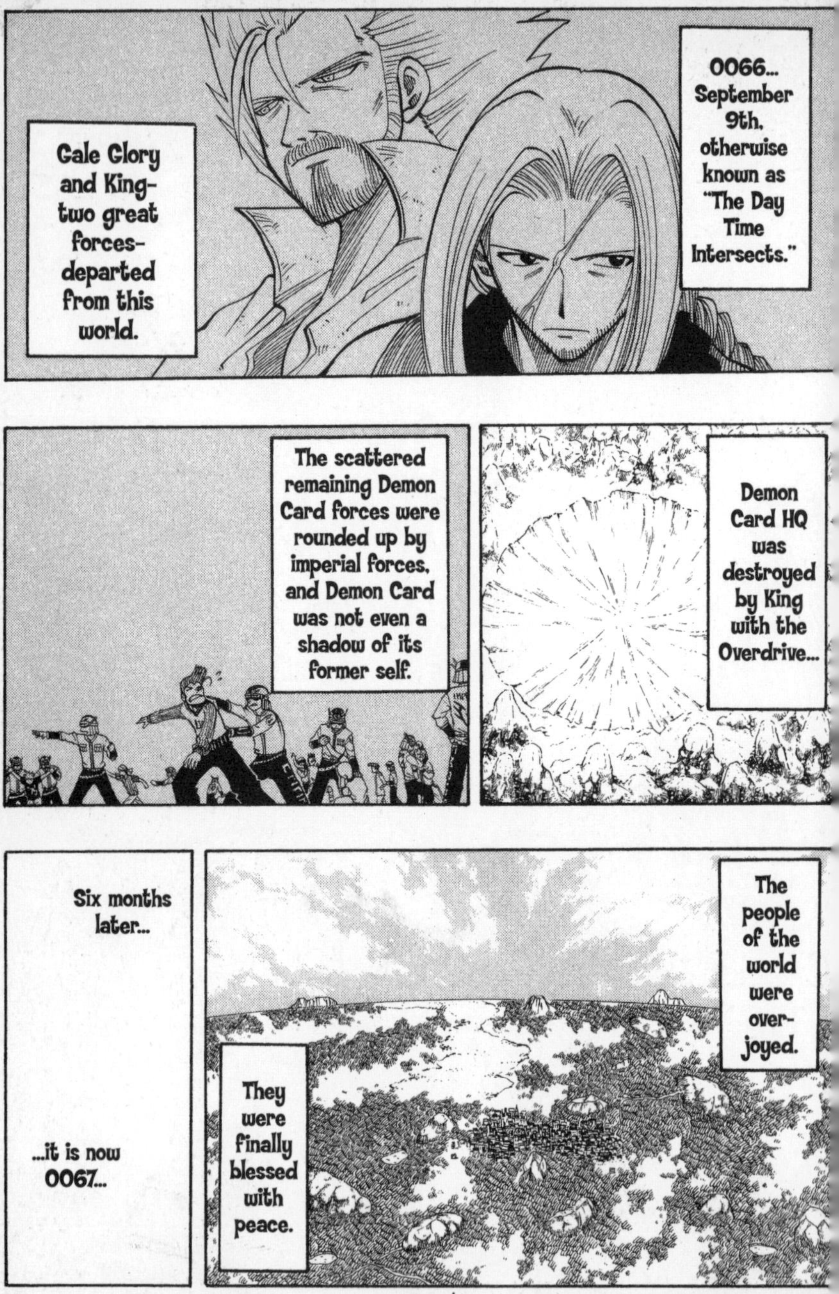
0066... September 9th, otherwise known as "The Day Time Intersects."
Gale Glory and King-two great forces-departed from this world.
Demon Card HQ was destroyed by King with the Overdrive...
The scattered remaining Demon Card forces were rounded up by imperial forces, and Demon Card was not even a shadow of its former self.
The people of the world were over-joyed.
They were finally blessed with peace.
Six months later...
...it is now 0067...

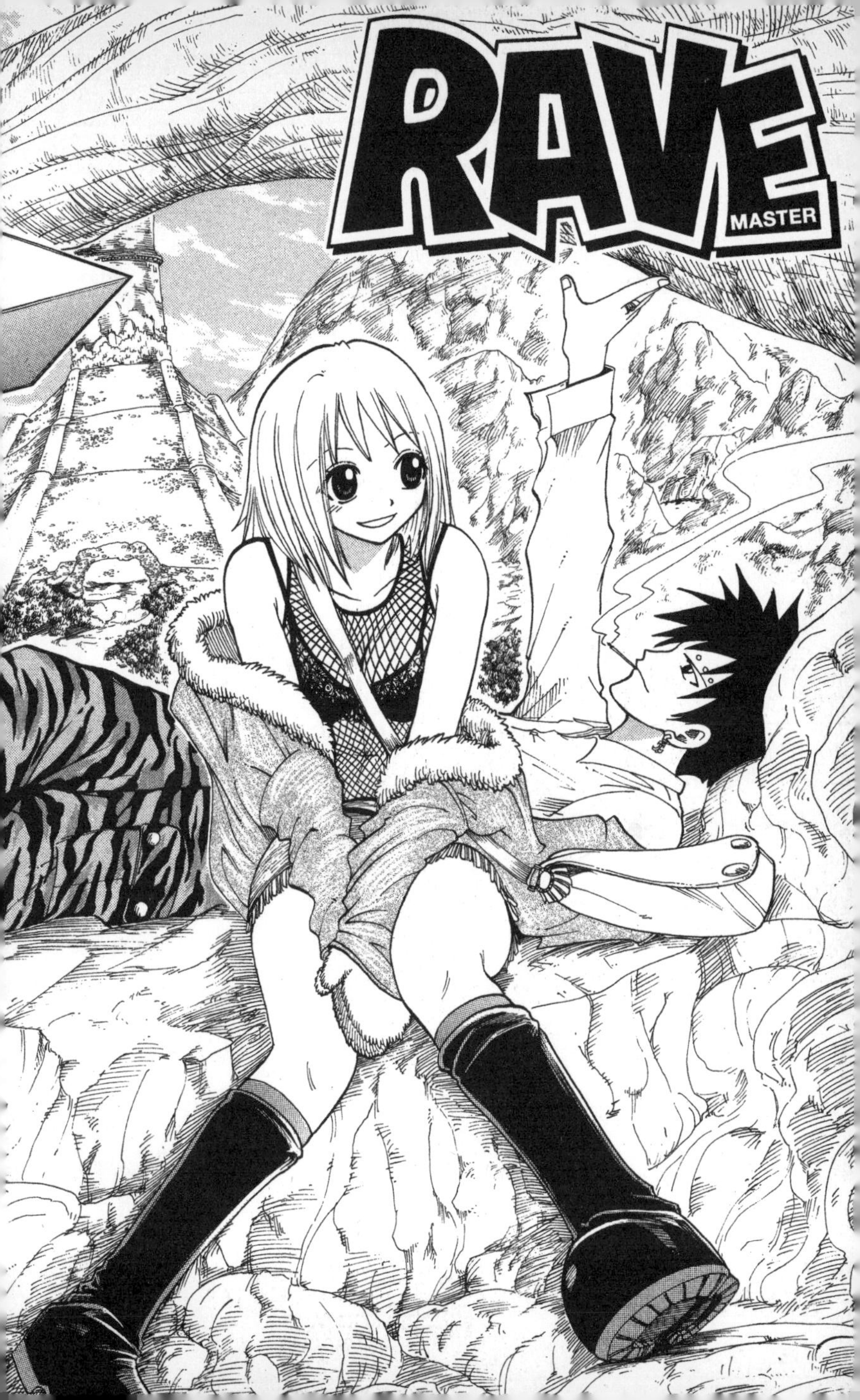
RAVE
MASTER

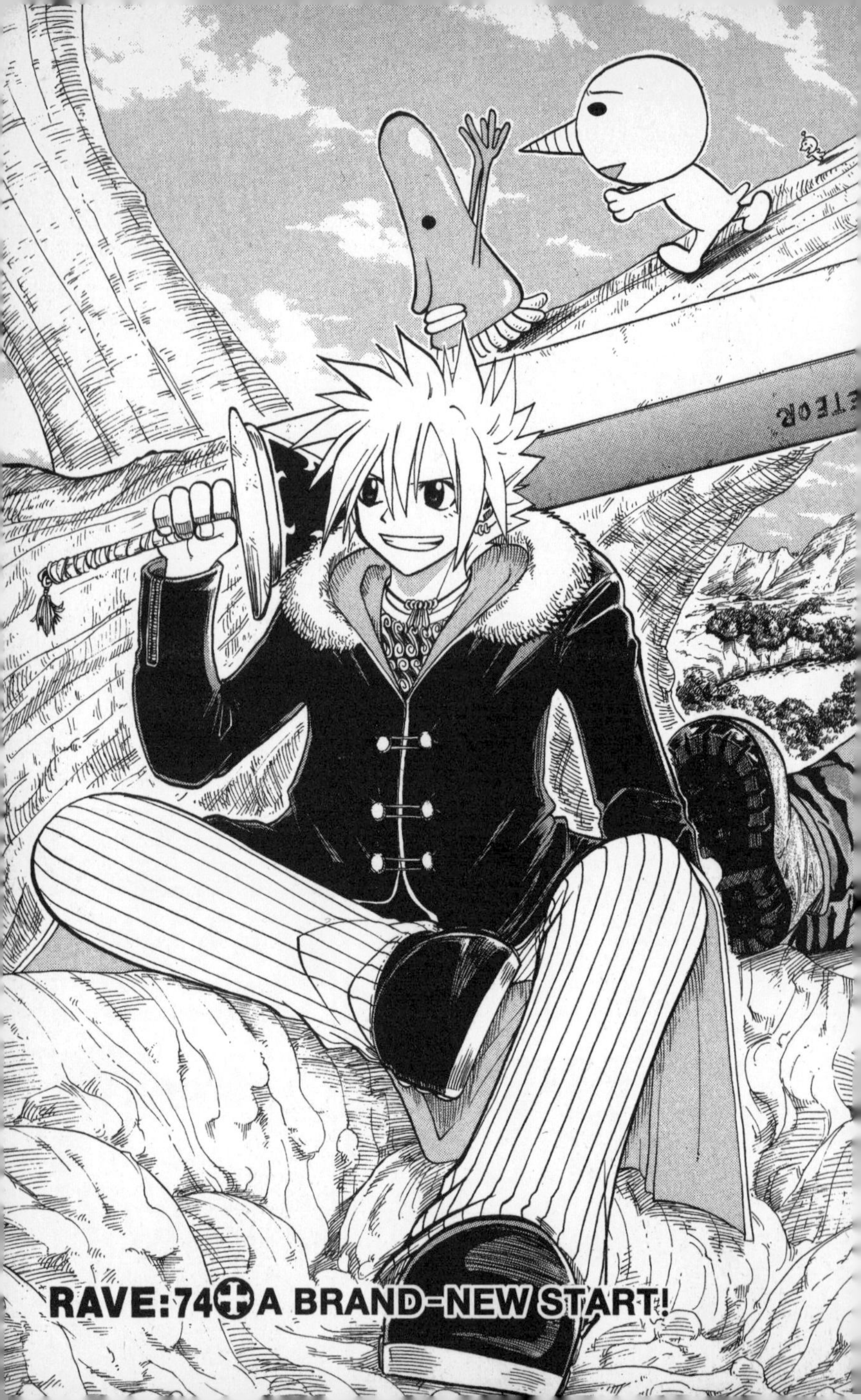
RAVE:74 A BRAND-NEW START!

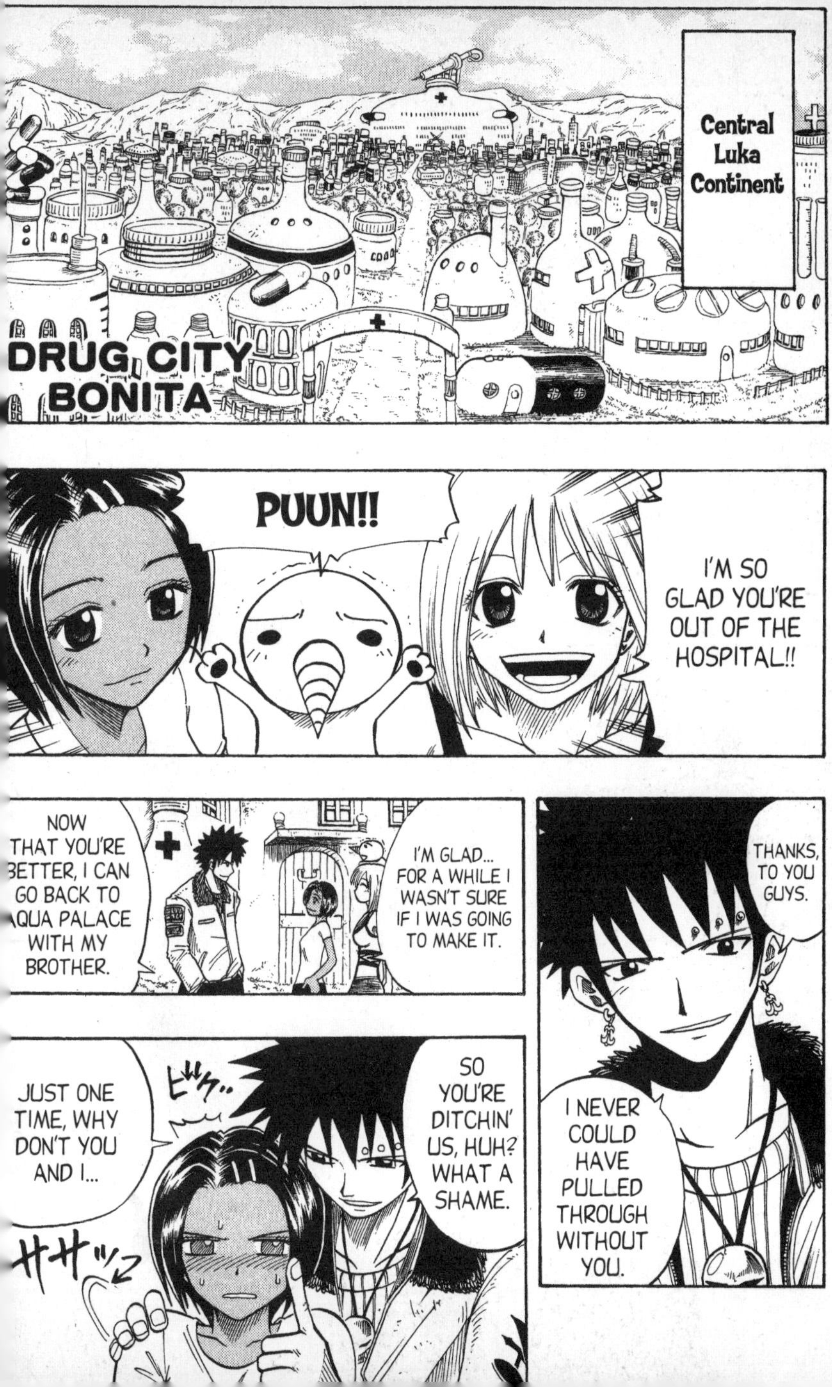
Central Luka Continent
DRUG CITY BONITA
I'M SO GLAD YOU'RE OUT OF THE HOSPITAL!!
PUUN!!
THANKS, TO YOU GUYS.
I NEVER COULD HAVE PULLED THROUGH WITHOUT YOU.
I'M GLAD... FOR A WHILE I WASN'T SURE IF I WAS GOING TO MAKE IT.
NOW THAT YOU'RE BETTER, I CAN GO BACK TO AQUA PALACE WITH MY BROTHER.
SO YOU'RE DITCHIN' US, HUH? WHAT A SHAME.
ビクッ..
JUST ONE TIME, WHY DON'T YOU AND I...
ササッ

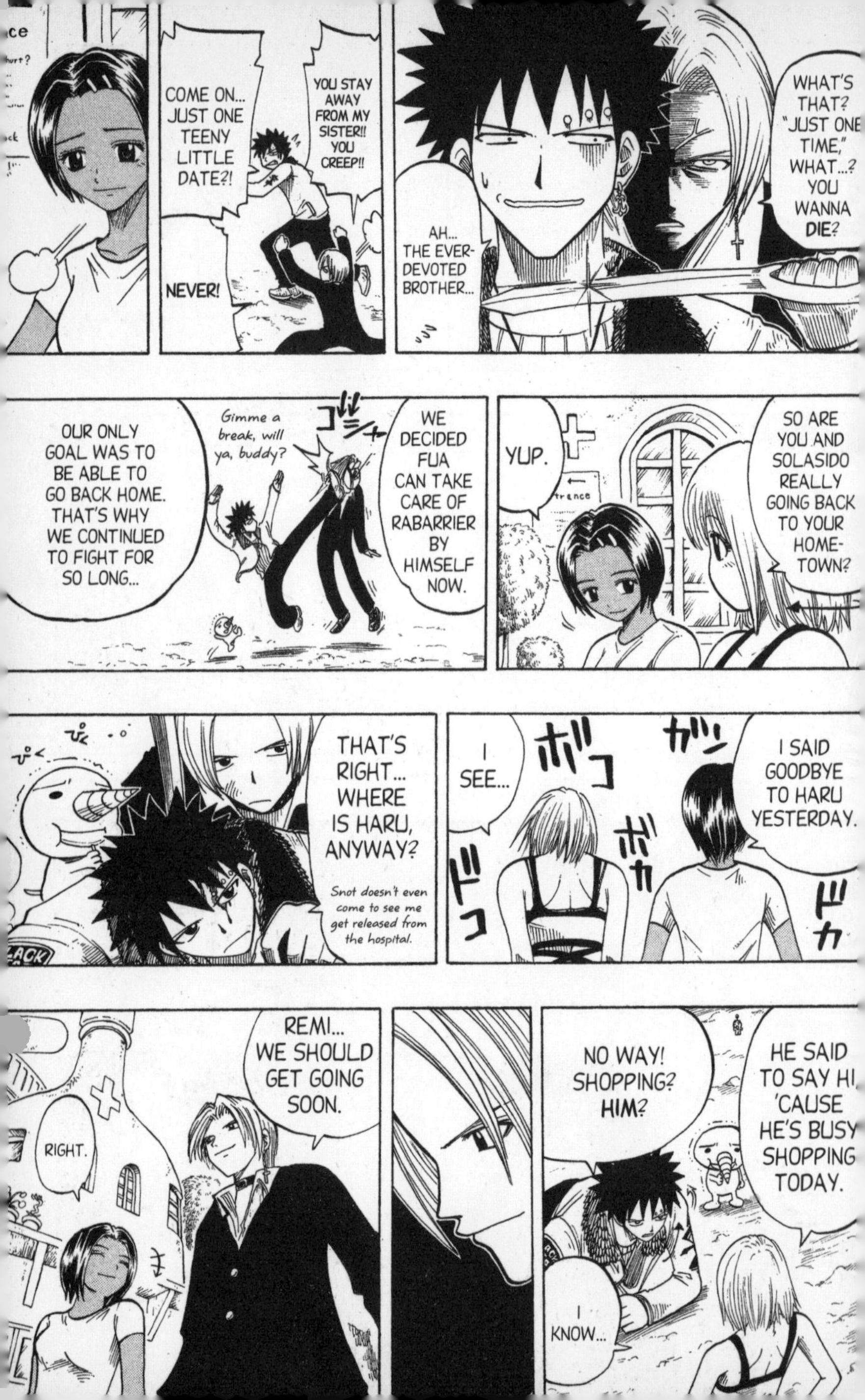
WHAT'S THAT? "JUST ONE TIME," WHAT...? YOU WANNA DIE?
AH... THE EVER-DEVOTED BROTHER...
YOU STAY AWAY FROM MY SISTER!! YOU CREEP!!
COME ON... JUST ONE TEENY LITTLE DATE?!
NEVER!
SO ARE YOU AND SOLASIDO REALLY GOING BACK TO YOUR HOME-TOWN?
YUP.
WE DECIDED FUA CAN TAKE CARE OF RABARRIER BY HIMSELF NOW.
Gimme a break, will ya, buddy?
OUR ONLY GOAL WAS TO BE ABLE TO GO BACK HOME. THAT'S WHY WE CONTINUED TO FIGHT FOR SO LONG...
I SAID GOODBYE TO HARU YESTERDAY.
I SEE...
THAT'S RIGHT... WHERE IS HARU, ANYWAY?
Snot doesn't even come to see me get released from the hospital.
HE SAID TO SAY HI, 'CAUSE HE'S BUSY SHOPPING TODAY.
NO WAY! SHOPPING? HIM?
I KNOW...
REMI... WE SHOULD GET GOING SOON.
RIGHT.

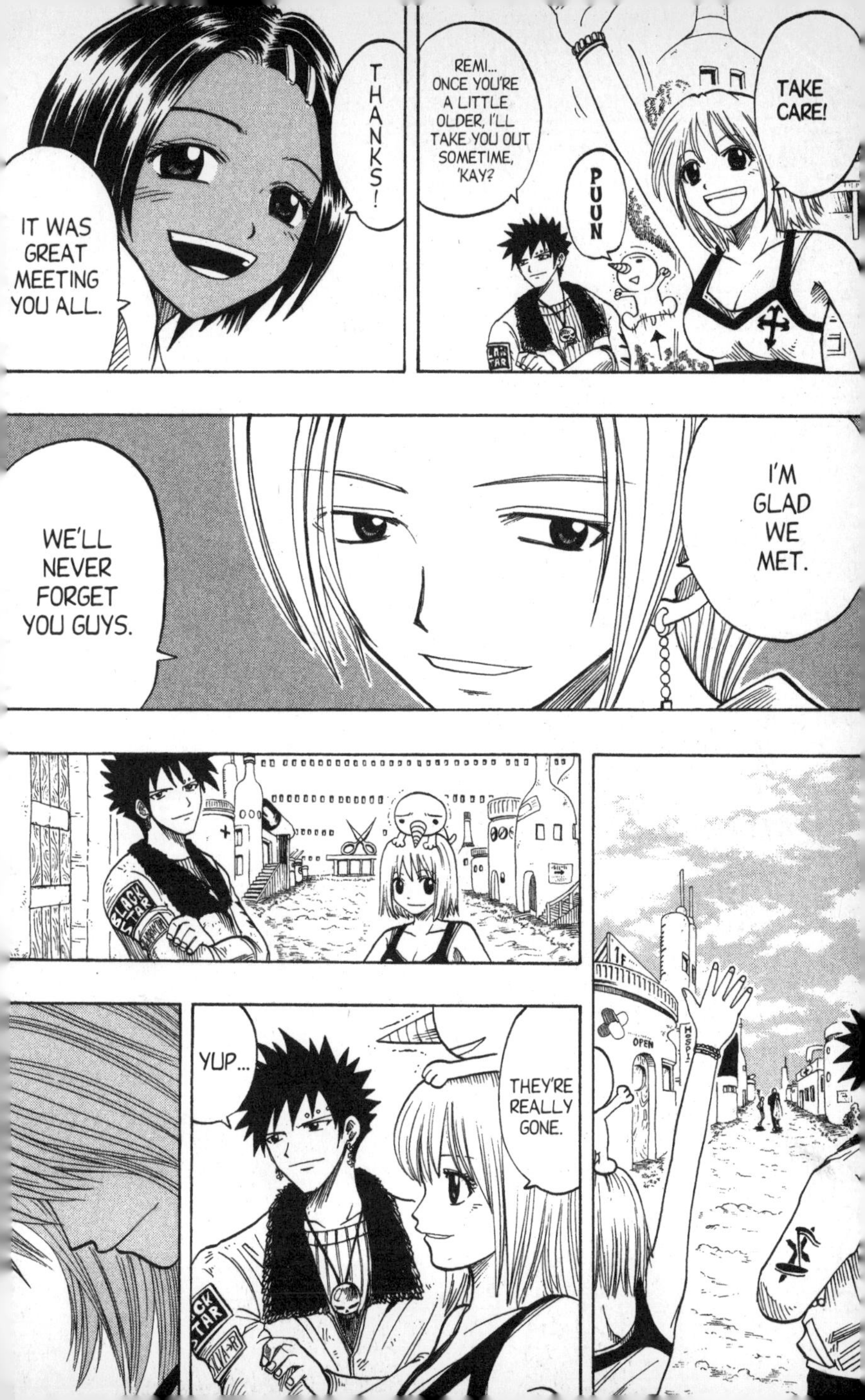
TAKE CARE!
REMI... ONCE YOU'RE A LITTLE OLDER, I'LL TAKE YOU OUT SOMETIME, 'KAY?
PUUN
THANKS!
IT WAS GREAT MEETING YOU ALL.
I'M GLAD WE MET.
WE'LL NEVER FORGET YOU GUYS.
1F
OPEN
BLACK STAR
THEY'RE REALLY GONE.
YUP...

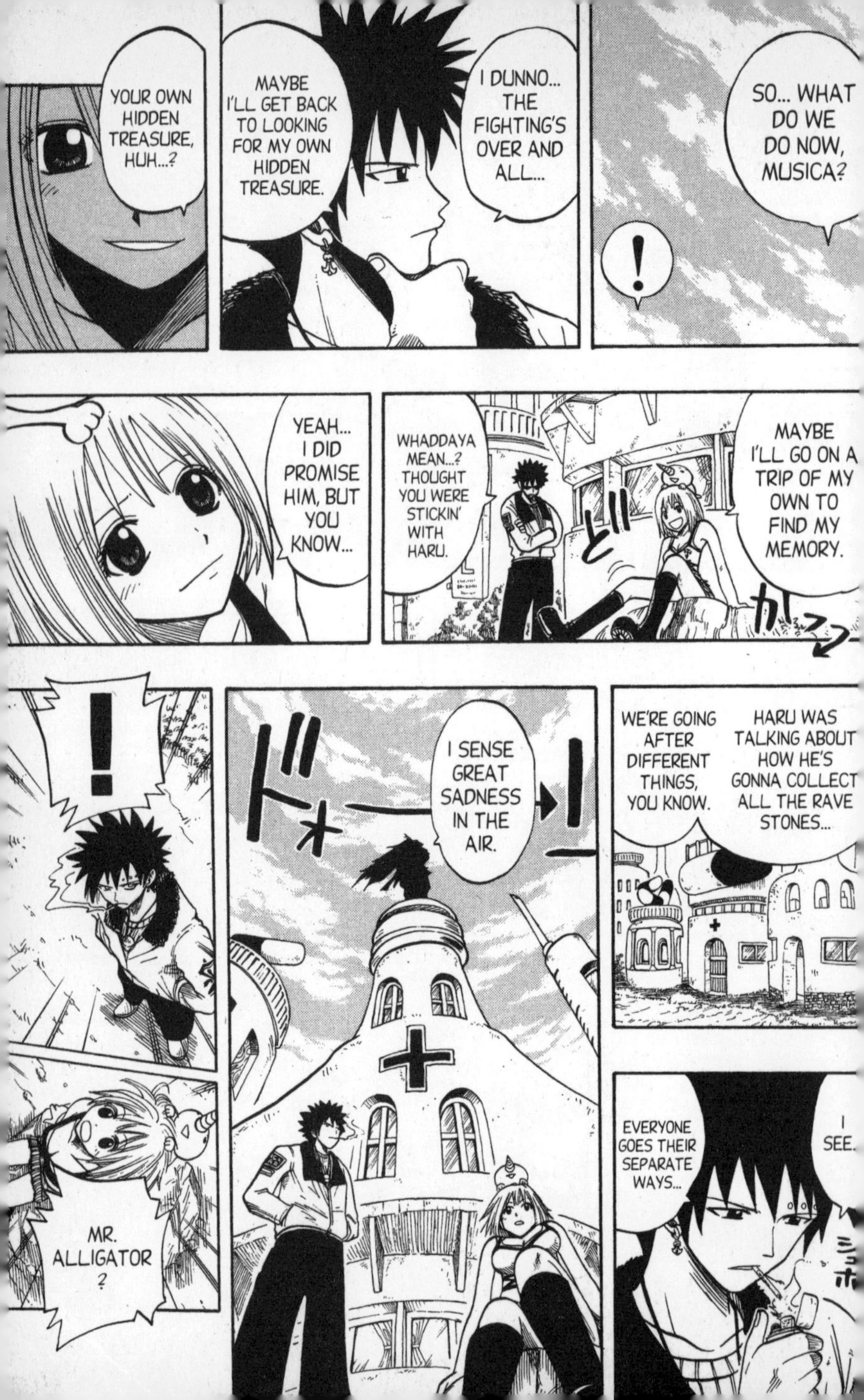
SO... WHAT DO WE DO NOW, MUSICA?
!
I DUNNO... THE FIGHTING'S OVER AND ALL...
MAYBE I'LL GET BACK TO LOOKING FOR MY OWN HIDDEN TREASURE.
YOUR OWN HIDDEN TREASURE, HUH...?
MAYBE I'LL GO ON A TRIP OF MY OWN TO FIND MY MEMORY.
WHADDAYA MEAN...? THOUGHT YOU WERE STICKIN' WITH HARU.
YEAH... I DID PROMISE HIM, BUT YOU KNOW...
HARU WAS TALKING ABOUT HOW HE'S GONNA COLLECT ALL THE RAVE STONES...
WE'RE GOING AFTER DIFFERENT THINGS, YOU KNOW.
I SEE.
EVERYONE GOES THEIR SEPARATE WAYS...
I SENSE GREAT SADNESS IN THE AIR.
!
MR. ALLIGATOR?

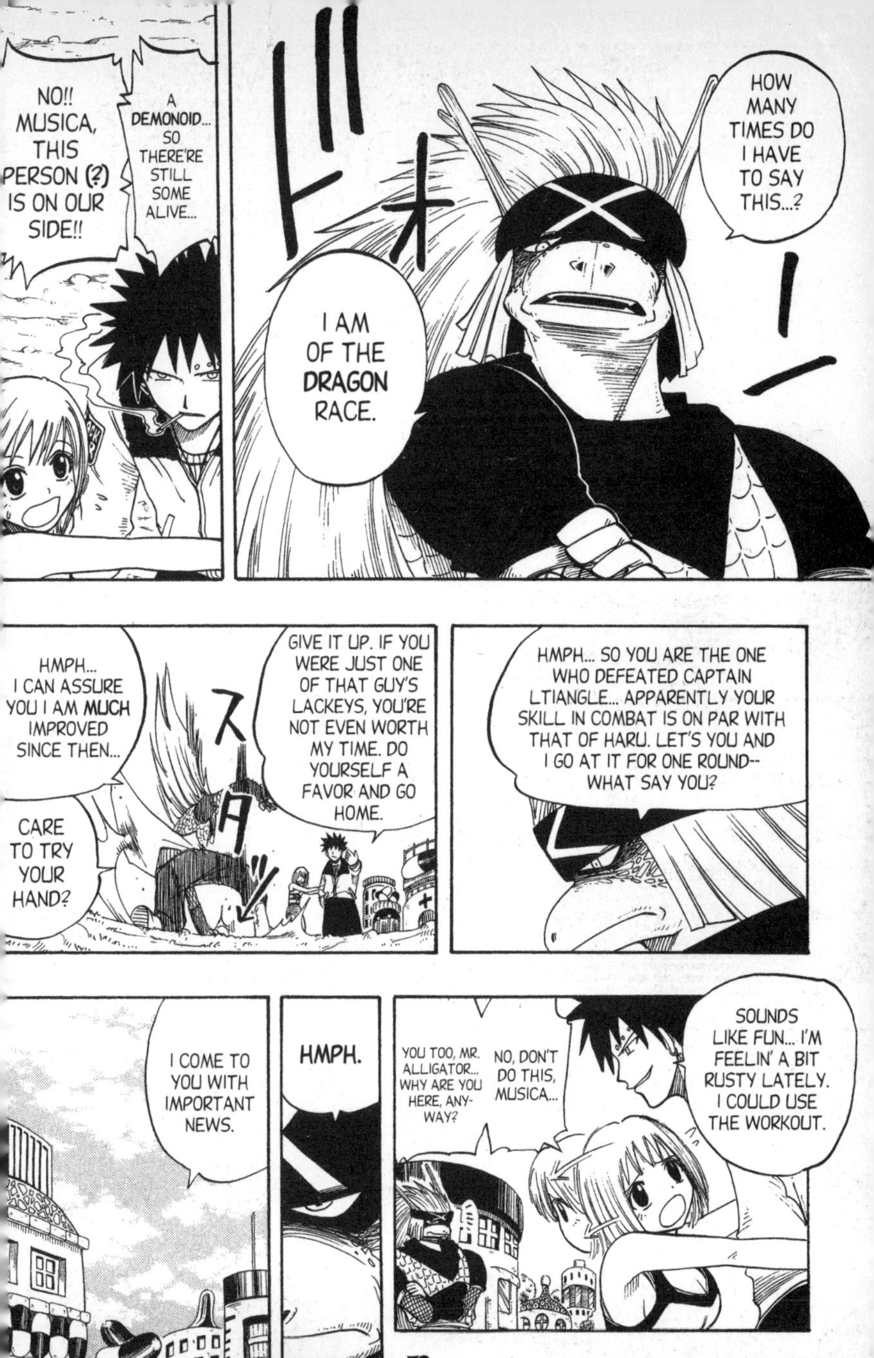

HOW MANY TIMES DO I HAVE TO SAY THIS...?
ドォ
I AM OF THE **DRAGON** RACE.
A **DEMONOID**... SO THERE'RE STILL SOME ALIVE...
NO!! MUSICA, THIS PERSON (?) IS ON OUR SIDE!!
HMPH... SO YOU ARE THE ONE WHO DEFEATED CAPTAIN LTIANGLE... APPARENTLY YOUR SKILL IN COMBAT IS ON PAR WITH THAT OF HARU. LET'S YOU AND I GO AT IT FOR ONE ROUND-- WHAT SAY YOU?
GIVE IT UP. IF YOU WERE JUST ONE OF THAT GUY'S LACKEYS, YOU'RE NOT EVEN WORTH MY TIME. DO YOURSELF A FAVOR AND GO HOME.
スタ
HMPH... I CAN ASSURE YOU I AM **MUCH** IMPROVED SINCE THEN...
CARE TO TRY YOUR HAND?
SOUNDS LIKE FUN... I'M FEELIN' A BIT RUSTY LATELY. I COULD USE THE WORKOUT.
NO, DON'T DO THIS, MUSICA...
YOU TOO, MR. ALLIGATOR... WHY ARE YOU HERE, ANY-WAY?
HMPH.
I COME TO YOU WITH IMPORTANT NEWS.

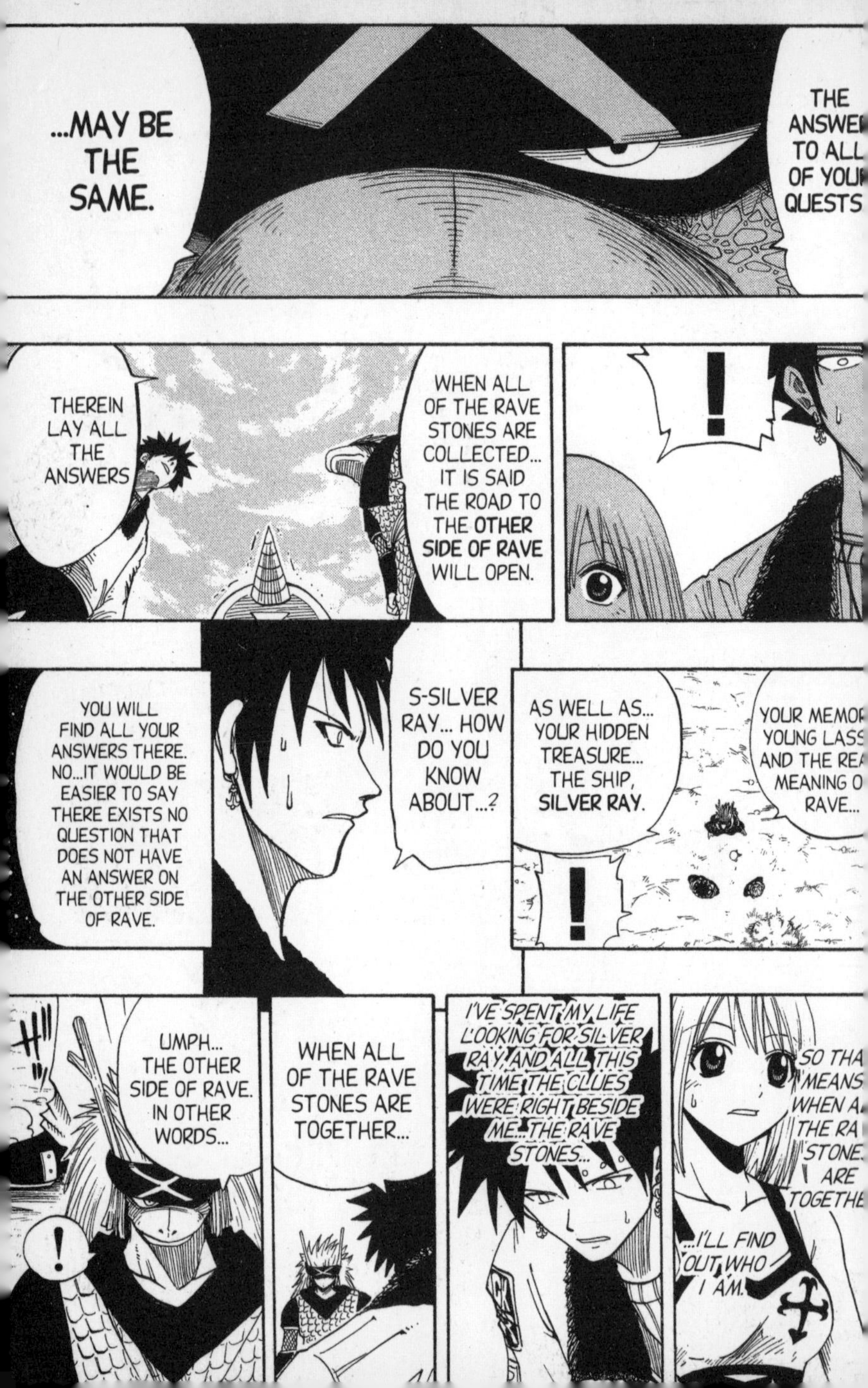
THE ANSWE TO ALL OF YOU QUESTS
...MAY BE THE SAME.
!
WHEN ALL OF THE RAVE STONES ARE COLLECTED... IT IS SAID THE ROAD TO THE **OTHER SIDE OF RAVE** WILL OPEN.
THEREIN LAY ALL THE ANSWERS
YOUR MEMOR YOUNG LASS AND THE REA MEANING O RAVE...
AS WELL AS... YOUR HIDDEN TREASURE... THE SHIP, **SILVER RAY**.
!
S-SILVER RAY... HOW DO YOU KNOW ABOUT...?
YOU WILL FIND ALL YOUR ANSWERS THERE. NO...IT WOULD BE EASIER TO SAY THERE EXISTS NO QUESTION THAT DOES NOT HAVE AN ANSWER ON THE OTHER SIDE OF RAVE.
SO THA MEANS WHEN A THE RA STONE ARE TOGETHE
...I'LL FIND OUT WHO I AM.
I'VE SPENT MY LIFE LOOKING FOR SILVER RAY, AND ALL THIS TIME THE CLUES WERE RIGHT BESIDE ME... THE RAVE STONES...
WHEN ALL OF THE RAVE STONES ARE TOGETHER...
UMPH... THE OTHER SIDE OF RAVE. IN OTHER WORDS...
!

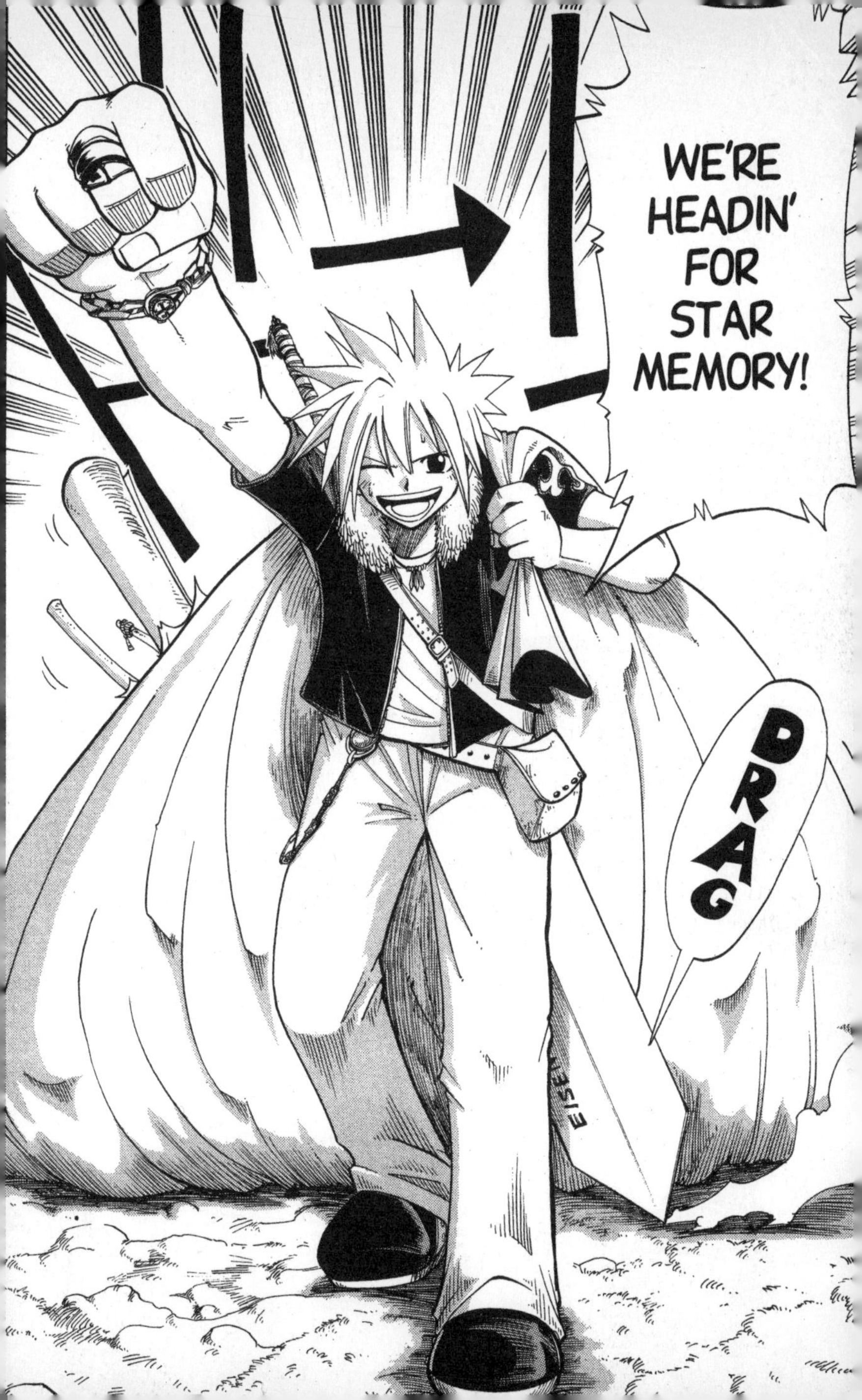
WE'RE HEADIN' FOR STAR MEMORY!
DRAG
EISEN

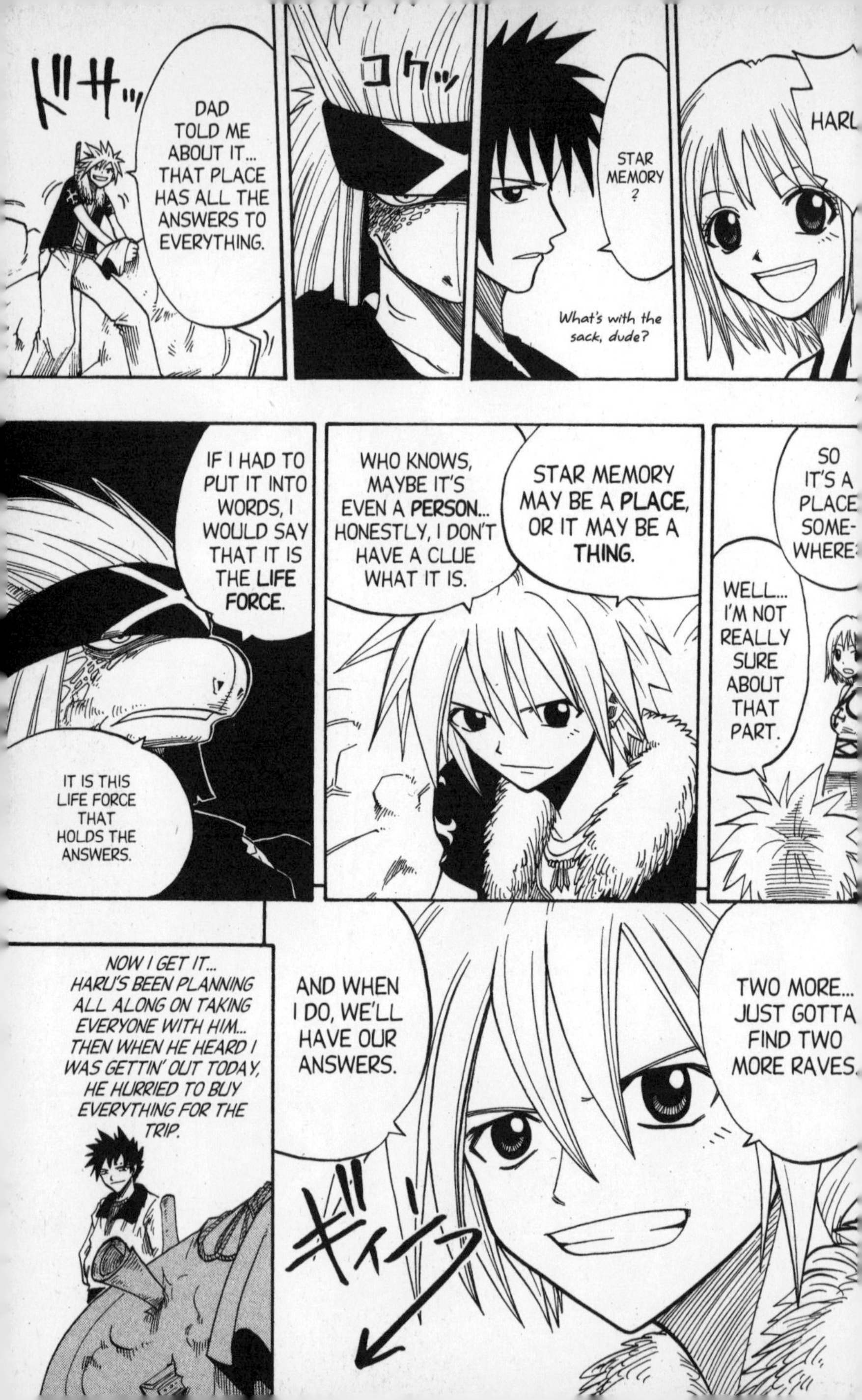
HARU
STAR MEMORY?
What's with the sack, dude?
コクッ
ドサッ
DAD TOLD ME ABOUT IT... THAT PLACE HAS ALL THE ANSWERS TO EVERYTHING.
SO IT'S A PLACE SOMEWHERE?
WELL... I'M NOT REALLY SURE ABOUT THAT PART.
STAR MEMORY MAY BE A **PLACE**, OR IT MAY BE A **THING**.
WHO KNOWS, MAYBE IT'S EVEN A **PERSON**... HONESTLY, I DON'T HAVE A CLUE WHAT IT IS.
IF I HAD TO PUT IT INTO WORDS, I WOULD SAY THAT IT IS THE **LIFE FORCE**.
IT IS THIS LIFE FORCE THAT HOLDS THE ANSWERS.
TWO MORE... JUST GOTTA FIND TWO MORE RAVES.
AND WHEN I DO, WE'LL HAVE OUR ANSWERS.
ギィーッ
NOW I GET IT... HARU'S BEEN PLANNING ALL ALONG ON TAKING EVERYONE WITH HIM... THEN WHEN HE HEARD I WAS GETTIN' OUT TODAY, HE HURRIED TO BUY EVERYTHING FOR THE TRIP.

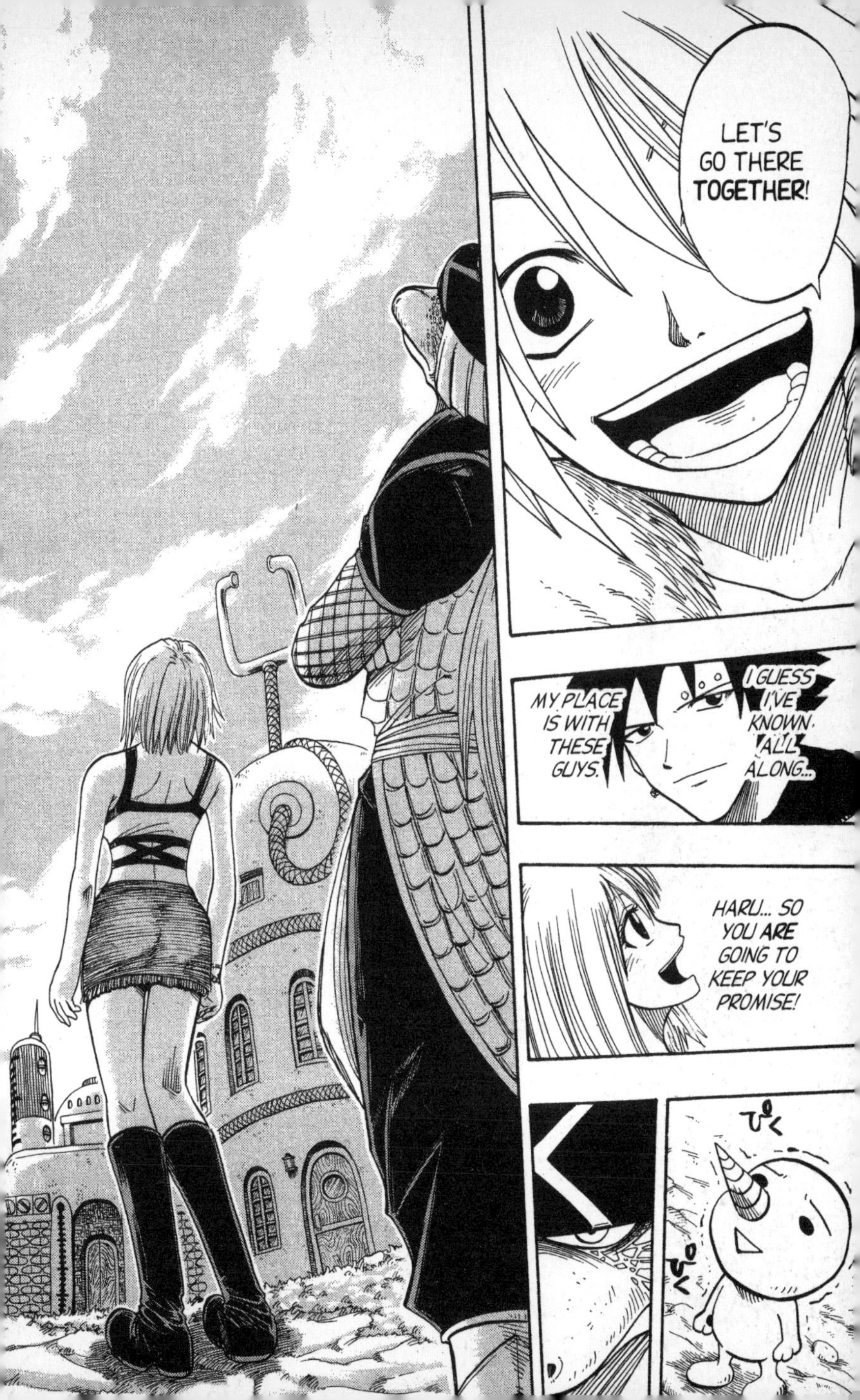
LET'S GO THERE TOGETHER!
I GUESS I'VE KNOWN ALL ALONG...
MY PLACE IS WITH THESE GUYS.
HARU... SO YOU ARE GOING TO KEEP YOUR PROMISE!

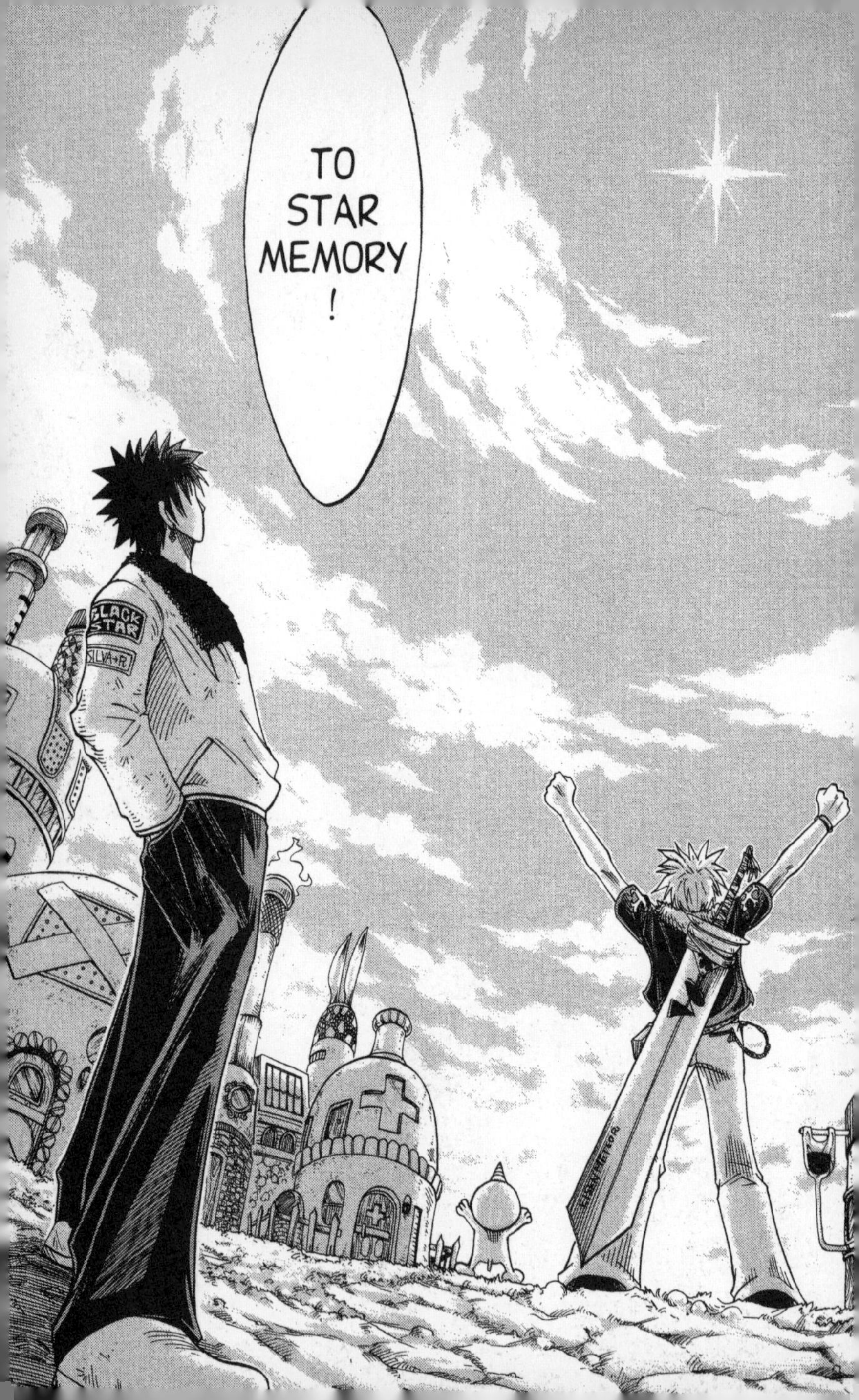
TO STAR MEMORY !
BLACK STAR

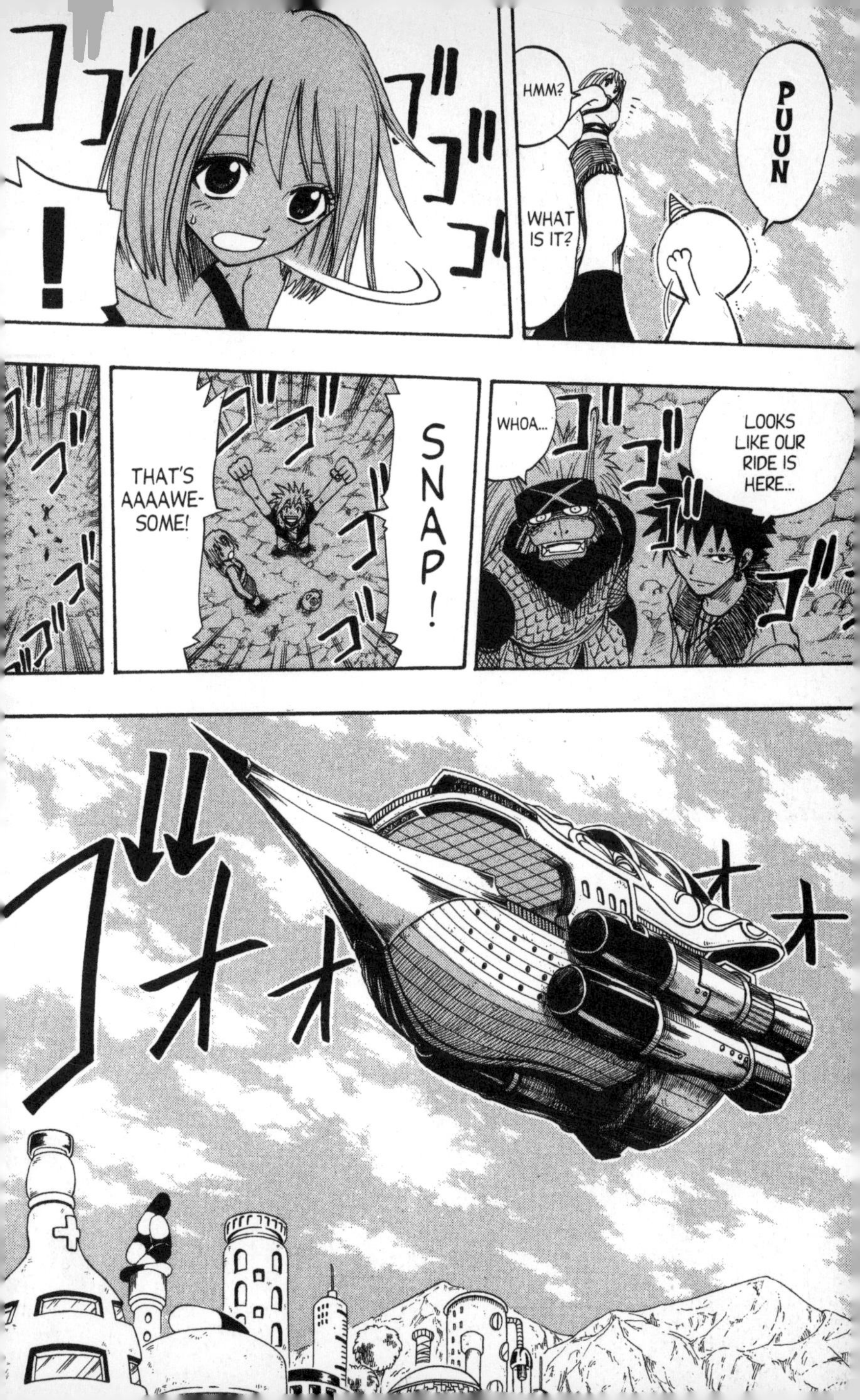
PUUN
HMM?
WHAT IS IT?
!
LOOKS LIKE OUR RIDE IS HERE...
WHOA...
SNAP!
THAT'S AAAAWE-SOME!

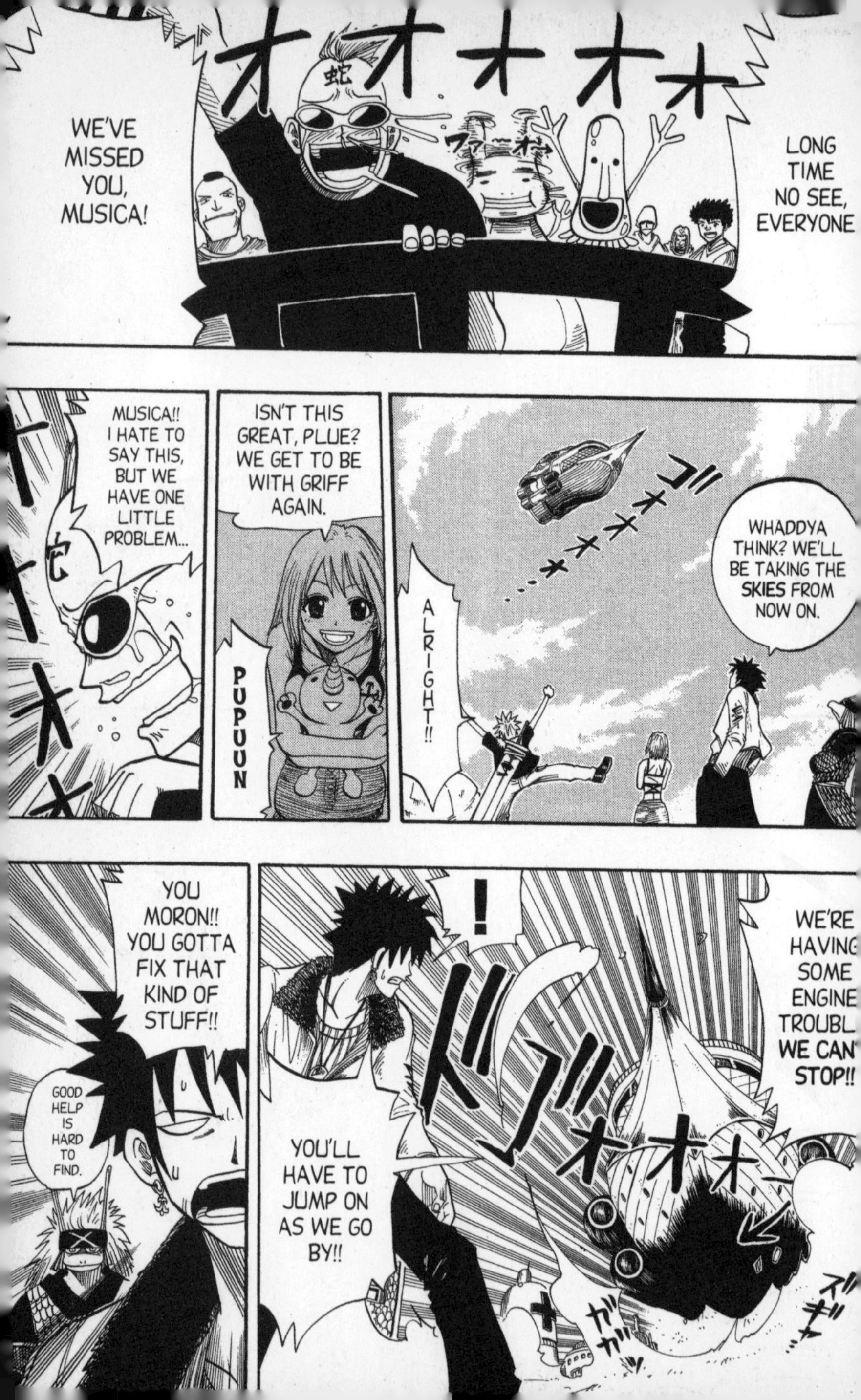

オオオオオ
LONG TIME NO SEE, EVERYONE
WE'VE MISSED YOU, MUSICA!
WHADDYA THINK? WE'LL BE TAKING THE SKIES FROM NOW ON.
ALRIGHT!!
ISN'T THIS GREAT, PLUE? WE GET TO BE WITH GRIFF AGAIN.
PUPUUN
MUSICA!! I HATE TO SAY THIS, BUT WE HAVE ONE LITTLE PROBLEM...
WE'RE HAVING SOME ENGINE TROUBL
WE CAN STOP!!
!
YOU'LL HAVE TO JUMP ON AS WE GO BY!!
YOU MORON!! YOU GOTTA FIX THAT KIND OF STUFF!!
GOOD HELP IS HARD TO FIND.

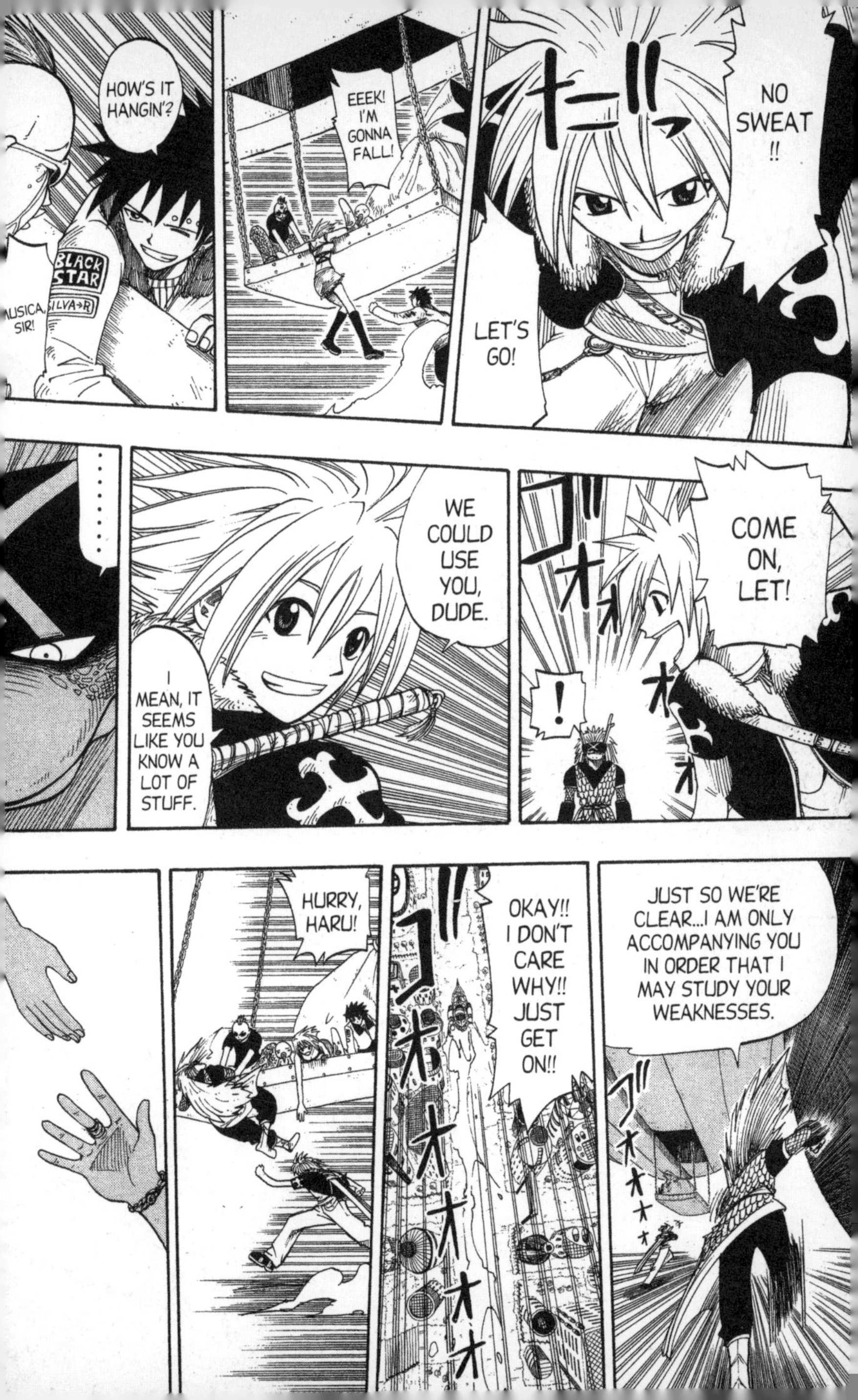
NO SWEAT!!
LET'S GO!
EEEK! I'M GONNA FALL!
HOW'S IT HANGIN'?
MUSICA, SIR!
BLACK STAR
SILVA→R
COME ON, LET!
!
WE COULD USE YOU, DUDE.
I MEAN, IT SEEMS LIKE YOU KNOW A LOT OF STUFF.
......
JUST SO WE'RE CLEAR...I AM ONLY ACCOMPANYING YOU IN ORDER THAT I MAY STUDY YOUR WEAKNESSES.
OKAY!! I DON'T CARE WHY!! JUST GET ON!!
HURRY, HARU!

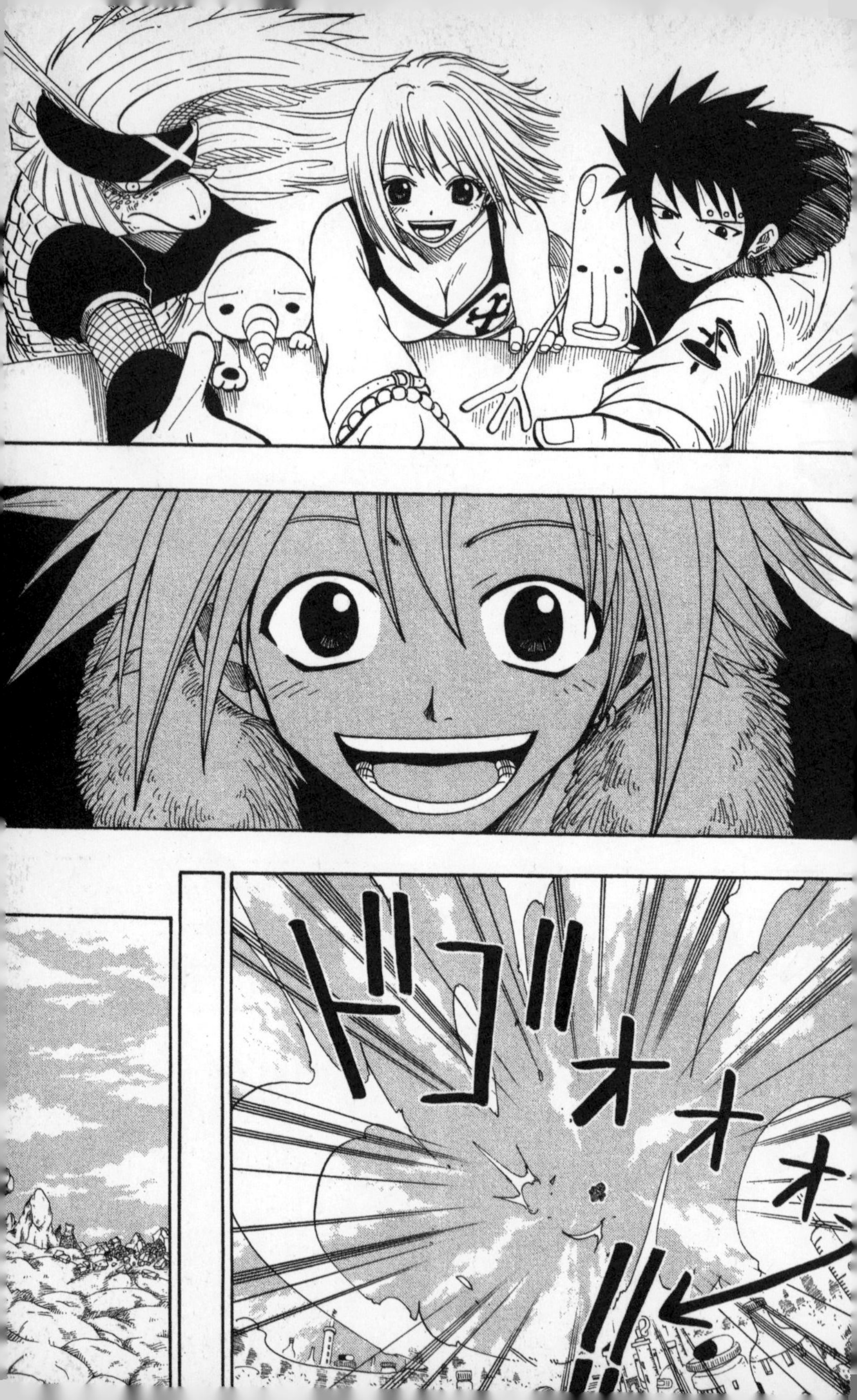
ドゴオオォ!!!

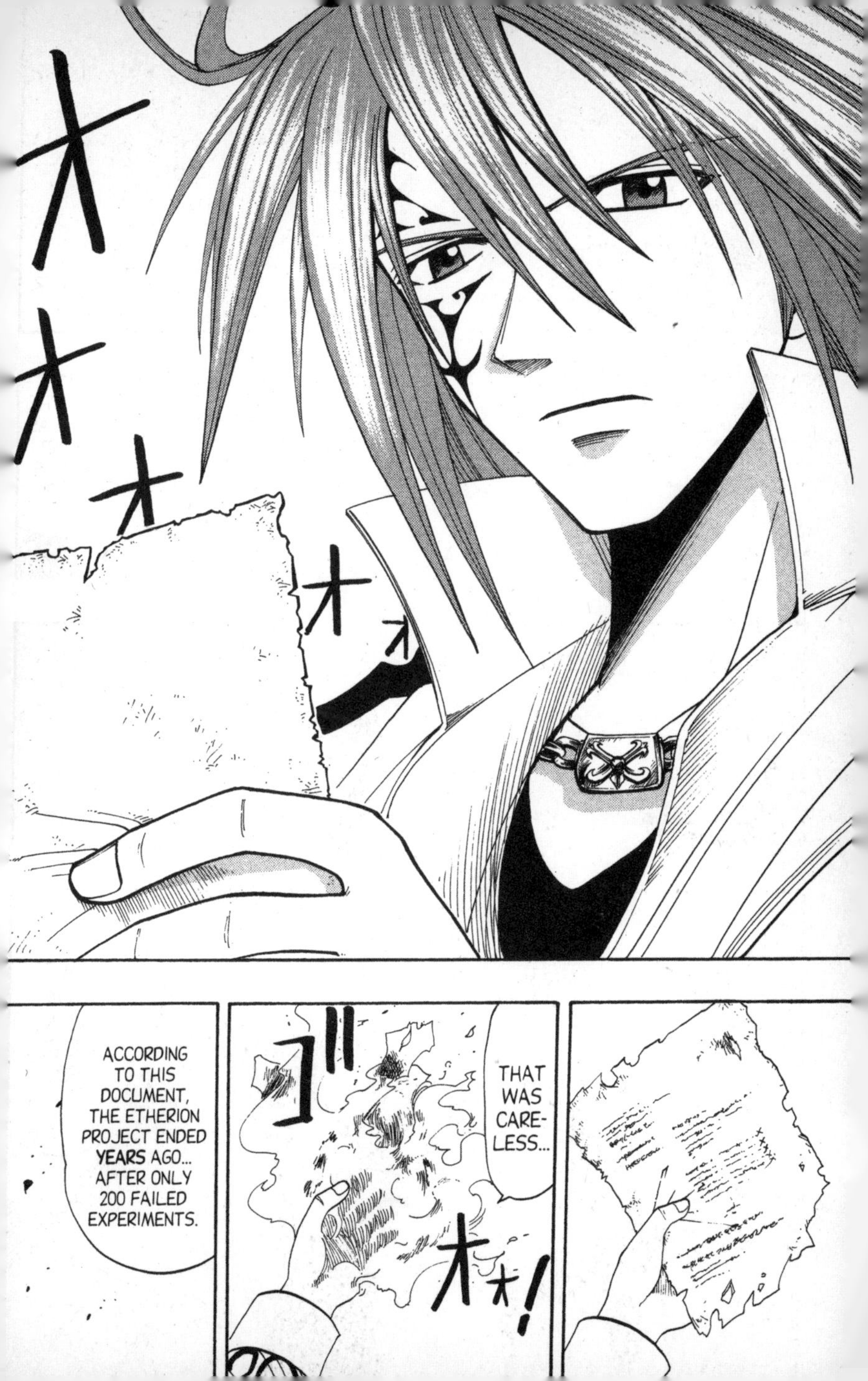
オオオオオ
THAT WAS CARE-LESS...
ゴオォ!
ACCORDING TO THIS DOCUMENT, THE ETHERION PROJECT ENDED **YEARS** AGO... AFTER ONLY 200 FAILED EXPERIMENTS.

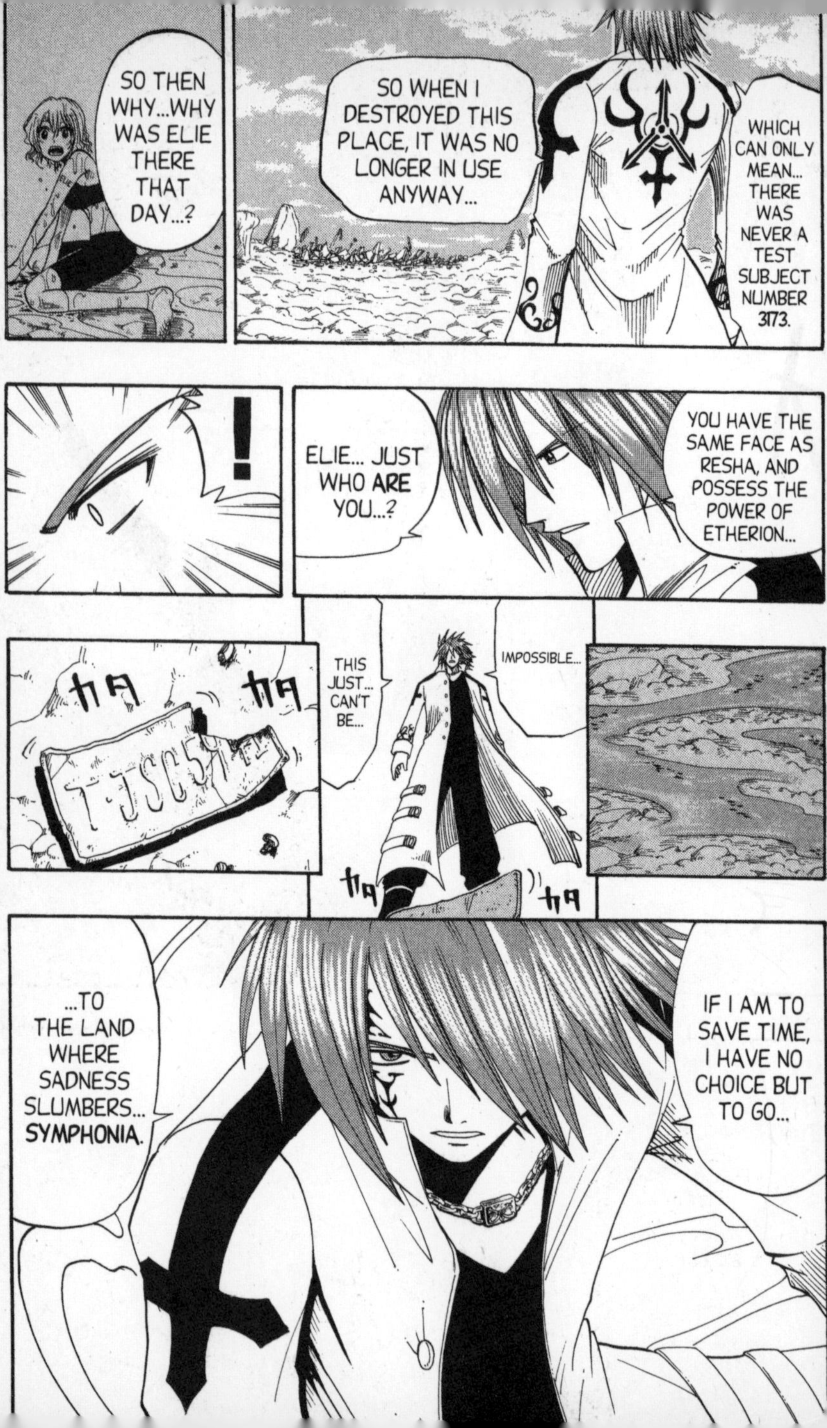
WHICH CAN ONLY MEAN... THERE WAS NEVER A TEST SUBJECT NUMBER 3173.
SO WHEN I DESTROYED THIS PLACE, IT WAS NO LONGER IN USE ANYWAY...
SO THEN WHY...WHY WAS ELIE THERE THAT DAY...?
YOU HAVE THE SAME FACE AS RESHA, AND POSSESS THE POWER OF ETHERION...
ELIE... JUST WHO **ARE** YOU...?
!
IMPOSSIBLE...
THIS JUST... CAN'T BE...
カタ
カタ
カタ
カタ
T-JSC5
IF I AM TO SAVE TIME, I HAVE NO CHOICE BUT TO GO...
...TO THE LAND WHERE SADNESS SLUMBERS... **SYMPHONIA.**

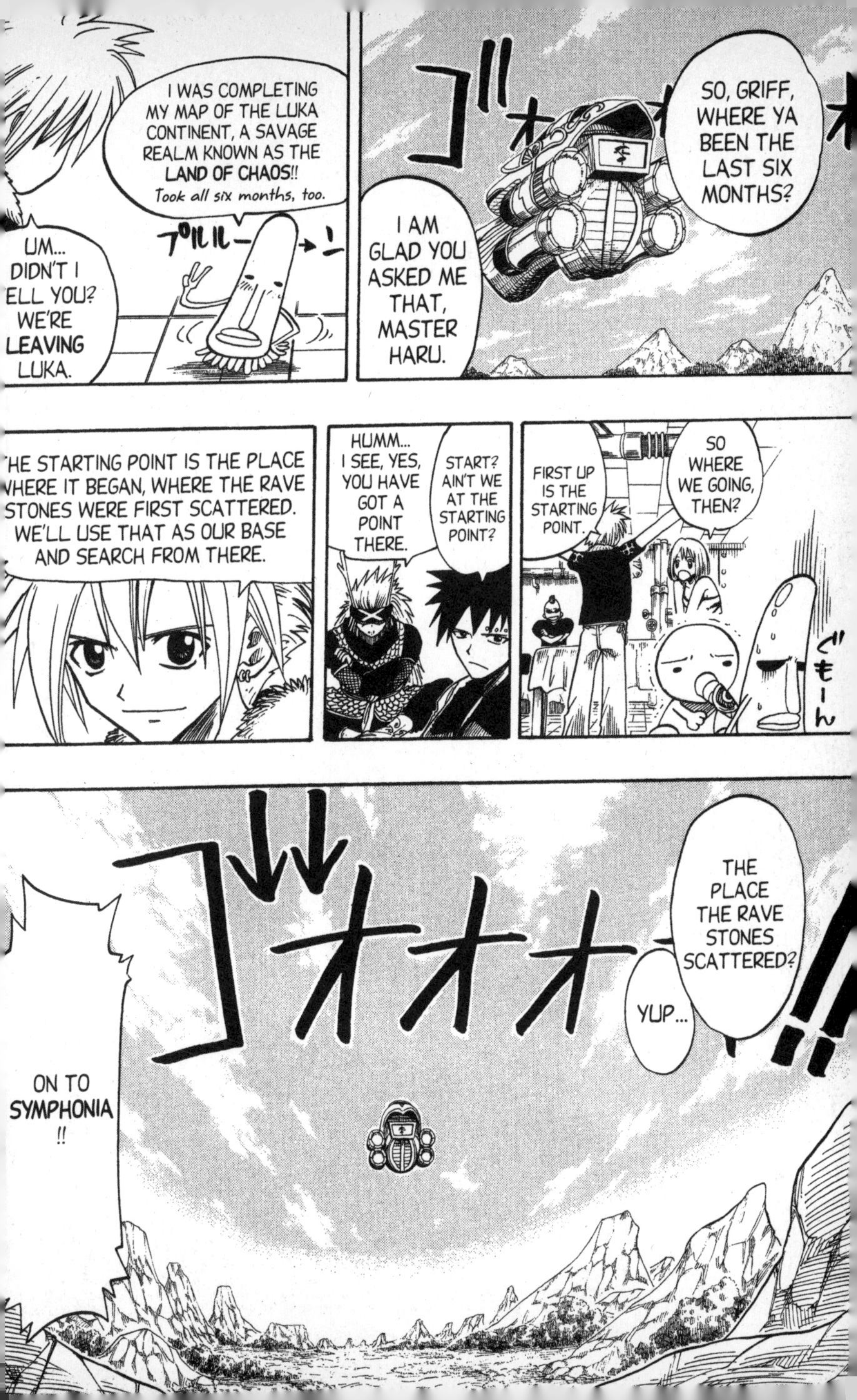
SO, GRIFF, WHERE YA BEEN THE LAST SIX MONTHS?
I AM GLAD YOU ASKED ME THAT, MASTER HARU.
I WAS COMPLETING MY MAP OF THE LUKA CONTINENT, A SAVAGE REALM KNOWN AS THE **LAND OF CHAOS**!! *Took all six months, too.*
UM... DIDN'T I TELL YOU? WE'RE **LEAVING** LUKA.
SO WHERE WE GOING, THEN?
FIRST UP IS THE STARTING POINT.
START? AIN'T WE AT THE STARTING POINT?
HUMM... I SEE, YES, YOU HAVE GOT A POINT THERE.
THE STARTING POINT IS THE PLACE WHERE IT BEGAN, WHERE THE RAVE STONES WERE FIRST SCATTERED. WE'LL USE THAT AS OUR BASE AND SEARCH FROM THERE.
ゴオオオ!!
THE PLACE THE RAVE STONES SCATTERED?
YUP...
ON TO **SYMPHONIA**!!

RAVE MASTER™

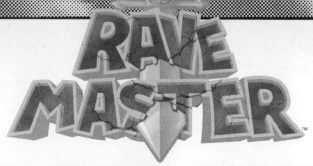

FLYING SHIP SILVER KNIGHTS

PURCHASED WITH THE MONEY FROM SELLING THEIR FORMER SHIP, THE *ADVENT* AND ALL THE MONEY IN THE SILVERHYTHM GANG'S SAVINGS. ESTIMATED VALUE, OVER 800 MILLION EDELS.

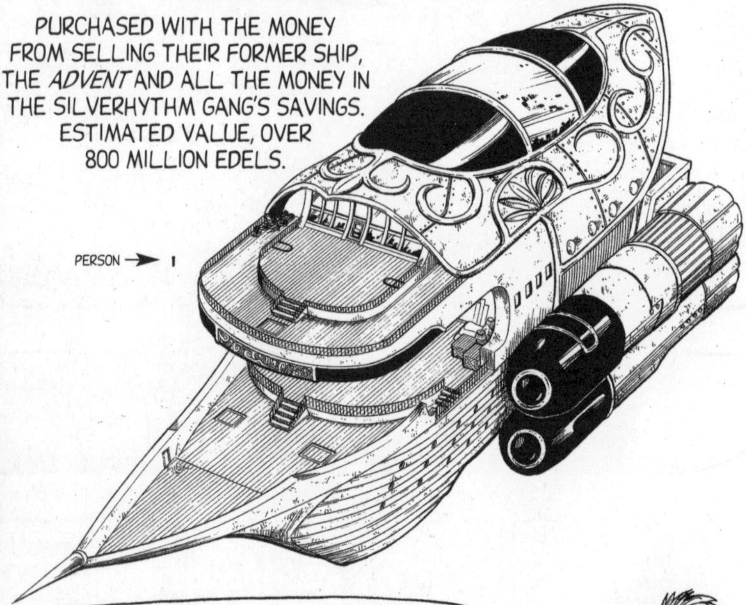
PERSON

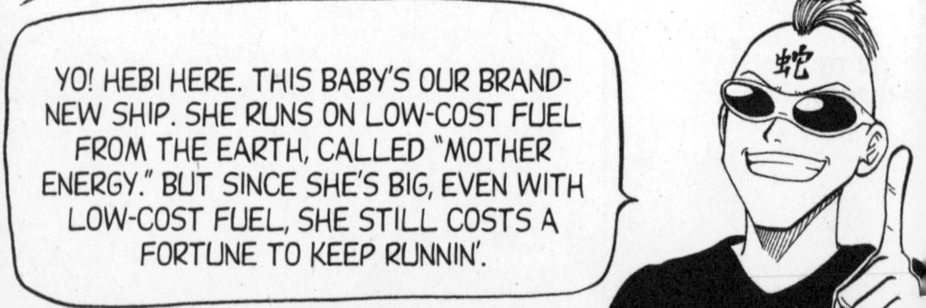
YO! HEBI HERE. THIS BABY'S OUR BRAND-NEW SHIP. SHE RUNS ON LOW-COST FUEL FROM THE EARTH, CALLED "MOTHER ENERGY." BUT SINCE SHE'S BIG, EVEN WITH LOW-COST FUEL, SHE STILL COSTS A FORTUNE TO KEEP RUNNIN'.
蛇

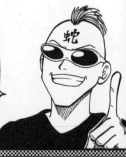

RAVE:75 THE SIDE ROADS ARE FULL OF DANGER?!

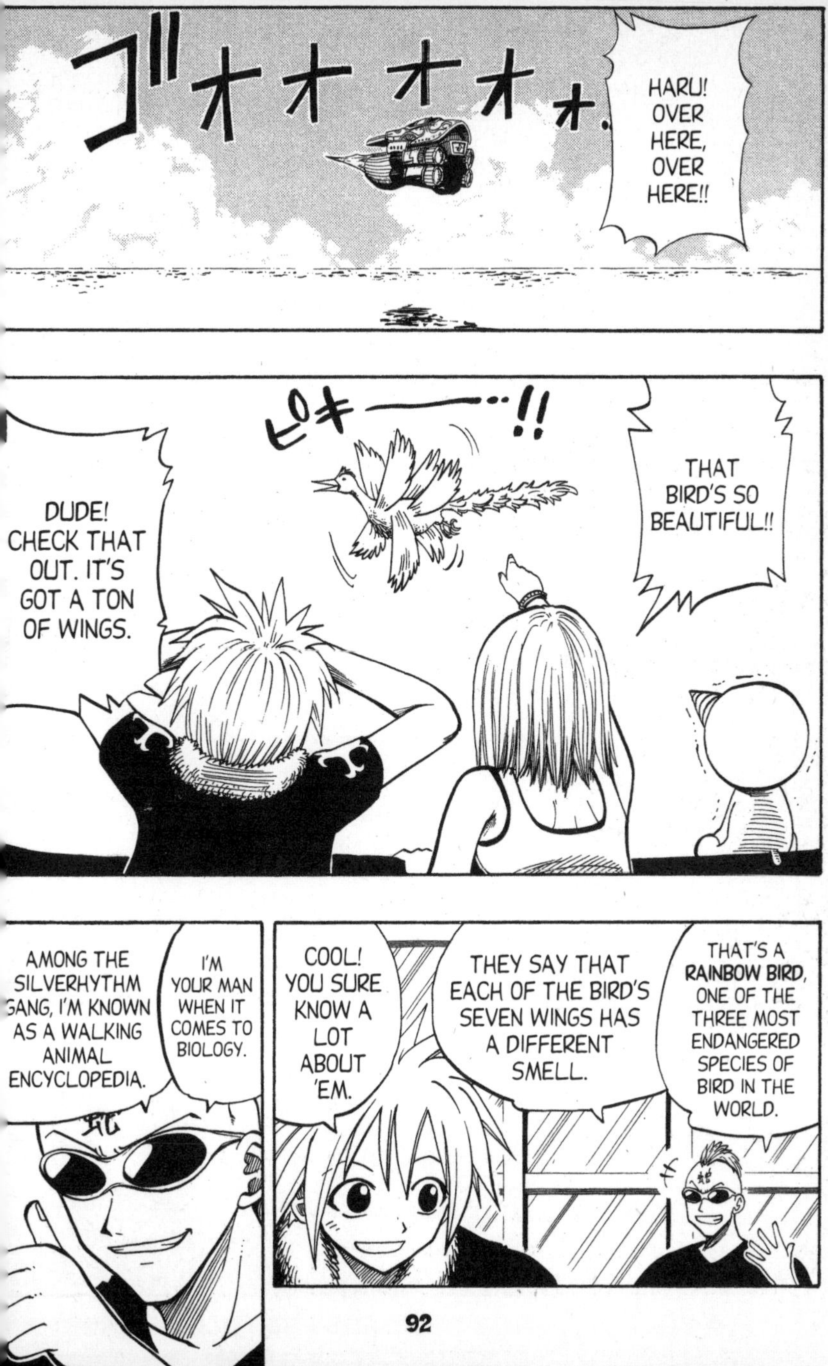
HARU! OVER HERE, OVER HERE!!
ゴオオオオオ
THAT BIRD'S SO BEAUTIFUL!!
ピキーー‥!!
DUDE! CHECK THAT OUT. IT'S GOT A TON OF WINGS.
THAT'S A **RAINBOW BIRD**, ONE OF THE THREE MOST ENDANGERED SPECIES OF BIRD IN THE WORLD.
THEY SAY THAT EACH OF THE BIRD'S SEVEN WINGS HAS A DIFFERENT SMELL.
COOL! YOU SURE KNOW A LOT ABOUT 'EM.
I'M YOUR MAN WHEN IT COMES TO BIOLOGY.
AMONG THE SILVERHYTHM GANG, I'M KNOWN AS A WALKING ANIMAL ENCYCLOPEDIA.

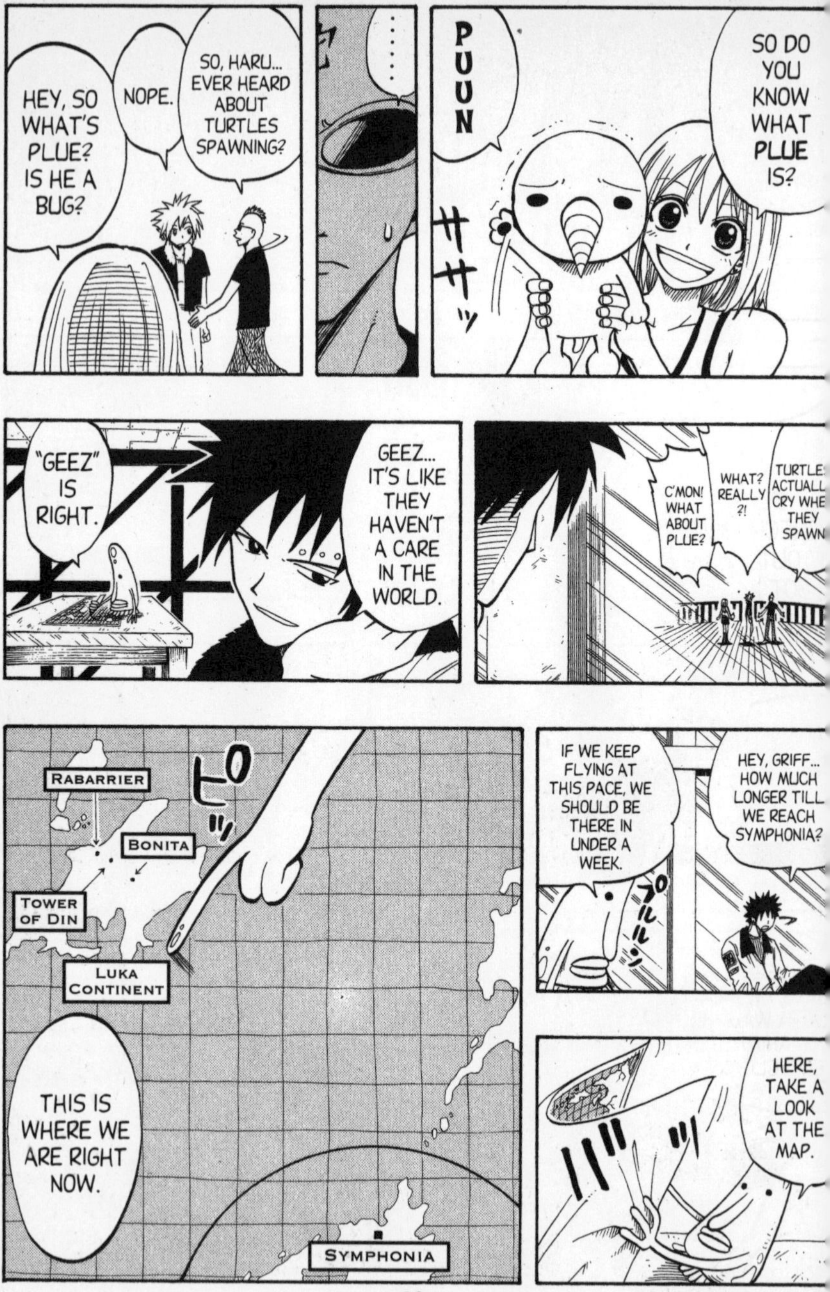
SO DO YOU KNOW WHAT PLUE IS?
PUUN
......
SO, HARU... EVER HEARD ABOUT TURTLES SPAWNING?
NOPE.
HEY, SO WHAT'S PLUE? IS HE A BUG?
TURTLE ACTUALL CRY WHE THEY SPAWN
WHAT? REALLY?!
C'MON! WHAT ABOUT PLUE?
GEEZ... IT'S LIKE THEY HAVEN'T A CARE IN THE WORLD.
"GEEZ" IS RIGHT.
HEY, GRIFF... HOW MUCH LONGER TILL WE REACH SYMPHONIA?
IF WE KEEP FLYING AT THIS PACE, WE SHOULD BE THERE IN UNDER A WEEK.
HERE, TAKE A LOOK AT THE MAP.
RABARRIER
BONITA
TOWER OF DIN
LUKA CONTINENT
THIS IS WHERE WE ARE RIGHT NOW.
SYMPHONIA

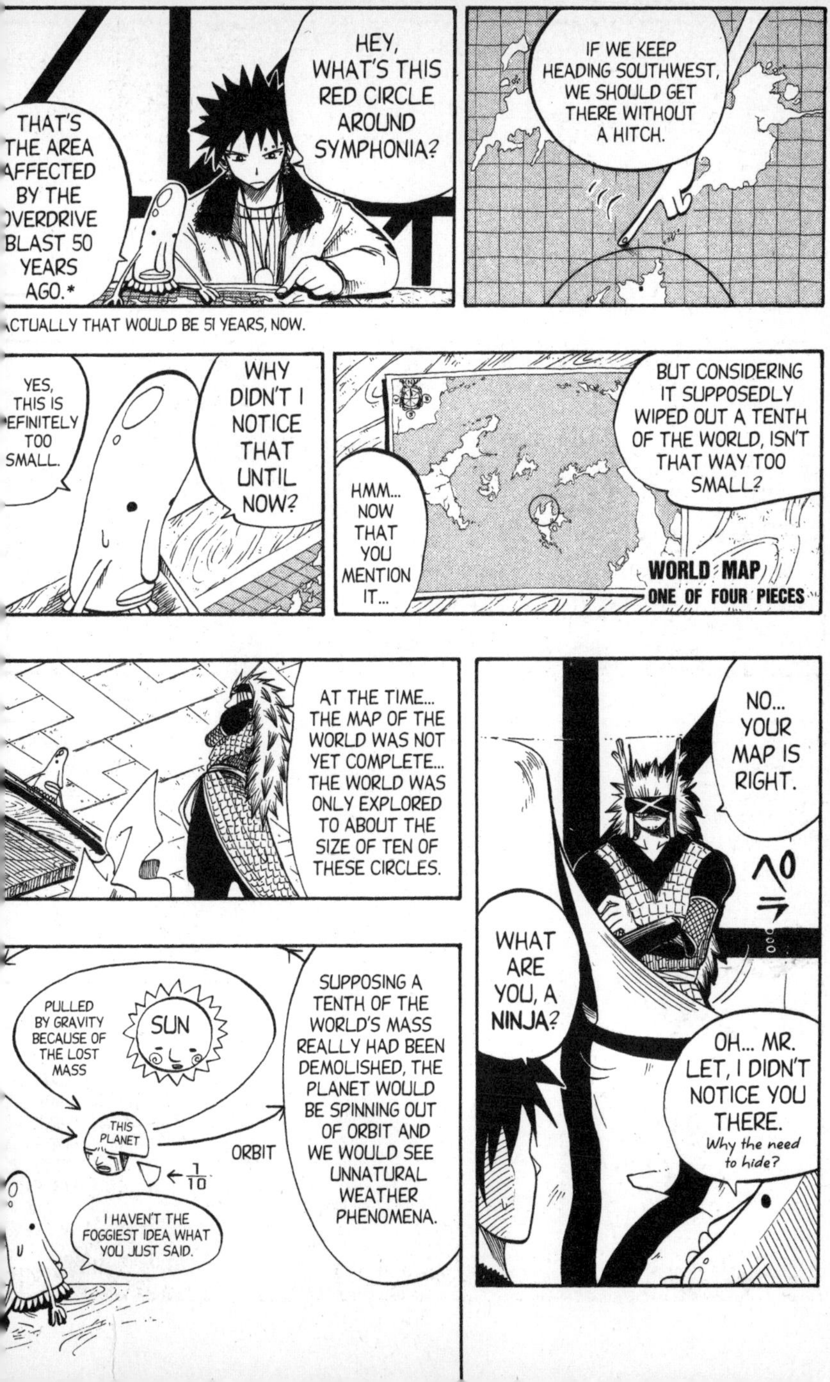

IF WE KEEP HEADING SOUTHWEST, WE SHOULD GET THERE WITHOUT A HITCH.
HEY, WHAT'S THIS RED CIRCLE AROUND SYMPHONIA?
THAT'S THE AREA AFFECTED BY THE OVERDRIVE BLAST 50 YEARS AGO.*
ACTUALLY THAT WOULD BE 51 YEARS, NOW.
BUT CONSIDERING IT SUPPOSEDLY WIPED OUT A TENTH OF THE WORLD, ISN'T THAT WAY TOO SMALL?
HMM... NOW THAT YOU MENTION IT...
WORLD MAP
ONE OF FOUR PIECES
WHY DIDN'T I NOTICE THAT UNTIL NOW?
YES, THIS IS DEFINITELY TOO SMALL.
NO... YOUR MAP IS RIGHT.
WHAT ARE YOU, A NINJA?
OH... MR. LET, I DIDN'T NOTICE YOU THERE.
Why the need to hide?
AT THE TIME... THE MAP OF THE WORLD WAS NOT YET COMPLETE... THE WORLD WAS ONLY EXPLORED TO ABOUT THE SIZE OF TEN OF THESE CIRCLES.
SUPPOSING A TENTH OF THE WORLD'S MASS REALLY HAD BEEN DEMOLISHED, THE PLANET WOULD BE SPINNING OUT OF ORBIT AND WE WOULD SEE UNNATURAL WEATHER PHENOMENA.
PULLED BY GRAVITY BECAUSE OF THE LOST MASS
SUN
THIS PLANET
ORBIT
1/10
I HAVEN'T THE FOGGIEST IDEA WHAT YOU JUST SAID.

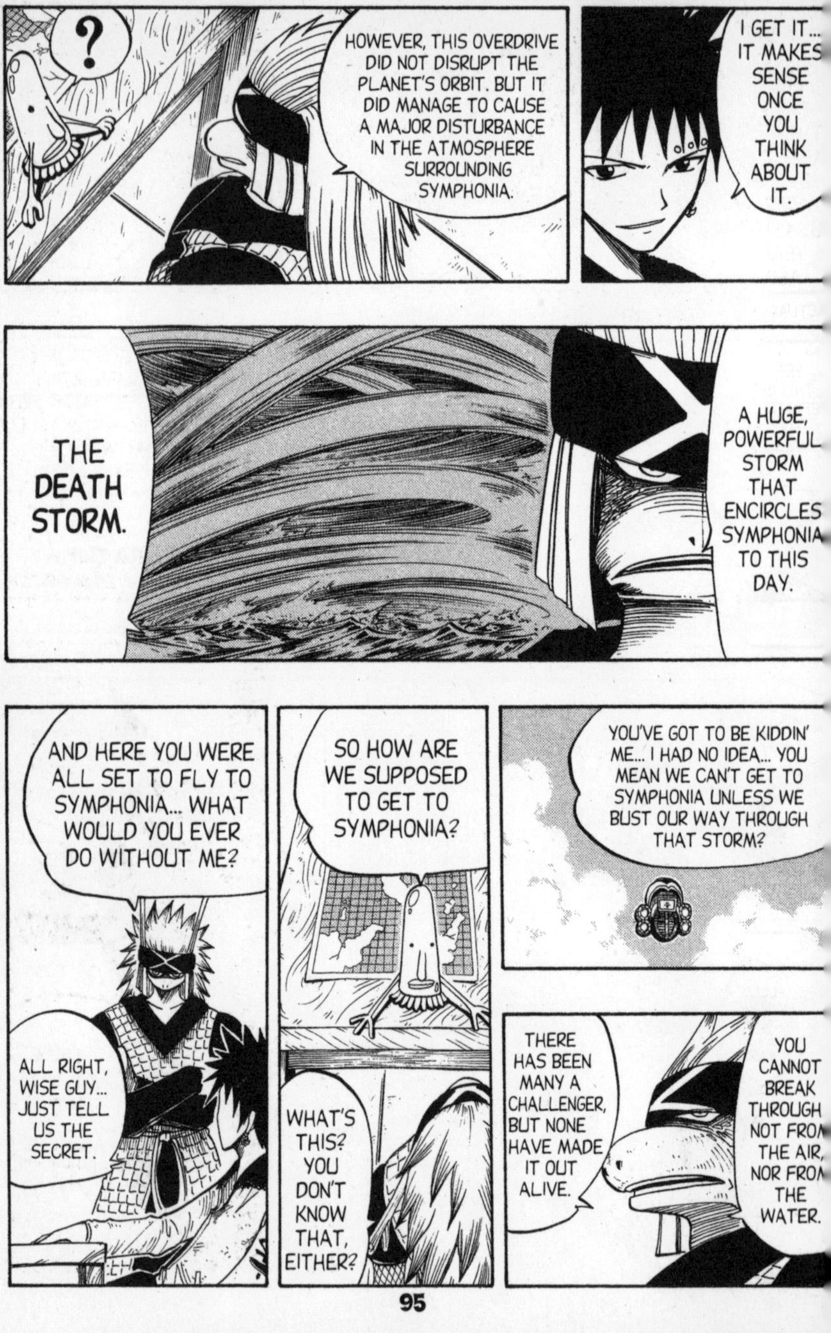
I GET IT... IT MAKES SENSE ONCE YOU THINK ABOUT IT.
?
HOWEVER, THIS OVERDRIVE DID NOT DISRUPT THE PLANET'S ORBIT. BUT IT DID MANAGE TO CAUSE A MAJOR DISTURBANCE IN THE ATMOSPHERE SURROUNDING SYMPHONIA.
A HUGE, POWERFUL STORM THAT ENCIRCLES SYMPHONIA TO THIS DAY.
THE DEATH STORM.
YOU'VE GOT TO BE KIDDIN' ME... I HAD NO IDEA... YOU MEAN WE CAN'T GET TO SYMPHONIA UNLESS WE BUST OUR WAY THROUGH THAT STORM?
YOU CANNOT BREAK THROUGH NOT FROM THE AIR, NOR FROM THE WATER.
THERE HAS BEEN MANY A CHALLENGER, BUT NONE HAVE MADE IT OUT ALIVE.
SO HOW ARE WE SUPPOSED TO GET TO SYMPHONIA?
WHAT'S THIS? YOU DON'T KNOW THAT, EITHER?
AND HERE YOU WERE ALL SET TO FLY TO SYMPHONIA... WHAT WOULD YOU EVER DO WITHOUT ME?
ALL RIGHT, WISE GUY... JUST TELL US THE SECRET.

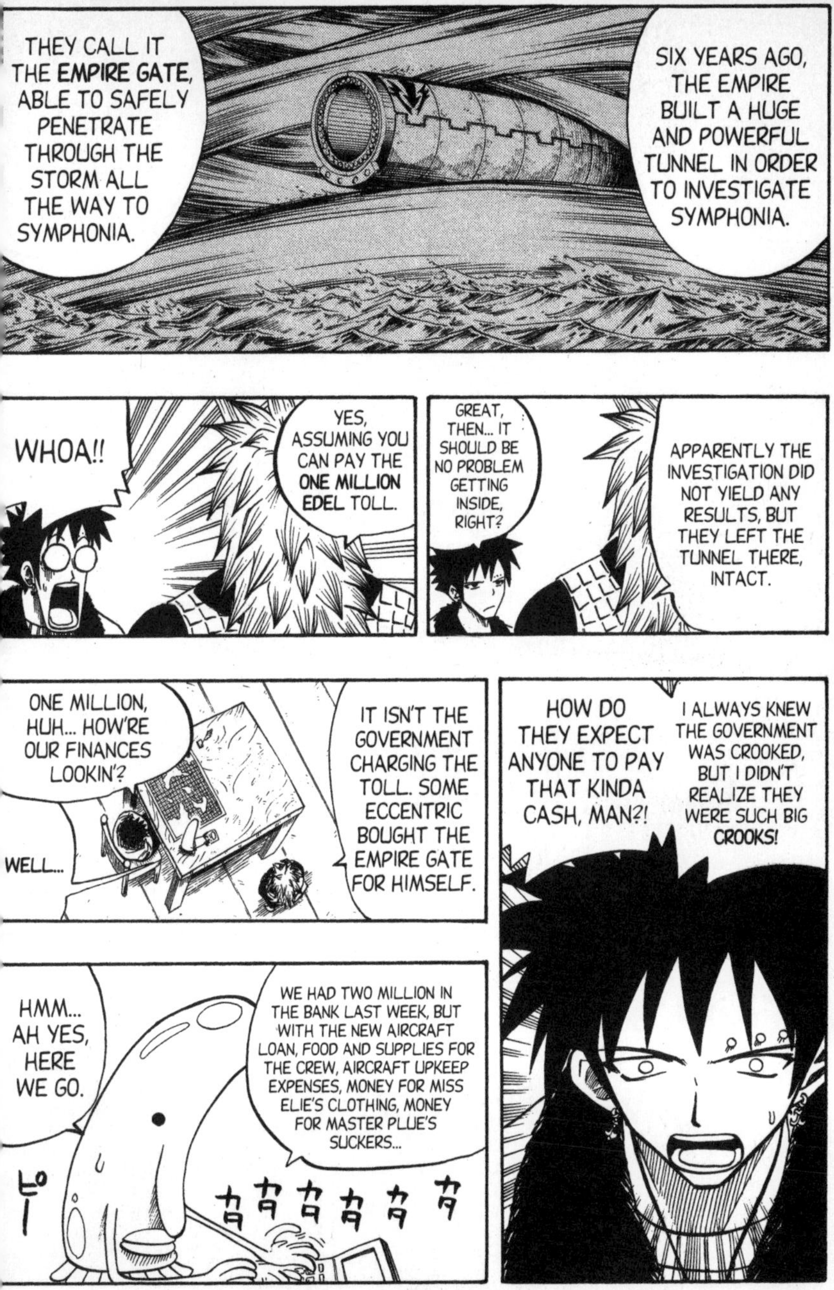
SIX YEARS AGO, THE EMPIRE BUILT A HUGE AND POWERFUL TUNNEL IN ORDER TO INVESTIGATE SYMPHONIA.
THEY CALL IT THE **EMPIRE GATE**, ABLE TO SAFELY PENETRATE THROUGH THE STORM ALL THE WAY TO SYMPHONIA.
APPARENTLY THE INVESTIGATION DID NOT YIELD ANY RESULTS, BUT THEY LEFT THE TUNNEL THERE, INTACT.
GREAT, THEN... IT SHOULD BE NO PROBLEM GETTING INSIDE, RIGHT?
YES, ASSUMING YOU CAN PAY THE **ONE MILLION EDEL** TOLL.
WHOA!!
I ALWAYS KNEW THE GOVERNMENT WAS CROOKED, BUT I DIDN'T REALIZE THEY WERE SUCH BIG **CROOKS!**
HOW DO THEY EXPECT ANYONE TO PAY THAT KINDA CASH, MAN?!
IT ISN'T THE GOVERNMENT CHARGING THE TOLL. SOME ECCENTRIC BOUGHT THE EMPIRE GATE FOR HIMSELF.
ONE MILLION, HUH... HOW'RE OUR FINANCES LOOKIN'?
WELL...
WE HAD TWO MILLION IN THE BANK LAST WEEK, BUT WITH THE NEW AIRCRAFT LOAN, FOOD AND SUPPLIES FOR THE CREW, AIRCRAFT UPKEEP EXPENSES, MONEY FOR MISS ELIE'S CLOTHING, MONEY FOR MASTER PLUE'S SUCKERS...
HMM... AH YES, HERE WE GO.
カタカタカタカタカタカタ
ピー

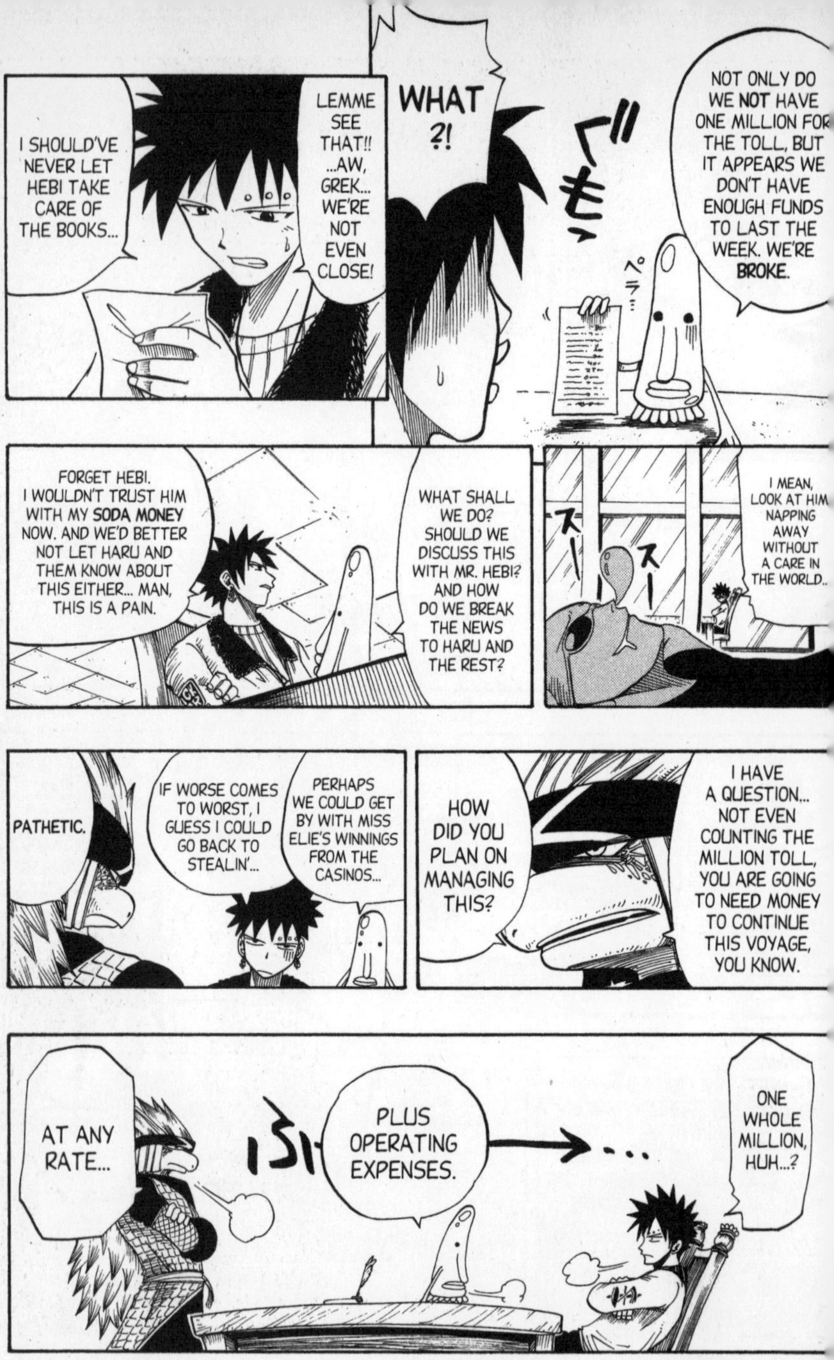
NOT ONLY DO WE NOT HAVE ONE MILLION FOR THE TOLL, BUT IT APPEARS WE DON'T HAVE ENOUGH FUNDS TO LAST THE WEEK. WE'RE BROKE.
ペラ
WHAT ?!
LEMME SEE THAT!! ...AW, GREK... WE'RE NOT EVEN CLOSE!
I SHOULD'VE NEVER LET HEBI TAKE CARE OF THE BOOKS...
I MEAN, LOOK AT HIM NAPPING AWAY WITHOUT A CARE IN THE WORLD..
スー
スー
WHAT SHALL WE DO? SHOULD WE DISCUSS THIS WITH MR. HEBI? AND HOW DO WE BREAK THE NEWS TO HARU AND THE REST?
FORGET HEBI. I WOULDN'T TRUST HIM WITH MY SODA MONEY NOW. AND WE'D BETTER NOT LET HARU AND THEM KNOW ABOUT THIS EITHER... MAN, THIS IS A PAIN.
I HAVE A QUESTION... NOT EVEN COUNTING THE MILLION TOLL, YOU ARE GOING TO NEED MONEY TO CONTINUE THIS VOYAGE, YOU KNOW.
HOW DID YOU PLAN ON MANAGING THIS?
PERHAPS WE COULD GET BY WITH MISS ELIE'S WINNINGS FROM THE CASINOS...
IF WORSE COMES TO WORST, I GUESS I COULD GO BACK TO STEALIN'...
PATHETIC.
ONE WHOLE MILLION, HUH...?
...
PLUS OPERATING EXPENSES.
AT ANY RATE...

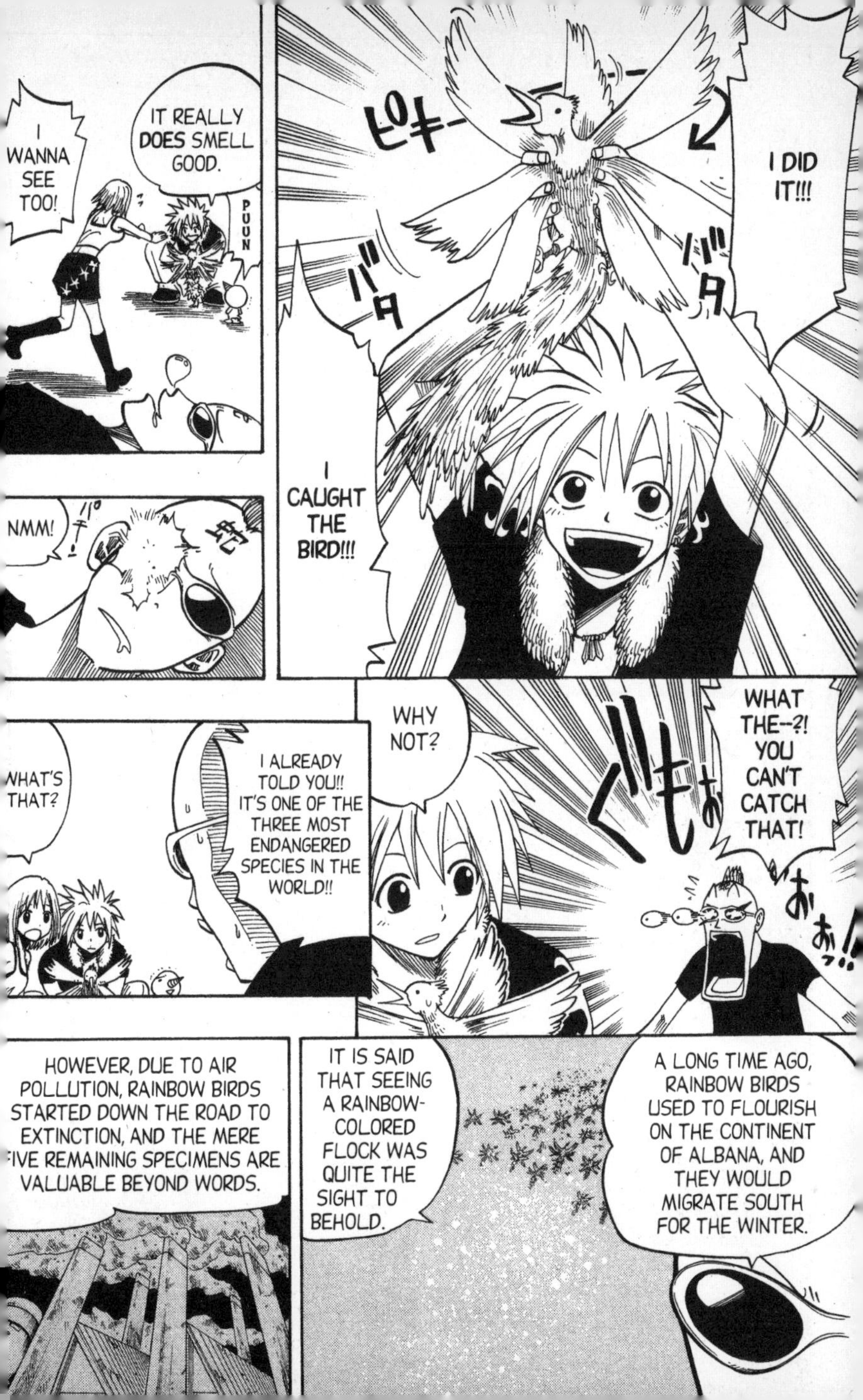

I DID IT!!!
I CAUGHT THE BIRD!!!
IT REALLY DOES SMELL GOOD.
PUUN
I WANNA SEE TOO!
NMM!
WHAT THE--?! YOU CAN'T CATCH THAT!
WHY NOT?
I ALREADY TOLD YOU!! IT'S ONE OF THE THREE MOST ENDANGERED SPECIES IN THE WORLD!!
WHAT'S THAT?
A LONG TIME AGO, RAINBOW BIRDS USED TO FLOURISH ON THE CONTINENT OF ALBANA, AND THEY WOULD MIGRATE SOUTH FOR THE WINTER.
IT IS SAID THAT SEEING A RAINBOW-COLORED FLOCK WAS QUITE THE SIGHT TO BEHOLD.
HOWEVER, DUE TO AIR POLLUTION, RAINBOW BIRDS STARTED DOWN THE ROAD TO EXTINCTION, AND THE MERE FIVE REMAINING SPECIMENS ARE VALUABLE BEYOND WORDS.

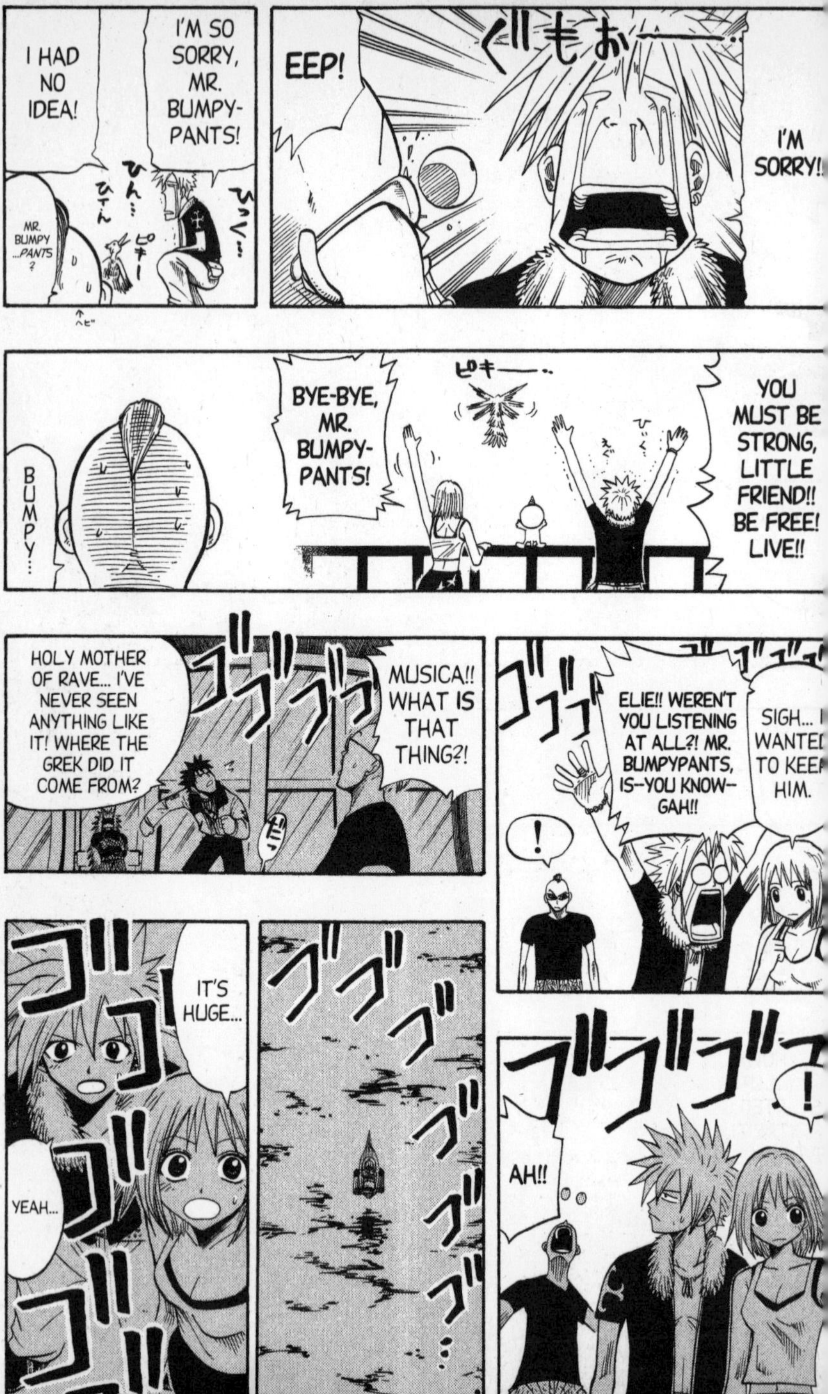
I'M SORRY!!
EEP!
I'M SO SORRY, MR. BUMPY-PANTS!
I HAD NO IDEA!
MR. BUMPY ...PANTS?
YOU MUST BE STRONG, LITTLE FRIEND!! BE FREE! LIVE!!
BYE-BYE, MR. BUMPY-PANTS!
BUMPY...
SIGH... I WANTED TO KEEP HIM.
ELIE!! WEREN'T YOU LISTENING AT ALL?! MR. BUMPYPANTS, IS--YOU KNOW--GAH!!
!
MUSICA!! WHAT IS THAT THING?!
HOLY MOTHER OF RAVE... I'VE NEVER SEEN ANYTHING LIKE IT! WHERE THE GREK DID IT COME FROM?
!
AH!!
IT'S HUGE...
YEAH...

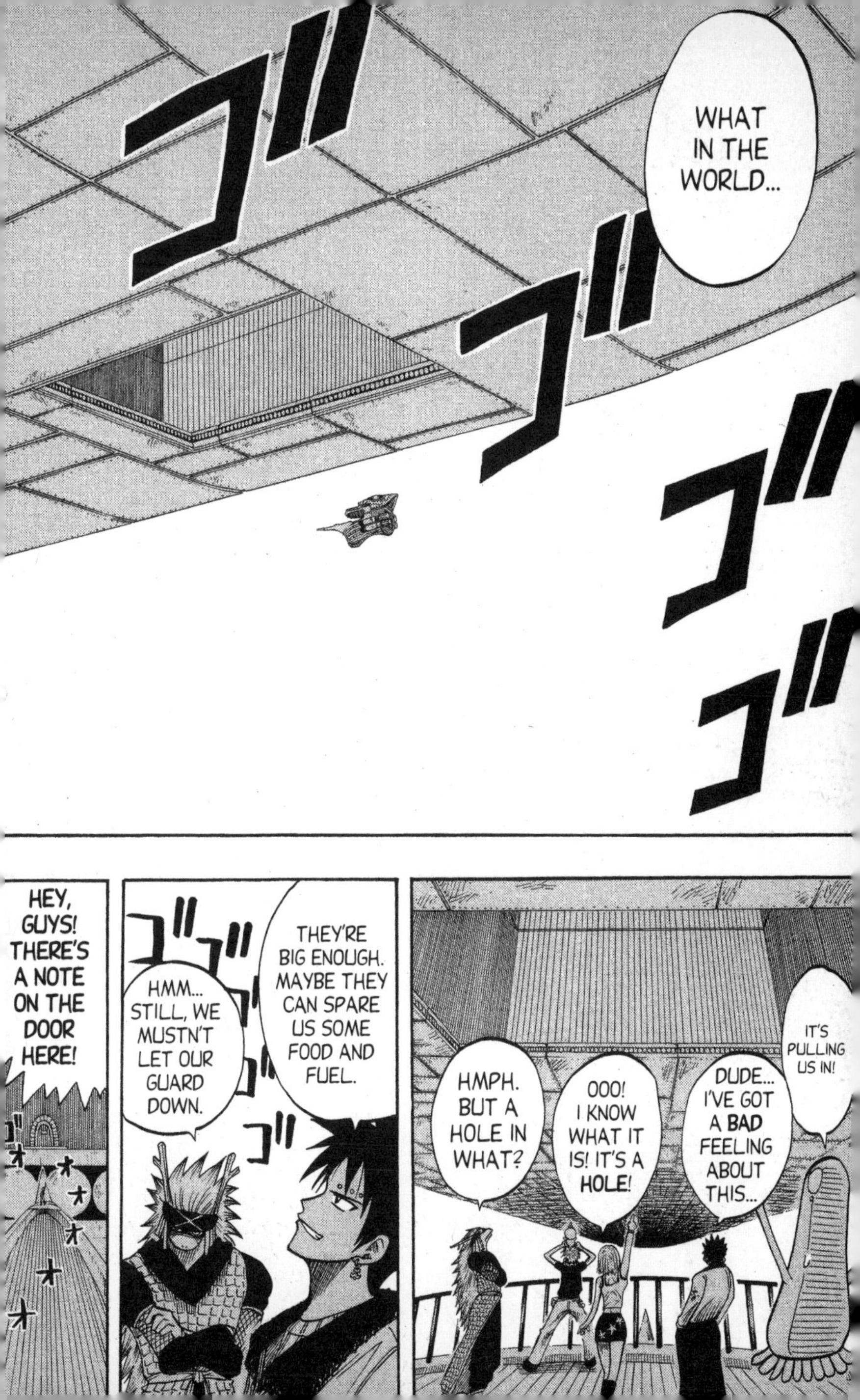

WHAT IN THE WORLD...
ゴゴゴゴ
IT'S PULLING US IN!
DUDE... I'VE GOT A **BAD** FEELING ABOUT THIS...
OOO! I KNOW WHAT IT IS! IT'S A **HOLE**!
HMPH. BUT A HOLE IN WHAT?
THEY'RE BIG ENOUGH. MAYBE THEY CAN SPARE US SOME FOOD AND FUEL.
HMM... STILL, WE MUSTN'T LET OUR GUARD DOWN.
HEY, GUYS! THERE'S A NOTE ON THE DOOR HERE!

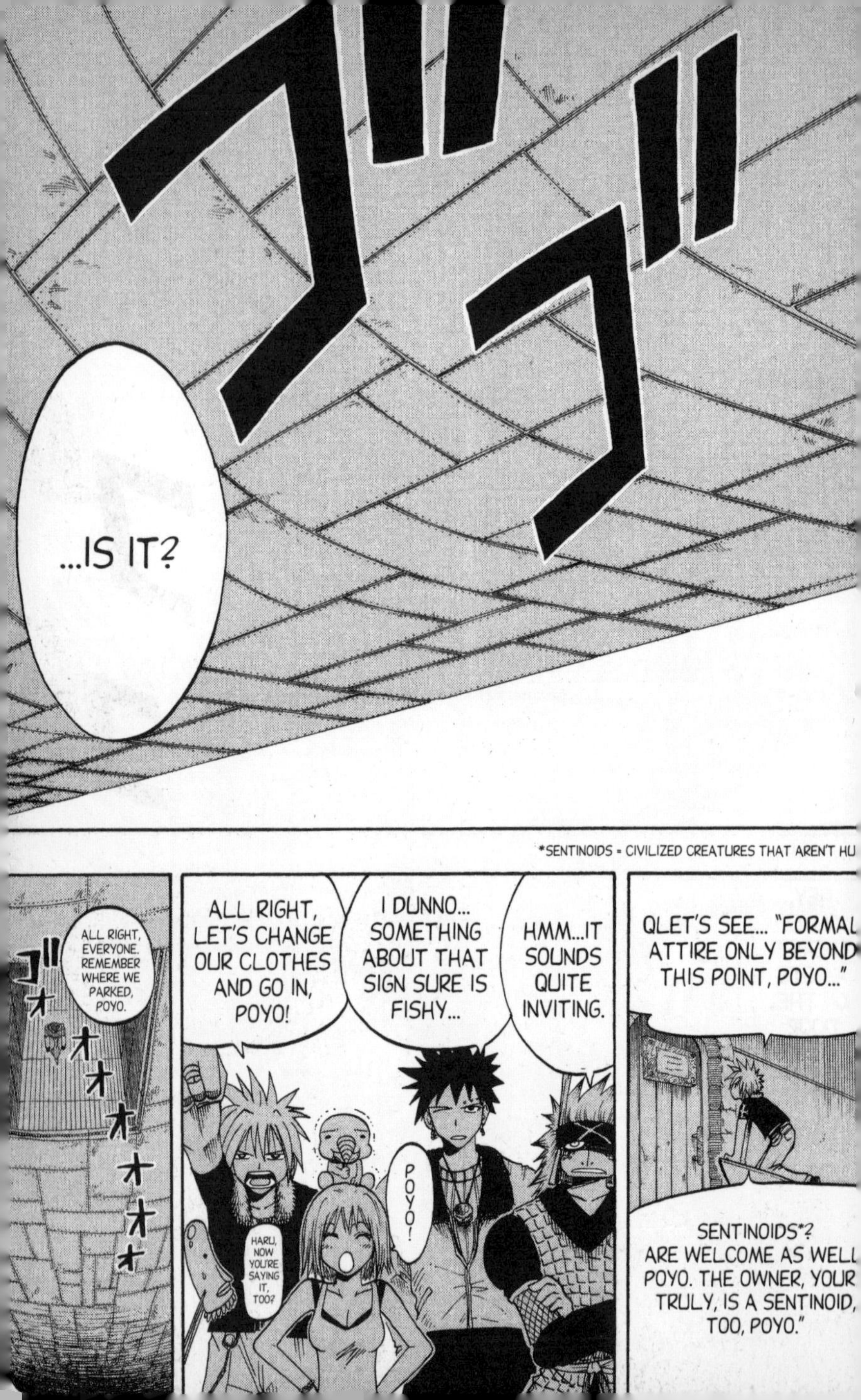
ゴゴ
...IS IT?
QLET'S SEE... "FORMAL ATTIRE ONLY BEYOND THIS POINT, POYO..."
SENTINOIDS*? ARE WELCOME AS WELL POYO. THE OWNER, YOUR TRULY, IS A SENTINOID, TOO, POYO."
HMM...IT SOUNDS QUITE INVITING.
I DUNNO... SOMETHING ABOUT THAT SIGN SURE IS FISHY...
ALL RIGHT, LET'S CHANGE OUR CLOTHES AND GO IN, POYO!
POYO!
HARU, NOW YOU'RE SAYING IT, TOO?
ALL RIGHT, EVERYONE. REMEMBER WHERE WE PARKED, POYO.
ゴオオオオオオオ

*SENTINOIDS = CIVILIZED CREATURES THAT AREN'T HU

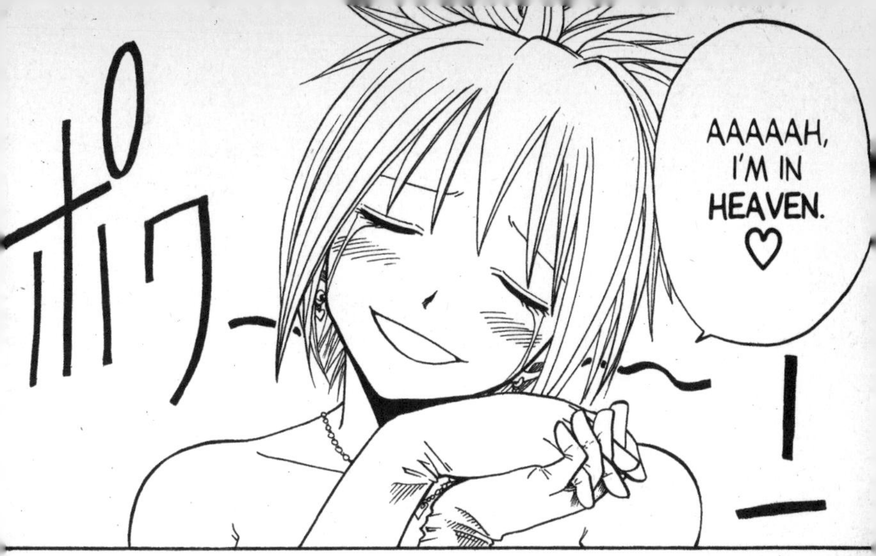
ポワ〜〜〜ー
AAAAAH, I'M IN HEAVEN. ♡
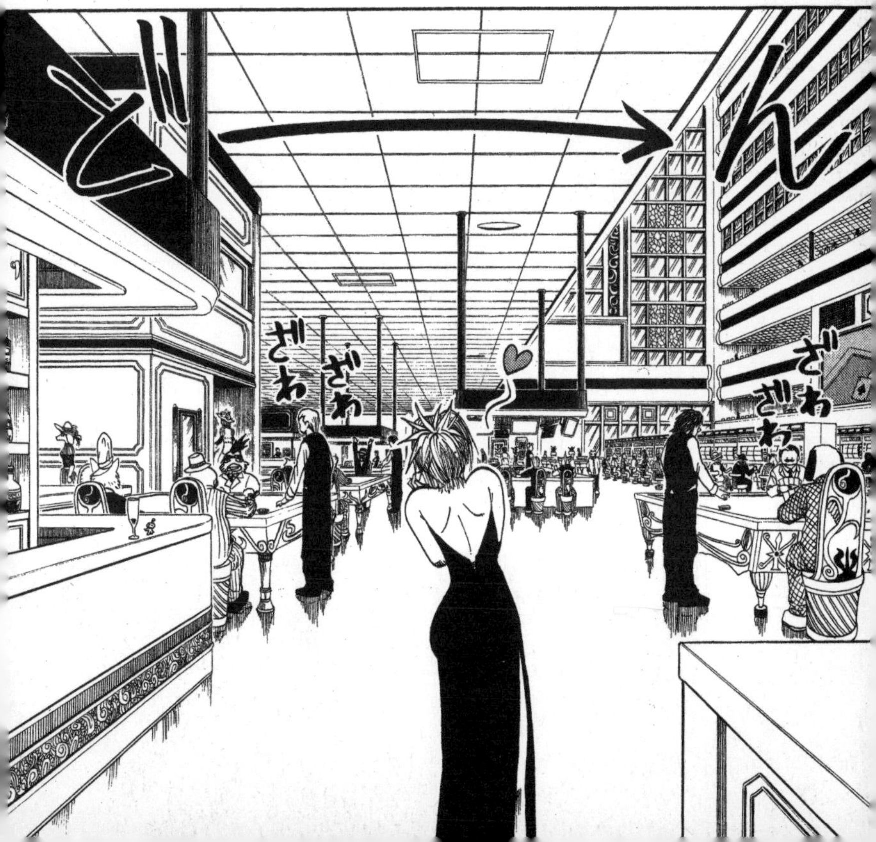
どーーん
ざわ ざわ
ざわ ざわ

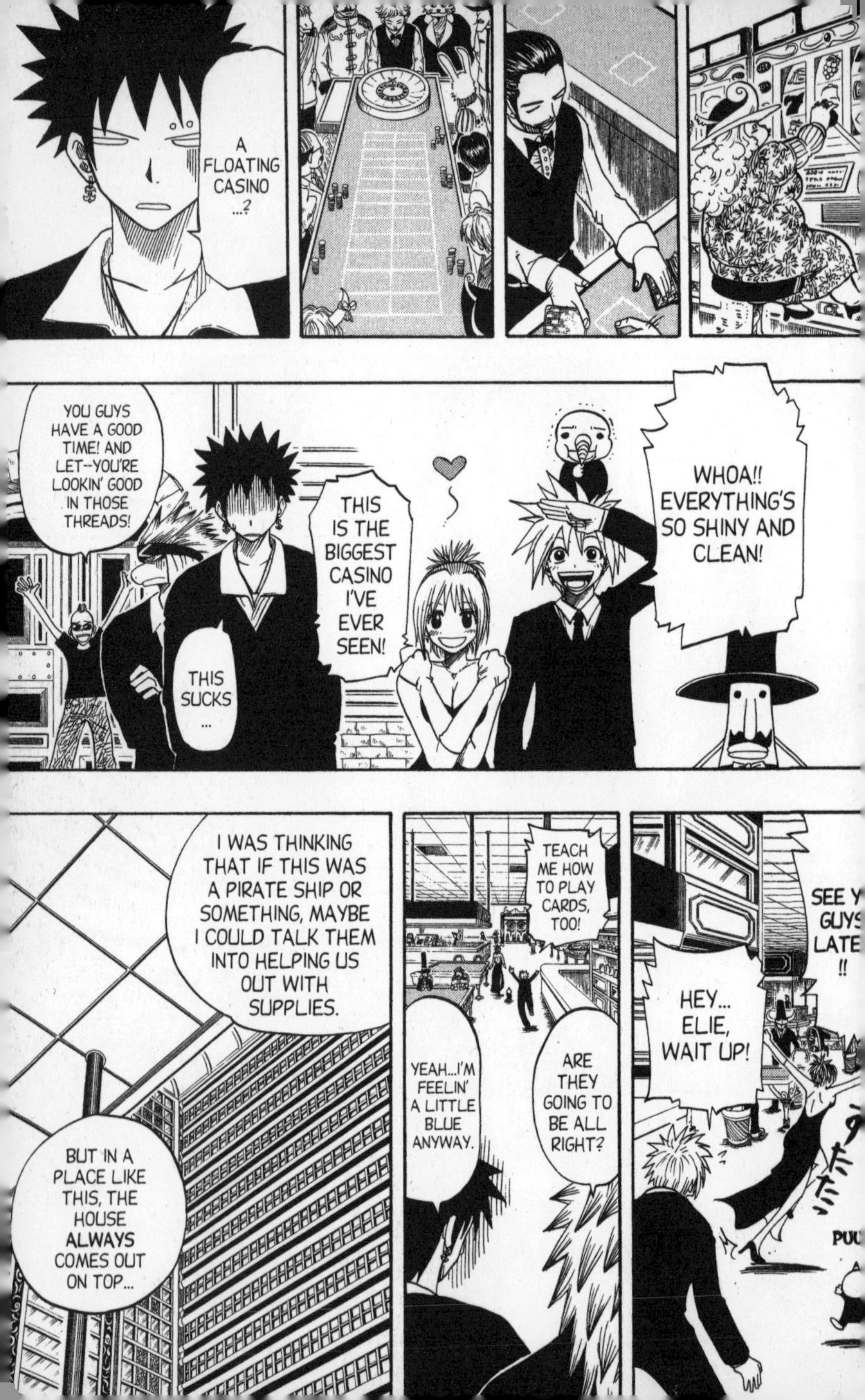
A FLOATING CASINO ...?
WHOA!! EVERYTHING'S SO SHINY AND CLEAN!
THIS IS THE BIGGEST CASINO I'VE EVER SEEN!
YOU GUYS HAVE A GOOD TIME! AND LET--YOU'RE LOOKIN' GOOD IN THOSE THREADS!
THIS SUCKS ...
SEE Y GUYS LATE !!
HEY... ELIE, WAIT UP!
PUU
TEACH ME HOW TO PLAY CARDS, TOO!
ARE THEY GOING TO BE ALL RIGHT?
YEAH...I'M FEELIN' A LITTLE BLUE ANYWAY.
I WAS THINKING THAT IF THIS WAS A PIRATE SHIP OR SOMETHING, MAYBE I COULD TALK THEM INTO HELPING US OUT WITH SUPPLIES.
BUT IN A PLACE LIKE THIS, THE HOUSE **ALWAYS** COMES OUT ON TOP...

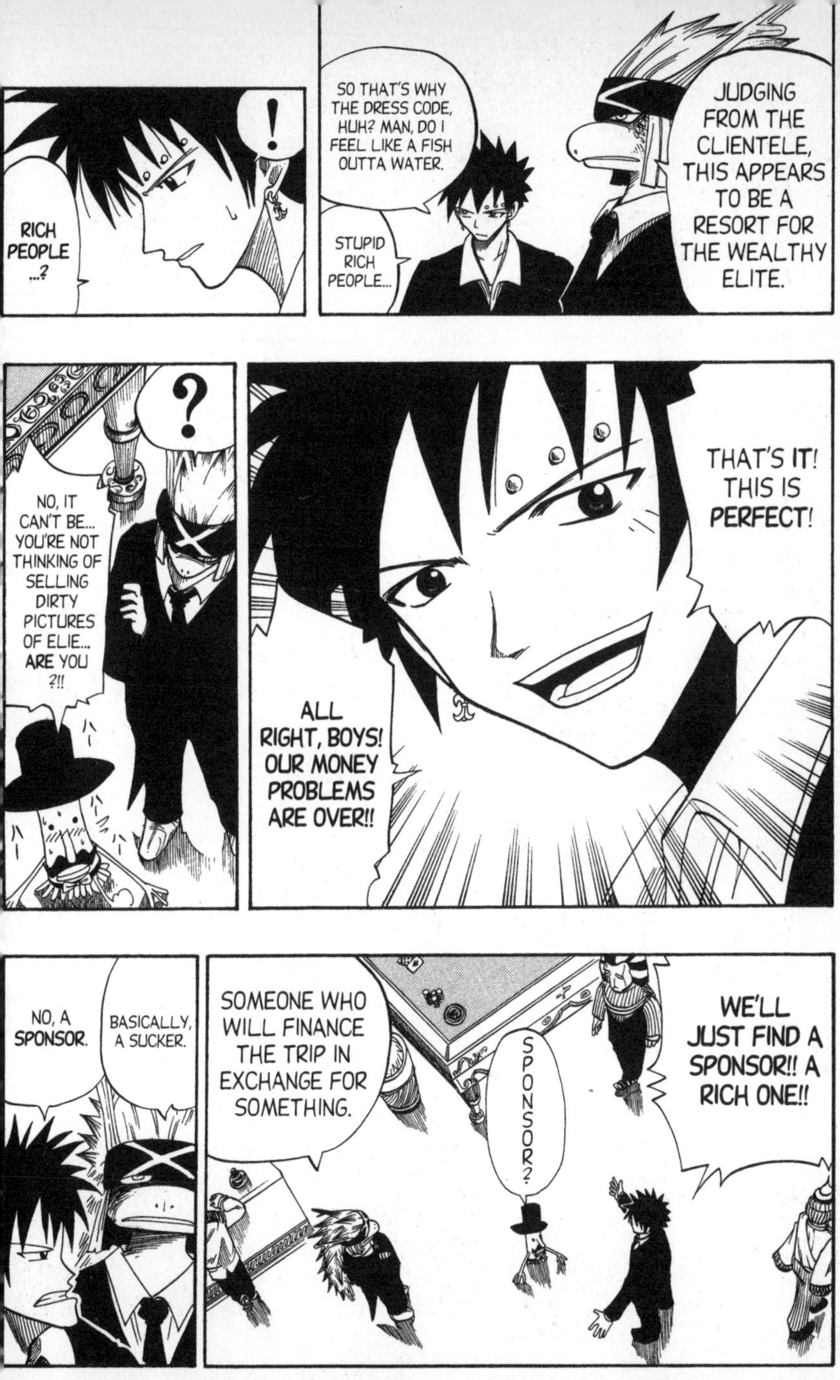
JUDGING FROM THE CLIENTELE, THIS APPEARS TO BE A RESORT FOR THE WEALTHY ELITE.
SO THAT'S WHY THE DRESS CODE, HUH? MAN, DO I FEEL LIKE A FISH OUTTA WATER.
STUPID RICH PEOPLE...
!
RICH PEOPLE ...?
THAT'S IT! THIS IS PERFECT!
ALL RIGHT, BOYS! OUR MONEY PROBLEMS ARE OVER!!
?
NO, IT CAN'T BE... YOU'RE NOT THINKING OF SELLING DIRTY PICTURES OF ELIE... ARE YOU ?!!
WE'LL JUST FIND A SPONSOR!! A RICH ONE!!
SPONSOR?
SOMEONE WHO WILL FINANCE THE TRIP IN EXCHANGE FOR SOMETHING.
BASICALLY, A SUCKER.
NO, A SPONSOR.

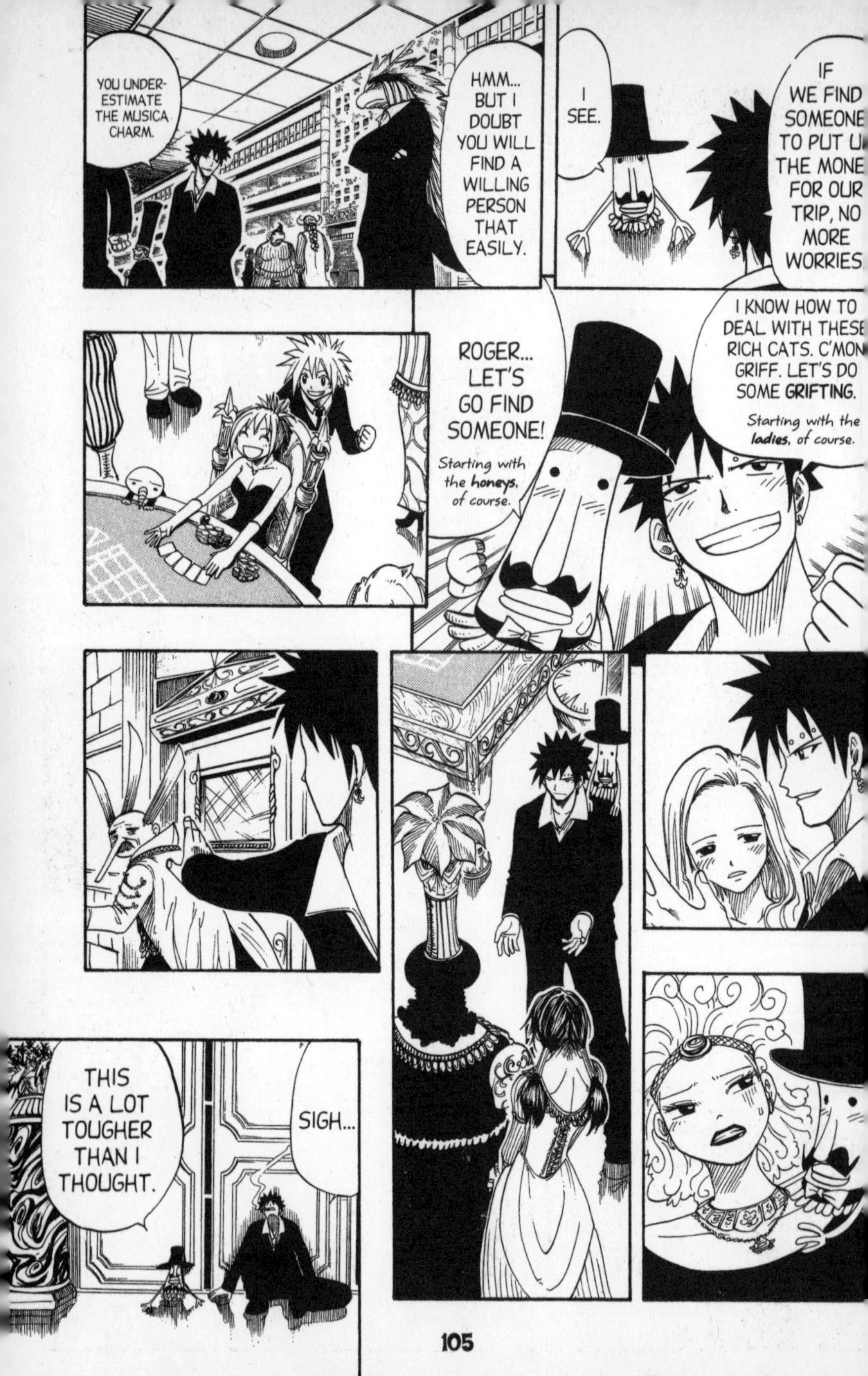
IF WE FIND SOMEONE TO PUT U THE MONE FOR OUR TRIP, NO MORE WORRIES.
I SEE.
HMM... BUT I DOUBT YOU WILL FIND A WILLING PERSON THAT EASILY.
YOU UNDER-ESTIMATE THE MUSICA CHARM.
I KNOW HOW TO DEAL WITH THESE RICH CATS. C'MON GRIFF. LET'S DO SOME GRIFTING.
Starting with the ladies, of course.
ROGER... LET'S GO FIND SOMEONE!
Starting with the honeys, of course.
SIGH...
THIS IS A LOT TOUGHER THAN I THOUGHT.

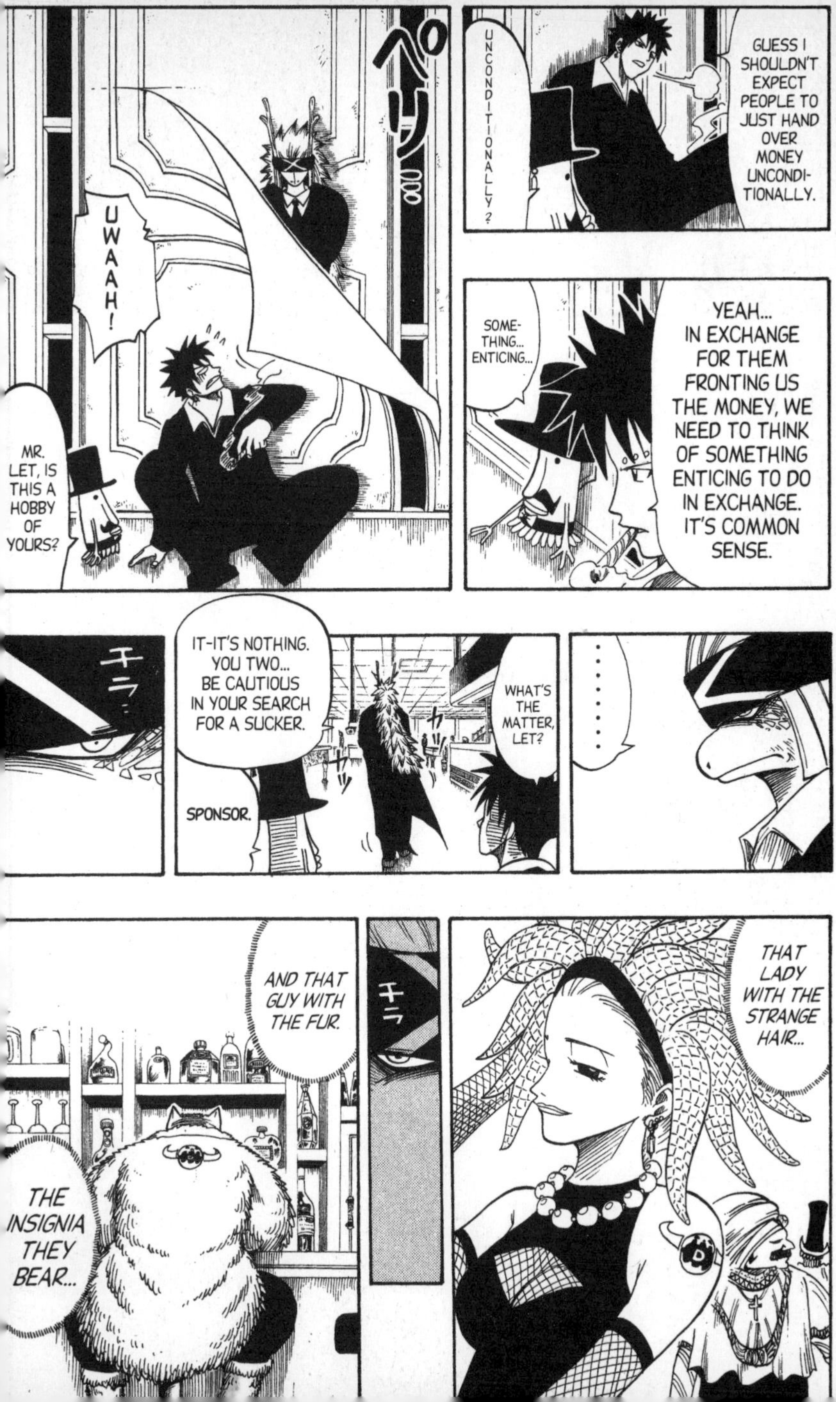
GUESS I SHOULDN'T EXPECT PEOPLE TO JUST HAND OVER MONEY UNCONDITIONALLY.
UNCONDITIONALLY?
YEAH... IN EXCHANGE FOR THEM FRONTING US THE MONEY, WE NEED TO THINK OF SOMETHING ENTICING TO DO IN EXCHANGE. IT'S COMMON SENSE.
SOME-THING... ENTICING...
ペリッ
UWAAAH!
MR. LET, IS THIS A HOBBY OF YOURS?
....
WHAT'S THE MATTER, LET?
IT-IT'S NOTHING. YOU TWO... BE CAUTIOUS IN YOUR SEARCH FOR A SUCKER.
SPONSOR.
チラ
THAT LADY WITH THE STRANGE HAIR...
チラ
AND THAT GUY WITH THE FUR.
THE INSIGNIA THEY BEAR...

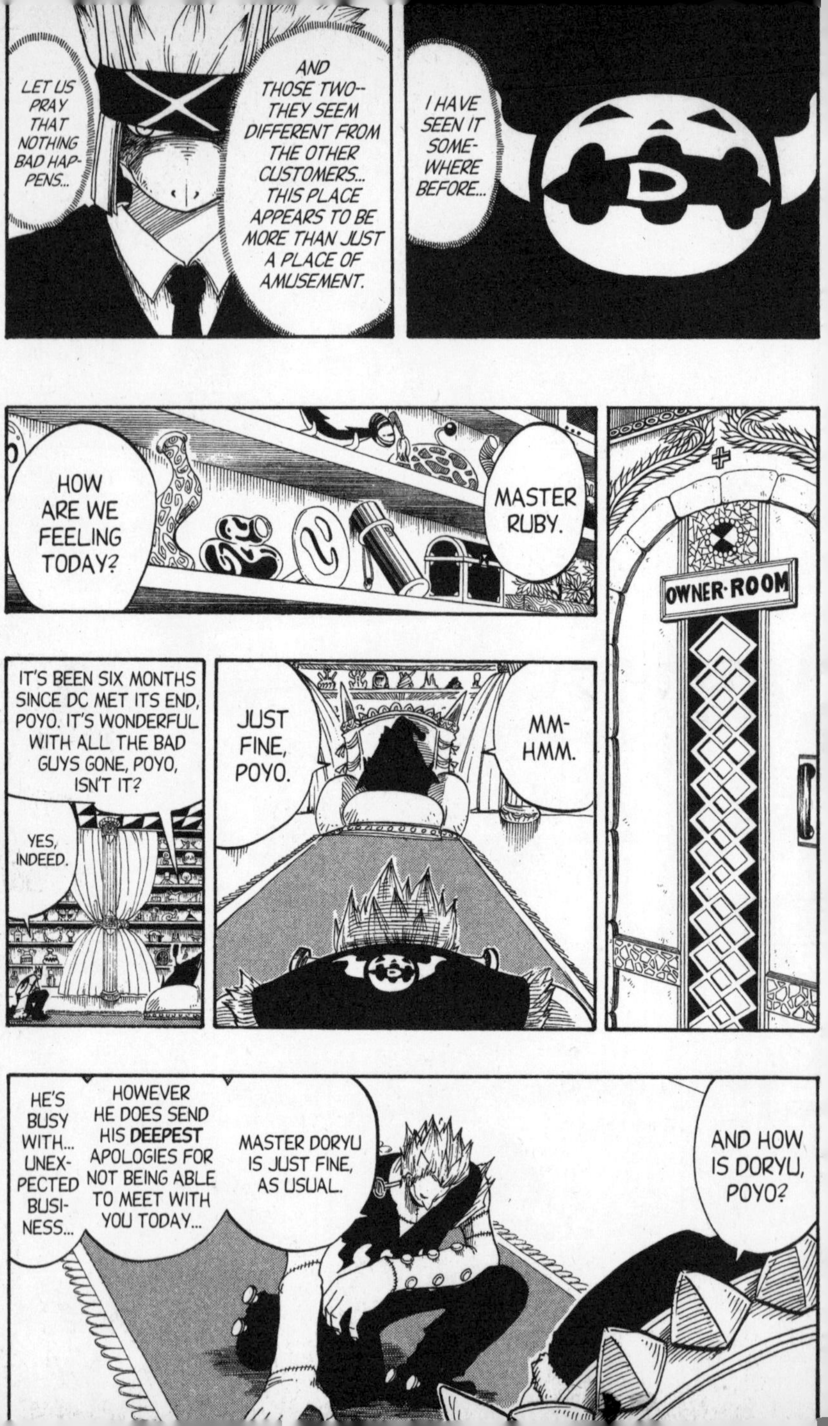

I HAVE SEEN IT SOMEWHERE BEFORE...
AND THOSE TWO-- THEY SEEM DIFFERENT FROM THE OTHER CUSTOMERS... THIS PLACE APPEARS TO BE MORE THAN JUST A PLACE OF AMUSEMENT.
LET US PRAY THAT NOTHING BAD HAPPENS...
OWNER·ROOM
MASTER RUBY.
HOW ARE WE FEELING TODAY?
MM-HMM.
JUST FINE, POYO.
IT'S BEEN SIX MONTHS SINCE DC MET ITS END, POYO. IT'S WONDERFUL WITH ALL THE BAD GUYS GONE, POYO, ISN'T IT?
YES, INDEED.
AND HOW IS DORYU, POYO?
MASTER DORYU IS JUST FINE, AS USUAL.
HOWEVER HE DOES SEND HIS **DEEPEST** APOLOGIES FOR NOT BEING ABLE TO MEET WITH YOU TODAY...
HE'S BUSY WITH... UNEXPECTED BUSINESS...

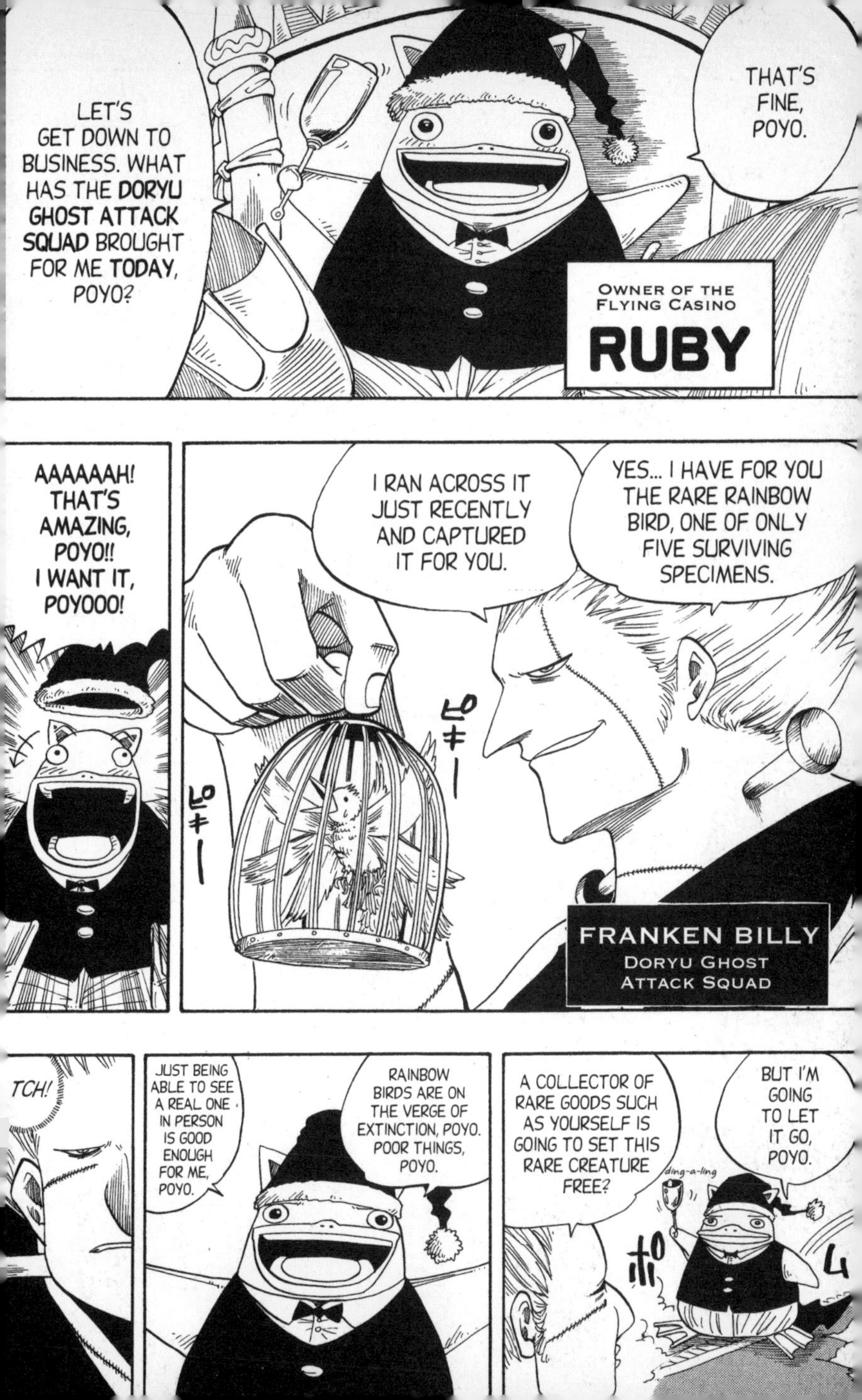
THAT'S FINE, POYO.
LET'S GET DOWN TO BUSINESS. WHAT HAS THE DORYU GHOST ATTACK SQUAD BROUGHT FOR ME TODAY, POYO?
OWNER OF THE FLYING CASINO
RUBY
YES... I HAVE FOR YOU THE RARE RAINBOW BIRD, ONE OF ONLY FIVE SURVIVING SPECIMENS.
I RAN ACROSS IT JUST RECENTLY AND CAPTURED IT FOR YOU.
ピキー
ピキー
FRANKEN BILLY
DORYU GHOST ATTACK SQUAD
AAAAAAH! THAT'S AMAZING, POYO!! I WANT IT, POYOOO!
BUT I'M GOING TO LET IT GO, POYO.
A COLLECTOR OF RARE GOODS SUCH AS YOURSELF IS GOING TO SET THIS RARE CREATURE FREE?
ding-a-ling
RAINBOW BIRDS ARE ON THE VERGE OF EXTINCTION, POYO. POOR THINGS, POYO.
JUST BEING ABLE TO SEE A REAL ONE IN PERSON IS GOOD ENOUGH FOR ME, POYO.
TCH!

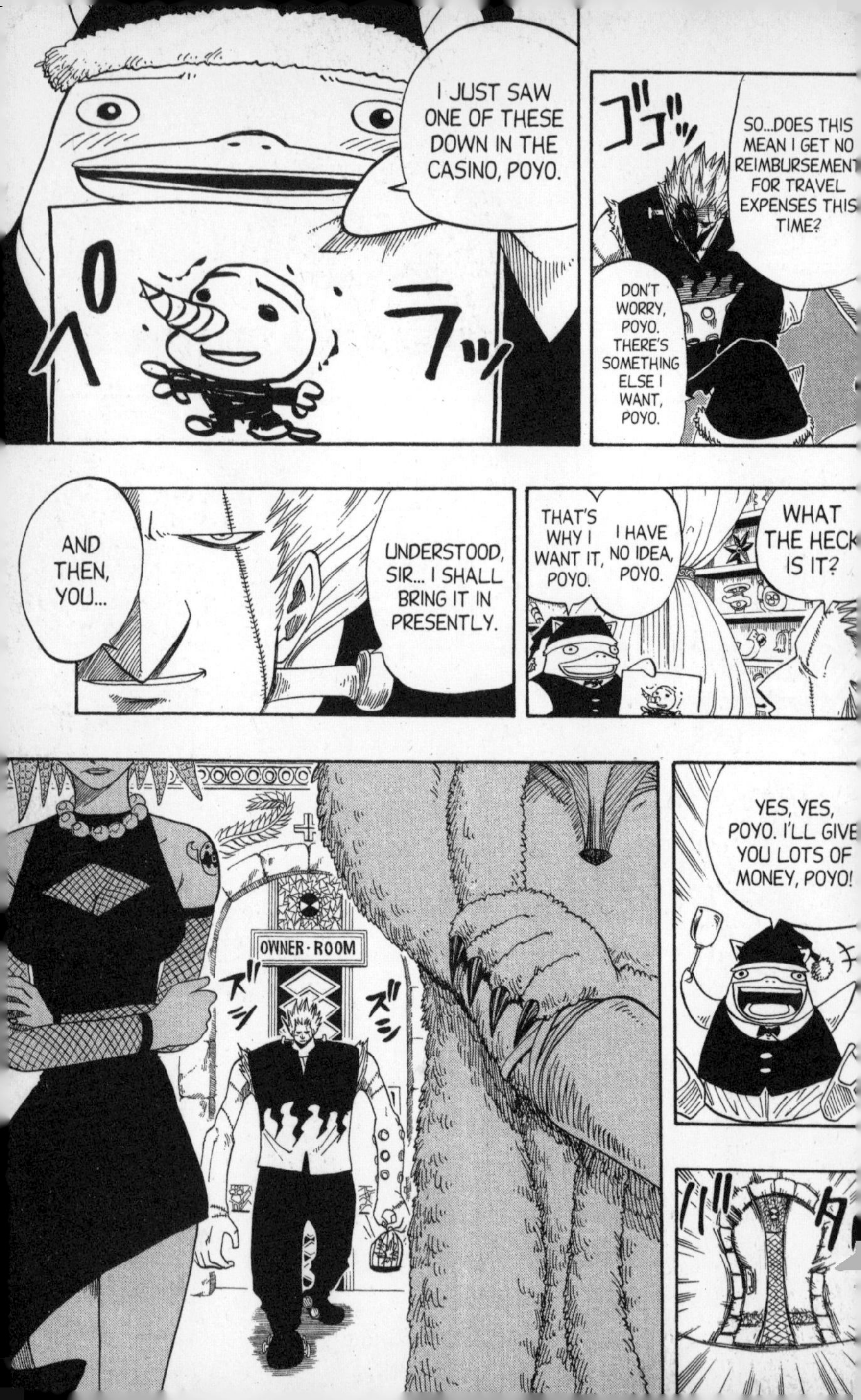
ゴゴッ
SO...DOES THIS MEAN I GET NO REIMBURSEMENT FOR TRAVEL EXPENSES THIS TIME?
DON'T WORRY, POYO. THERE'S SOMETHING ELSE I WANT, POYO.
I JUST SAW ONE OF THESE DOWN IN THE CASINO, POYO.
ペラッ
WHAT THE HECK IS IT?
I HAVE NO IDEA, POYO.
THAT'S WHY I WANT IT, POYO.
UNDERSTOOD, SIR... I SHALL BRING IT IN PRESENTLY.
AND THEN, YOU...
YES, YES, POYO. I'LL GIVE YOU LOTS OF MONEY, POYO!
バタ
OWNER・ROOM
ズシ
ズシ

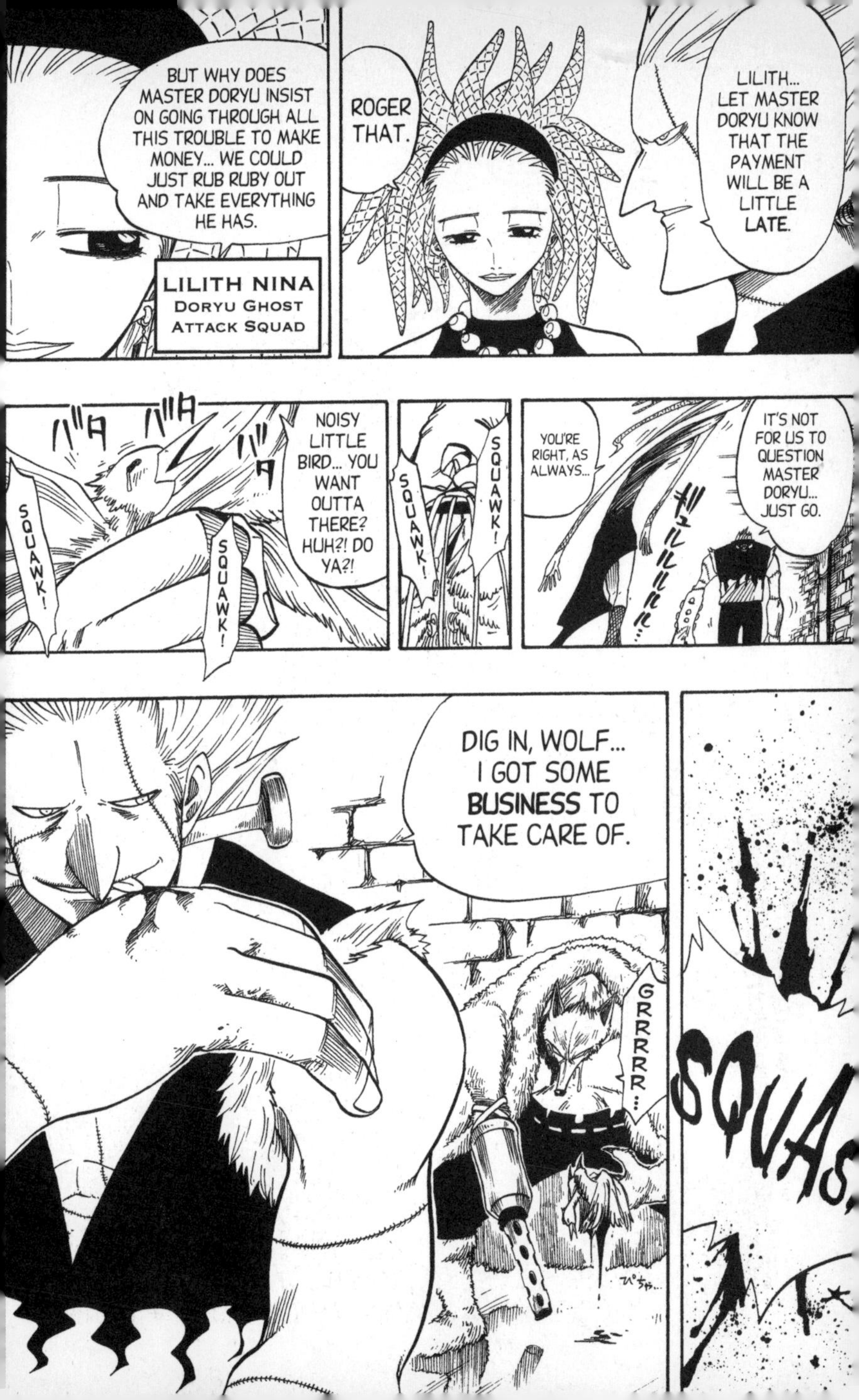
LILITH... LET MASTER DORYU KNOW THAT THE PAYMENT WILL BE A LITTLE LATE.
ROGER THAT.
BUT WHY DOES MASTER DORYU INSIST ON GOING THROUGH ALL THIS TROUBLE TO MAKE MONEY... WE COULD JUST RUB RUBY OUT AND TAKE EVERYTHING HE HAS.
LILITH NINA
DORYU GHOST ATTACK SQUAD
IT'S NOT FOR US TO QUESTION MASTER DORYU... JUST GO.
YOU'RE RIGHT, AS ALWAYS...
SQUAWK!
SQUAWK!
NOISY LITTLE BIRD... YOU WANT OUTTA THERE? HUH?! DO YA?!
バタ バタ バタ
SQUAWK!
SQUAWK!
SQUAS...
DIG IN, WOLF... I GOT SOME BUSINESS TO TAKE CARE OF.
GRRRRR...

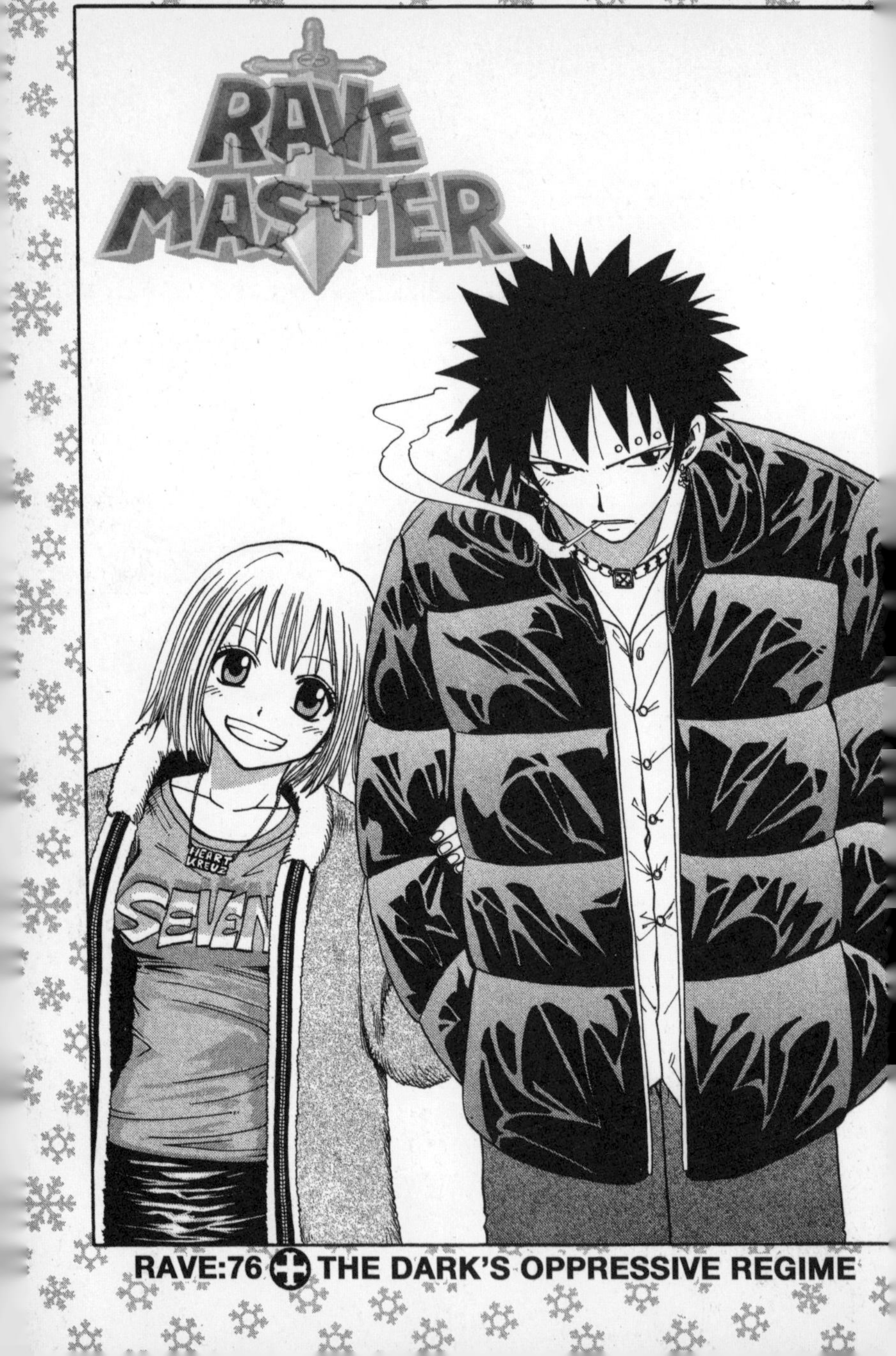
RAVE MASTER
HEART KREUZ
SEVEN

RAVE:76 ✚ THE DARK'S OPPRESSIVE REGIME

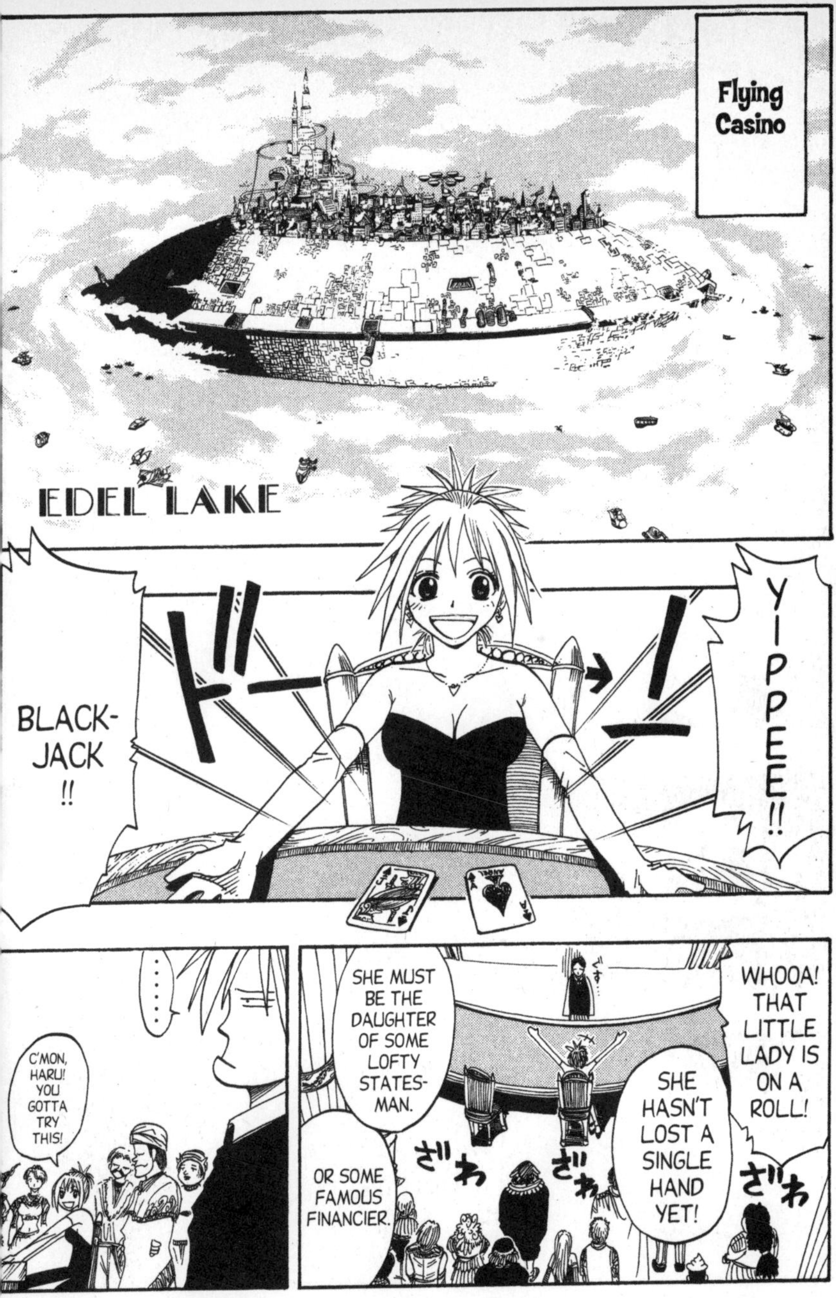
Flying Casino
EDEL LAKE
YIPPEE!!
BLACK-JACK!!
WHOOA! THAT LITTLE LADY IS ON A ROLL!
ざわ
SHE HASN'T LOST A SINGLE HAND YET!
ざわ
SHE MUST BE THE DAUGHTER OF SOME LOFTY STATESMAN.
OR SOME FAMOUS FINANCIER.
ざわ
......
C'MON, HARU! YOU GOTTA TRY THIS!

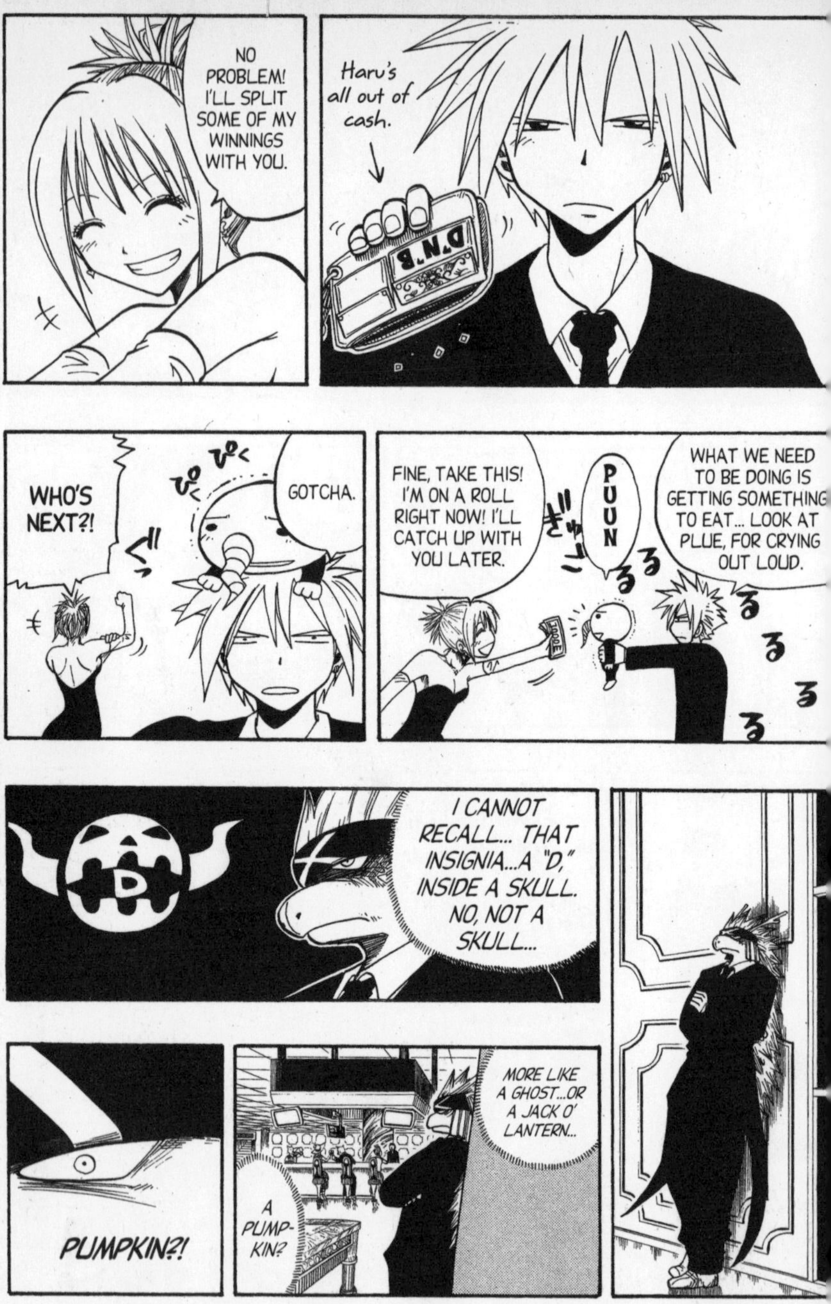

Haru's all out of cash.
NO PROBLEM! I'LL SPLIT SOME OF MY WINNINGS WITH YOU.
WHAT WE NEED TO BE DOING IS GETTING SOMETHING TO EAT... LOOK AT PLUE, FOR CRYING OUT LOUD.
PUUN
FINE, TAKE THIS! I'M ON A ROLL RIGHT NOW! I'LL CATCH UP WITH YOU LATER.
GOTCHA.
WHO'S NEXT?!
I CANNOT RECALL... THAT INSIGNIA...A "D," INSIDE A SKULL. NO, NOT A SKULL...
MORE LIKE A GHOST...OR A JACK O' LANTERN...
A PUMPKIN?
PUMPKIN?!

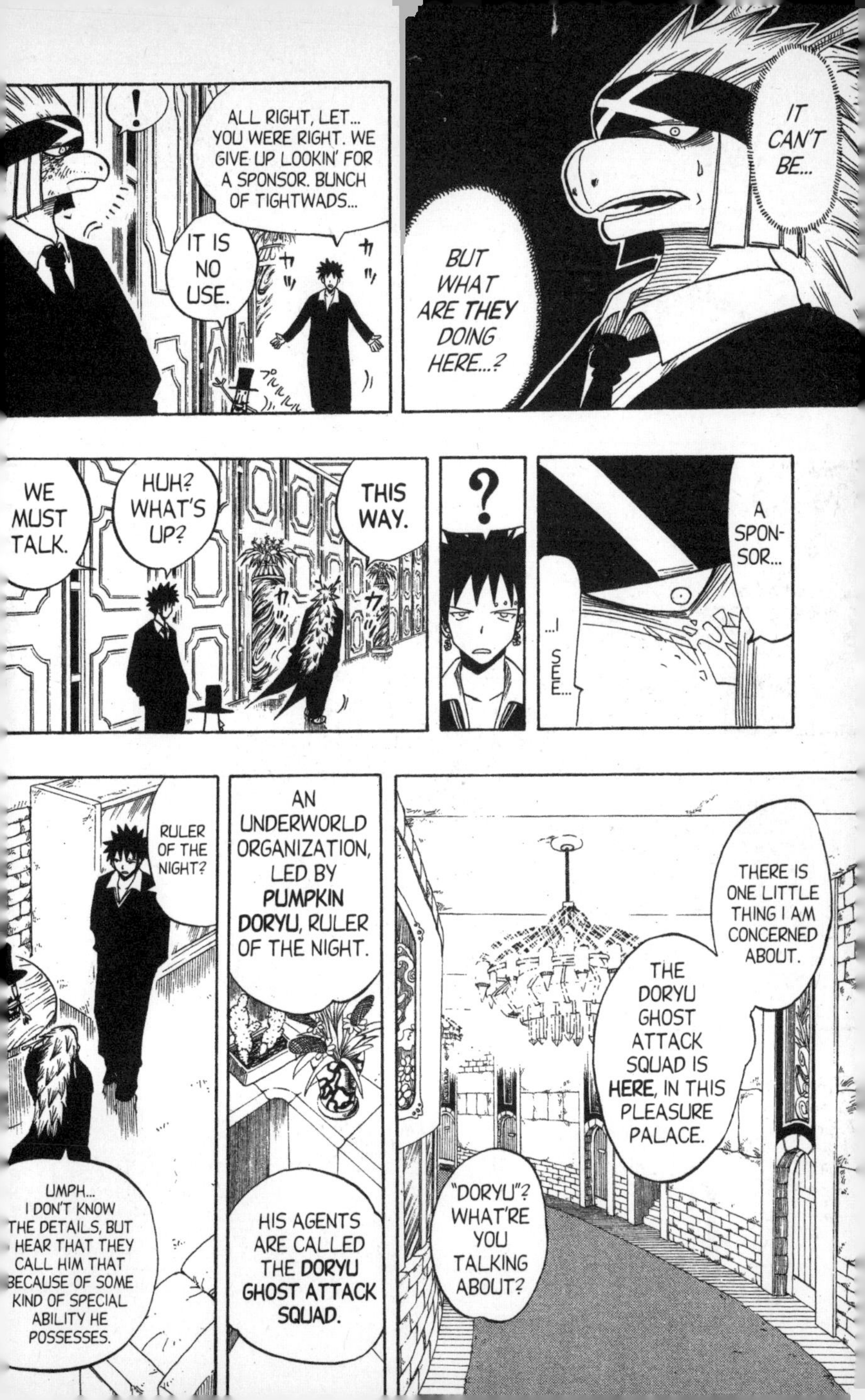
IT CAN'T BE...
BUT WHAT ARE THEY DOING HERE...?
!
ALL RIGHT, LET... YOU WERE RIGHT. WE GIVE UP LOOKIN' FOR A SPONSOR. BUNCH OF TIGHTWADS...
IT IS NO USE.
A SPONSOR...
...I SEE...
?
THIS WAY.
HUH? WHAT'S UP?
WE MUST TALK.
THERE IS ONE LITTLE THING I AM CONCERNED ABOUT.
THE DORYU GHOST ATTACK SQUAD IS HERE, IN THIS PLEASURE PALACE.
"DORYU"? WHAT'RE YOU TALKING ABOUT?
AN UNDERWORLD ORGANIZATION, LED BY PUMPKIN DORYU, RULER OF THE NIGHT.
HIS AGENTS ARE CALLED THE DORYU GHOST ATTACK SQUAD.
RULER OF THE NIGHT?
UMPH... I DON'T KNOW THE DETAILS, BUT I HEAR THAT THEY CALL HIM THAT BECAUSE OF SOME KIND OF SPECIAL ABILITY HE POSSESSES.

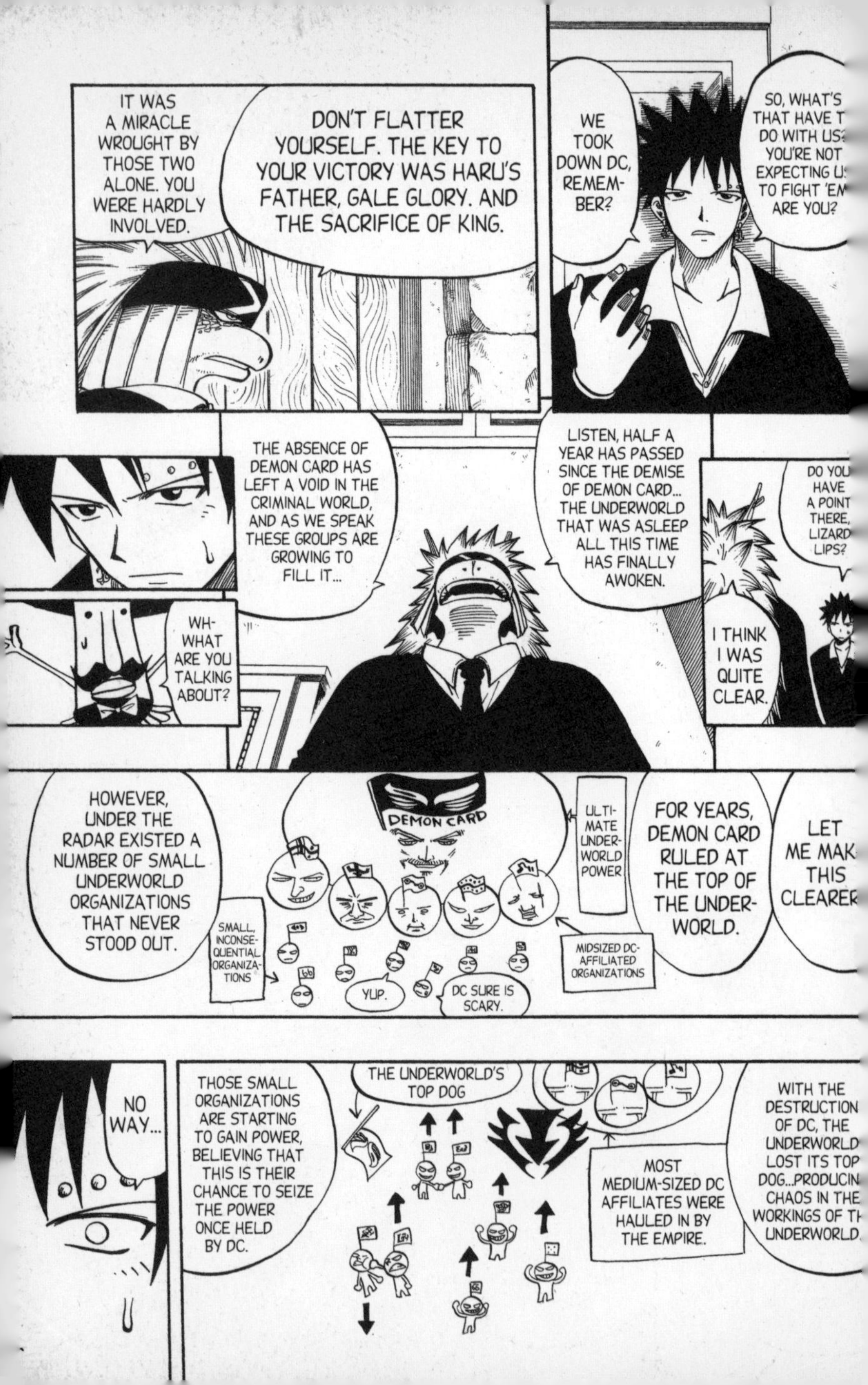
SO, WHAT'S THAT HAVE T DO WITH US? YOU'RE NOT EXPECTING US TO FIGHT 'EM ARE YOU?
WE TOOK DOWN DC, REMEMBER?
DON'T FLATTER YOURSELF. THE KEY TO YOUR VICTORY WAS HARU'S FATHER, GALE GLORY. AND THE SACRIFICE OF KING.
IT WAS A MIRACLE WROUGHT BY THOSE TWO ALONE. YOU WERE HARDLY INVOLVED.
DO YOU HAVE A POINT THERE, LIZARD LIPS?
I THINK I WAS QUITE CLEAR.
LISTEN, HALF A YEAR HAS PASSED SINCE THE DEMISE OF DEMON CARD... THE UNDERWORLD THAT WAS ASLEEP ALL THIS TIME HAS FINALLY AWOKEN.
THE ABSENCE OF DEMON CARD HAS LEFT A VOID IN THE CRIMINAL WORLD, AND AS WE SPEAK THESE GROUPS ARE GROWING TO FILL IT...
WH- WHAT ARE YOU TALKING ABOUT?
LET ME MAK THIS CLEARER
FOR YEARS, DEMON CARD RULED AT THE TOP OF THE UNDERWORLD.
ULTIMATE UNDERWORLD POWER
DEMON CARD
MIDSIZED DC-AFFILIATED ORGANIZATIONS
DC SURE IS SCARY.
YUP.
SMALL, INCONSEQUENTIAL ORGANIZATIONS
HOWEVER, UNDER THE RADAR EXISTED A NUMBER OF SMALL UNDERWORLD ORGANIZATIONS THAT NEVER STOOD OUT.
WITH THE DESTRUCTION OF DC, THE UNDERWORLD LOST ITS TOP DOG...PRODUCIN CHAOS IN THE WORKINGS OF T UNDERWORLD.
MOST MEDIUM-SIZED DC AFFILIATES WERE HAULED IN BY THE EMPIRE.
THE UNDERWORLD'S TOP DOG
THOSE SMALL ORGANIZATIONS ARE STARTING TO GAIN POWER, BELIEVING THAT THIS IS THEIR CHANCE TO SEIZE THE POWER ONCE HELD BY DC.
NO WAY...

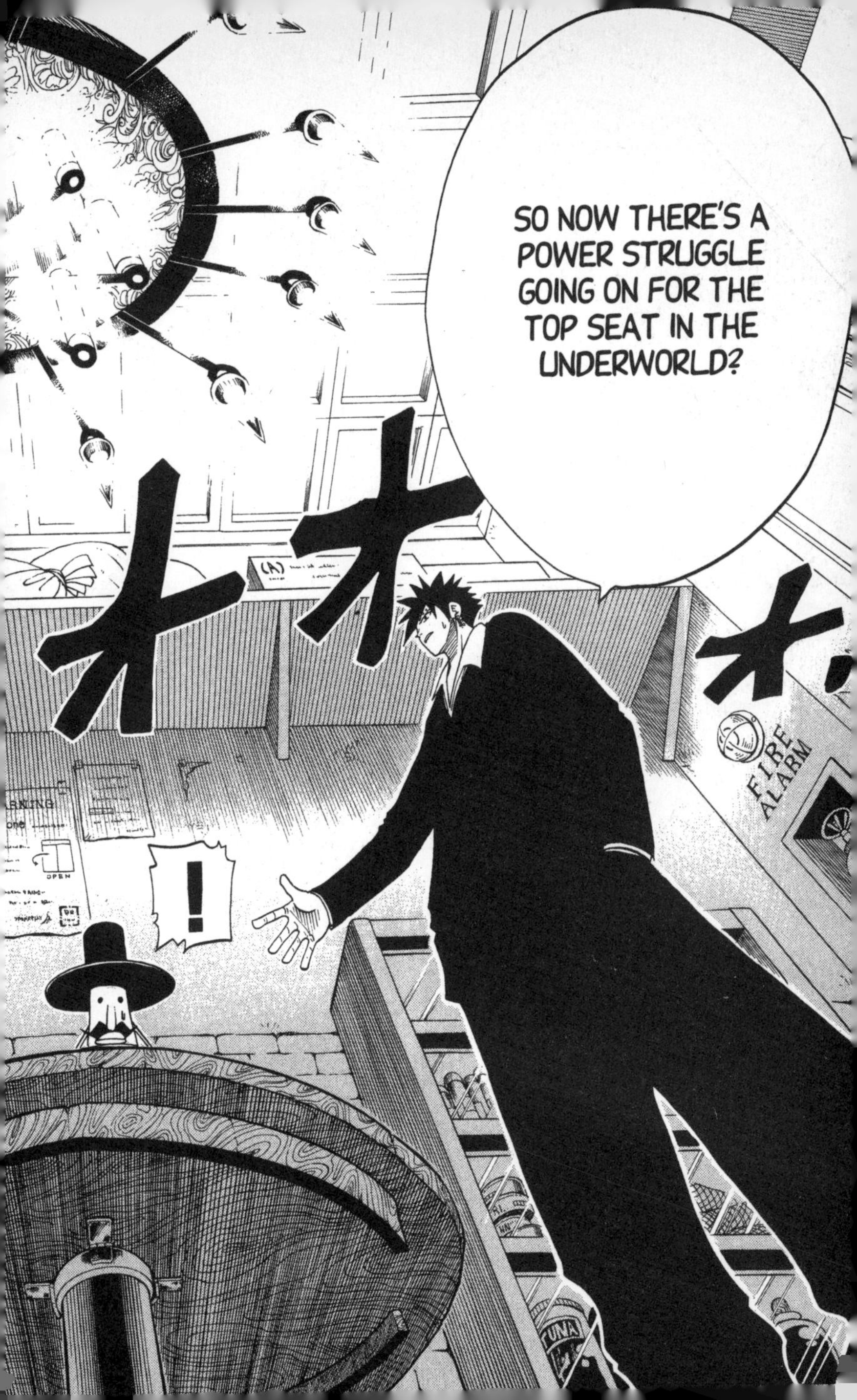
SO NOW THERE'S A POWER STRUGGLE GOING ON FOR THE TOP SEAT IN THE UNDERWORLD?
!
FIRE ALARM

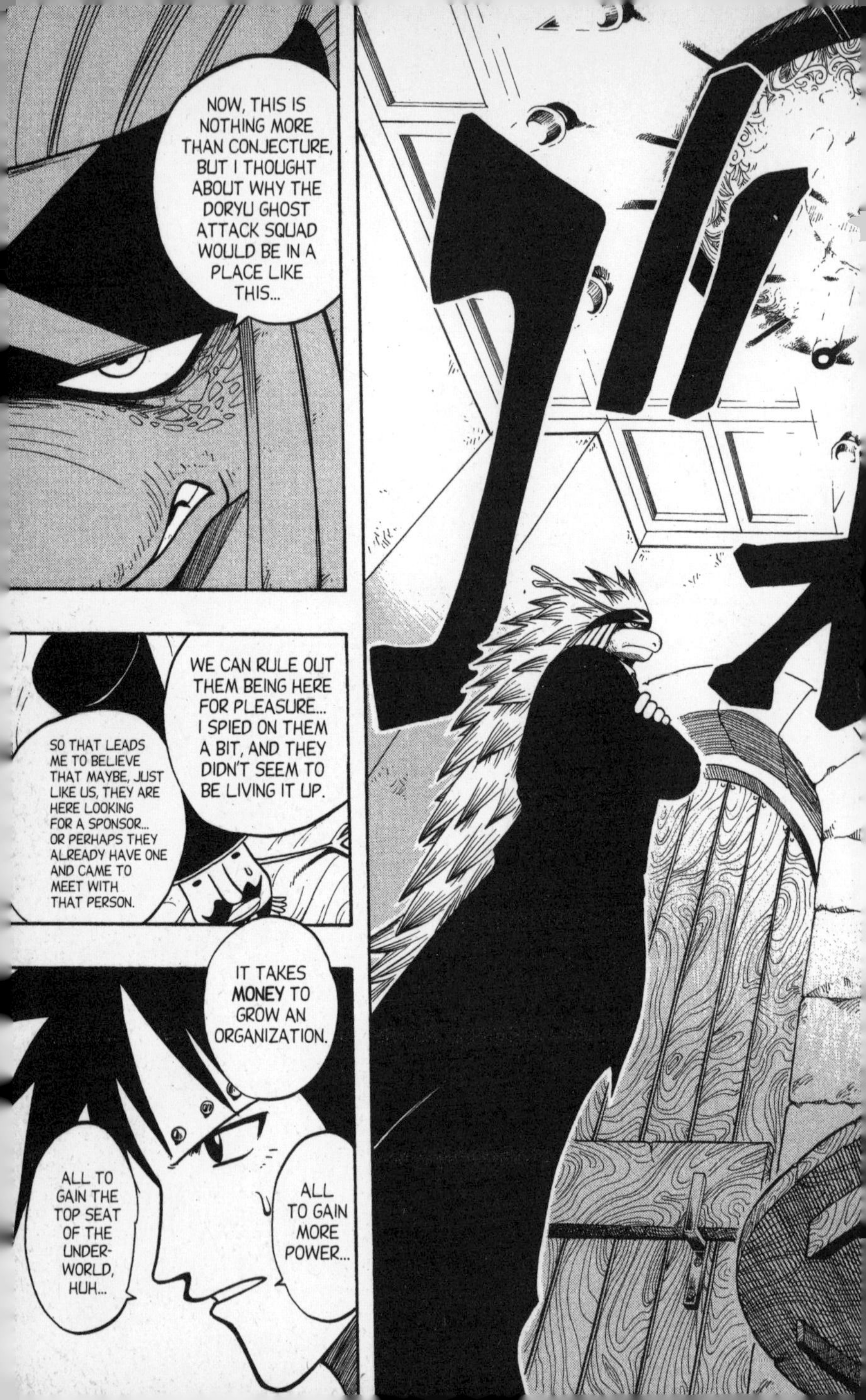
NOW, THIS IS NOTHING MORE THAN CONJECTURE, BUT I THOUGHT ABOUT WHY THE DORYU GHOST ATTACK SQUAD WOULD BE IN A PLACE LIKE THIS...
WE CAN RULE OUT THEM BEING HERE FOR PLEASURE... I SPIED ON THEM A BIT, AND THEY DIDN'T SEEM TO BE LIVING IT UP.
SO THAT LEADS ME TO BELIEVE THAT MAYBE, JUST LIKE US, THEY ARE HERE LOOKING FOR A SPONSOR... OR PERHAPS THEY ALREADY HAVE ONE AND CAME TO MEET WITH THAT PERSON.
IT TAKES **MONEY** TO GROW AN ORGANIZATION.
ALL TO GAIN MORE POWER...
ALL TO GAIN THE TOP SEAT OF THE UNDER-WORLD, HUH...

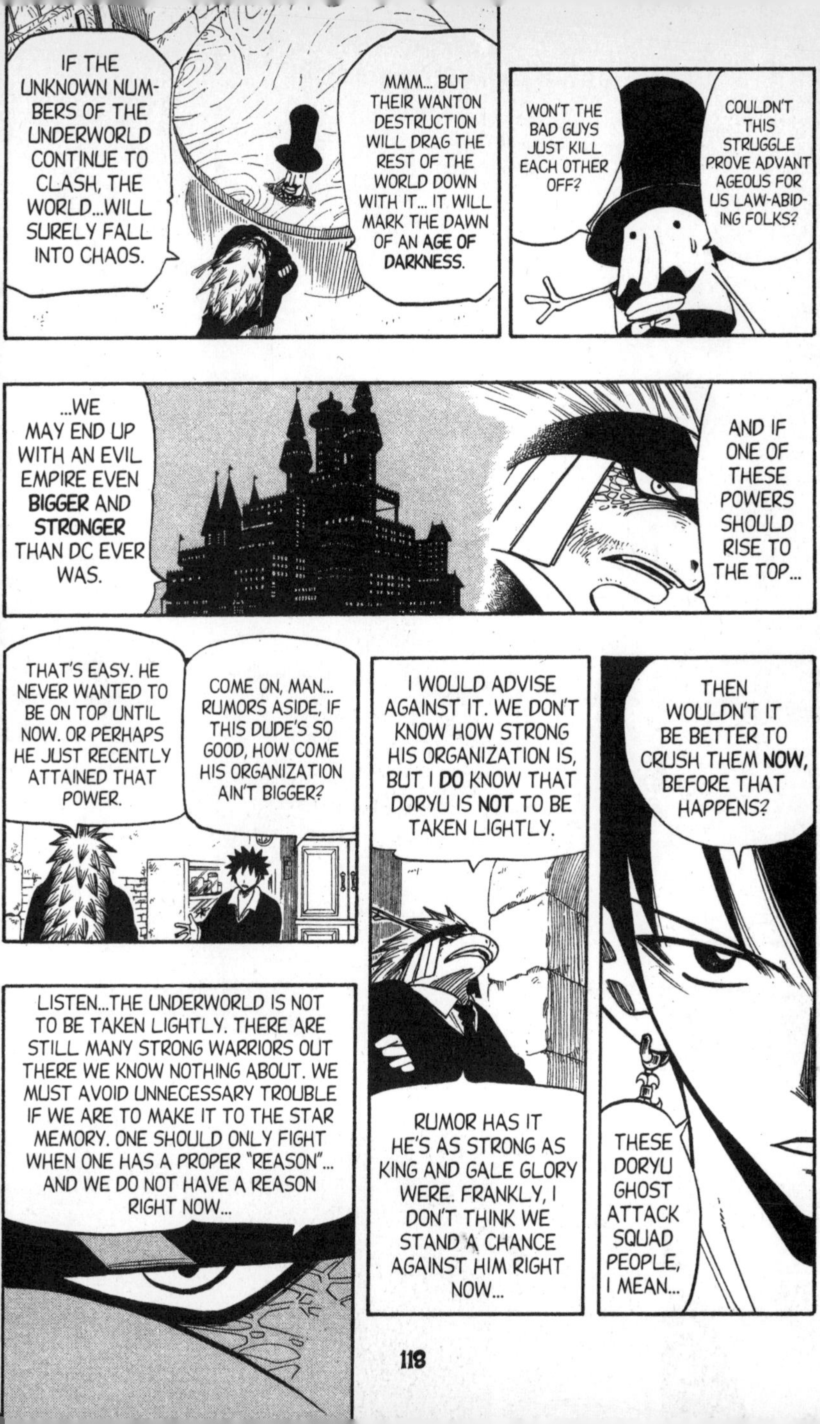
COULDN'T THIS STRUGGLE PROVE ADVANTAGEOUS FOR US LAW-ABIDING FOLKS?
WON'T THE BAD GUYS JUST KILL EACH OTHER OFF?
MMM... BUT THEIR WANTON DESTRUCTION WILL DRAG THE REST OF THE WORLD DOWN WITH IT... IT WILL MARK THE DAWN OF AN AGE OF DARKNESS.
IF THE UNKNOWN NUMBERS OF THE UNDERWORLD CONTINUE TO CLASH, THE WORLD...WILL SURELY FALL INTO CHAOS.
AND IF ONE OF THESE POWERS SHOULD RISE TO THE TOP...
...WE MAY END UP WITH AN EVIL EMPIRE EVEN BIGGER AND STRONGER THAN DC EVER WAS.
THEN WOULDN'T IT BE BETTER TO CRUSH THEM NOW, BEFORE THAT HAPPENS?
THESE DORYU GHOST ATTACK SQUAD PEOPLE, I MEAN...
I WOULD ADVISE AGAINST IT. WE DON'T KNOW HOW STRONG HIS ORGANIZATION IS, BUT I DO KNOW THAT DORYU IS NOT TO BE TAKEN LIGHTLY.
RUMOR HAS IT HE'S AS STRONG AS KING AND GALE GLORY WERE. FRANKLY, I DON'T THINK WE STAND A CHANCE AGAINST HIM RIGHT NOW...
COME ON, MAN... RUMORS ASIDE, IF THIS DUDE'S SO GOOD, HOW COME HIS ORGANIZATION AIN'T BIGGER?
THAT'S EASY. HE NEVER WANTED TO BE ON TOP UNTIL NOW. OR PERHAPS HE JUST RECENTLY ATTAINED THAT POWER.
LISTEN...THE UNDERWORLD IS NOT TO BE TAKEN LIGHTLY. THERE ARE STILL MANY STRONG WARRIORS OUT THERE WE KNOW NOTHING ABOUT. WE MUST AVOID UNNECESSARY TROUBLE IF WE ARE TO MAKE IT TO THE STAR MEMORY. ONE SHOULD ONLY FIGHT WHEN ONE HAS A PROPER "REASON"... AND WE DO NOT HAVE A REASON RIGHT NOW...

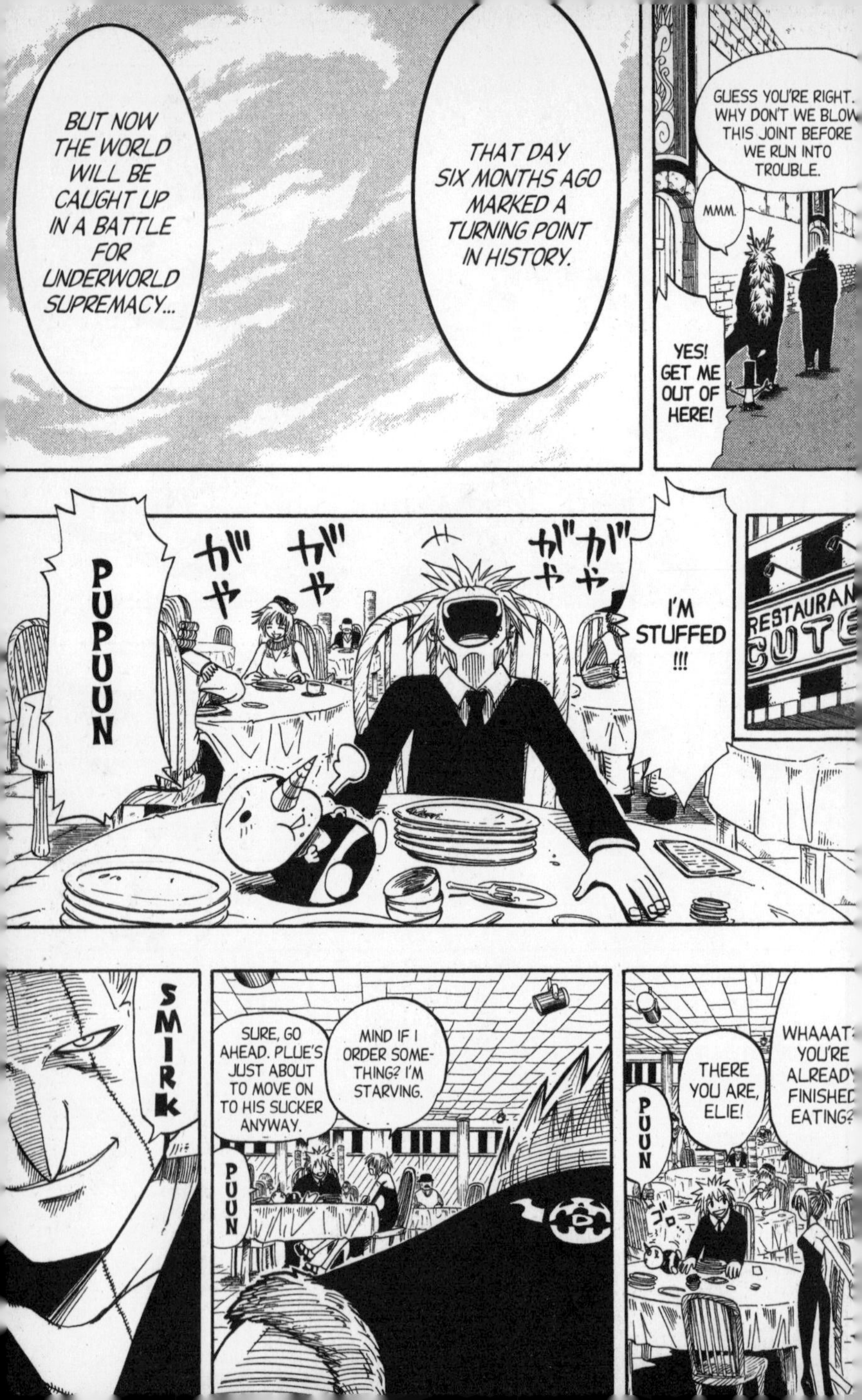
GUESS YOU'RE RIGHT. WHY DON'T WE BLOW THIS JOINT BEFORE WE RUN INTO TROUBLE.
MMM.
YES! GET ME OUT OF HERE!
THAT DAY SIX MONTHS AGO MARKED A TURNING POINT IN HISTORY.
BUT NOW THE WORLD WILL BE CAUGHT UP IN A BATTLE FOR UNDERWORLD SUPREMACY...
RESTAURAN
CUTE
I'M STUFFED !!!
ガヤ
ガヤ
ガヤ
ガヤ
PUPUUUN
WHAAAT? YOU'RE ALREADY FINISHED EATING?
THERE YOU ARE, ELIE!
PUUN
MIND IF I ORDER SOME-THING? I'M STARVING.
SURE, GO AHEAD. PLUE'S JUST ABOUT TO MOVE ON TO HIS SUCKER ANYWAY.
PUUN
SMIRK

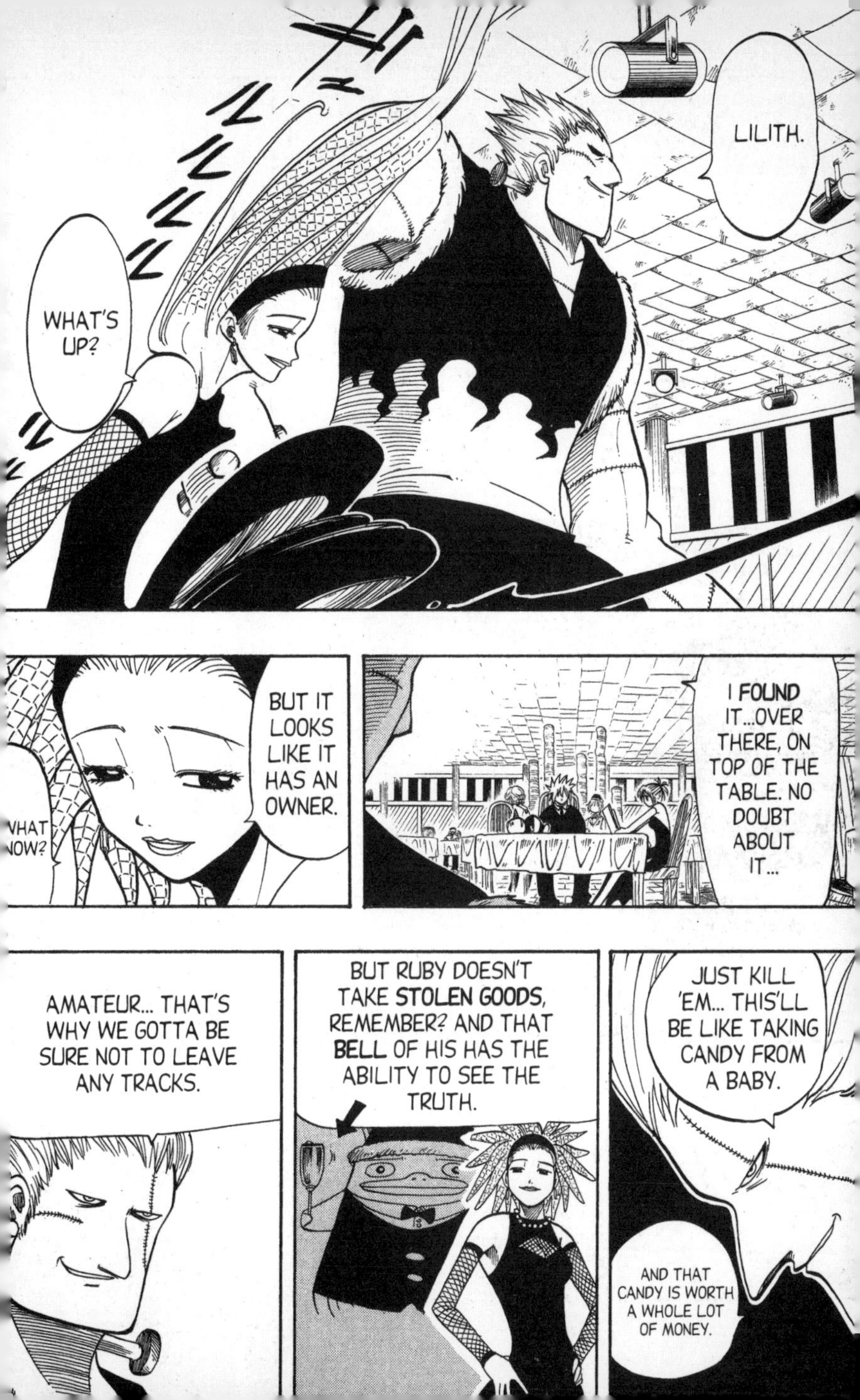
LILITH.
WHAT'S UP?
I FOUND IT...OVER THERE, ON TOP OF THE TABLE. NO DOUBT ABOUT IT...
BUT IT LOOKS LIKE IT HAS AN OWNER.
WHAT NOW?
JUST KILL 'EM... THIS'LL BE LIKE TAKING CANDY FROM A BABY.
AND THAT CANDY IS WORTH A WHOLE LOT OF MONEY.
BUT RUBY DOESN'T TAKE STOLEN GOODS, REMEMBER? AND THAT BELL OF HIS HAS THE ABILITY TO SEE THE TRUTH.
AMATEUR... THAT'S WHY WE GOTTA BE SURE NOT TO LEAVE ANY TRACKS.

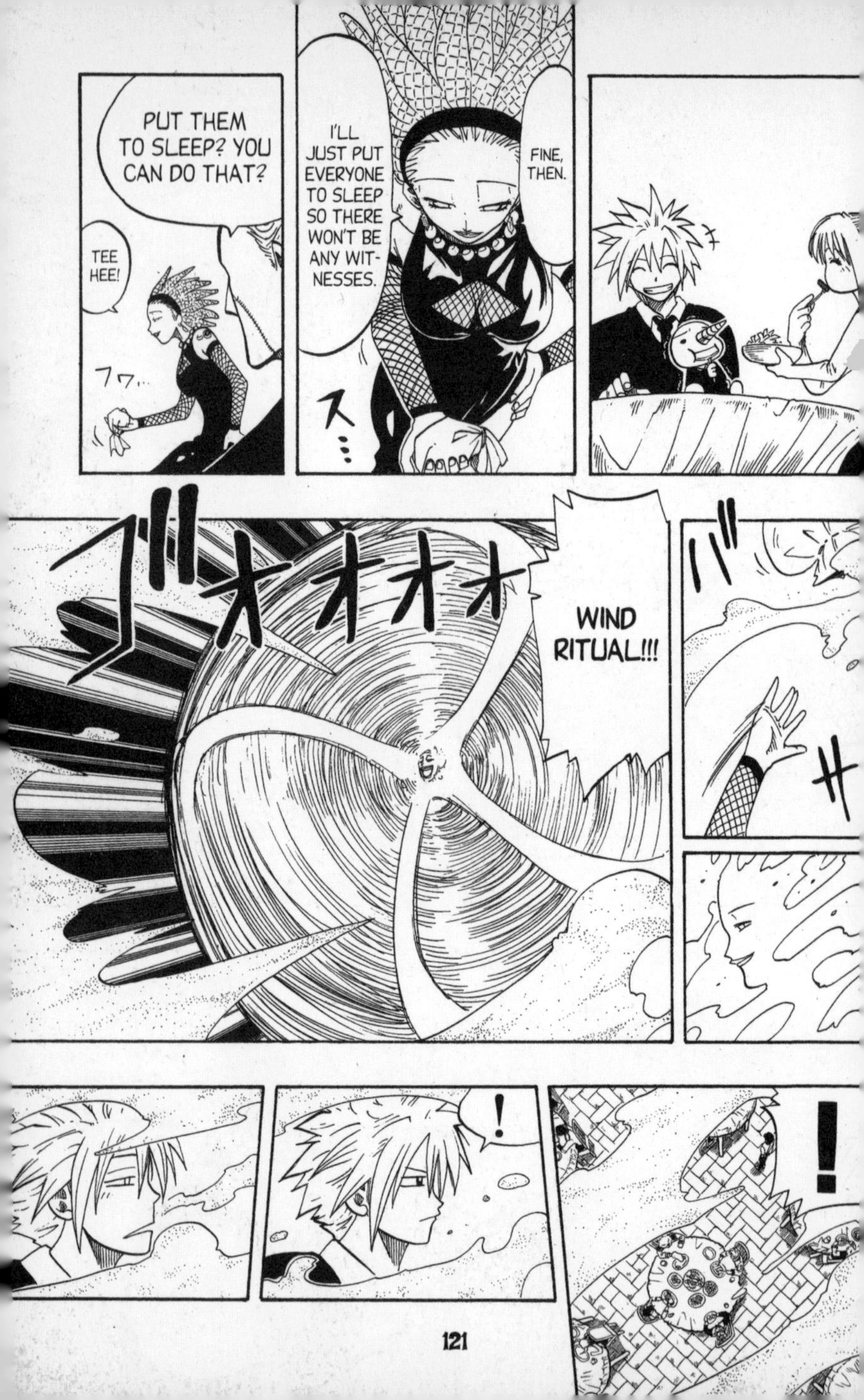
FINE, THEN.
I'LL JUST PUT EVERYONE TO SLEEP SO THERE WON'T BE ANY WITNESSES.
ス…
PUT THEM TO SLEEP? YOU CAN DO THAT?
TEE HEE!
フワ…
バ
サ
WIND RITUAL!!!
ゴオオオオ
!
!

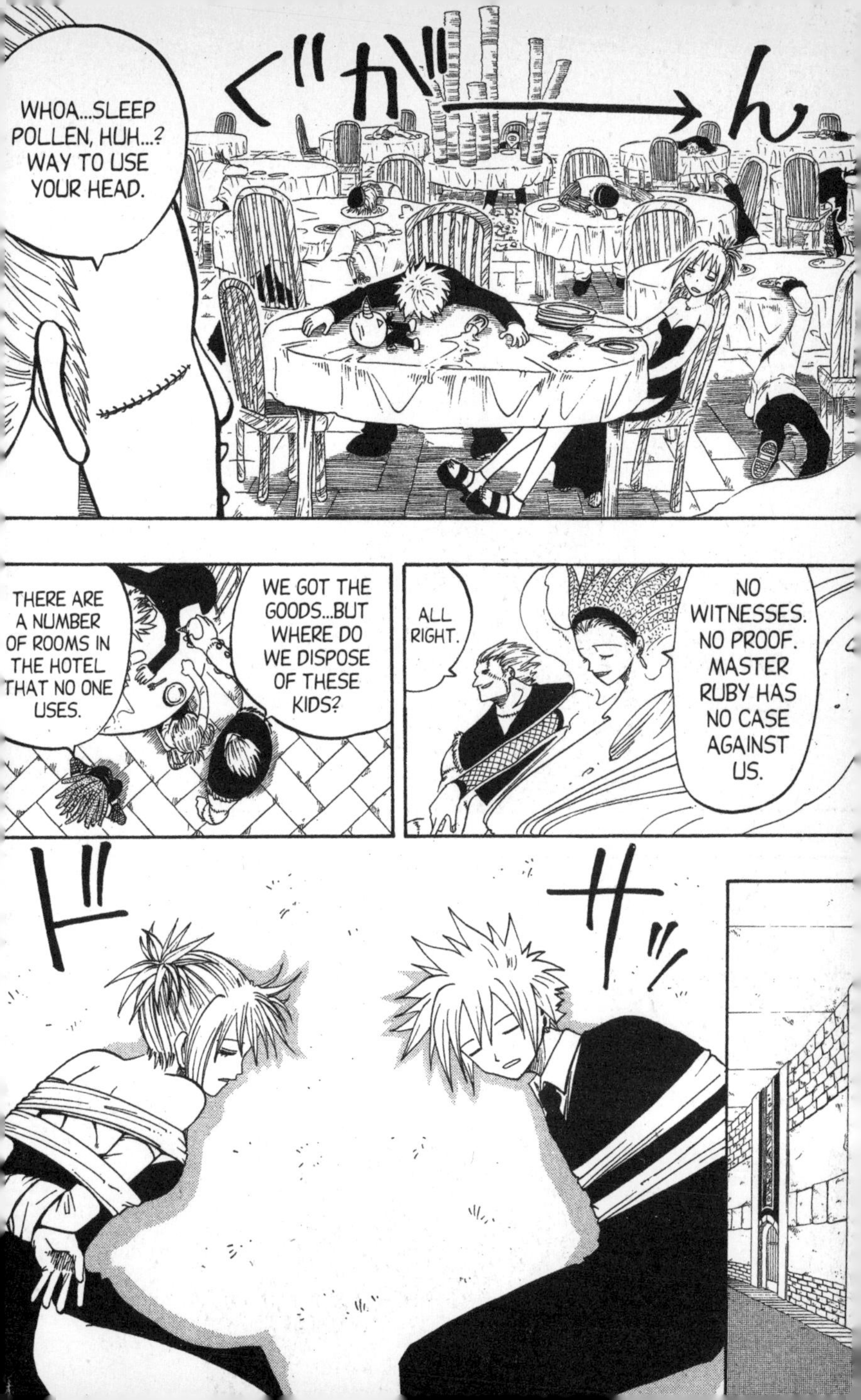
ぐがーん
WHOA...SLEEP POLLEN, HUH...? WAY TO USE YOUR HEAD.
NO WITNESSES. NO PROOF. MASTER RUBY HAS NO CASE AGAINST US.
ALL RIGHT.
WE GOT THE GOODS...BUT WHERE DO WE DISPOSE OF THESE KIDS?
THERE ARE A NUMBER OF ROOMS IN THE HOTEL THAT NO ONE USES.
サッ
ド

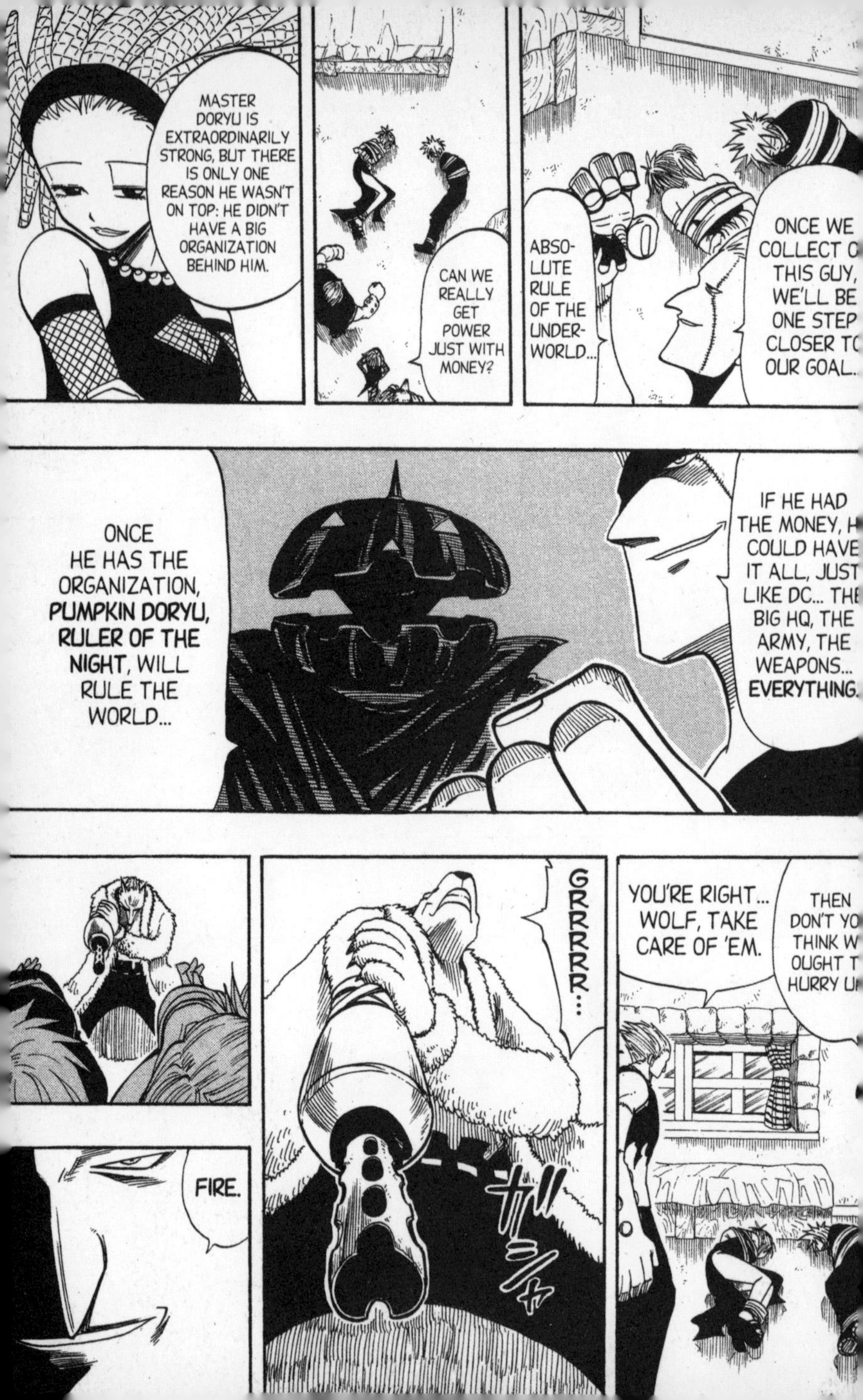
ONCE WE COLLECT O THIS GUY, WE'LL BE ONE STEP CLOSER TC OUR GOAL...
ABSO-LUTE RULE OF THE UNDER-WORLD...
CAN WE REALLY GET POWER JUST WITH MONEY?
MASTER DORYU IS EXTRAORDINARILY STRONG, BUT THERE IS ONLY ONE REASON HE WASN'T ON TOP: HE DIDN'T HAVE A BIG ORGANIZATION BEHIND HIM.
IF HE HAD THE MONEY, H COULD HAVE IT ALL, JUST LIKE DC... TH BIG HQ, THE ARMY, THE WEAPONS... **EVERYTHING.**
ONCE HE HAS THE ORGANIZATION, **PUMPKIN DORYU, RULER OF THE NIGHT**, WILL RULE THE WORLD...
THEN DON'T YO THINK W OUGHT T HURRY U
YOU'RE RIGHT... WOLF, TAKE CARE OF 'EM.
GRRRRR...
FIRE.

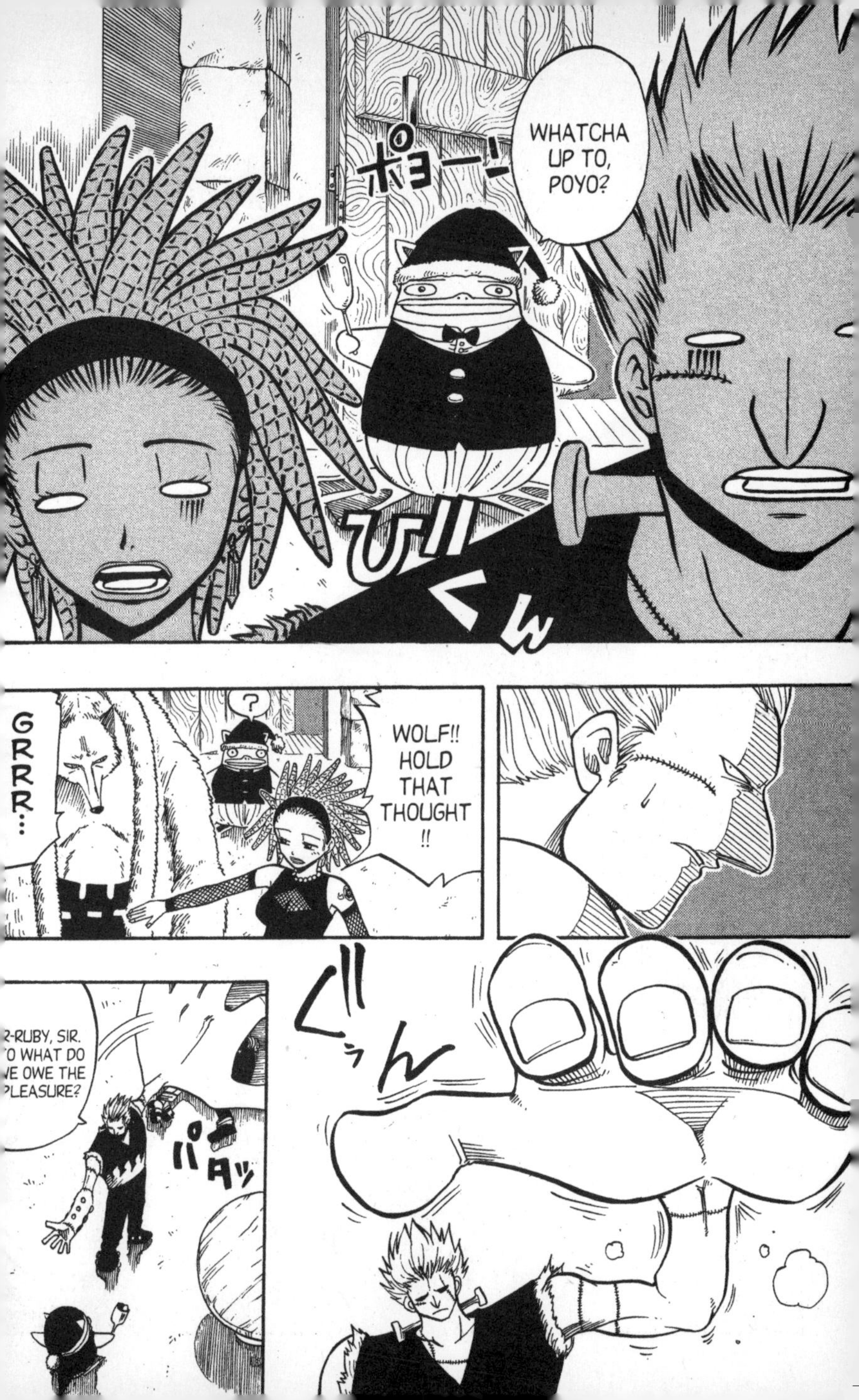
WHATCHA UP TO, POYO?
びくん
WOLF!! HOLD THAT THOUGHT!!
GRRR...
R-RUBY, SIR. TO WHAT DO WE OWE THE PLEASURE?
パタッ

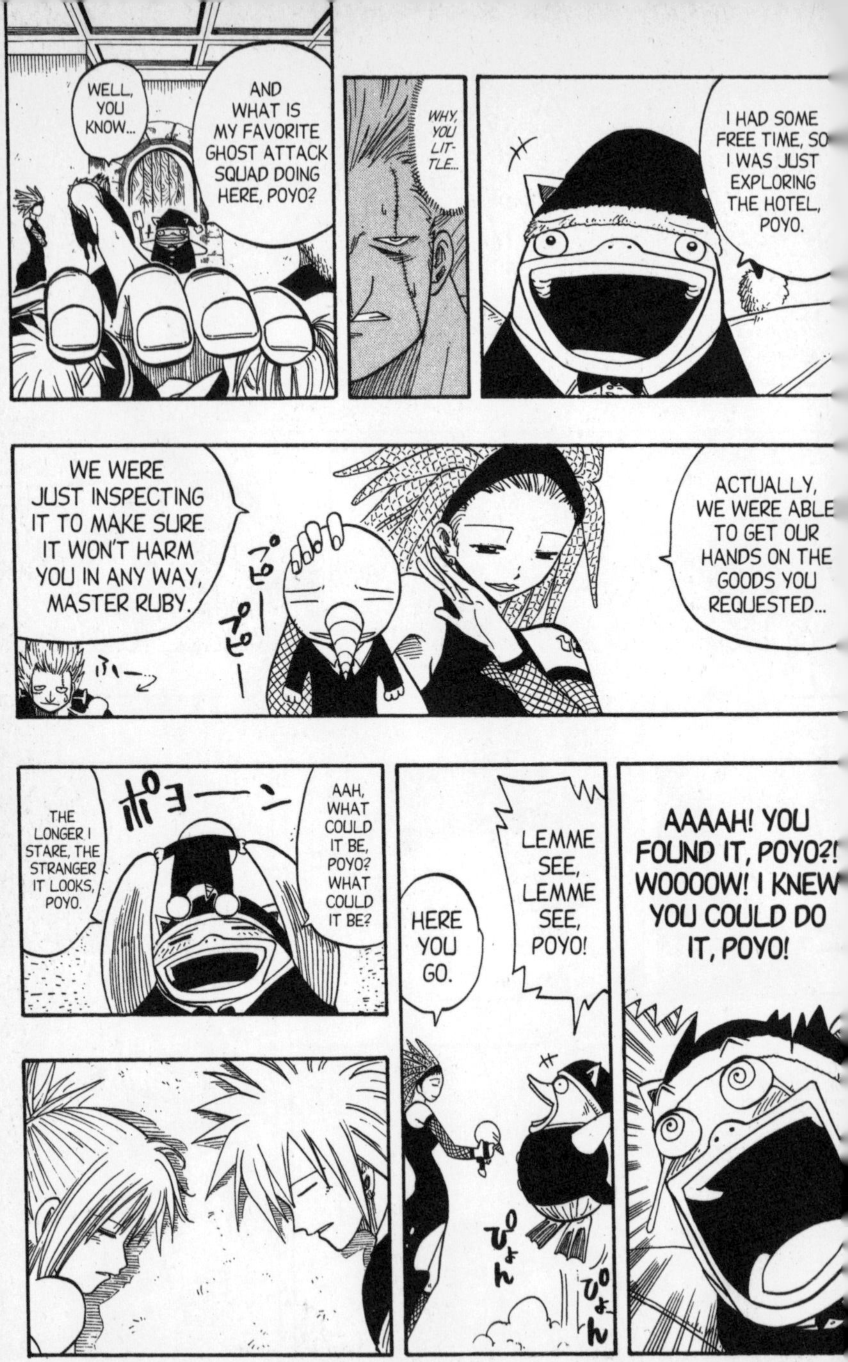
I HAD SOME FREE TIME, SO I WAS JUST EXPLORING THE HOTEL, POYO.
WHY, YOU LIT-TLE...
AND WHAT IS MY FAVORITE GHOST ATTACK SQUAD DOING HERE, POYO?
WELL, YOU KNOW...
ACTUALLY, WE WERE ABLE TO GET OUR HANDS ON THE GOODS YOU REQUESTED...
プピープピー
WE WERE JUST INSPECTING IT TO MAKE SURE IT WON'T HARM YOU IN ANY WAY, MASTER RUBY.
ふー
AAAAH! YOU FOUND IT, POYO?! WOOOOW! I KNEW YOU COULD DO IT, POYO!
LEMME SEE, LEMME SEE, POYO!
HERE YOU GO.
ぴょん
ぴょん
AAH, WHAT COULD IT BE, POYO? WHAT COULD IT BE?
ポヨーーン
THE LONGER I STARE, THE STRANGER IT LOOKS, POYO.

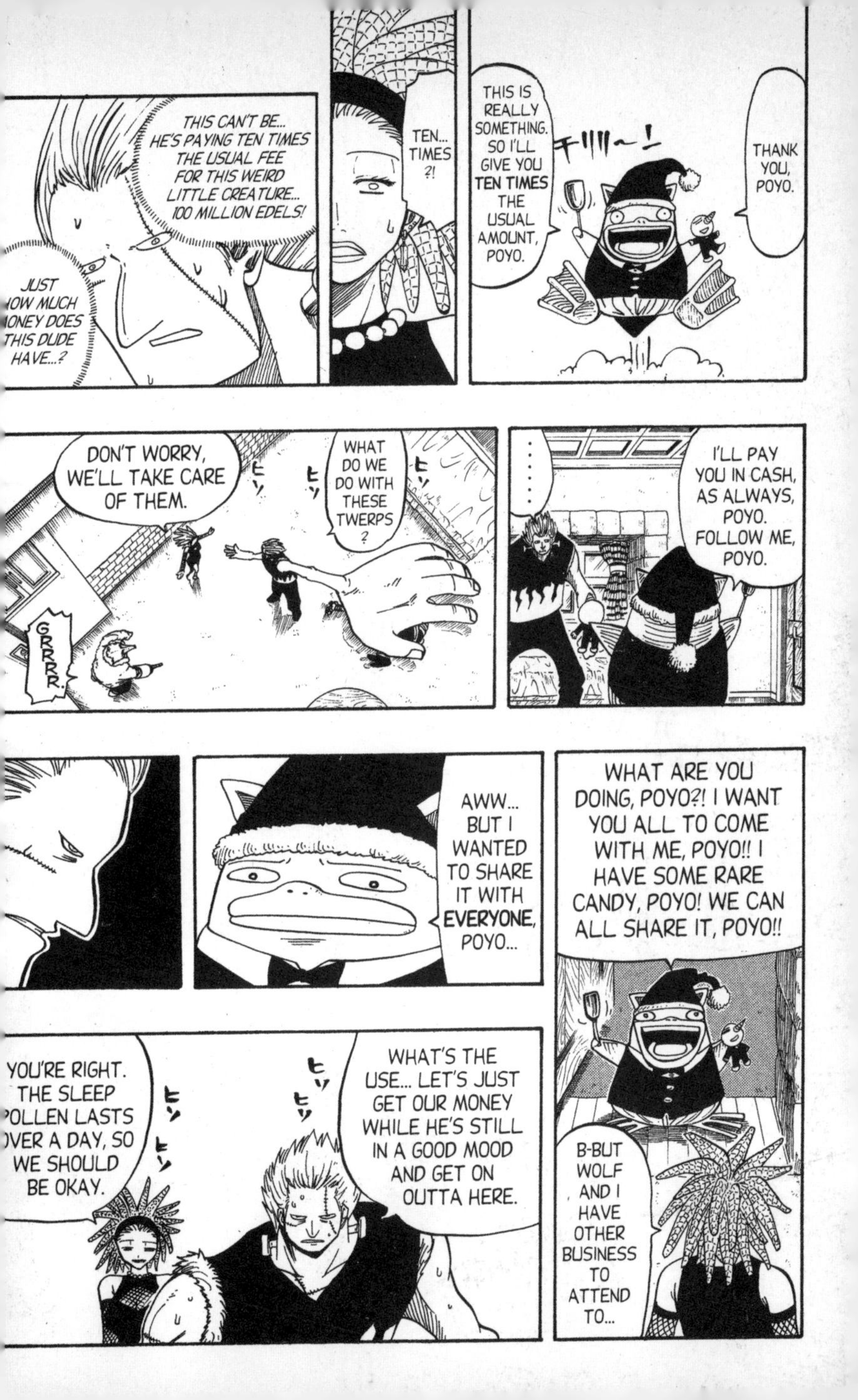
THANK YOU, POYO.
THIS IS REALLY SOMETHING. SO I'LL GIVE YOU **TEN TIMES** THE USUAL AMOUNT, POYO.
TEN... TIMES?!
THIS CAN'T BE... HE'S PAYING TEN TIMES THE USUAL FEE FOR THIS WEIRD LITTLE CREATURE... 100 MILLION EDELS!
JUST HOW MUCH MONEY DOES THIS DUDE HAVE...?
I'LL PAY YOU IN CASH, AS ALWAYS, POYO. FOLLOW ME, POYO.
......
WHAT DO WE DO WITH THESE TWERPS?
DON'T WORRY, WE'LL TAKE CARE OF THEM.
GRRRR.
WHAT ARE YOU DOING, POYO?! I WANT YOU ALL TO COME WITH ME, POYO!! I HAVE SOME RARE CANDY, POYO! WE CAN ALL SHARE IT, POYO!!
B-BUT WOLF AND I HAVE OTHER BUSINESS TO ATTEND TO...
AWW... BUT I WANTED TO SHARE IT WITH **EVERYONE**, POYO...
WHAT'S THE USE... LET'S JUST GET OUR MONEY WHILE HE'S STILL IN A GOOD MOOD AND GET ON OUTTA HERE.
YOU'RE RIGHT. THE SLEEP POLLEN LASTS OVER A DAY, SO WE SHOULD BE OKAY.

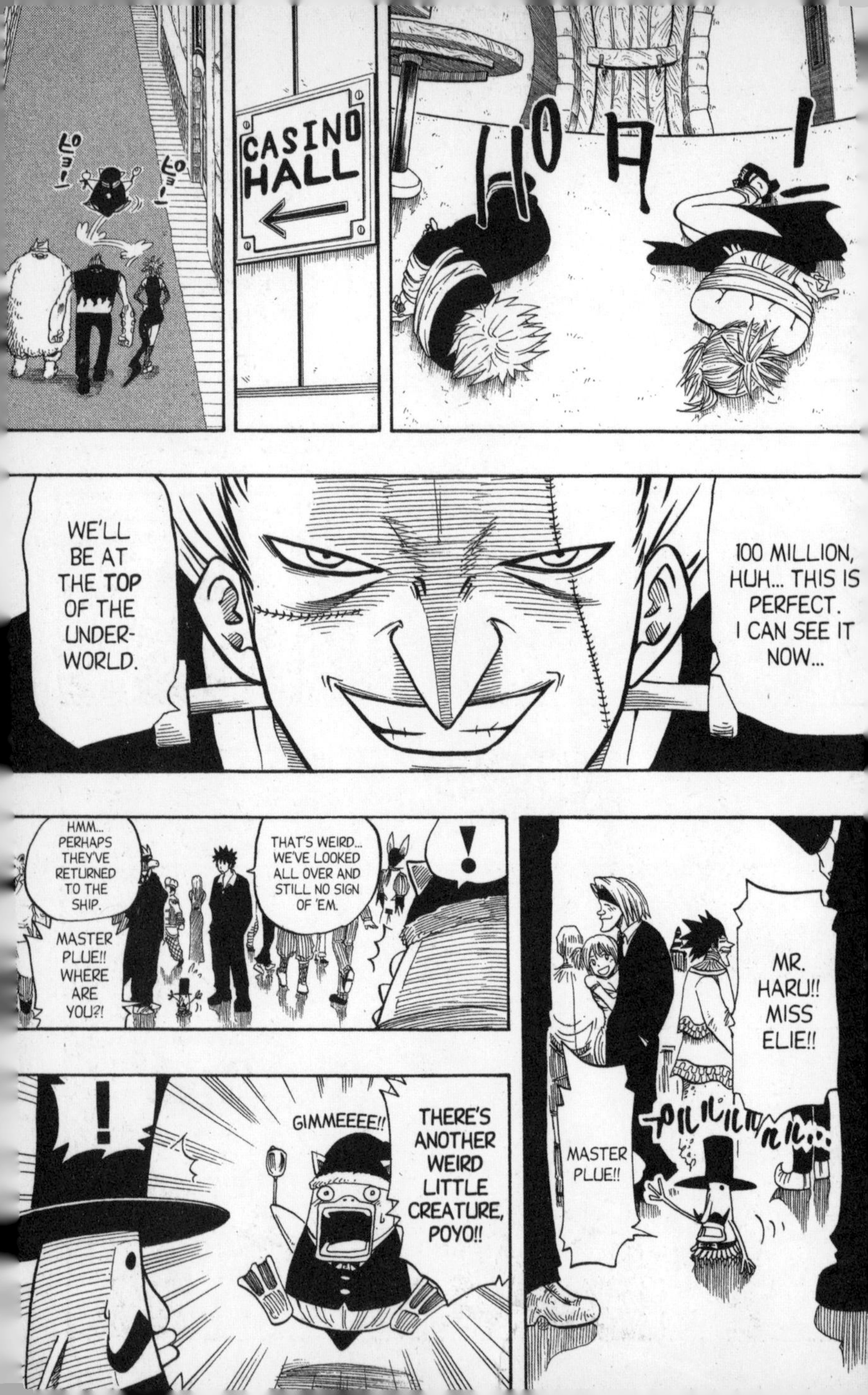
CASINO HALL
100 MILLION, HUH... THIS IS PERFECT. I CAN SEE IT NOW...
WE'LL BE AT THE TOP OF THE UNDERWORLD.
MR. HARU!! MISS ELIE!!
PILILILILI...
MASTER PLUE!!
!
THAT'S WEIRD... WE'VE LOOKED ALL OVER AND STILL NO SIGN OF 'EM.
HMM... PERHAPS THEY'VE RETURNED TO THE SHIP.
MASTER PLUE!! WHERE ARE YOU?!
THERE'S ANOTHER WEIRD LITTLE CREATURE, POYO!!
GIMMEEEE!!
!

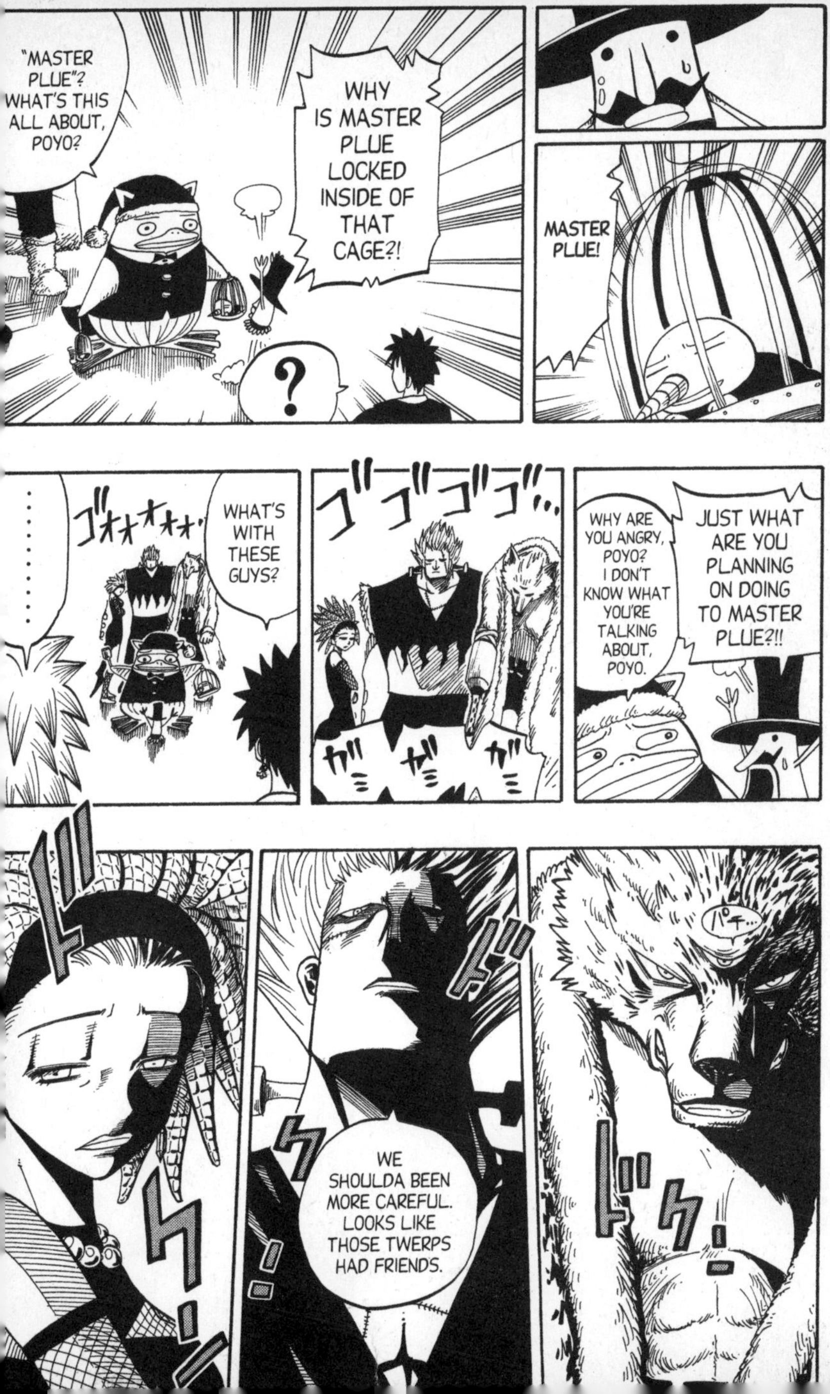
MASTER PLUE!
WHY IS MASTER PLUE LOCKED INSIDE OF THAT CAGE?!
"MASTER PLUE"? WHAT'S THIS ALL ABOUT, POYO?
?
JUST WHAT ARE YOU PLANNING ON DOING TO MASTER PLUE?!!
WHY ARE YOU ANGRY, POYO? I DON'T KNOW WHAT YOU'RE TALKING ABOUT, POYO.
ゴゴゴゴ…
WHAT'S WITH THESE GUYS?
……
WE SHOULDA BEEN MORE CAREFUL. LOOKS LIKE THOSE TWERPS HAD FRIENDS.

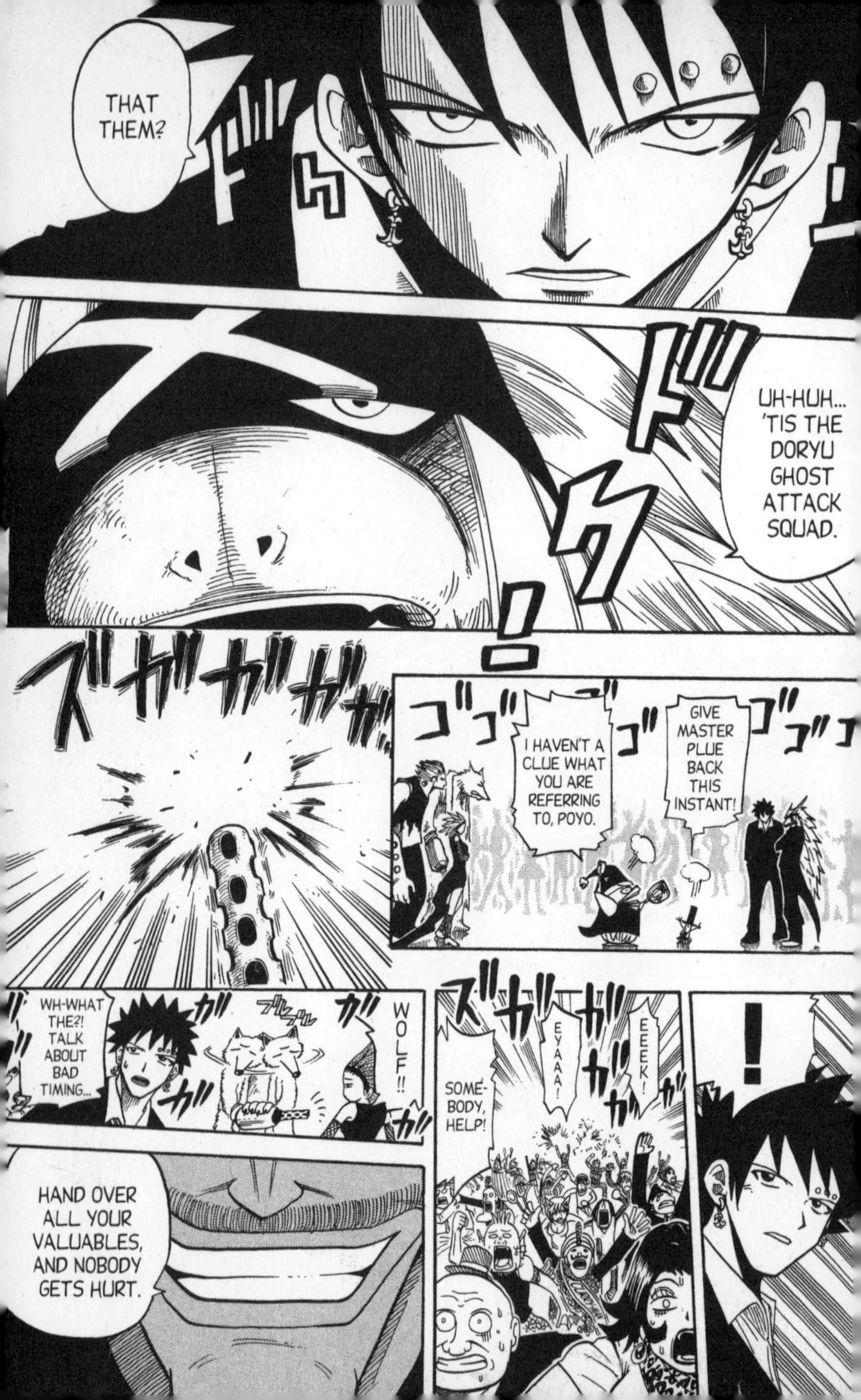
THAT THEM?
UH-HUH... 'TIS THE DORYU GHOST ATTACK SQUAD.
GIVE MASTER PLUE BACK THIS INSTANT!
I HAVEN'T A CLUE WHAT YOU ARE REFERRING TO, POYO.
!
EEEK!
EYAAA!
SOMEBODY, HELP!
WOLF!!
WH-WHAT THE?! TALK ABOUT BAD TIMING...
HAND OVER ALL YOUR VALUABLES, AND NOBODY GETS HURT.

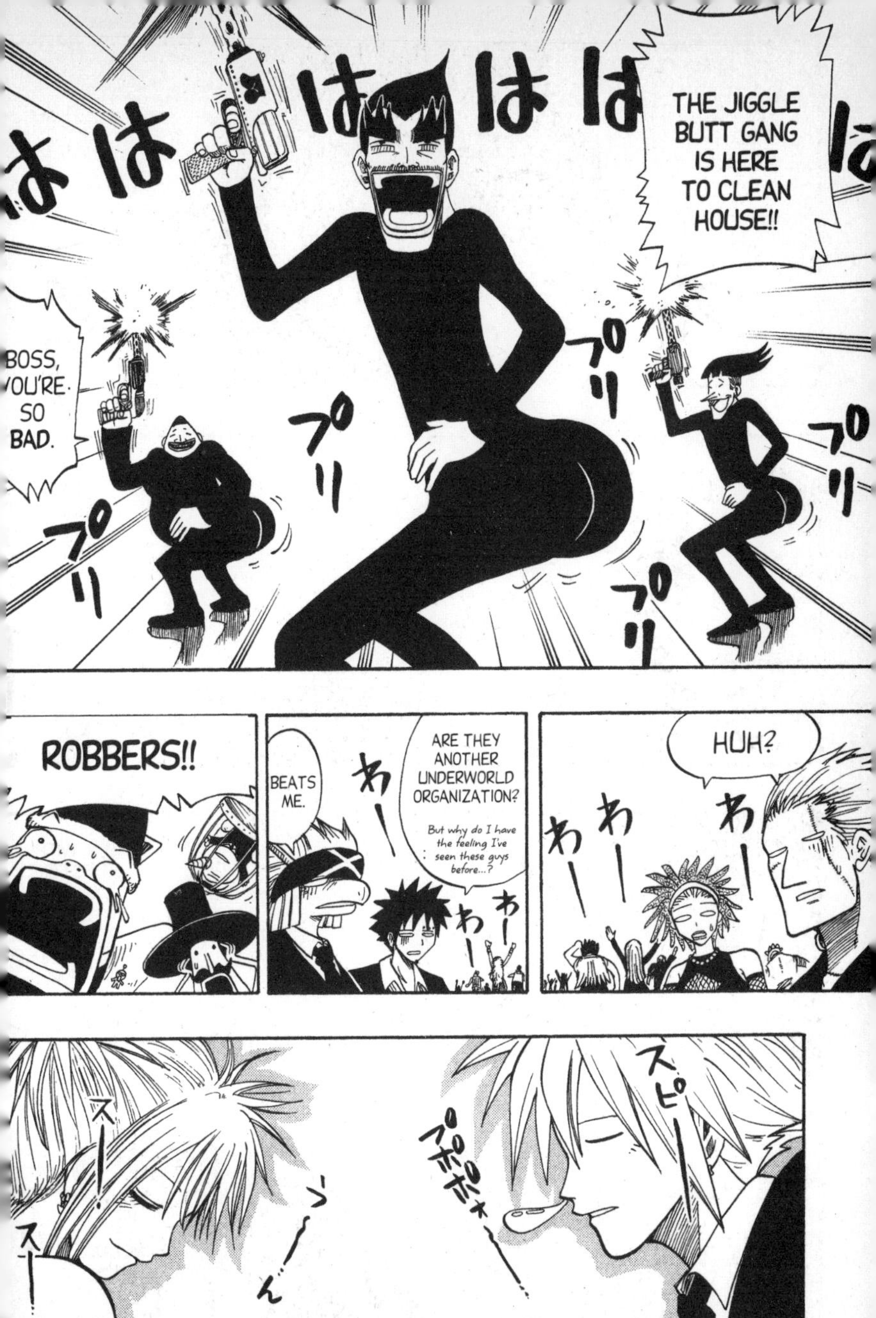
THE JIGGLE BUTT GANG IS HERE TO CLEAN HOUSE!!
BOSS, YOU'RE SO BAD.
HUH?
ARE THEY ANOTHER UNDERWORLD ORGANIZATION?
But why do I have the feeling I've seen these guys before...?
BEATS ME.
ROBBERS!!

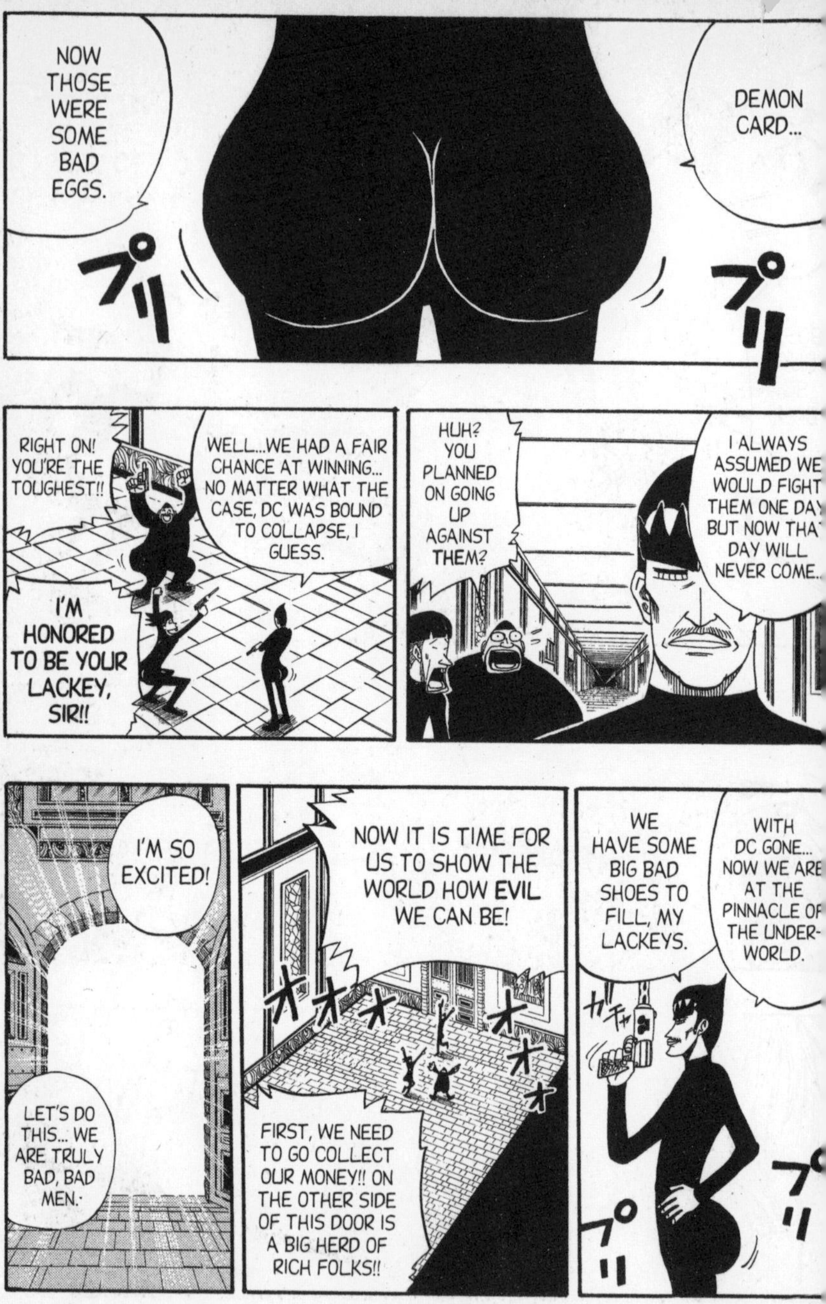
DEMON CARD...
NOW THOSE WERE SOME BAD EGGS.
プリ
プリ
I ALWAYS ASSUMED WE WOULD FIGHT THEM ONE DAY BUT NOW THAT DAY WILL NEVER COME...
HUH? YOU PLANNED ON GOING UP AGAINST THEM?
WELL...WE HAD A FAIR CHANCE AT WINNING... NO MATTER WHAT THE CASE, DC WAS BOUND TO COLLAPSE, I GUESS.
RIGHT ON! YOU'RE THE TOUGHEST!!
I'M HONORED TO BE YOUR LACKEY, SIR!!
WITH DC GONE... NOW WE ARE AT THE PINNACLE OF THE UNDER-WORLD.
WE HAVE SOME BIG BAD SHOES TO FILL, MY LACKEYS.
ガチャ
プリ
プリ
NOW IT IS TIME FOR US TO SHOW THE WORLD HOW EVIL WE CAN BE!
オオオ
オオオ
FIRST, WE NEED TO GO COLLECT OUR MONEY!! ON THE OTHER SIDE OF THIS DOOR IS A BIG HERD OF RICH FOLKS!!
I'M SO EXCITED!
LET'S DO THIS... WE ARE TRULY BAD, BAD MEN.

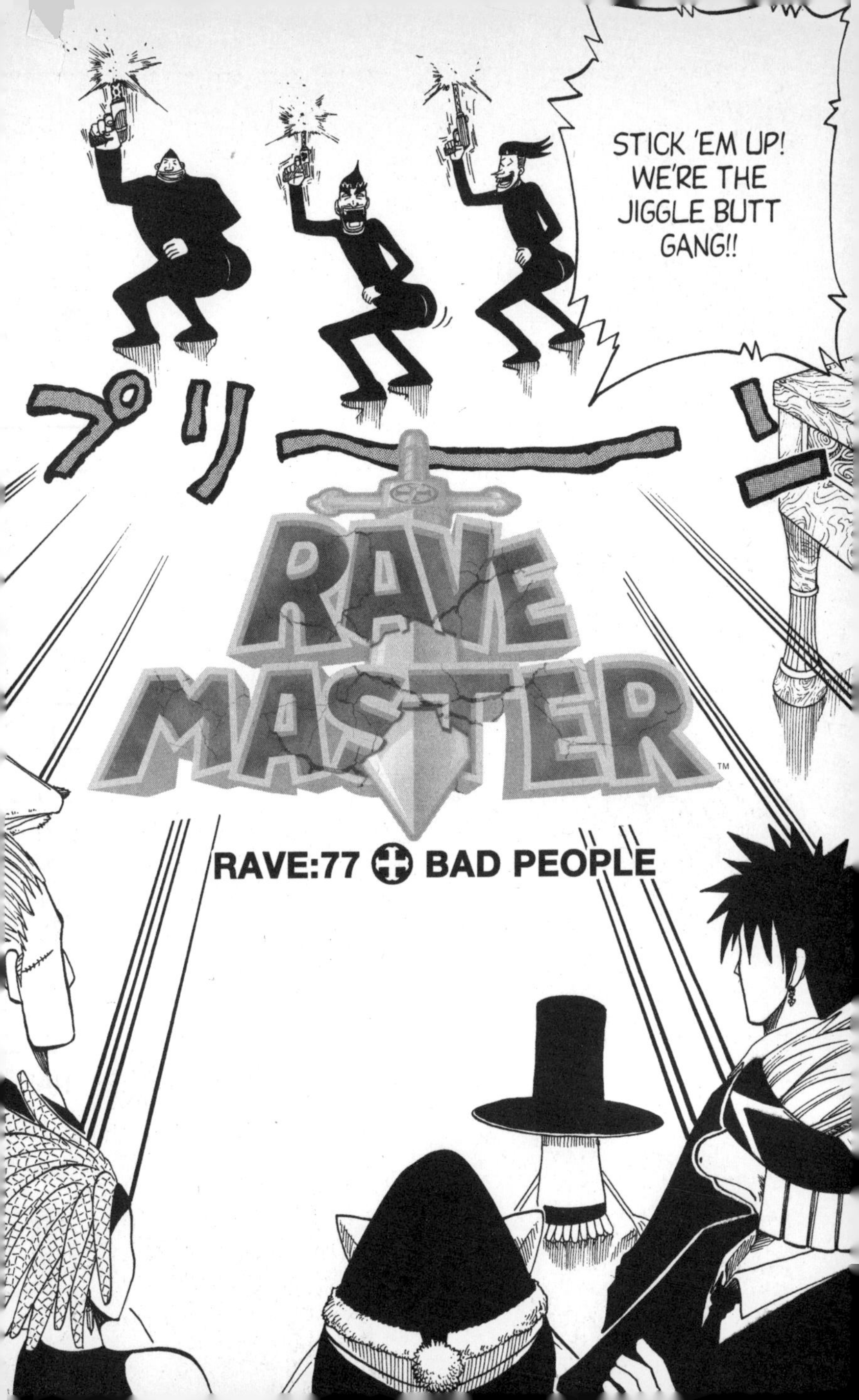
STICK 'EM UP! WE'RE THE JIGGLE BUTT GANG!!
プリーーー
RAVE MASTER™
RAVE:77 BAD PEOPLE

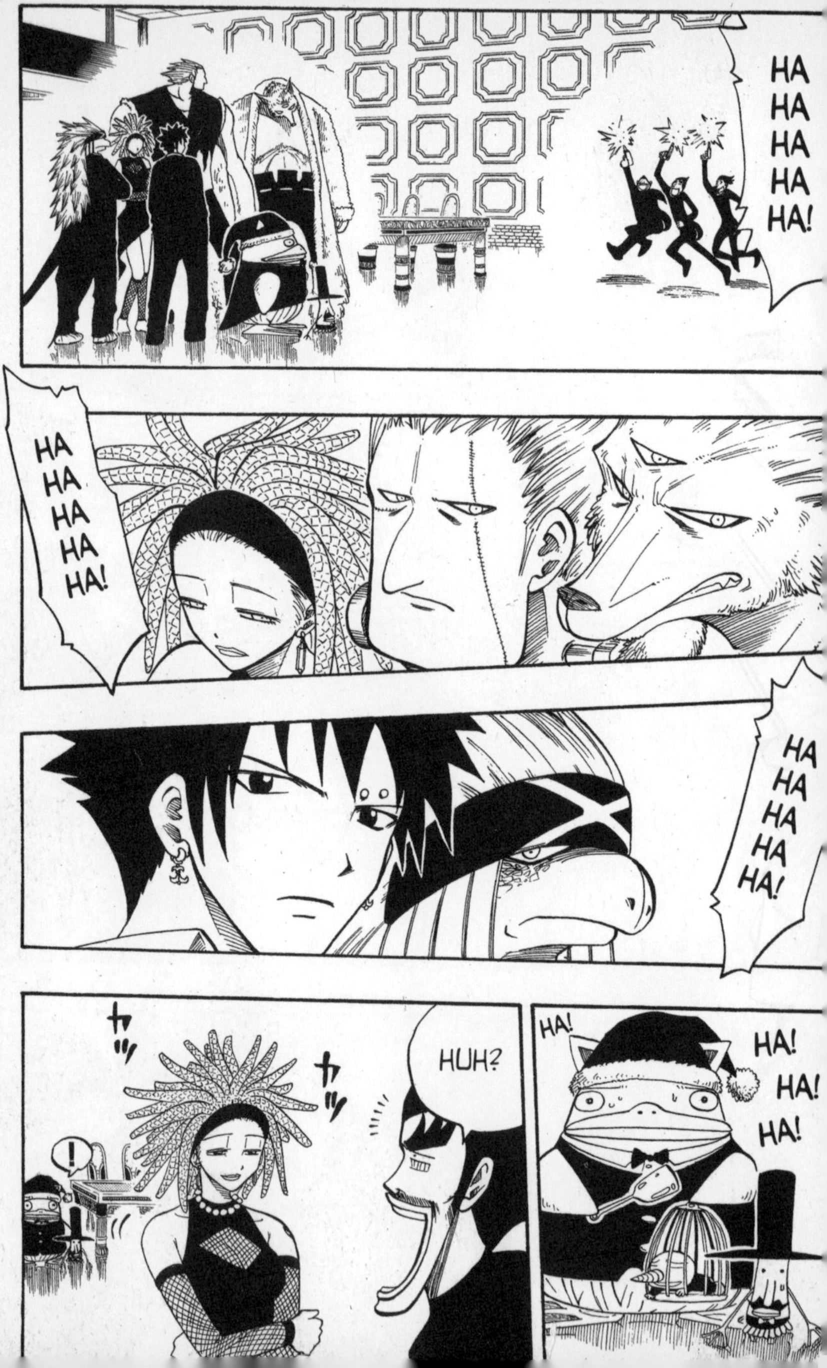
HA HA HA HA HA!
HA HA HA HA HA!
HA HA HA HA HA HA!
HA! HA! HA!
HA!
HUH?
カッ カッ
!

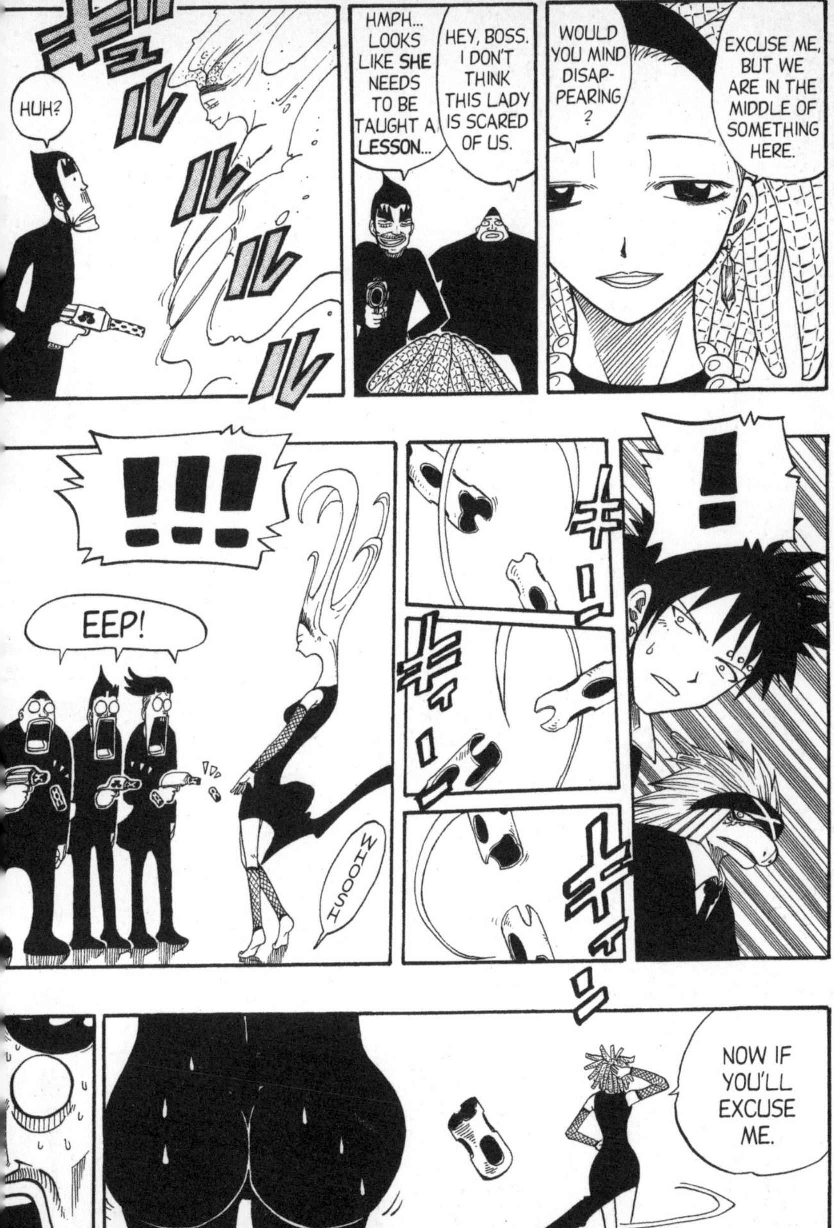
EXCUSE ME, BUT WE ARE IN THE MIDDLE OF SOMETHING HERE.
WOULD YOU MIND DISAPPEARING?
HEY, BOSS. I DON'T THINK THIS LADY IS SCARED OF US.
HMPH... LOOKS LIKE SHE NEEDS TO BE TAUGHT A LESSON...
HUH?
!
!!!
EEP!
WHOOSH
NOW IF YOU'LL EXCUSE ME.

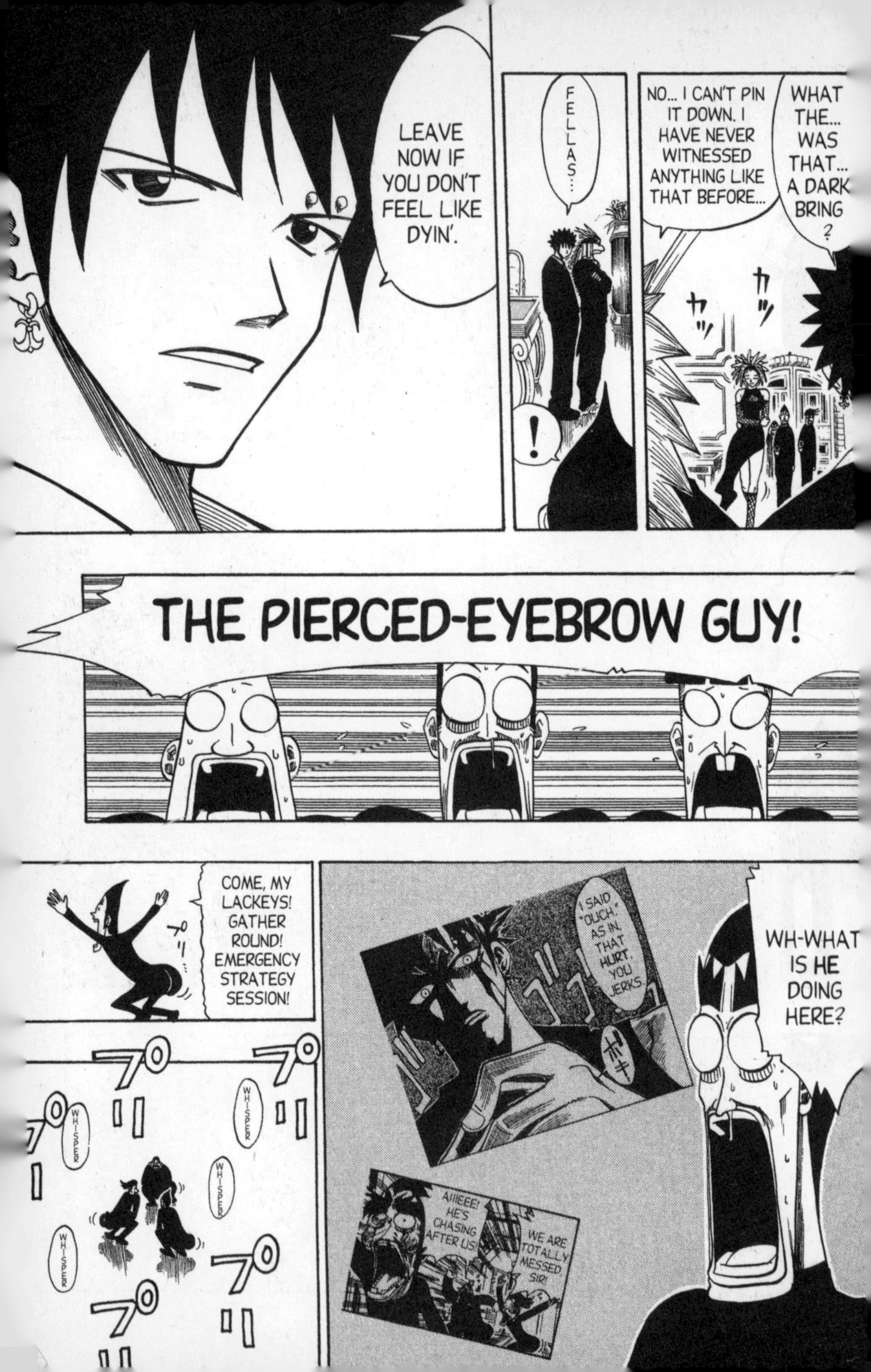
WHAT THE... WAS THAT... A DARK BRING?
NO... I CAN'T PIN IT DOWN. I HAVE NEVER WITNESSED ANYTHING LIKE THAT BEFORE...
カッ
カッ
FELLAS...
!
LEAVE NOW IF YOU DON'T FEEL LIKE DYIN'.
THE PIERCED-EYEBROW GUY!
WH-WHAT IS HE DOING HERE?
I SAID "OUCH," AS IN, THAT HURT, YOU JERKS.
AIIIEEE! HE'S CHASING AFTER US!
WE ARE TOTALLY MESSED SIR!
COME, MY LACKEYS! GATHER ROUND! EMERGENCY STRATEGY SESSION!
WHISPER
WHISPER
WHISPER
WHISPER

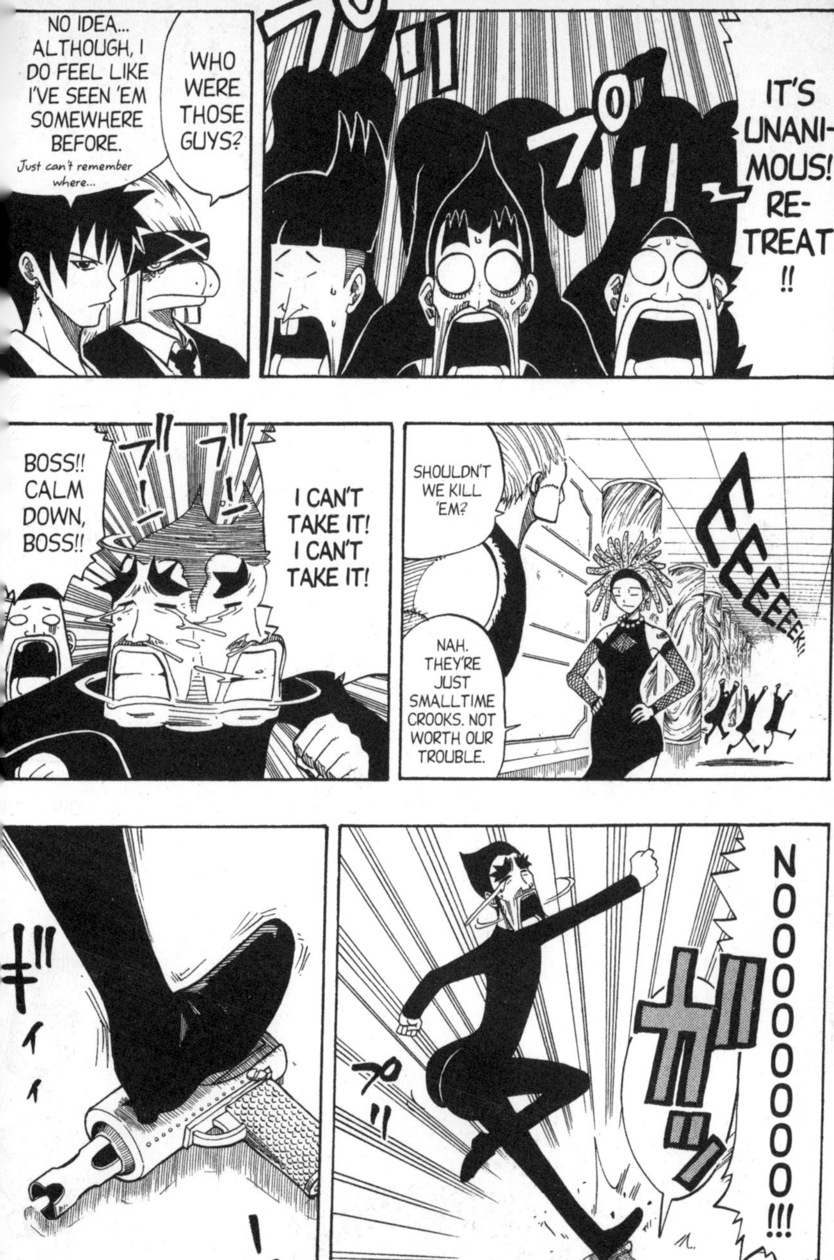
IT'S UNANI-MOUS! RE-TREAT!!
WHO WERE THOSE GUYS?
NO IDEA... ALTHOUGH, I DO FEEL LIKE I'VE SEEN 'EM SOMEWHERE BEFORE.
Just can't remember where...
EEEEEEK!!
SHOULDN'T WE KILL 'EM?
NAH. THEY'RE JUST SMALLTIME CROOKS. NOT WORTH OUR TROUBLE.
I CAN'T TAKE IT! I CAN'T TAKE IT!
BOSS!! CALM DOWN, BOSS!!
NOOOOOOOOOO!!!

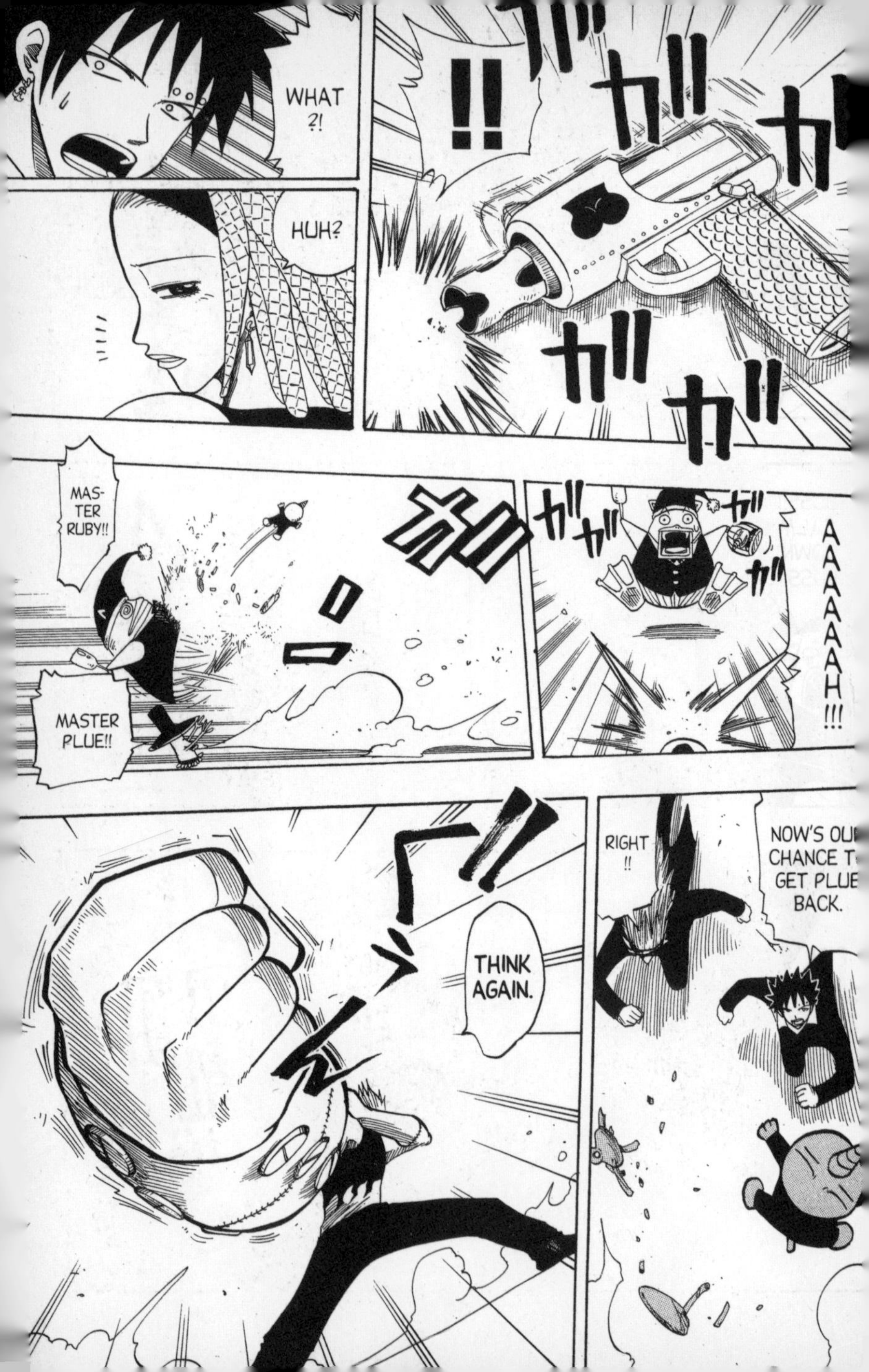

!!
WHAT ?!
HUH?
AAAAAAAH!!!
MAS-TER RUBY!!
MASTER PLUE!!
NOW'S OU
CHANCE T
GET PLUE
BACK.
RIGHT !!
THINK AGAIN.

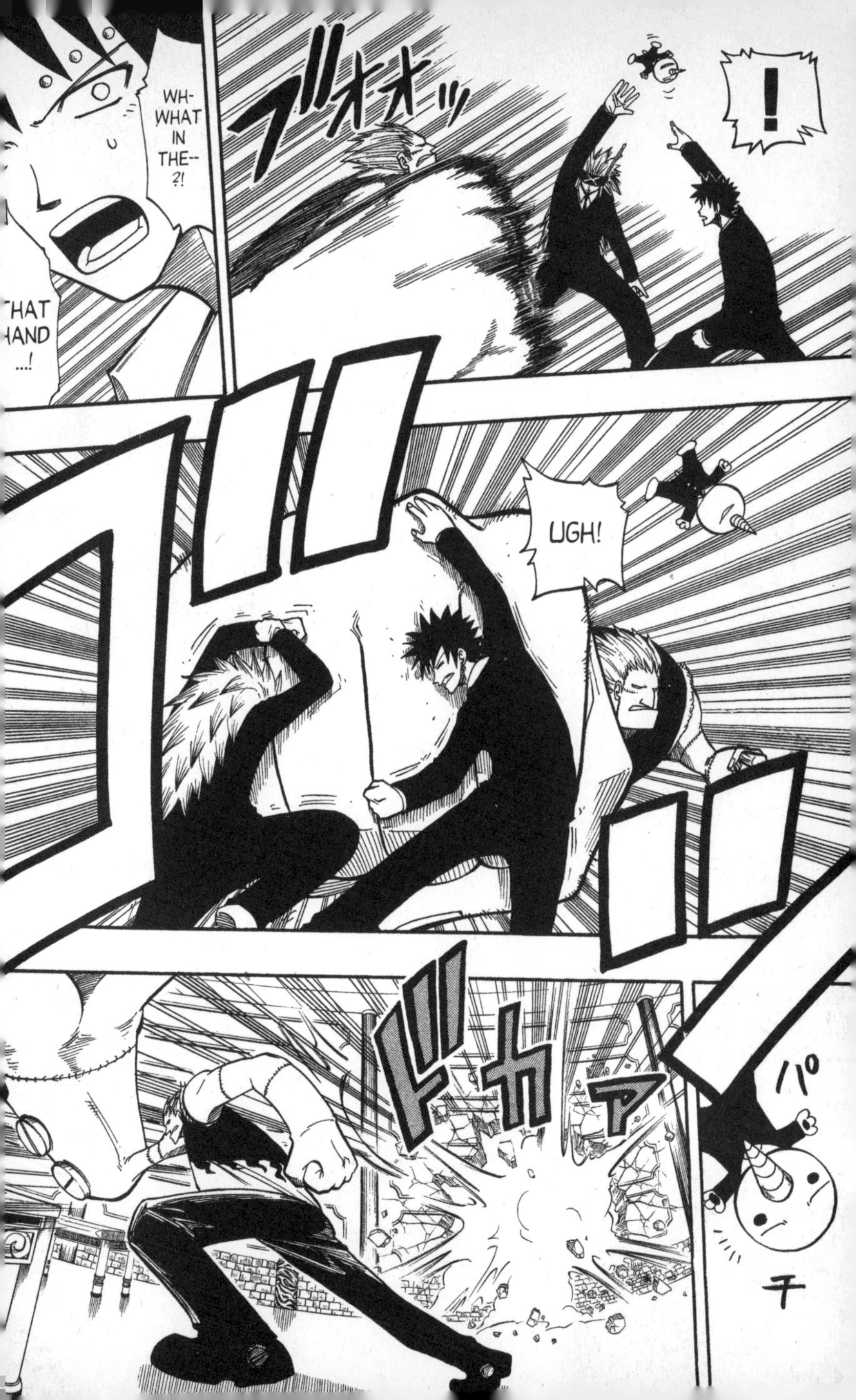
!
ブオオッ
WH-WHAT IN THE--?!
THAT HAND ...!
UGH!
ドカァ
パ
チ

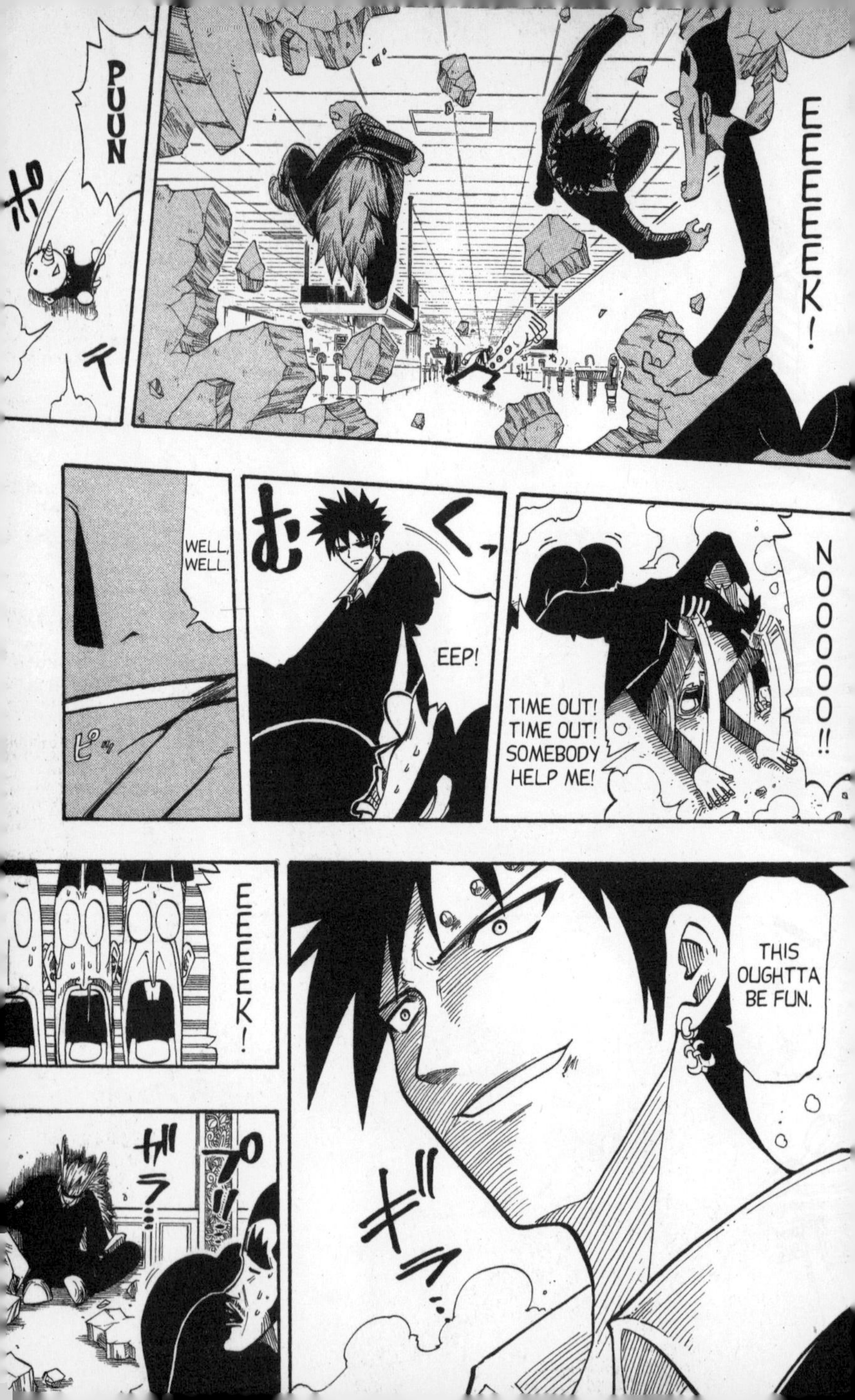
EEEEEEK!
PUUN
NOOOOOO!!
TIME OUT! TIME OUT! SOMEBODY HELP ME!
EEP!
WELL, WELL.
THIS OUGHTTA BE FUN.
EEEEEK!

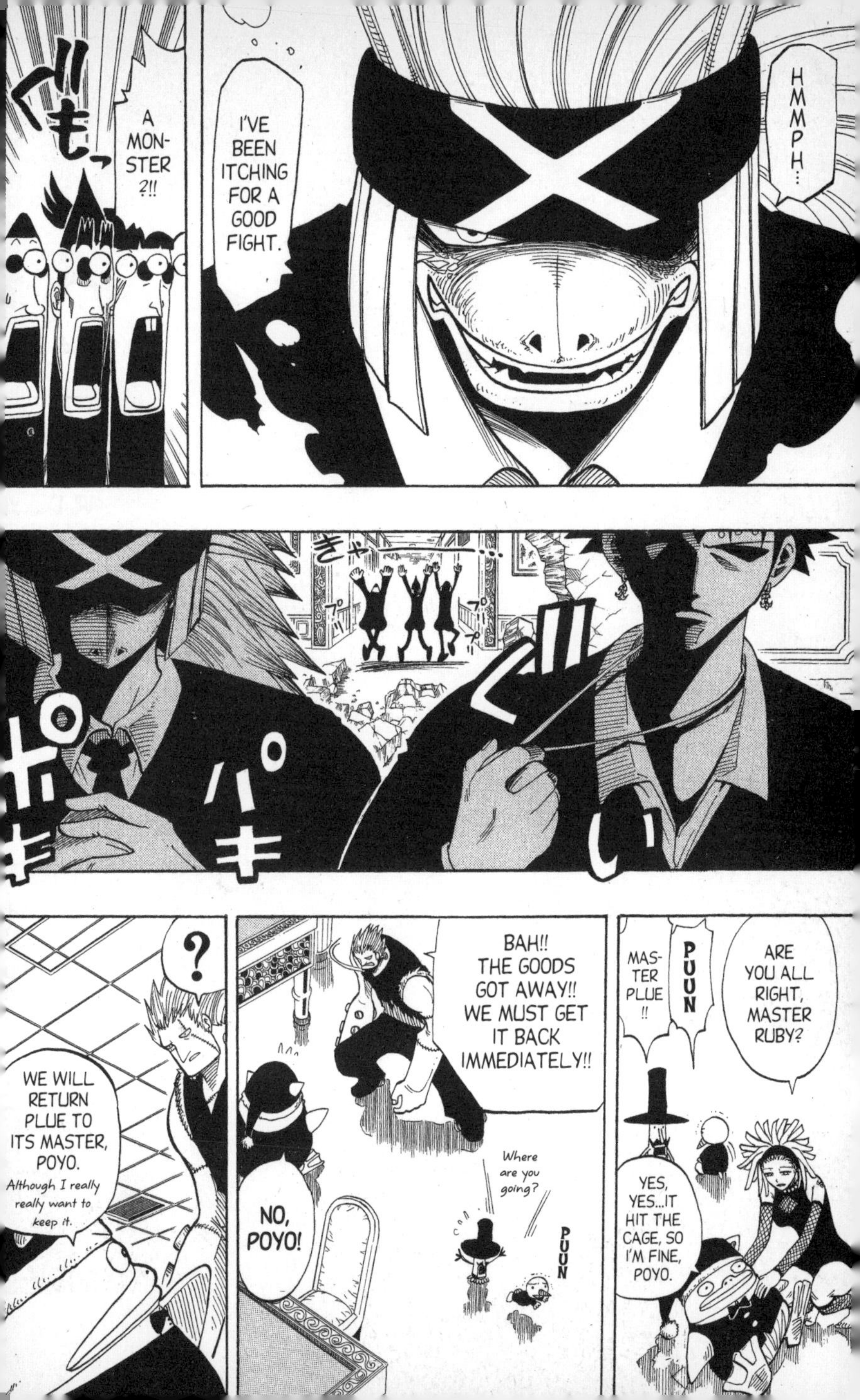
HMMPH...
I'VE BEEN ITCHING FOR A GOOD FIGHT.
A MONSTER?!!
ARE YOU ALL RIGHT, MASTER RUBY?
PUUN
MASTER PLUE!!
YES, YES...IT HIT THE CAGE, SO I'M FINE, POYO.
BAH!! THE GOODS GOT AWAY!! WE MUST GET IT BACK IMMEDIATELY!!
Where are you going?
PUUN
NO, POYO!
?
WE WILL RETURN PLUE TO ITS MASTER, POYO.
Although I really really want to keep it.

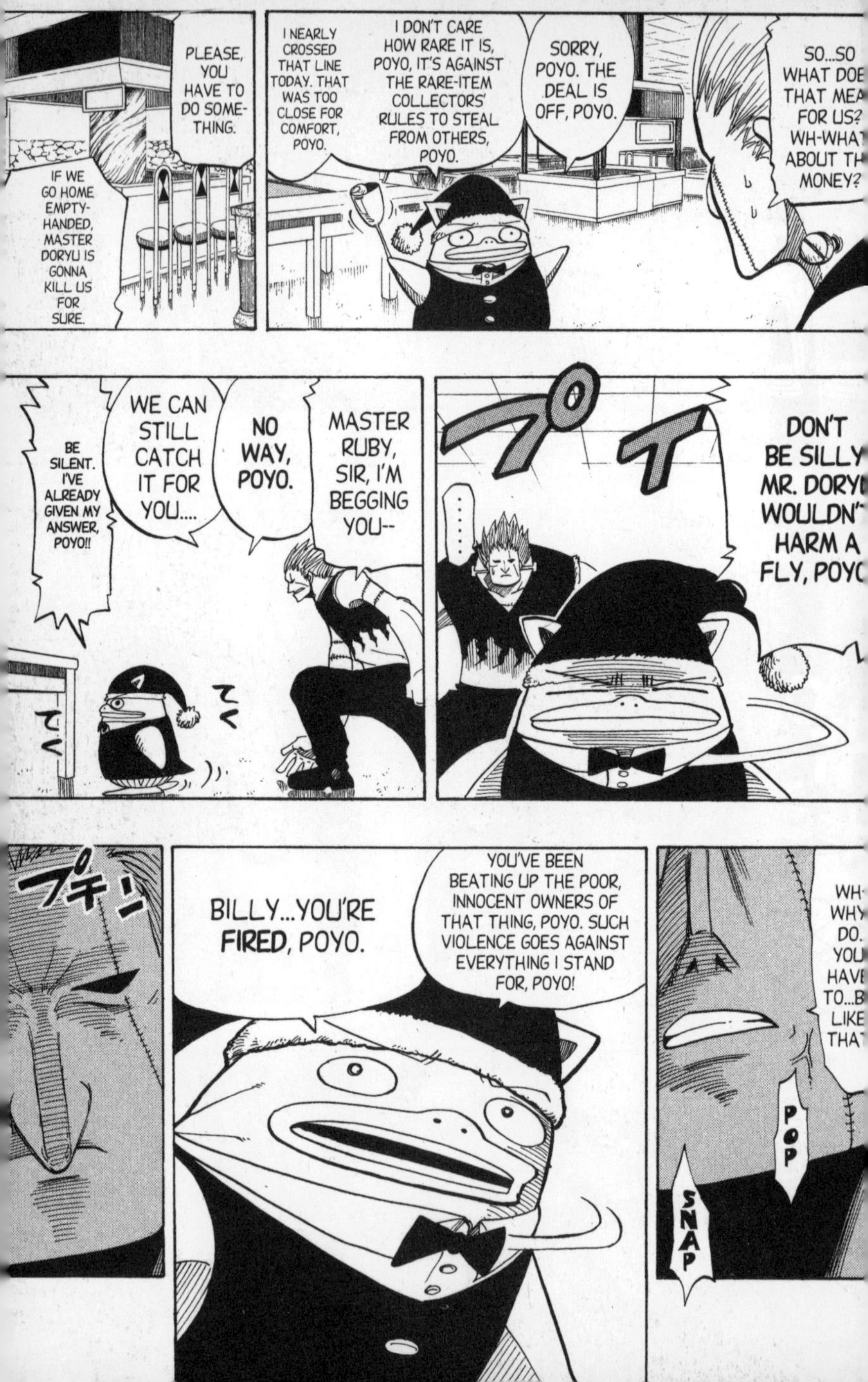
SO...SO WHAT DOE THAT MEA FOR US? WH-WHAT ABOUT TH MONEY?
SORRY, POYO. THE DEAL IS OFF, POYO.
I DON'T CARE HOW RARE IT IS, POYO, IT'S AGAINST THE RARE-ITEM COLLECTORS' RULES TO STEAL FROM OTHERS, POYO.
I NEARLY CROSSED THAT LINE TODAY. THAT WAS TOO CLOSE FOR COMFORT, POYO.
PLEASE, YOU HAVE TO DO SOME-THING.
IF WE GO HOME EMPTY-HANDED, MASTER DORYU IS GONNA KILL US FOR SURE.
プイ
DON'T BE SILLY MR. DORYU WOULDN'T HARM A FLY, POYO
......
MASTER RUBY, SIR, I'M BEGGING YOU--
NO WAY, POYO.
WE CAN STILL CATCH IT FOR YOU....
BE SILENT. I'VE ALREADY GIVEN MY ANSWER, POYO!!
てく
てく
WH- WHY DO. YOU HAVE TO...B LIKE THAT
POP
SNAP
YOU'VE BEEN BEATING UP THE POOR, INNOCENT OWNERS OF THAT THING, POYO. SUCH VIOLENCE GOES AGAINST EVERYTHING I STAND FOR, POYO!
BILLY...YOU'RE **FIRED**, POYO.
プチン

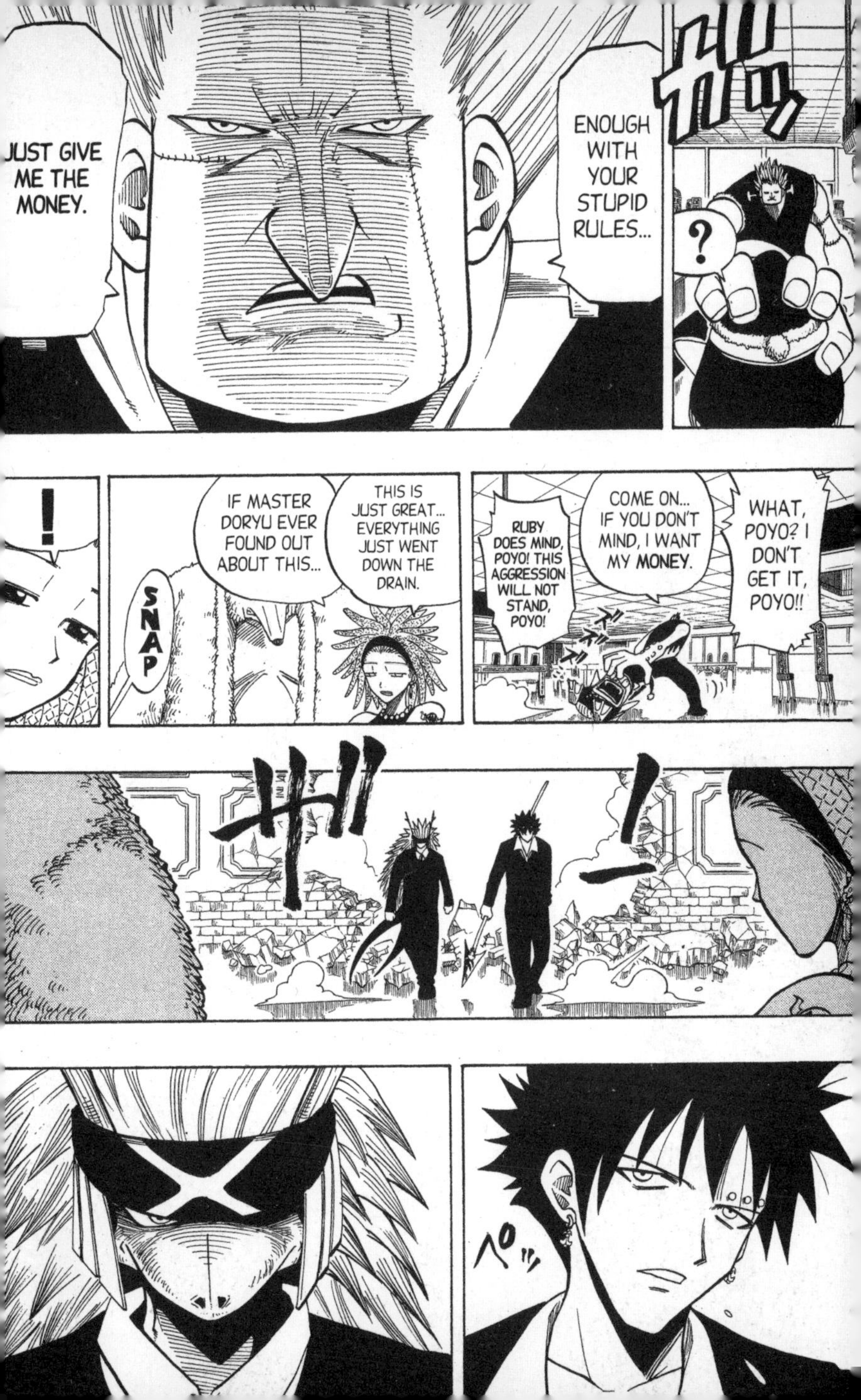
?
ENOUGH WITH YOUR STUPID RULES...
JUST GIVE ME THE MONEY.
WHAT, POYO? I DON'T GET IT, POYO!!
COME ON... IF YOU DON'T MIND, I WANT MY MONEY.
RUBY DOES MIND, POYO! THIS AGGRESSION WILL NOT STAND, POYO!
THIS IS JUST GREAT... EVERYTHING JUST WENT DOWN THE DRAIN.
IF MASTER DORYU EVER FOUND OUT ABOUT THIS...
SNAP
!

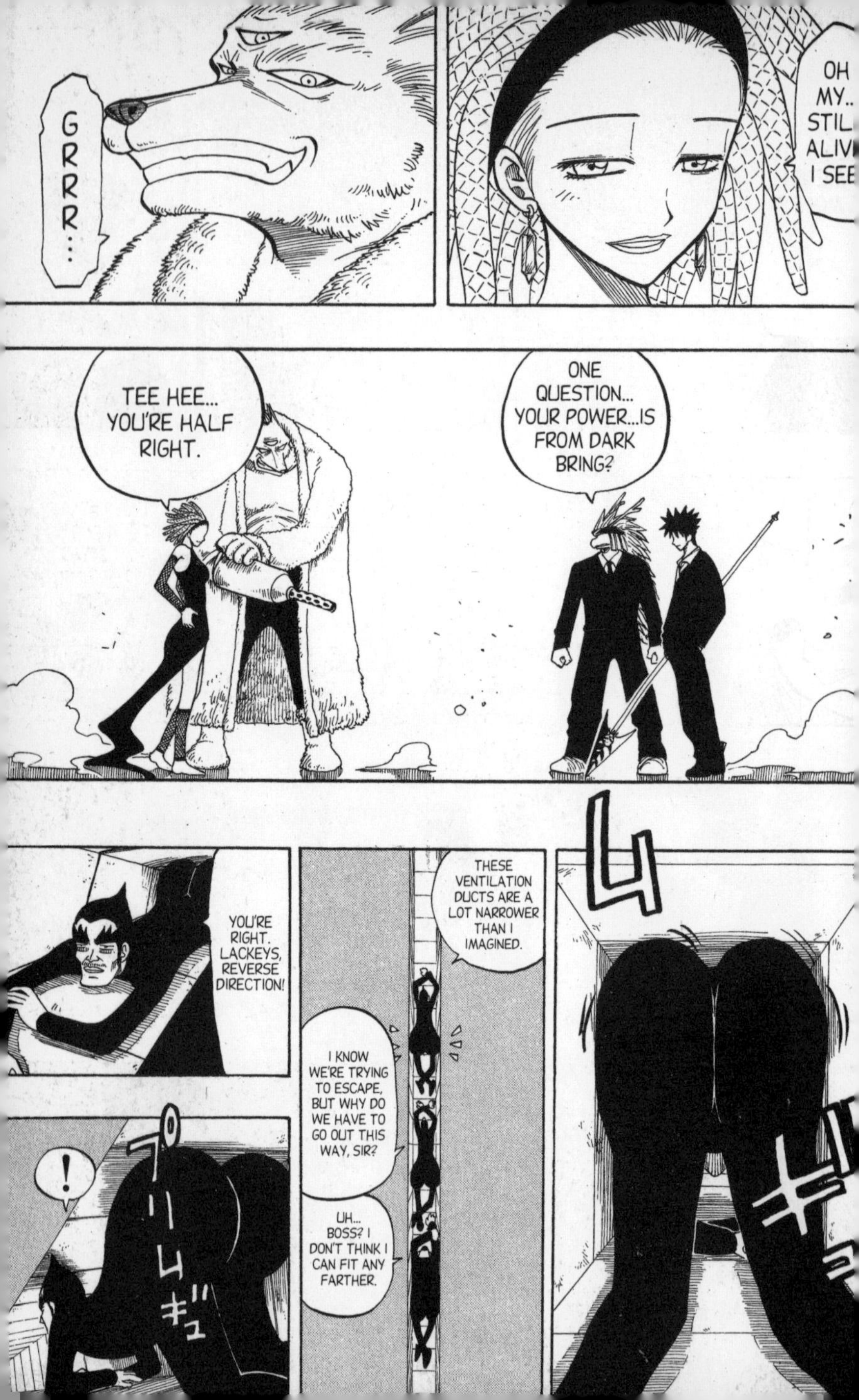
OH MY.. STIL ALIV I SEE
GRRR...
ONE QUESTION... YOUR POWER...IS FROM DARK BRING?
TEE HEE... YOU'RE HALF RIGHT.
THESE VENTILATION DUCTS ARE A LOT NARROWER THAN I IMAGINED.
I KNOW WE'RE TRYING TO ESCAPE, BUT WHY DO WE HAVE TO GO OUT THIS WAY, SIR?
UH... BOSS? I DON'T THINK I CAN FIT ANY FARTHER.
YOU'RE RIGHT. LACKEYS, REVERSE DIRECTION!
!

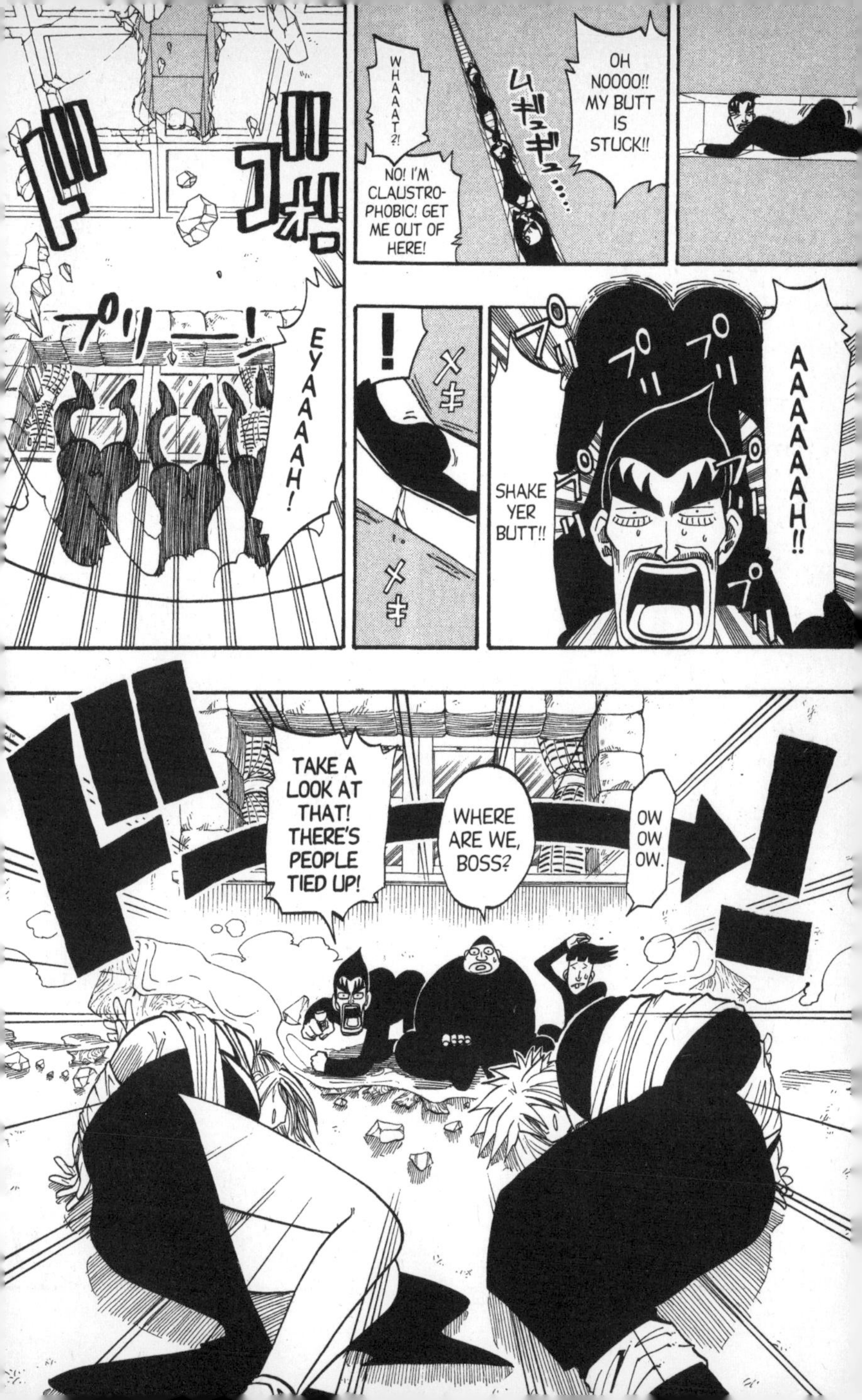
OH NOOOO!! MY BUTT IS STUCK!!
WHAAAAT?!
NO! I'M CLAUSTROPHOBIC! GET ME OUT OF HERE!
AAAAAAAH!!
SHAKE YER BUTT!!
!
EYAAAAAAH!
OW OW OW.
WHERE ARE WE, BOSS?
TAKE A LOOK AT THAT! THERE'S PEOPLE TIED UP!

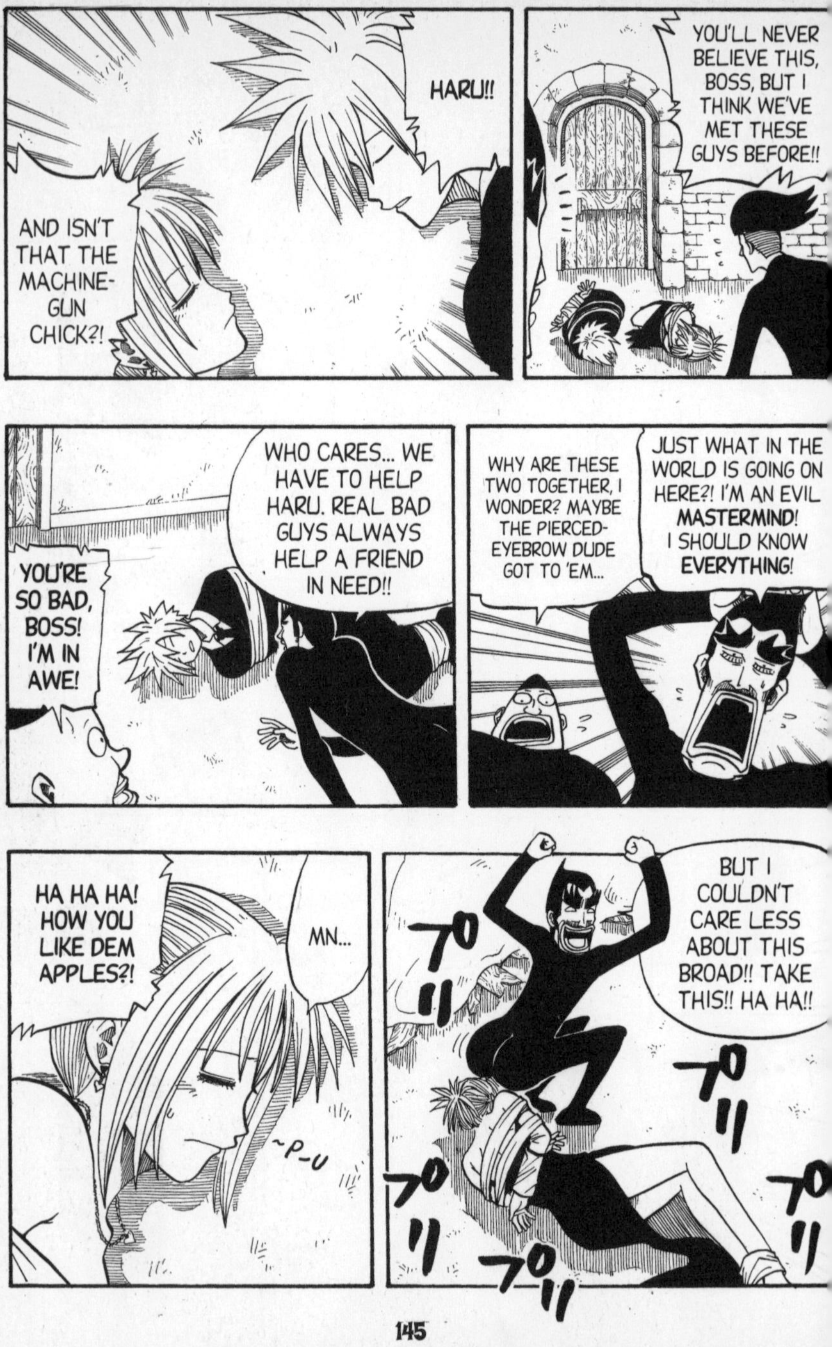
YOU'LL NEVER BELIEVE THIS, BOSS, BUT I THINK WE'VE MET THESE GUYS BEFORE!!
HARU!!
AND ISN'T THAT THE MACHINE-GUN CHICK?!
JUST WHAT IN THE WORLD IS GOING ON HERE?! I'M AN EVIL MASTERMIND! I SHOULD KNOW EVERYTHING!
WHY ARE THESE TWO TOGETHER, I WONDER? MAYBE THE PIERCED-EYEBROW DUDE GOT TO 'EM...
WHO CARES... WE HAVE TO HELP HARU. REAL BAD GUYS ALWAYS HELP A FRIEND IN NEED!!
YOU'RE SO BAD, BOSS! I'M IN AWE!
BUT I COULDN'T CARE LESS ABOUT THIS BROAD!! TAKE THIS!! HA HA!!
プリ
プリ
プリ
プリ
プリ
MN...
HA HA HA! HOW YOU LIKE DEM APPLES?!
~P-U

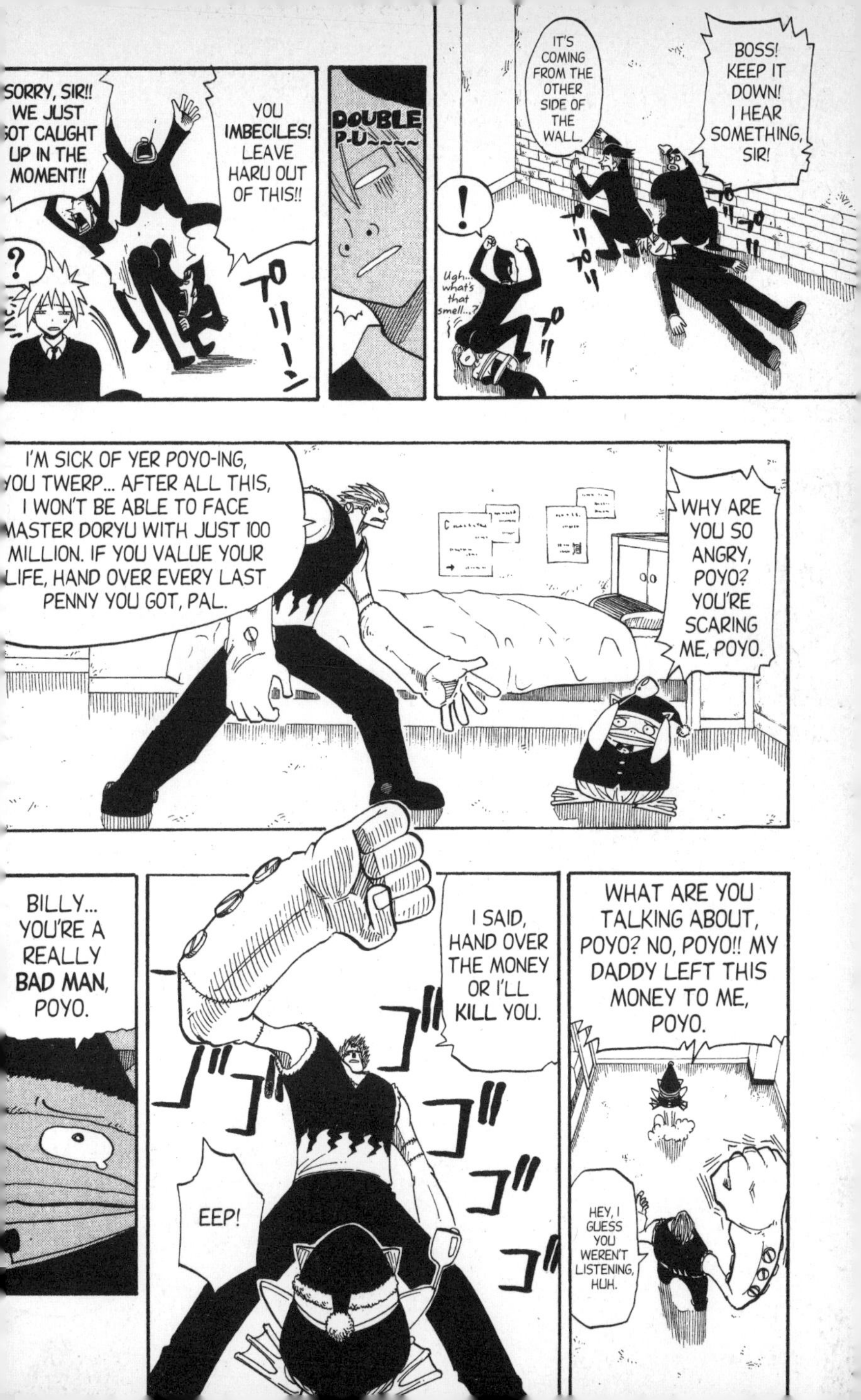
BOSS! KEEP IT DOWN! I HEAR SOMETHING, SIR!
IT'S COMING FROM THE OTHER SIDE OF THE WALL.
!
Ugh... what's that smell...?
DOUBLE P-U~~~~
YOU IMBECILES! LEAVE HARU OUT OF THIS!!
SORRY, SIR!! WE JUST GOT CAUGHT UP IN THE MOMENT!!
?
WHY ARE YOU SO ANGRY, POYO? YOU'RE SCARING ME, POYO.
I'M SICK OF YER POYO-ING, YOU TWERP... AFTER ALL THIS, I WON'T BE ABLE TO FACE MASTER DORYU WITH JUST 100 MILLION. IF YOU VALUE YOUR LIFE, HAND OVER EVERY LAST PENNY YOU GOT, PAL.
WHAT ARE YOU TALKING ABOUT, POYO? NO, POYO!! MY DADDY LEFT THIS MONEY TO ME, POYO.
HEY, I GUESS YOU WEREN'T LISTENING, HUH.
I SAID, HAND OVER THE MONEY OR I'LL KILL YOU.
EEP!
BILLY... YOU'RE A REALLY BAD MAN, POYO.

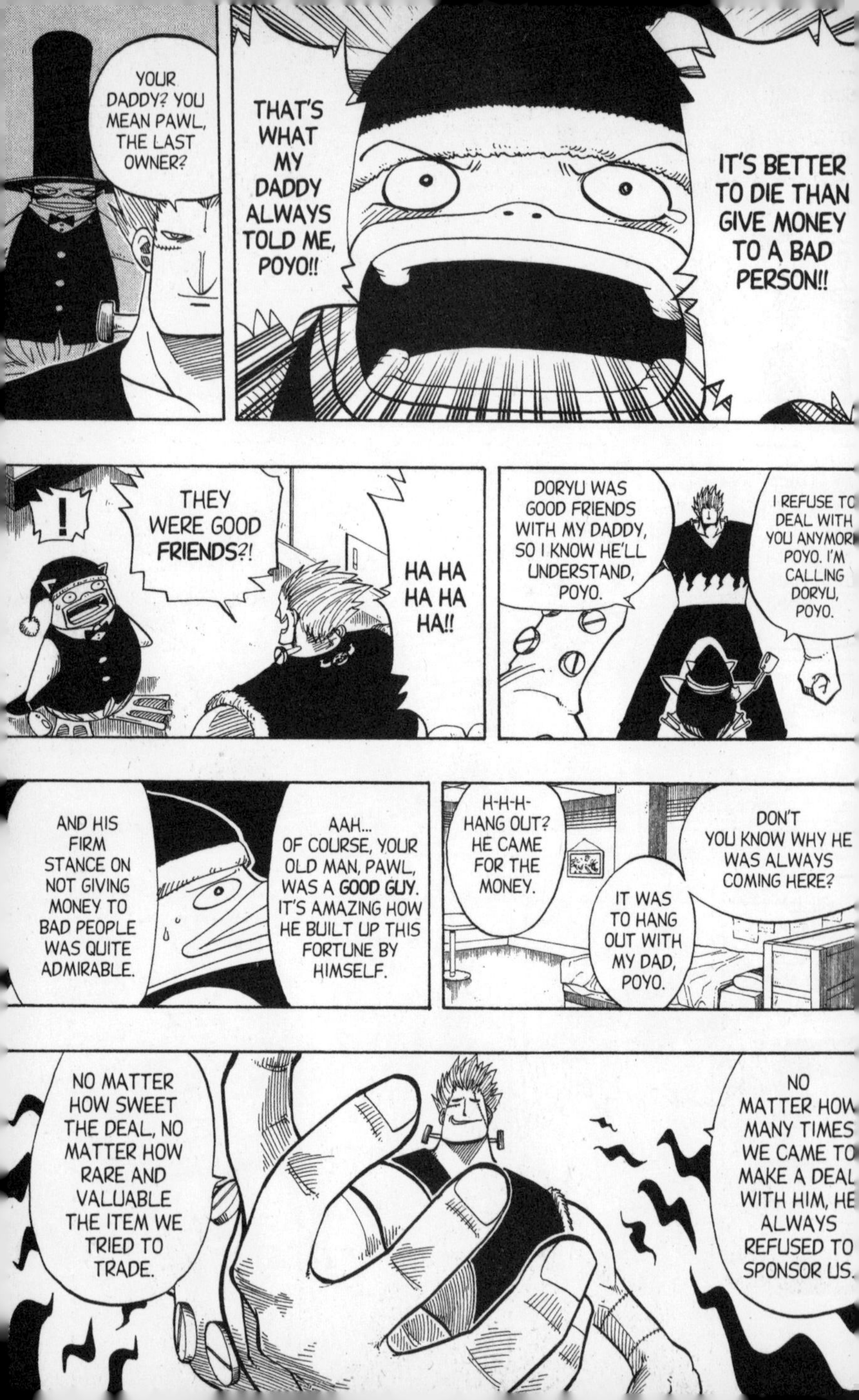
IT'S BETTER TO DIE THAN GIVE MONEY TO A BAD PERSON!!
THAT'S WHAT MY DADDY ALWAYS TOLD ME, POYO!!
YOUR DADDY? YOU MEAN PAWL, THE LAST OWNER?
I REFUSE TO DEAL WITH YOU ANYMOR POYO. I'M CALLING DORYU, POYO.
DORYU WAS GOOD FRIENDS WITH MY DADDY, SO I KNOW HE'LL UNDERSTAND, POYO.
!
THEY WERE GOOD FRIENDS?!
HA HA HA HA HA!!
DON'T YOU KNOW WHY HE WAS ALWAYS COMING HERE?
IT WAS TO HANG OUT WITH MY DAD, POYO.
H-H-H-HANG OUT? HE CAME FOR THE MONEY.
AAH... OF COURSE, YOUR OLD MAN, PAWL, WAS A GOOD GUY. IT'S AMAZING HOW HE BUILT UP THIS FORTUNE BY HIMSELF.
AND HIS FIRM STANCE ON NOT GIVING MONEY TO BAD PEOPLE WAS QUITE ADMIRABLE.
NO MATTER HOW MANY TIMES WE CAME TO MAKE A DEAL WITH HIM, HE ALWAYS REFUSED TO SPONSOR US.
NO MATTER HOW SWEET THE DEAL, NO MATTER HOW RARE AND VALUABLE THE ITEM WE TRIED TO TRADE.

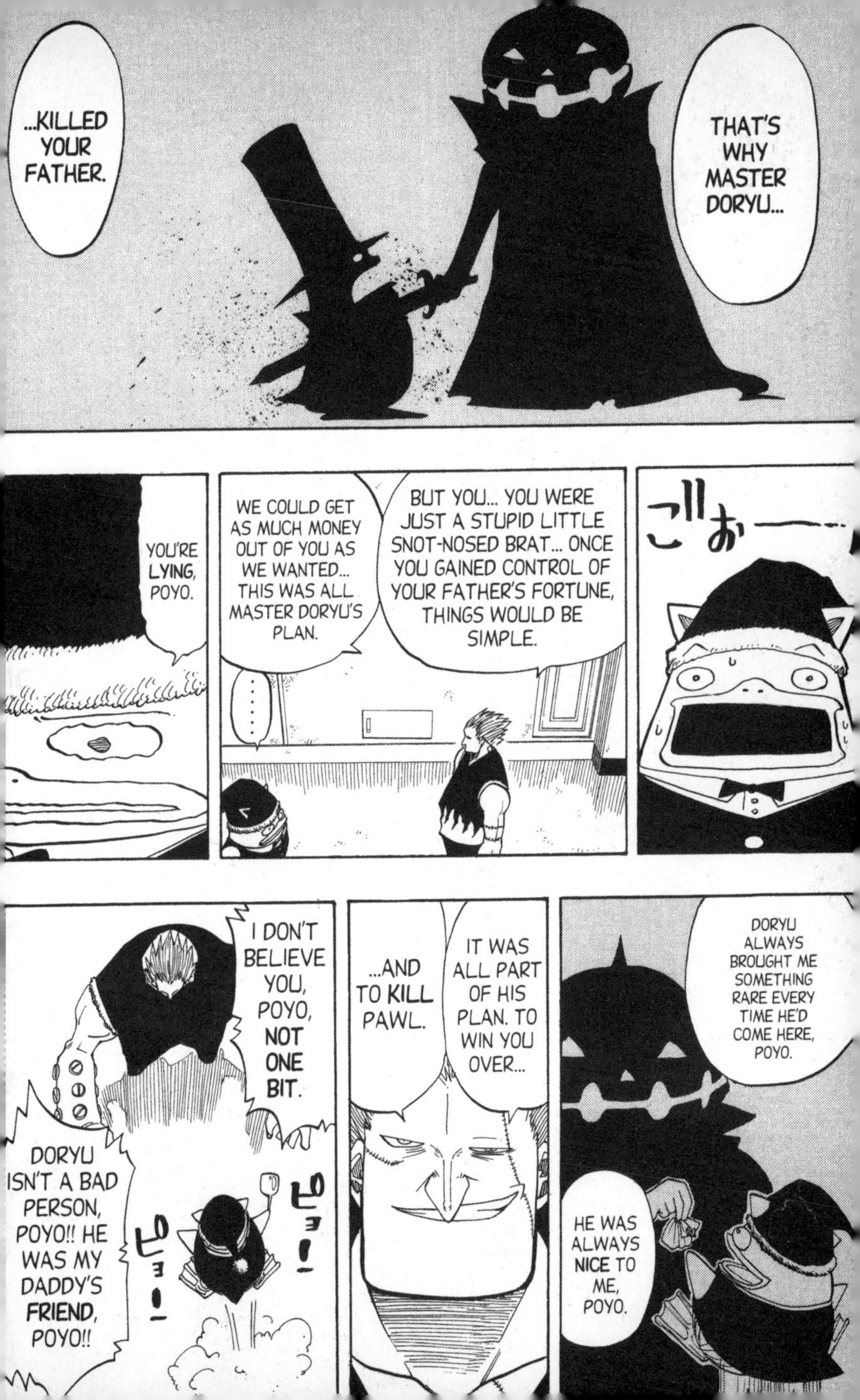
THAT'S WHY MASTER DORYU...
...KILLED YOUR FATHER.
ごぉーー
BUT YOU... YOU WERE JUST A STUPID LITTLE SNOT-NOSED BRAT... ONCE YOU GAINED CONTROL OF YOUR FATHER'S FORTUNE, THINGS WOULD BE SIMPLE.
WE COULD GET AS MUCH MONEY OUT OF YOU AS WE WANTED... THIS WAS ALL MASTER DORYU'S PLAN.
......
YOU'RE **LYING**, POYO.
DORYU ALWAYS BROUGHT ME SOMETHING RARE EVERY TIME HE'D COME HERE, POYO.
HE WAS ALWAYS **NICE** TO ME, POYO.
IT WAS ALL PART OF HIS PLAN. TO WIN YOU OVER...
...AND TO **KILL** PAWL.
I DON'T BELIEVE YOU, POYO, **NOT ONE BIT**.
DORYU ISN'T A BAD PERSON, POYO!! HE WAS MY DADDY'S **FRIEND**, POYO!!
ピョ！ピョ！

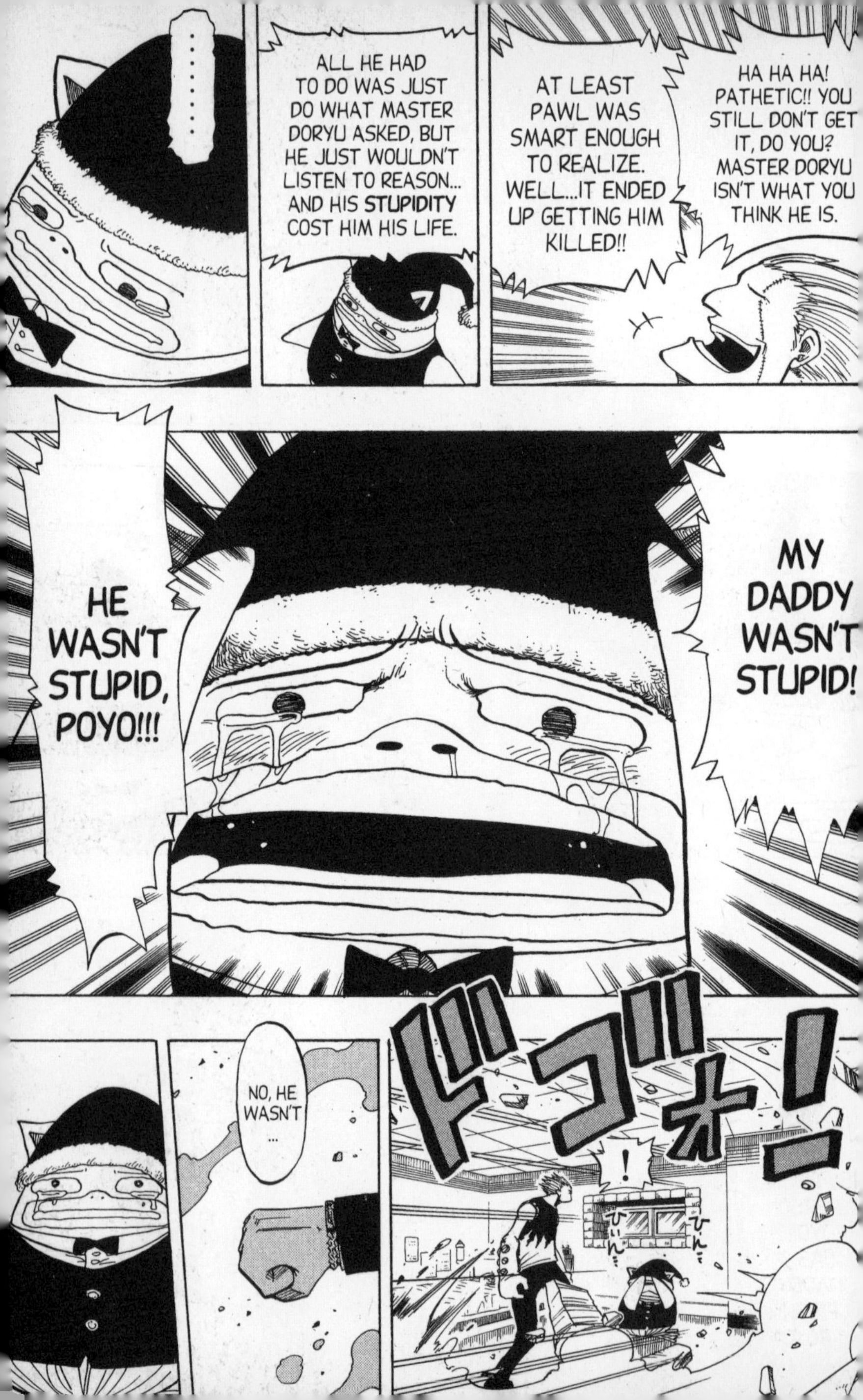
HA HA HA! PATHETIC!! YOU STILL DON'T GET IT, DO YOU? MASTER DORYU ISN'T WHAT YOU THINK HE IS.
AT LEAST PAWL WAS SMART ENOUGH TO REALIZE. WELL...IT ENDED UP GETTING HIM KILLED!!
ALL HE HAD TO DO WAS JUST DO WHAT MASTER DORYU ASKED, BUT HE JUST WOULDN'T LISTEN TO REASON... AND HIS **STUPIDITY** COST HIM HIS LIFE.
....
MY DADDY WASN'T STUPID!
HE WASN'T STUPID, POYO!!!
ドゴォ!
!
NO, HE WASN'T ...

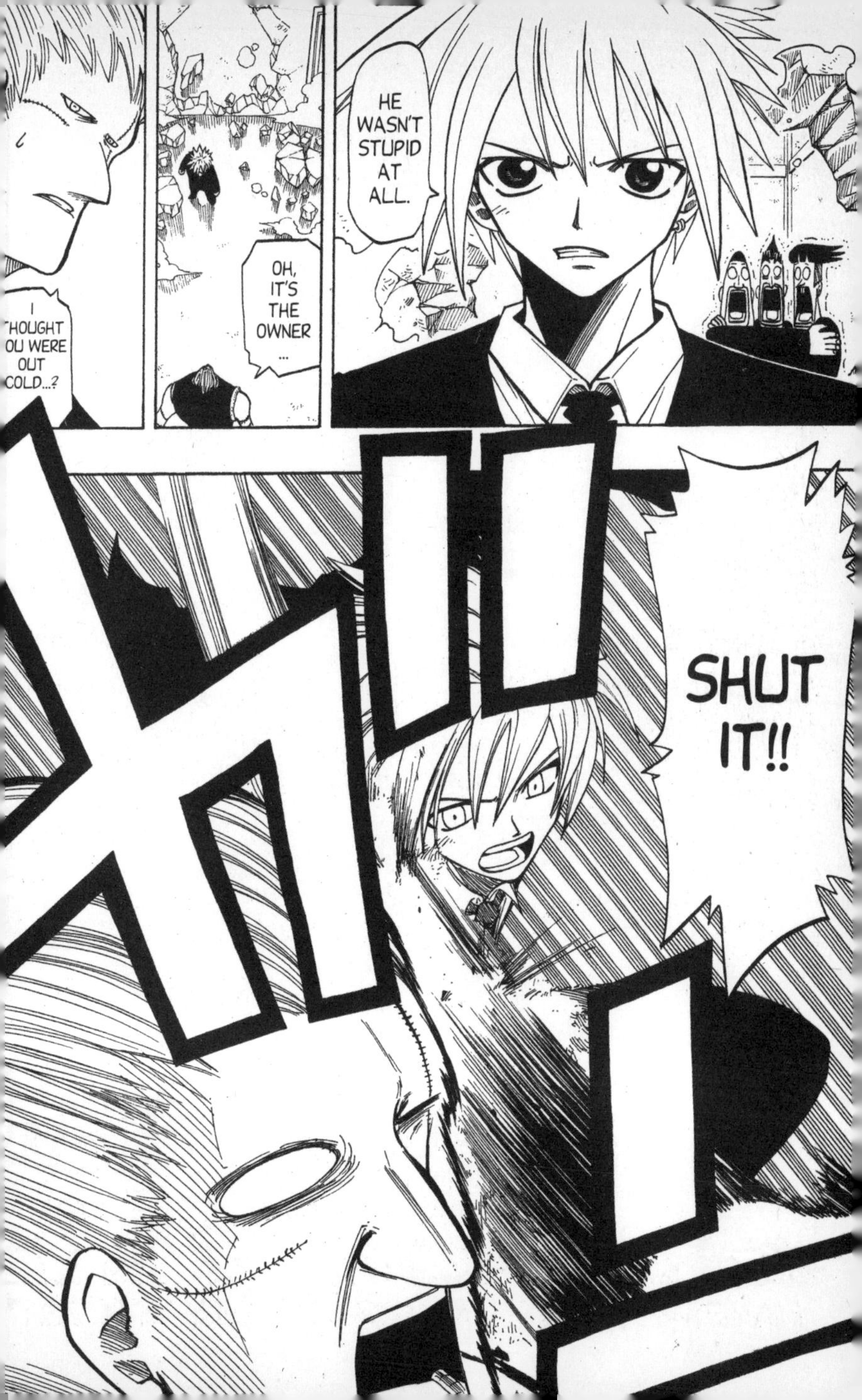
HE WASN'T STUPID AT ALL.
OH, IT'S THE OWNER ...
I HOUGHT OU WERE OUT COLD...?
SHUT IT!!

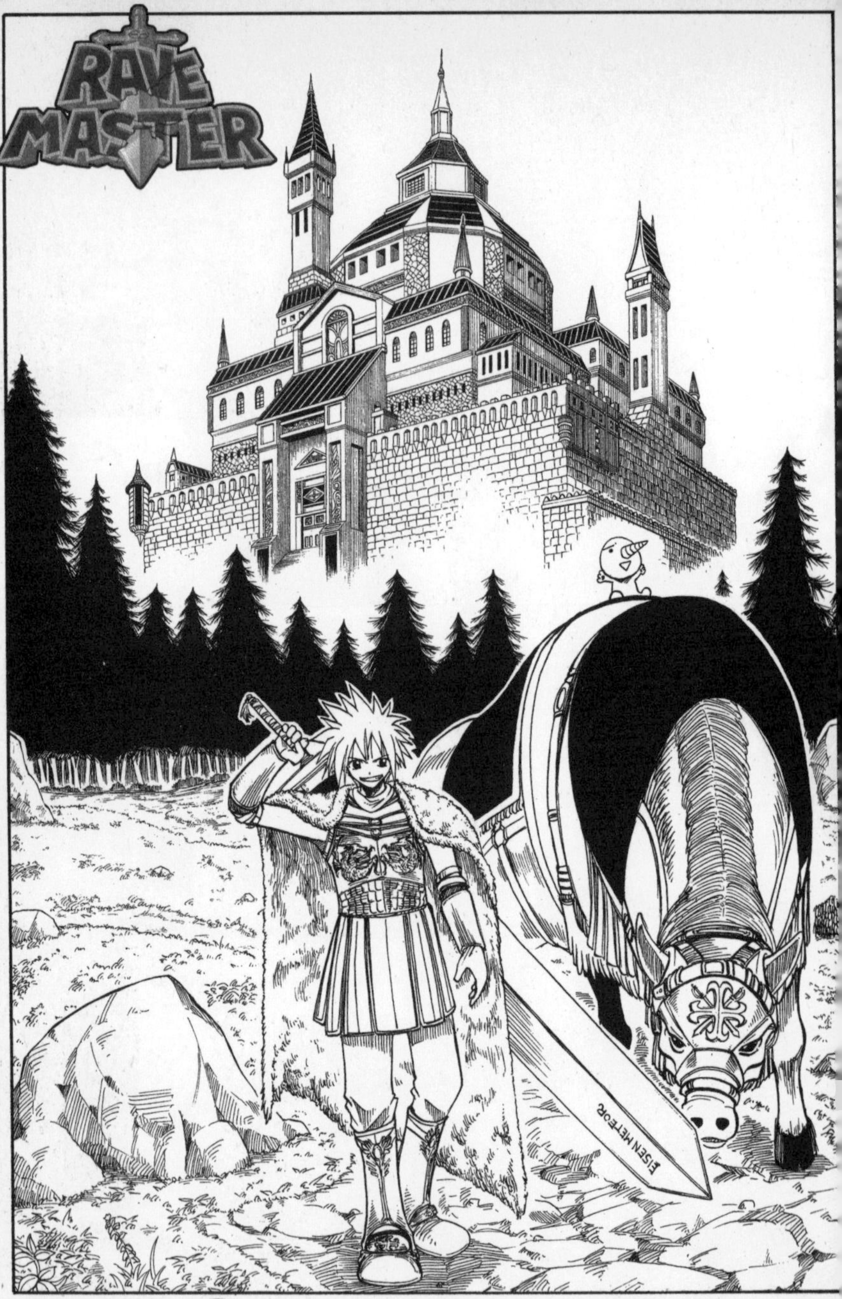
RAVE MASTER
EISEN METEOR

RAVE:78 ✠ THE COMING OF THE "STORM"

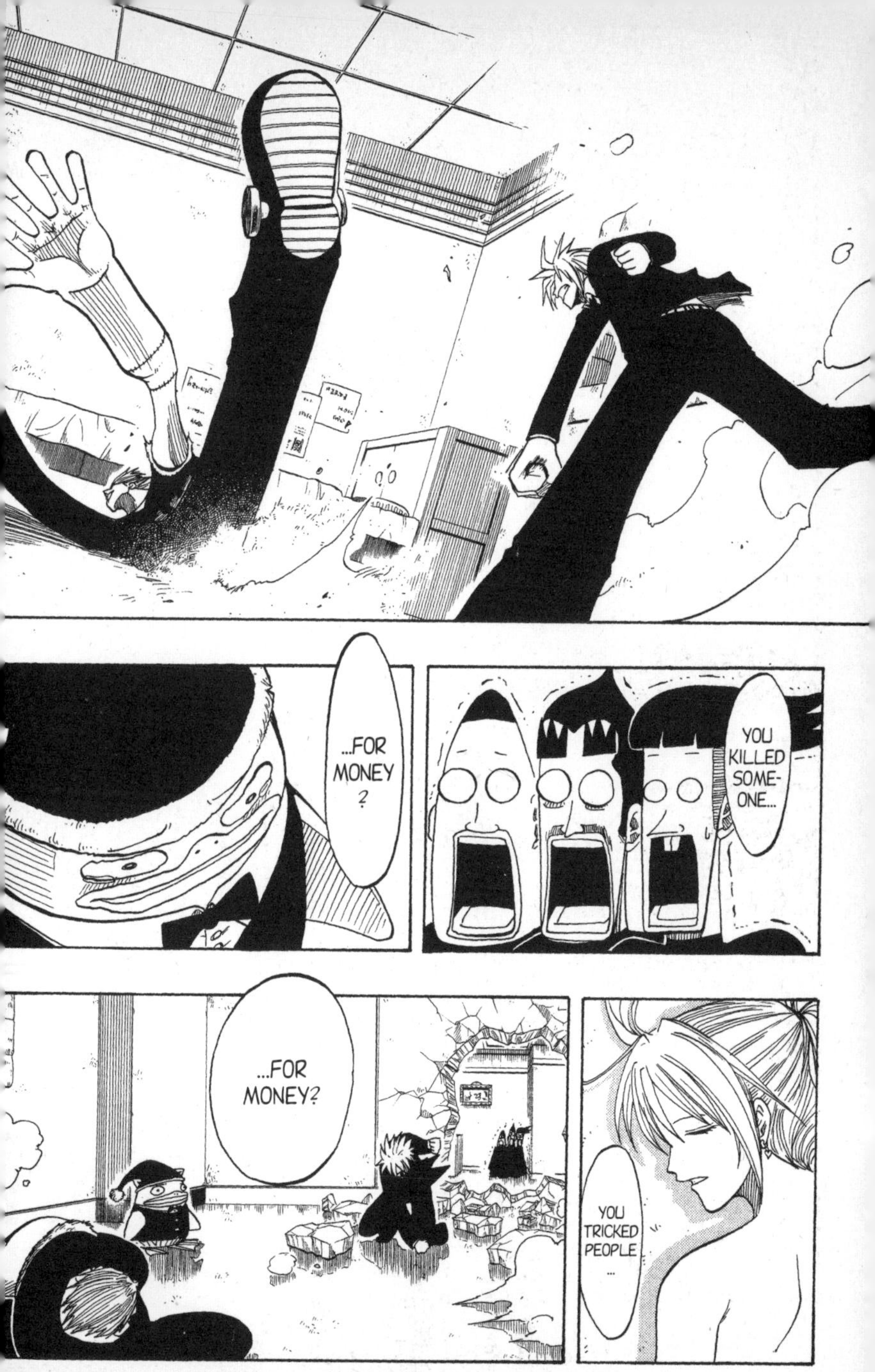
YOU KILLED SOME-ONE...
...FOR MONEY?
YOU TRICKED PEOPLE ...
...FOR MONEY?

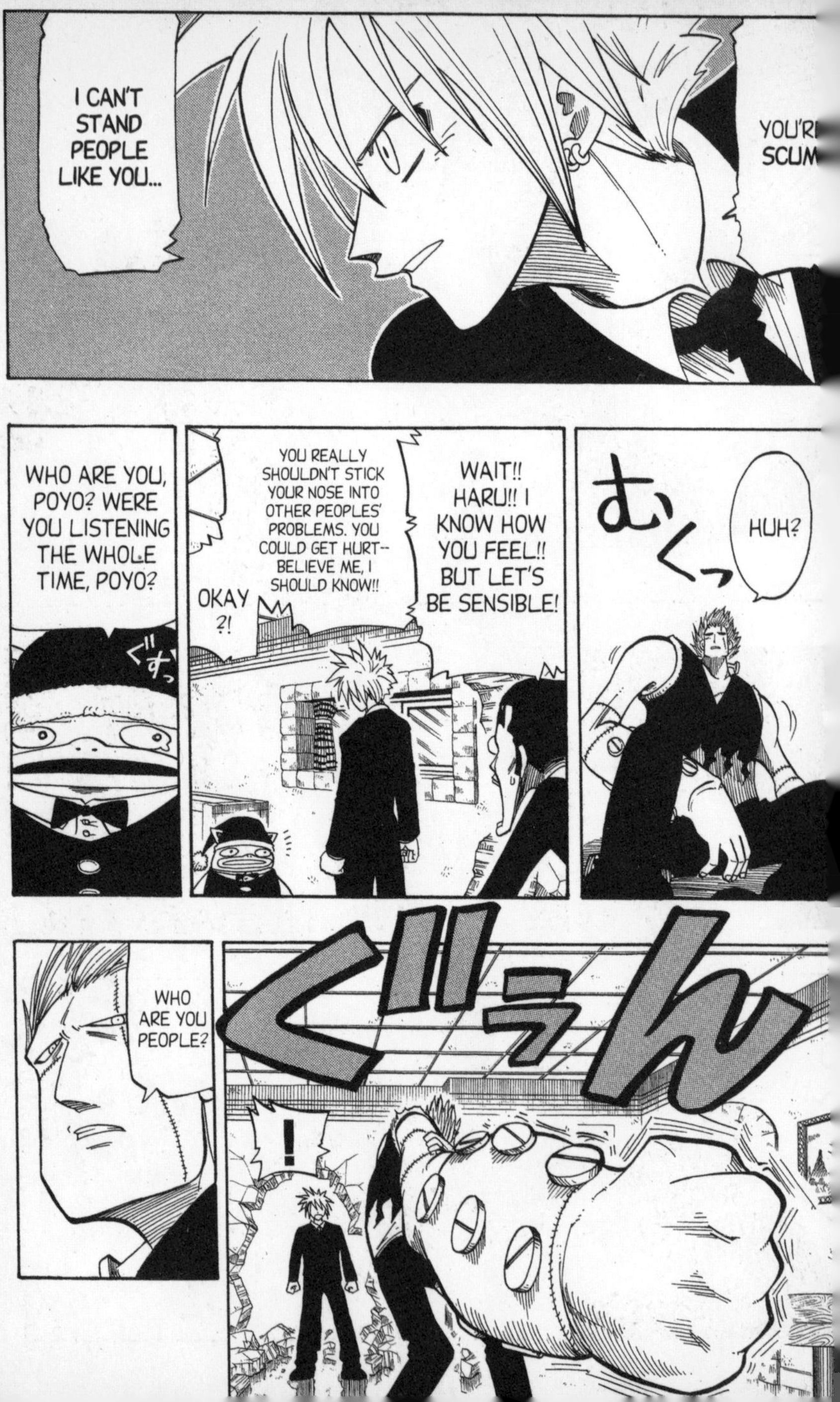
YOU'R
SCUM
I CAN'T STAND PEOPLE LIKE YOU...
むくっ
HUH?
WAIT!! HARU!! I KNOW HOW YOU FEEL!! BUT LET'S BE SENSIBLE!
YOU REALLY SHOULDN'T STICK YOUR NOSE INTO OTHER PEOPLES' PROBLEMS. YOU COULD GET HURT-- BELIEVE ME, I SHOULD KNOW!!
OKAY?!
WHO ARE YOU, POYO? WERE YOU LISTENING THE WHOLE TIME, POYO?
ぐすっ
ぐらん
!
WHO ARE YOU PEOPLE?

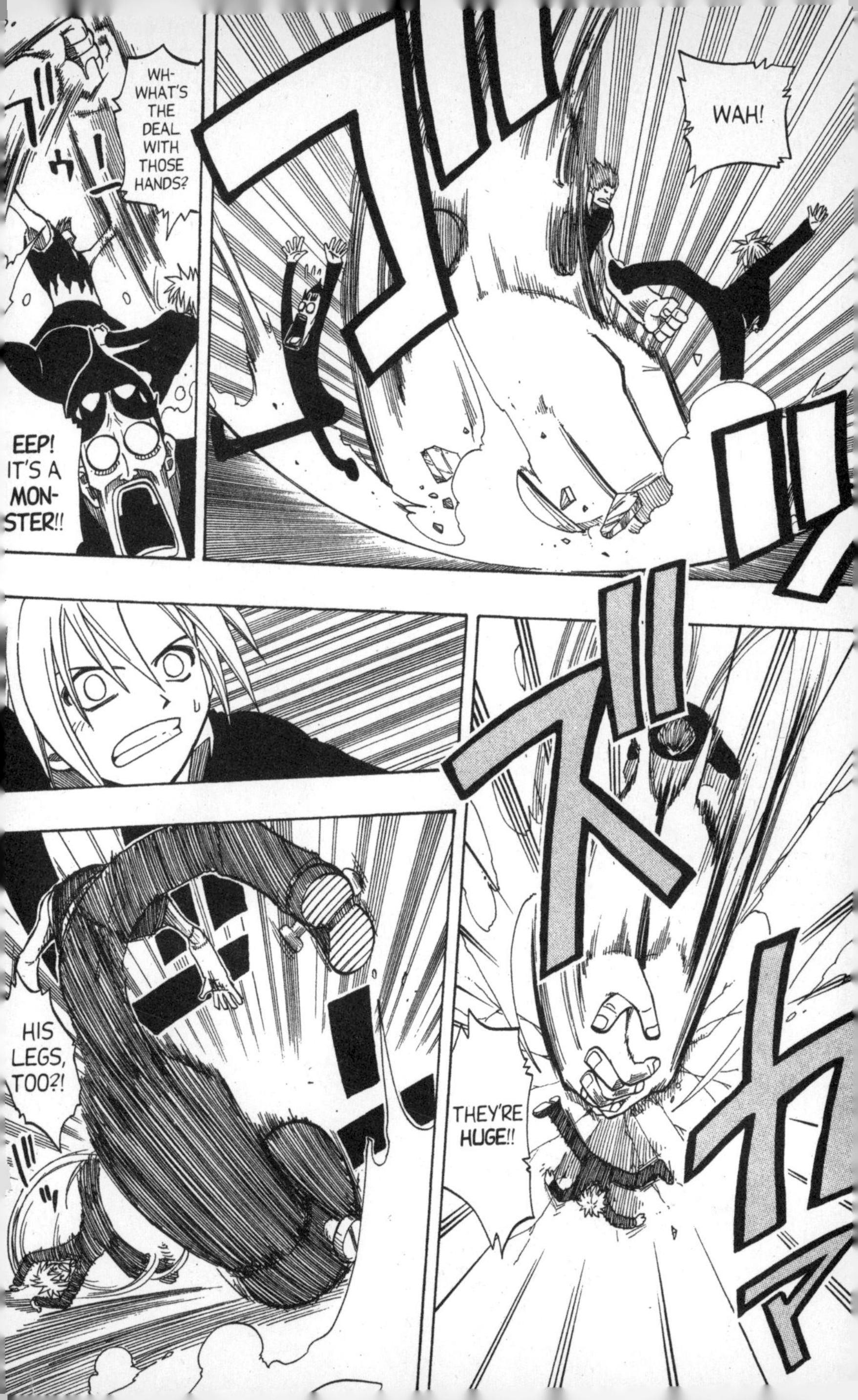
WAH!
WH-WHAT'S THE DEAL WITH THOSE HANDS?
EEP! IT'S A MON-STER!!
THEY'RE HUGE!!
HIS LEGS, TOO?!

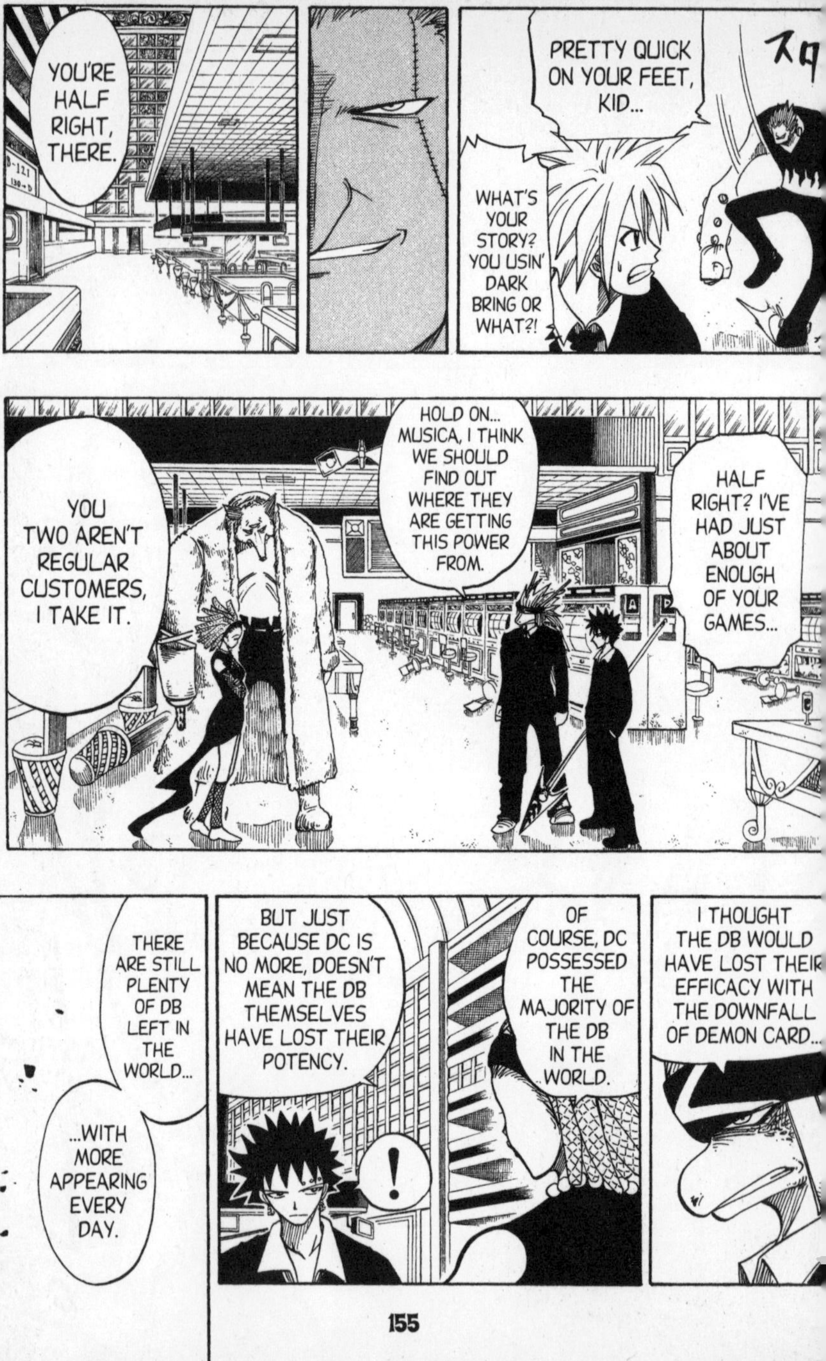
スロ
PRETTY QUICK ON YOUR FEET, KID...
WHAT'S YOUR STORY? YOU USIN' DARK BRING OR WHAT?!
YOU'RE HALF RIGHT, THERE.
HALF RIGHT? I'VE HAD JUST ABOUT ENOUGH OF YOUR GAMES...
HOLD ON... MUSICA, I THINK WE SHOULD FIND OUT WHERE THEY ARE GETTING THIS POWER FROM.
YOU TWO AREN'T REGULAR CUSTOMERS, I TAKE IT.
I THOUGHT THE DB WOULD HAVE LOST THEIR EFFICACY WITH THE DOWNFALL OF DEMON CARD...
OF COURSE, DC POSSESSED THE MAJORITY OF THE DB IN THE WORLD.
BUT JUST BECAUSE DC IS NO MORE, DOESN'T MEAN THE DB THEMSELVES HAVE LOST THEIR POTENCY.
!
THERE ARE STILL PLENTY OF DB LEFT IN THE WORLD...
...WITH MORE APPEARING EVERY DAY.

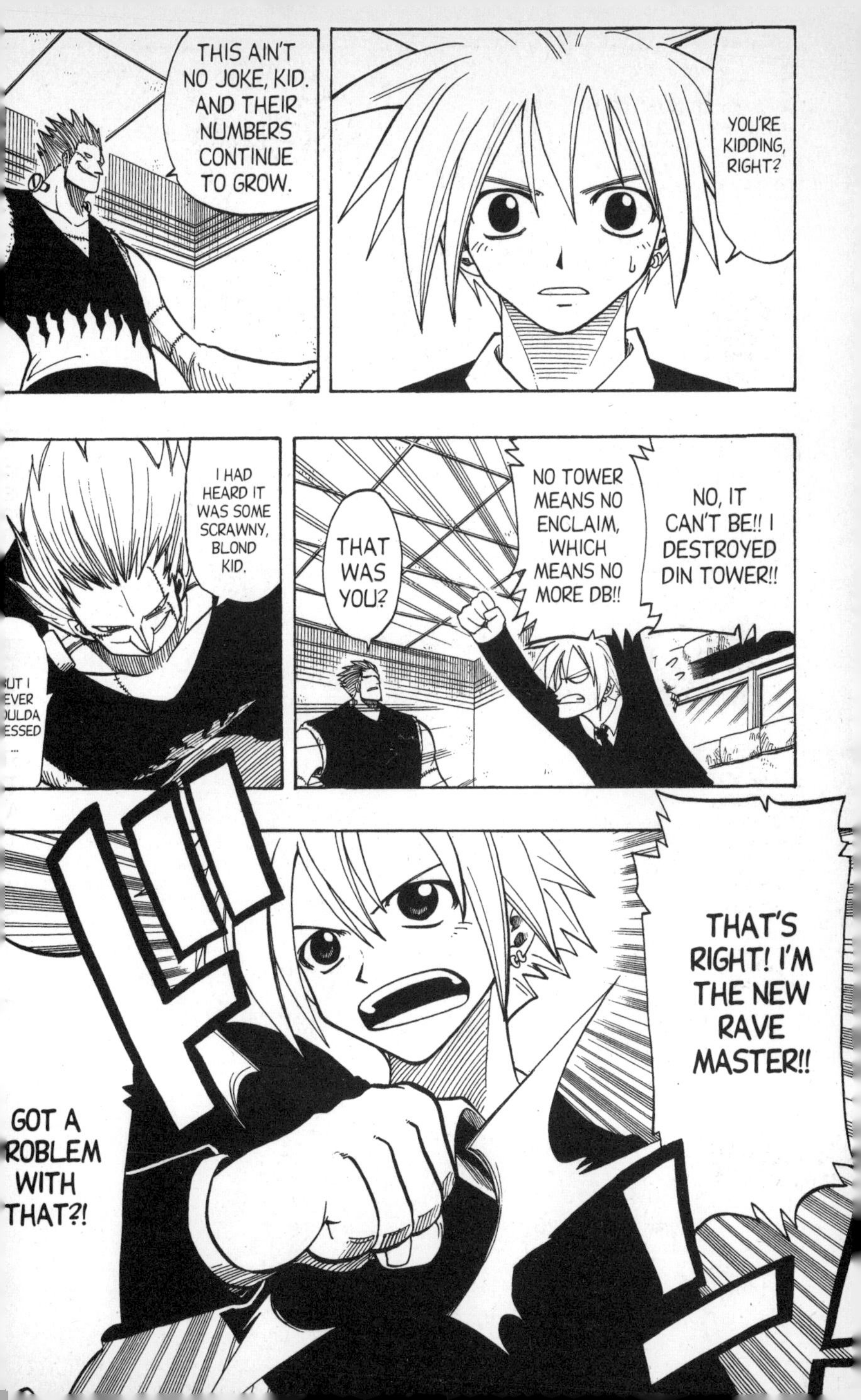
YOU'RE KIDDING, RIGHT?
THIS AIN'T NO JOKE, KID. AND THEIR NUMBERS CONTINUE TO GROW.
NO, IT CAN'T BE!! I DESTROYED DIN TOWER!!
NO TOWER MEANS NO ENCLAIM, WHICH MEANS NO MORE DB!!
THAT WAS YOU?
I HAD HEARD IT WAS SOME SCRAWNY, BLOND KID.
UT I EVER OULDA ESSED ...
THAT'S RIGHT! I'M THE NEW RAVE MASTER!!
GOT A ROBLEM WITH THAT?!

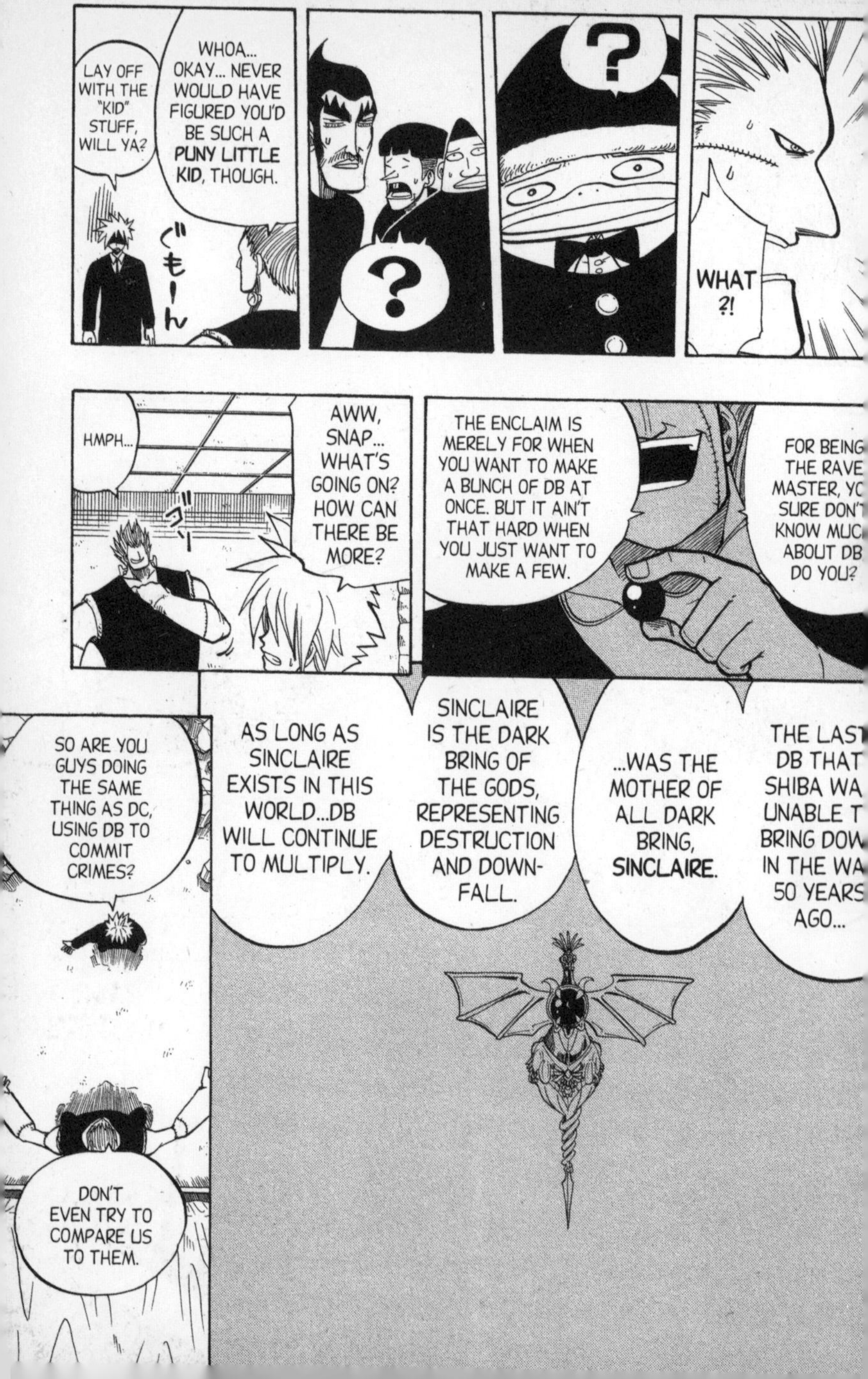
WHAT ?!
?
?
WHOA... OKAY... NEVER WOULD HAVE FIGURED YOU'D BE SUCH A **PUNY LITTLE KID**, THOUGH.
LAY OFF WITH THE "KID" STUFF, WILL YA?
ぐもーん
FOR BEING THE RAVE MASTER, YC SURE DON'T KNOW MUC ABOUT DB DO YOU?
THE ENCLAIM IS MERELY FOR WHEN YOU WANT TO MAKE A BUNCH OF DB AT ONCE. BUT IT AIN'T THAT HARD WHEN YOU JUST WANT TO MAKE A FEW.
AWW, SNAP... WHAT'S GOING ON? HOW CAN THERE BE MORE?
HMPH...
THE LAST DB THAT SHIBA WA UNABLE T BRING DOW IN THE WA 50 YEARS AGO...
...WAS THE MOTHER OF ALL DARK BRING, **SINCLAIRE**.
SINCLAIRE IS THE DARK BRING OF THE GODS, REPRESENTING DESTRUCTION AND DOWN-FALL.
AS LONG AS SINCLAIRE EXISTS IN THIS WORLD...DB WILL CONTINUE TO MULTIPLY.
SO ARE YOU GUYS DOING THE SAME THING AS DC, USING DB TO COMMIT CRIMES?
DON'T EVEN TRY TO COMPARE US TO THEM.

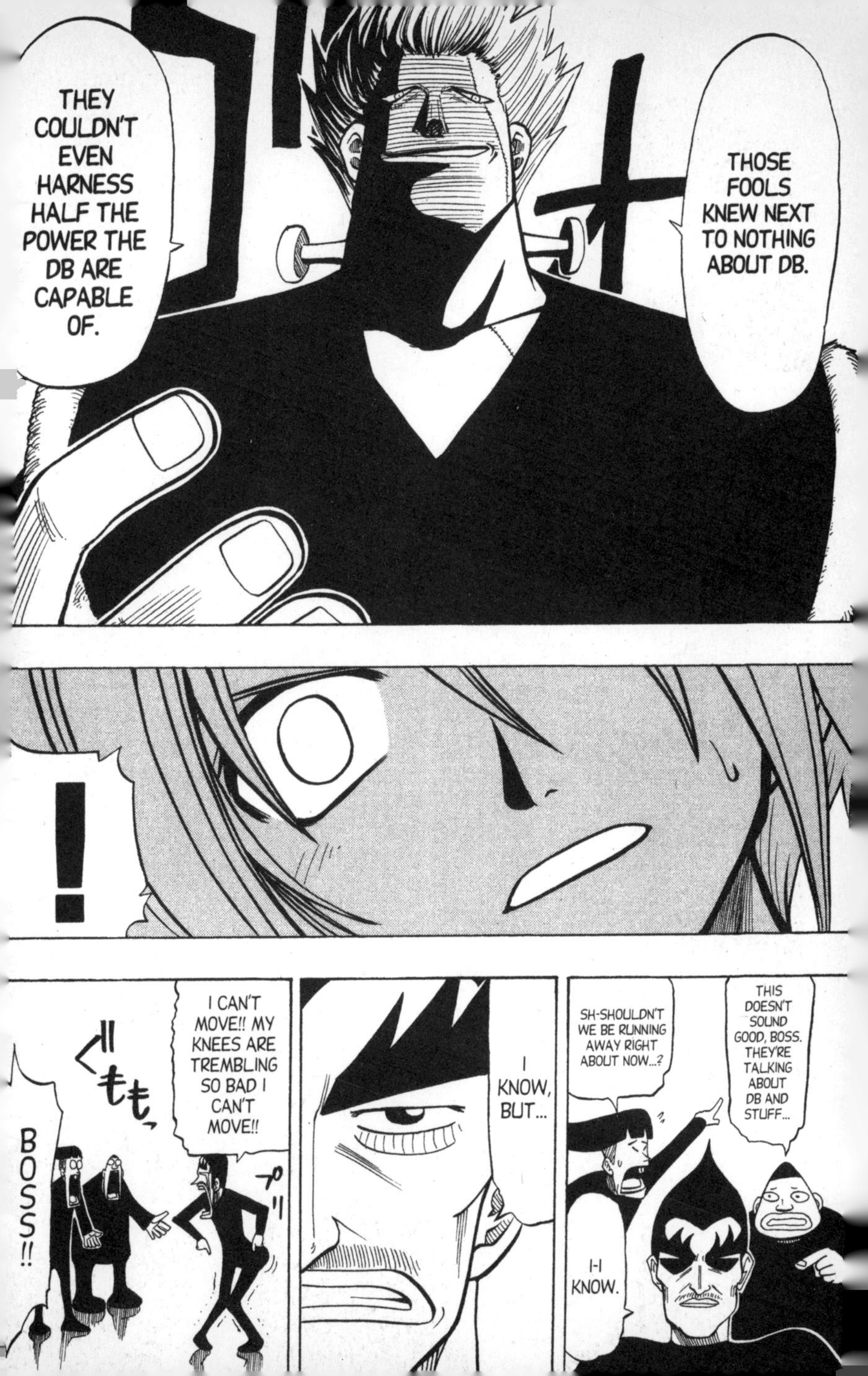
THOSE FOOLS KNEW NEXT TO NOTHING ABOUT DB.
THEY COULDN'T EVEN HARNESS HALF THE POWER THE DB ARE CAPABLE OF.
!
THIS DOESN'T SOUND GOOD, BOSS. THEY'RE TALKING ABOUT DB AND STUFF...
SH-SHOULDN'T WE BE RUNNING AWAY RIGHT ABOUT NOW...?
I-I KNOW.
I KNOW, BUT...
I CAN'T MOVE!! MY KNEES ARE TREMBLING SO BAD I CAN'T MOVE!!
BOSS!!

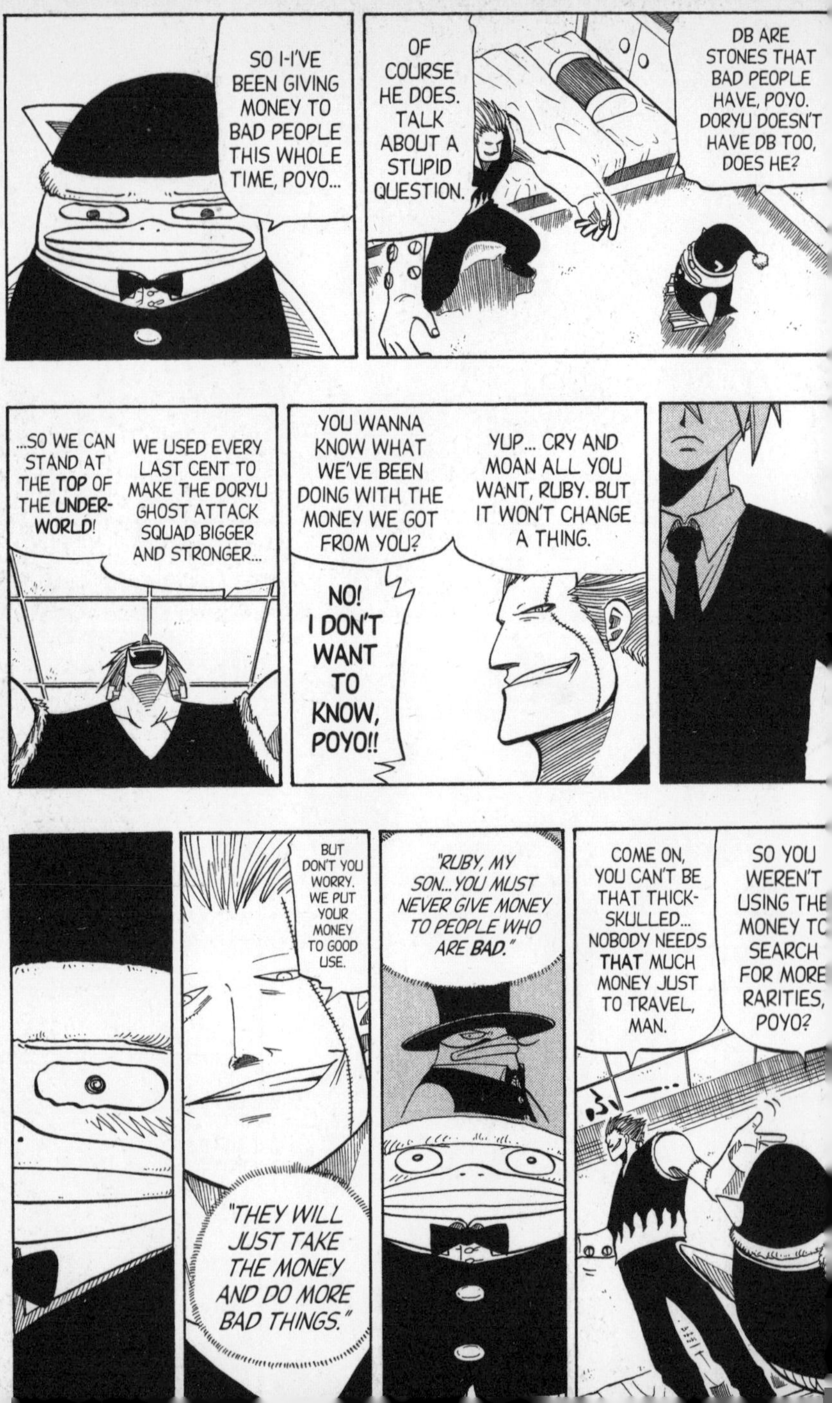
DB ARE STONES THAT BAD PEOPLE HAVE, POYO. DORYU DOESN'T HAVE DB TOO, DOES HE?
OF COURSE HE DOES. TALK ABOUT A STUPID QUESTION.
SO I-I'VE BEEN GIVING MONEY TO BAD PEOPLE THIS WHOLE TIME, POYO...
YUP... CRY AND MOAN ALL YOU WANT, RUBY. BUT IT WON'T CHANGE A THING.
YOU WANNA KNOW WHAT WE'VE BEEN DOING WITH THE MONEY WE GOT FROM YOU?
NO! I DON'T WANT TO KNOW, POYO!!
WE USED EVERY LAST CENT TO MAKE THE DORYU GHOST ATTACK SQUAD BIGGER AND STRONGER...
...SO WE CAN STAND AT THE TOP OF THE UNDERWORLD!
SO YOU WEREN'T USING THE MONEY TO SEARCH FOR MORE RARITIES, POYO?
COME ON, YOU CAN'T BE THAT THICK-SKULLED... NOBODY NEEDS THAT MUCH MONEY JUST TO TRAVEL, MAN.
"RUBY, MY SON... YOU MUST NEVER GIVE MONEY TO PEOPLE WHO ARE BAD."
BUT DON'T YOU WORRY. WE PUT YOUR MONEY TO GOOD USE.
"THEY WILL JUST TAKE THE MONEY AND DO MORE BAD THINGS."

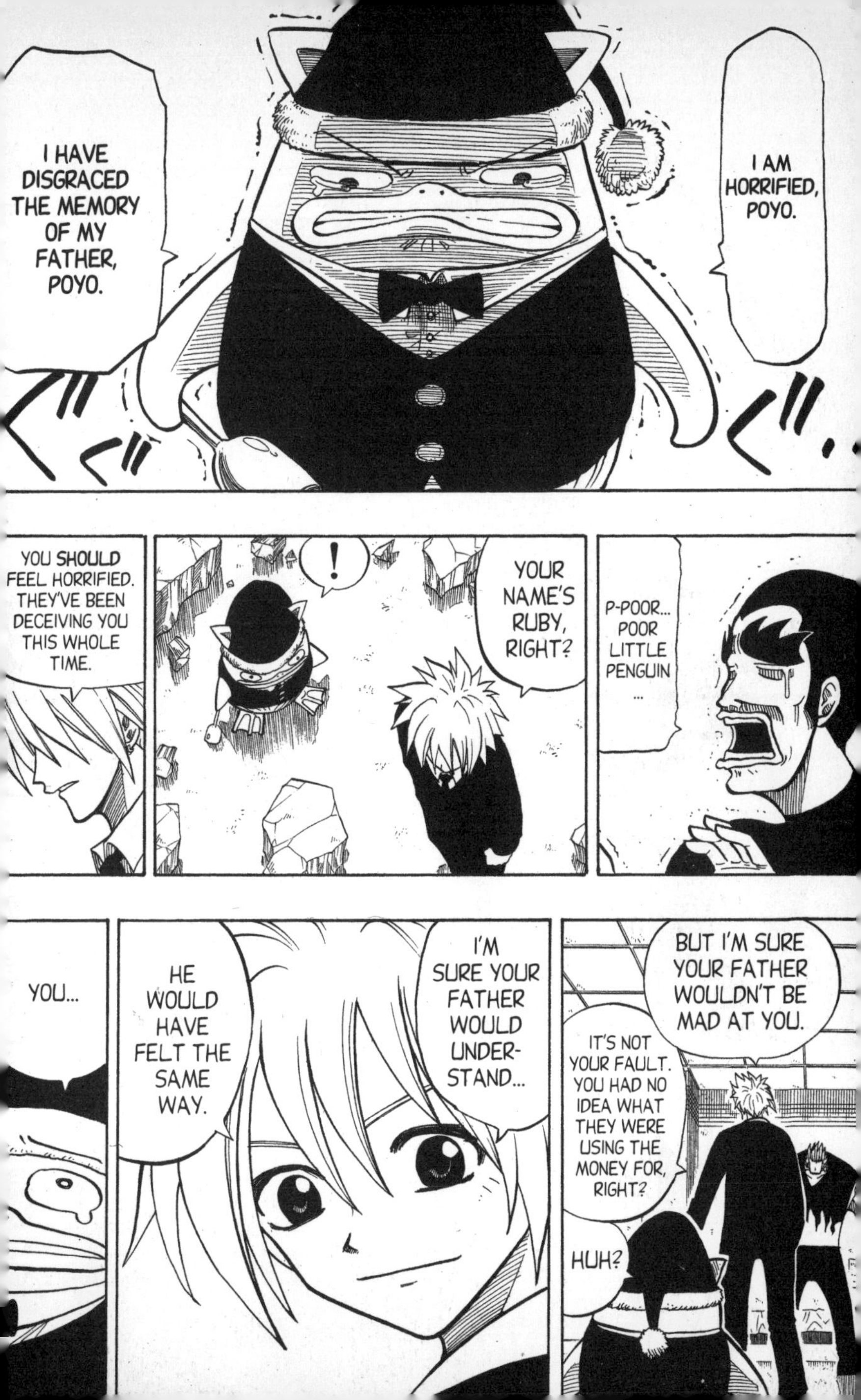
I AM HORRIFIED, POYO.
I HAVE DISGRACED THE MEMORY OF MY FATHER, POYO.
P-POOR... POOR LITTLE PENGUIN ...
!
YOUR NAME'S RUBY, RIGHT?
YOU **SHOULD** FEEL HORRIFIED. THEY'VE BEEN DECEIVING YOU THIS WHOLE TIME.
BUT I'M SURE YOUR FATHER WOULDN'T BE MAD AT YOU.
IT'S NOT YOUR FAULT. YOU HAD NO IDEA WHAT THEY WERE USING THE MONEY FOR, RIGHT?
HUH?
I'M SURE YOUR FATHER WOULD UNDER-STAND...
HE WOULD HAVE FELT THE SAME WAY.
YOU...

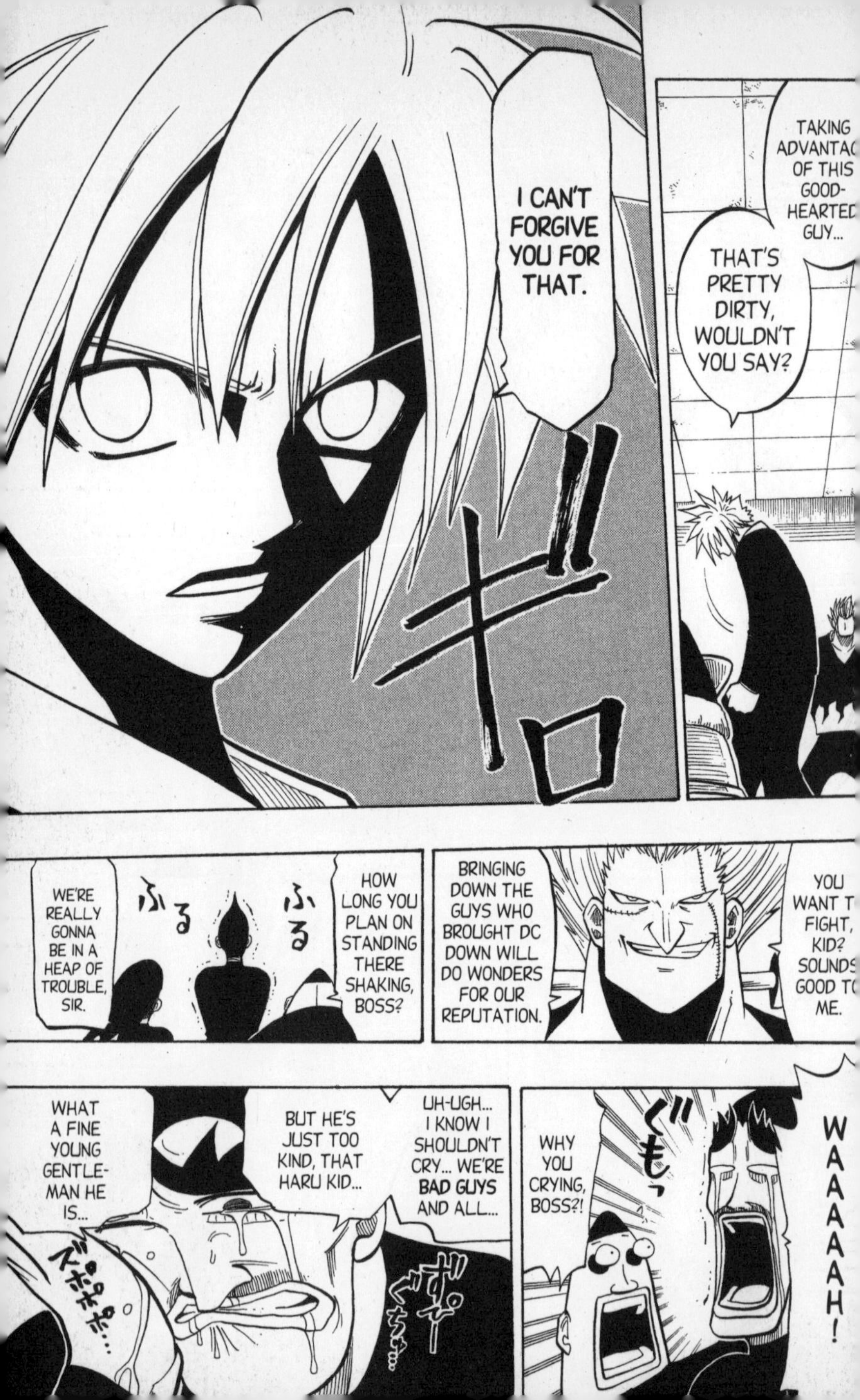
TAKING ADVANTAG OF THIS GOOD-HEARTED GUY...
THAT'S PRETTY DIRTY, WOULDN'T YOU SAY?
I CAN'T FORGIVE YOU FOR THAT.
ギロ
YOU WANT T FIGHT, KID? SOUNDS GOOD T ME.
BRINGING DOWN THE GUYS WHO BROUGHT DC DOWN WILL DO WONDERS FOR OUR REPUTATION.
HOW LONG YOU PLAN ON STANDING THERE SHAKING, BOSS?
ふる
ふる
WE'RE REALLY GONNA BE IN A HEAP OF TROUBLE, SIR.
WAAAAAH!
ぐもっ
WHY YOU CRYING, BOSS?!
UH-UGH... I KNOW I SHOULDN'T CRY... WE'RE **BAD GUYS** AND ALL...
BUT HE'S JUST TOO KIND, THAT HARU KID...
WHAT A FINE YOUNG GENTLE-MAN HE IS...
ずぴー
ぐちゅ...
ズポポポ...

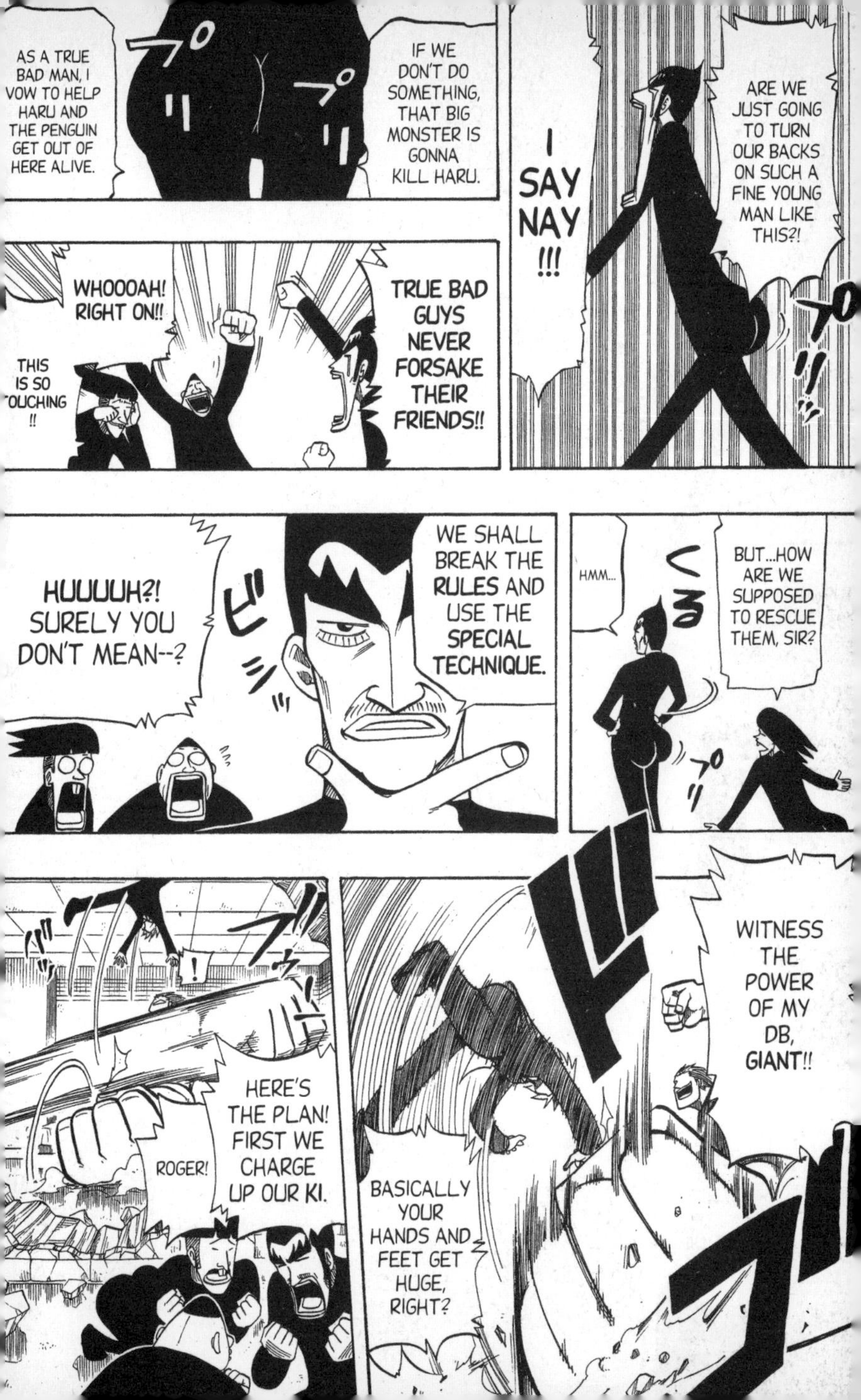
I SAY NAY !!!
ARE WE JUST GOING TO TURN OUR BACKS ON SUCH A FINE YOUNG MAN LIKE THIS?!
IF WE DON'T DO SOMETHING, THAT BIG MONSTER IS GONNA KILL HARU.
AS A TRUE BAD MAN, I VOW TO HELP HARU AND THE PENGUIN GET OUT OF HERE ALIVE.
TRUE BAD GUYS NEVER FORSAKE THEIR FRIENDS!!
WHOOOAH! RIGHT ON!!
THIS IS SO OUCHING !!
BUT...HOW ARE WE SUPPOSED TO RESCUE THEM, SIR?
HMM...
WE SHALL BREAK THE RULES AND USE THE SPECIAL TECHNIQUE.
HUUUUH?! SURELY YOU DON'T MEAN--?
WITNESS THE POWER OF MY DB, GIANT!!
BASICALLY YOUR HANDS AND FEET GET HUGE, RIGHT?
HERE'S THE PLAN! FIRST WE CHARGE UP OUR KI.
ROGER!

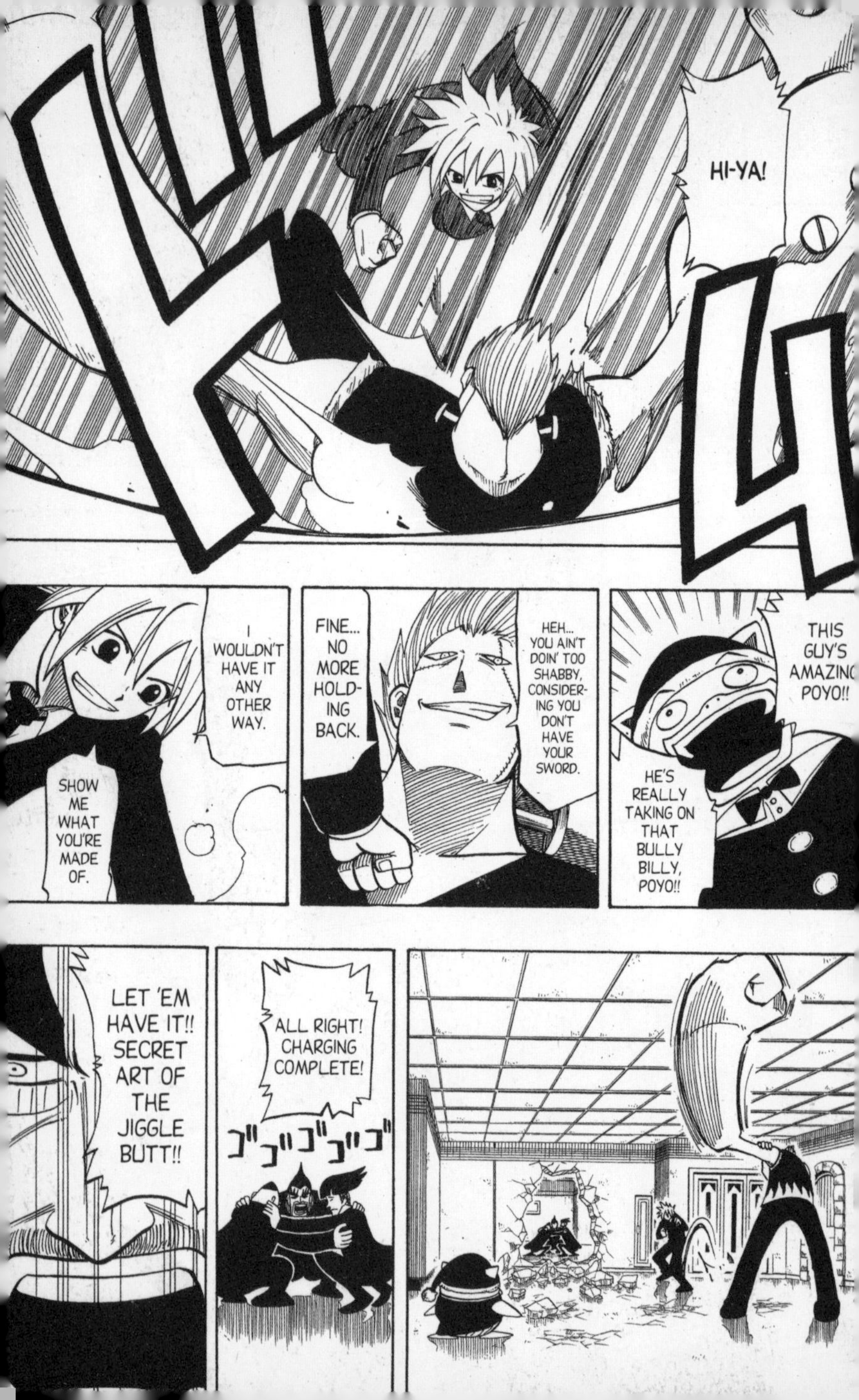
HI-YA!
THIS GUY'S AMAZING POYO!!
HE'S REALLY TAKING ON THAT BULLY BILLY, POYO!!
HEH... YOU AIN'T DOIN' TOO SHABBY, CONSIDERING YOU DON'T HAVE YOUR SWORD.
FINE... NO MORE HOLDING BACK.
I WOULDN'T HAVE IT ANY OTHER WAY.
SHOW ME WHAT YOU'RE MADE OF.
ALL RIGHT! CHARGING COMPLETE!
ゴゴゴゴゴ
LET 'EM HAVE IT!! SECRET ART OF THE JIGGLE BUTT!!

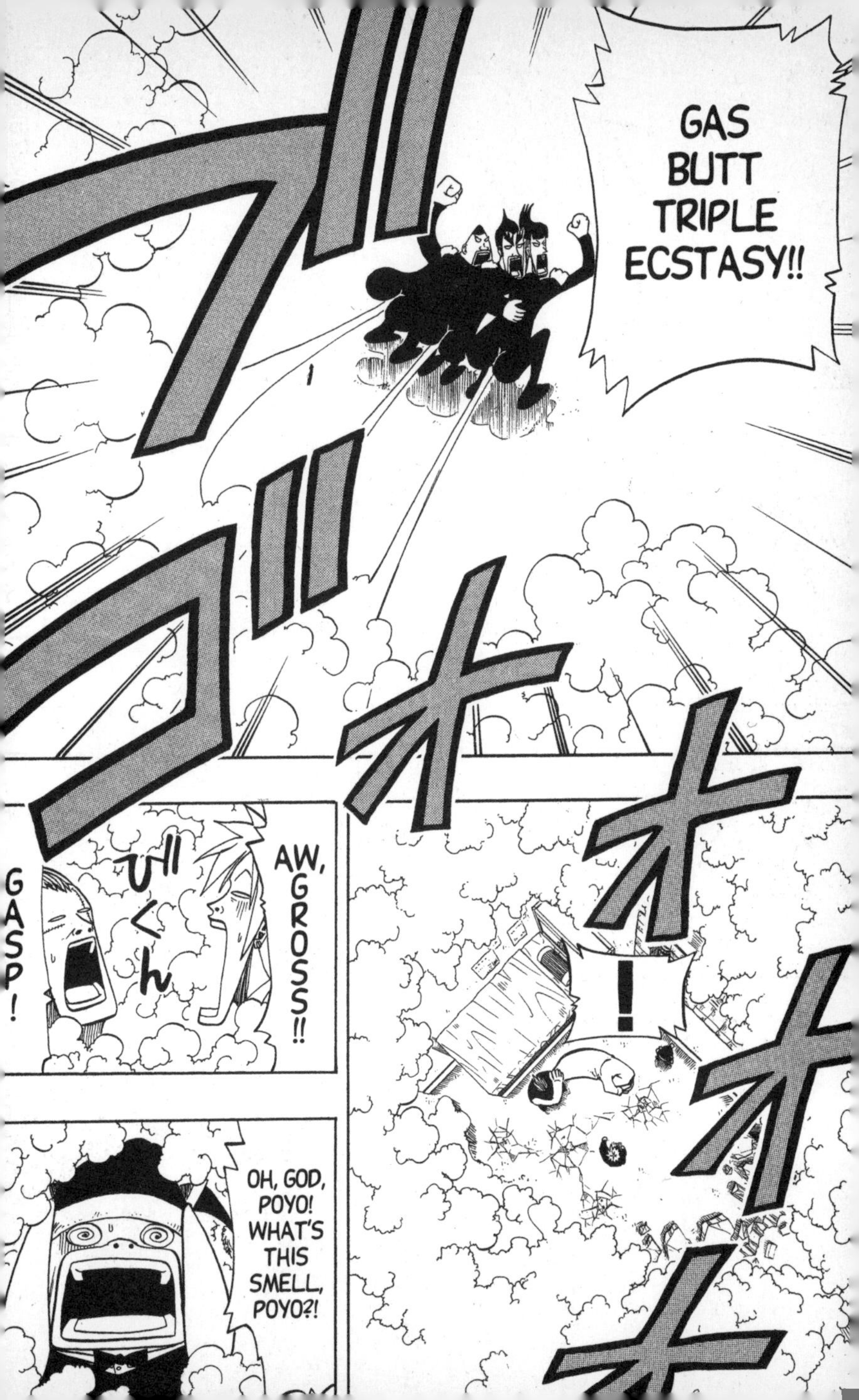
GAS BUTT TRIPLE ECSTASY!!
ブ
ゴオオオオ
!
AW, GROSS!!
GASP!
OH, GOD, POYO! WHAT'S THIS SMELL, POYO?!

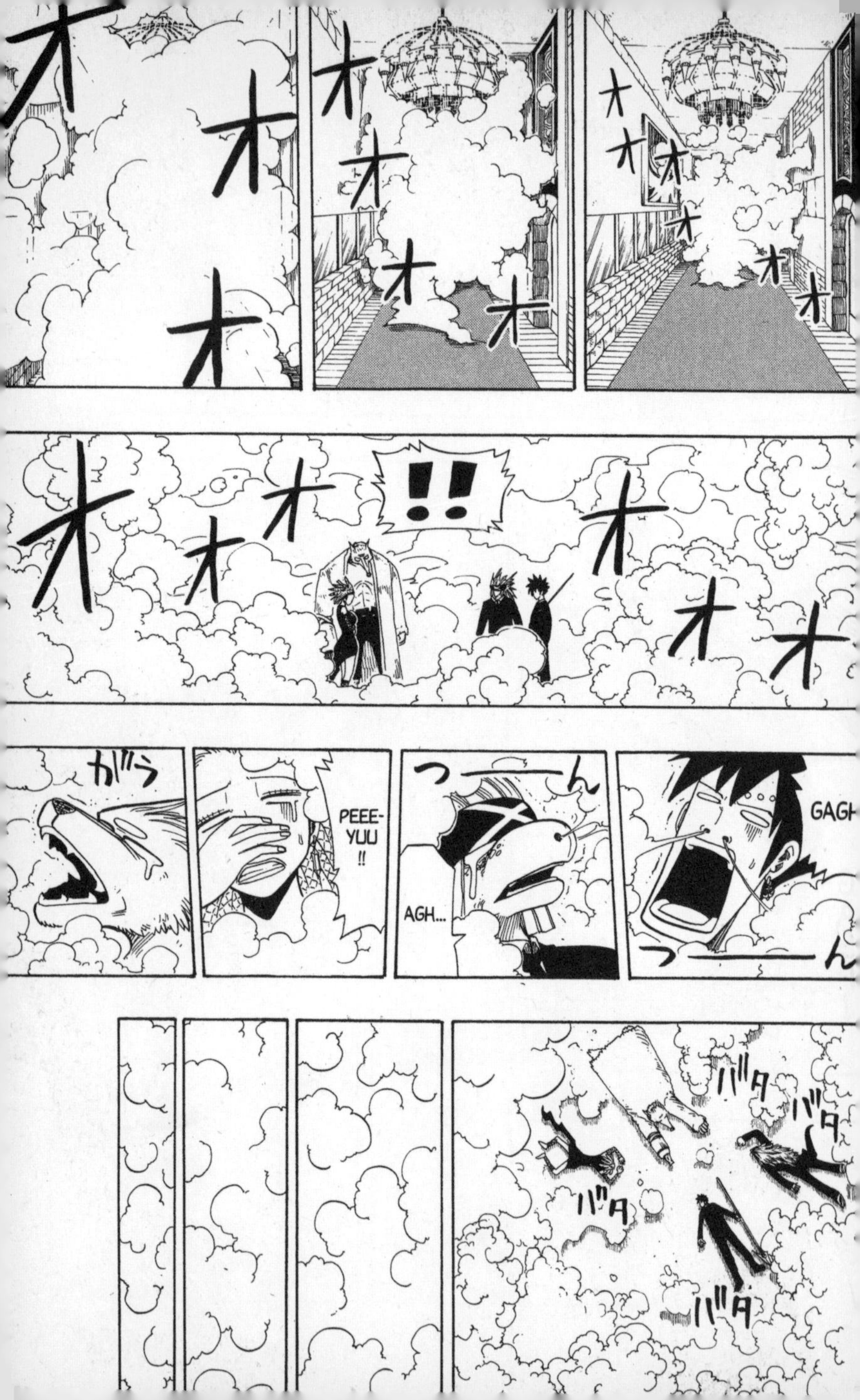

オオオオオオ
オオオオ
オオオ
!!
オオオオオ
GAGH
つーーん
つーーん
AGH...
PEEE-YUU !!
バタ
バタ
バタ
バタ

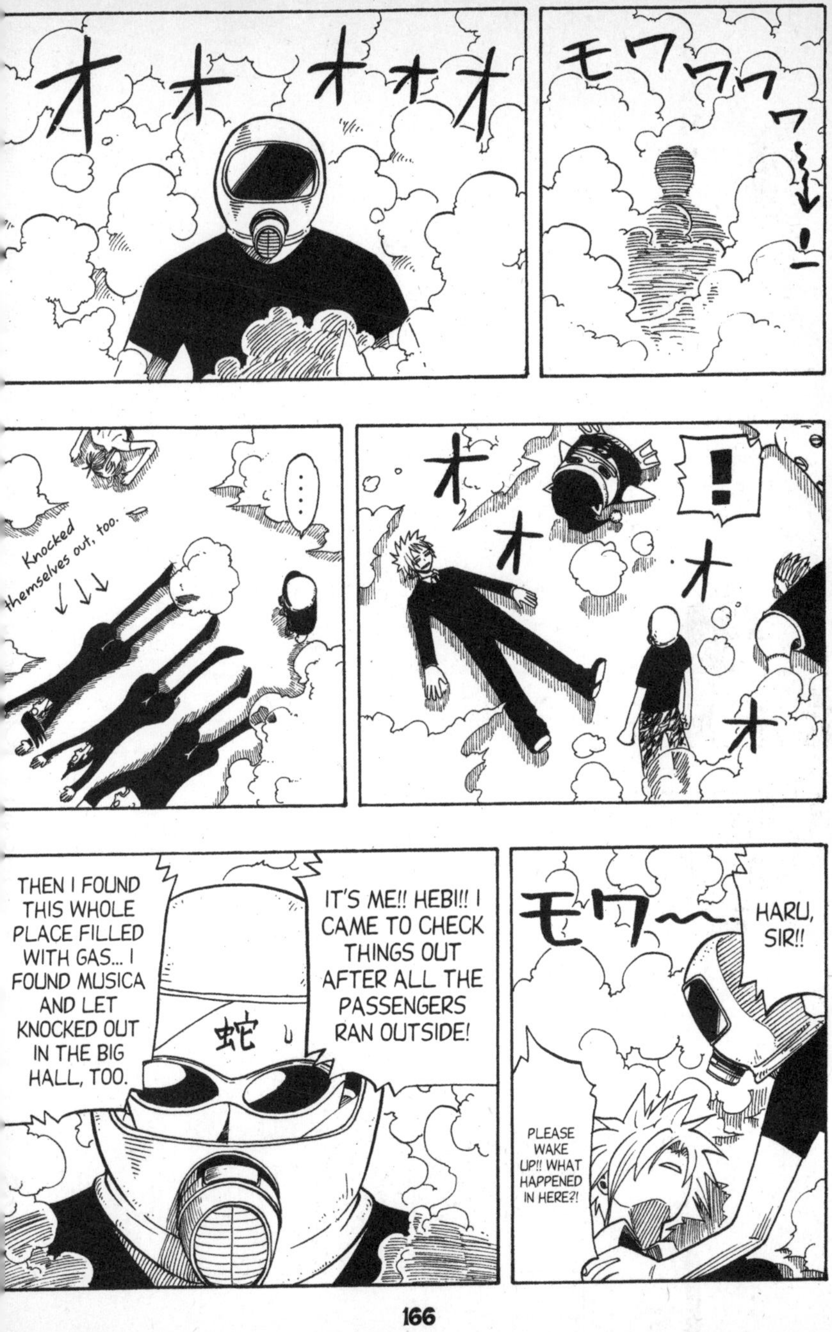
モワワワワ
!
オオオオオ
オ
!
オ
オ
オ
...
Knocked themselves out, too.
モワ~~
HARU, SIR!!
PLEASE WAKE UP!! WHAT HAPPENED IN HERE?!
IT'S ME!! HEBI!! I CAME TO CHECK THINGS OUT AFTER ALL THE PASSENGERS RAN OUTSIDE!
THEN I FOUND THIS WHOLE PLACE FILLED WITH GAS... I FOUND MUSICA AND LET KNOCKED OUT IN THE BIG HALL, TOO.
蛇

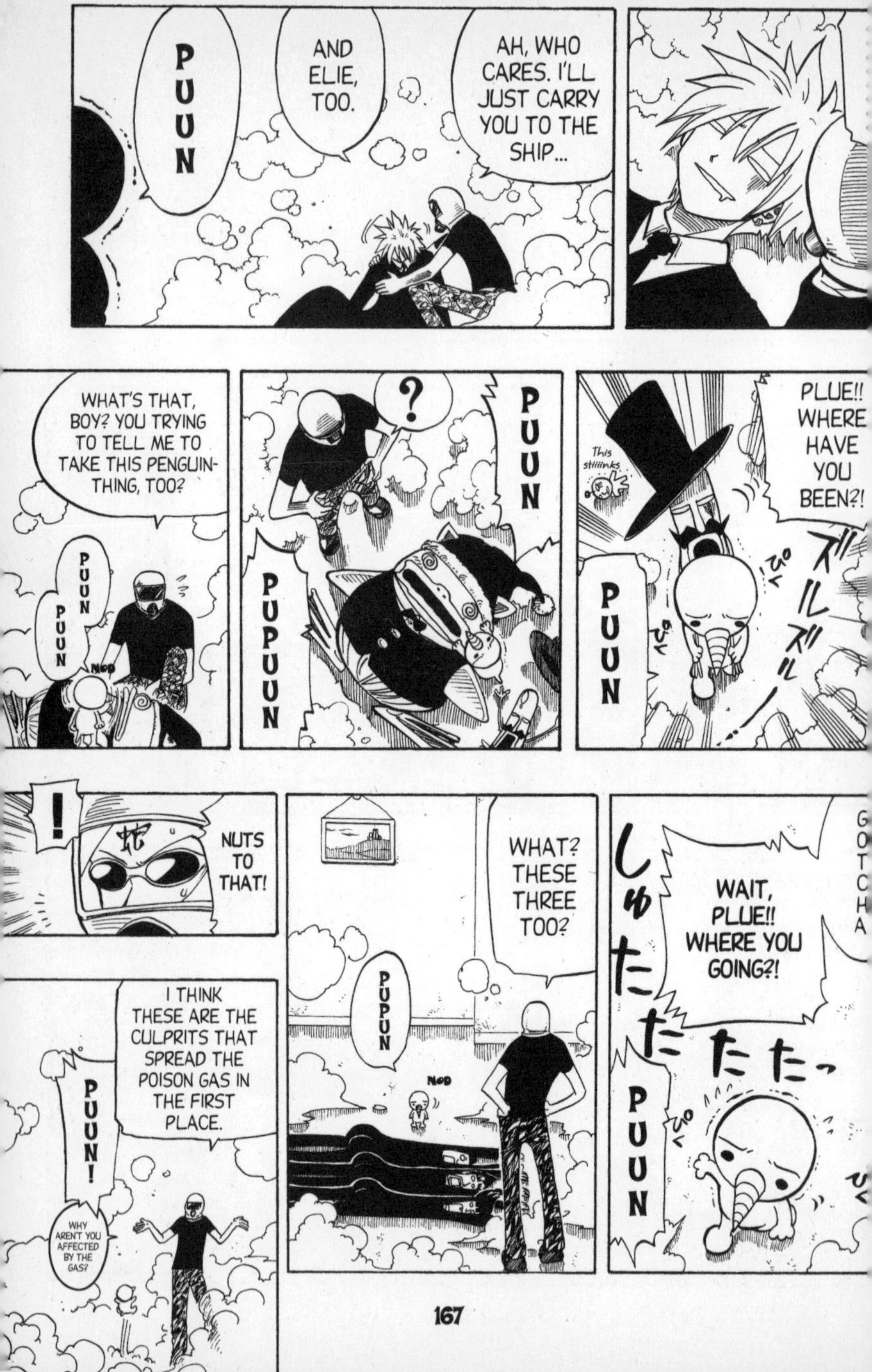
AH, WHO CARES. I'LL JUST CARRY YOU TO THE SHIP...
AND ELIE, TOO.
PUUN
PLUE!! WHERE HAVE YOU BEEN?!
This stiiiinks.
PUUN
PUUN
?
PUPUUN
WHAT'S THAT, BOY? YOU TRYING TO TELL ME TO TAKE THIS PENGUIN-THING, TOO?
PUUN
PUUN
NOD
GOTCHA
WAIT, PLUE!! WHERE YOU GOING?!
しゅたたたたっ
PUUN
WHAT? THESE THREE TOO?
PUPUN
NOD
!
NUTS TO THAT!
I THINK THESE ARE THE CULPRITS THAT SPREAD THE POISON GAS IN THE FIRST PLACE.
PUUN!
WHY AREN'T YOU AFFECTED BY THE GAS?

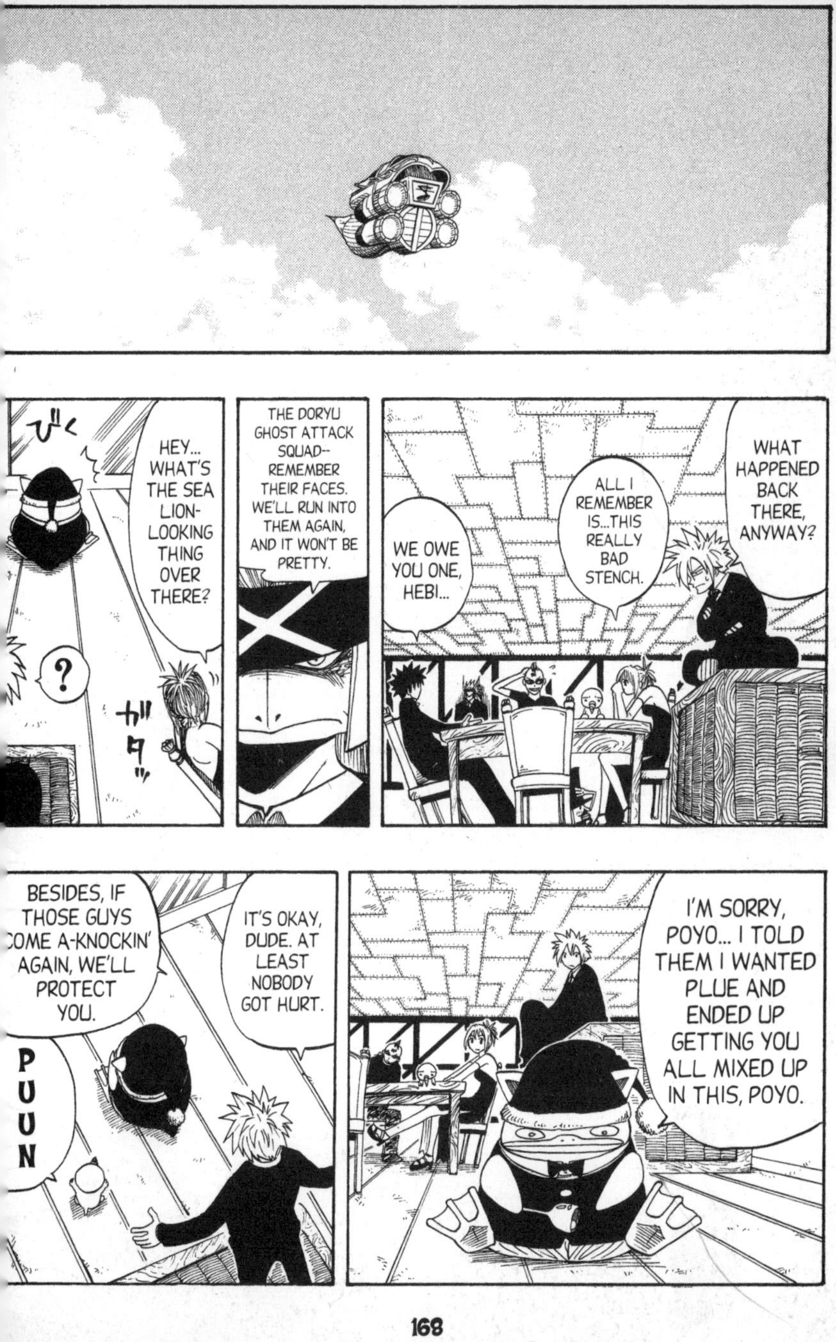

WHAT HAPPENED BACK THERE, ANYWAY?
ALL I REMEMBER IS...THIS REALLY BAD STENCH.
WE OWE YOU ONE, HEBI...
THE DORYU GHOST ATTACK SQUAD--REMEMBER THEIR FACES. WE'LL RUN INTO THEM AGAIN, AND IT WON'T BE PRETTY.
HEY... WHAT'S THE SEA LION-LOOKING THING OVER THERE?
?
I'M SORRY, POYO... I TOLD THEM I WANTED PLUE AND ENDED UP GETTING YOU ALL MIXED UP IN THIS, POYO.
IT'S OKAY, DUDE. AT LEAST NOBODY GOT HURT.
BESIDES, IF THOSE GUYS COME A-KNOCKIN' AGAIN, WE'LL PROTECT YOU.
PUUN

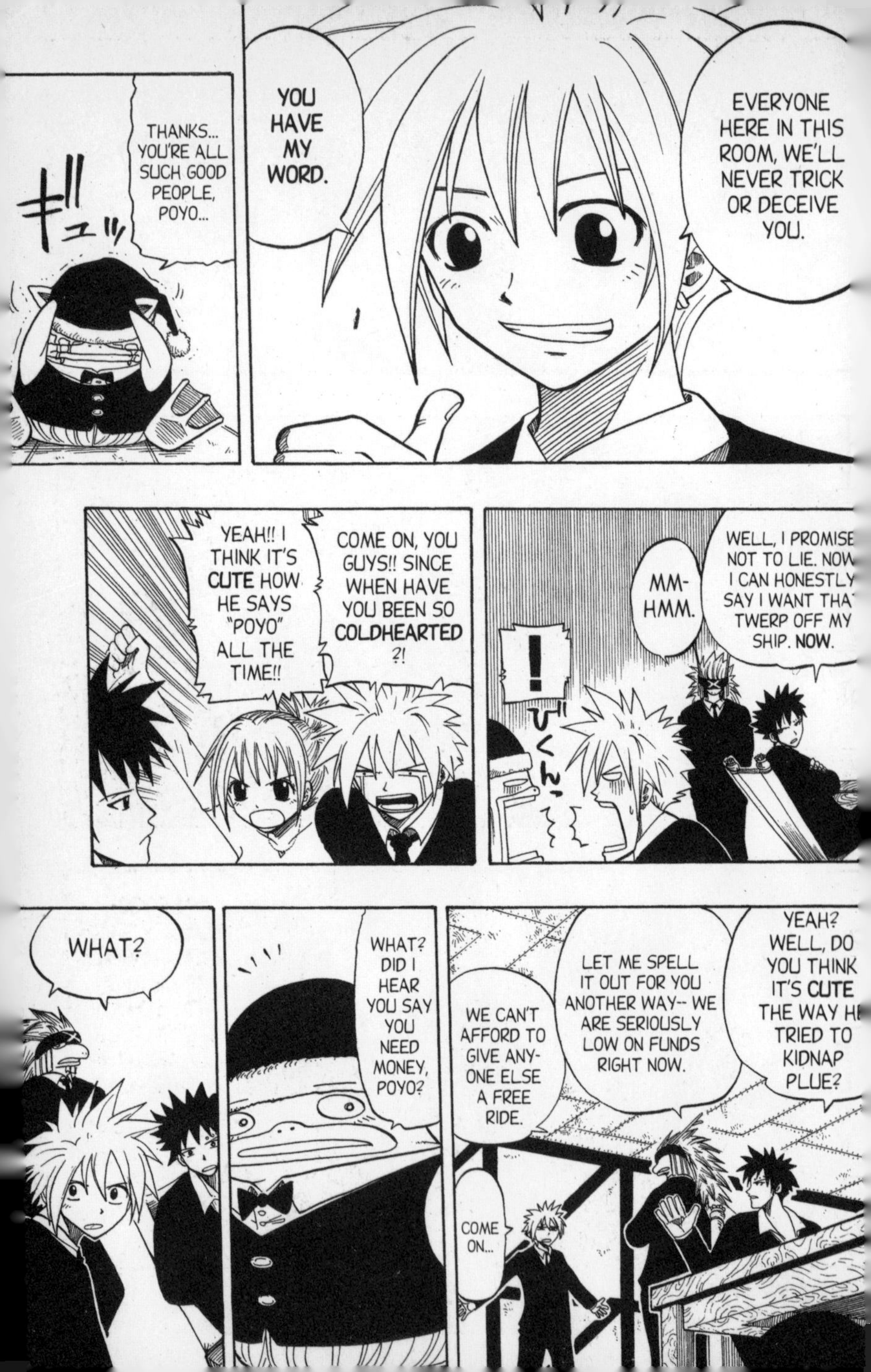

EVERYONE HERE IN THIS ROOM, WE'LL NEVER TRICK OR DECEIVE YOU.
YOU HAVE MY WORD.
THANKS... YOU'RE ALL SUCH GOOD PEOPLE, POYO...
ギュッ
WELL, I PROMISE NOT TO LIE. NOW I CAN HONESTLY SAY I WANT THA TWERP OFF MY SHIP. **NOW.**
MM-HMM.
!
びくんっ
COME ON, YOU GUYS!! SINCE WHEN HAVE YOU BEEN SO **COLDHEARTED**?!
YEAH!! I THINK IT'S **CUTE** HOW HE SAYS "POYO" ALL THE TIME!!
YEAH? WELL, DO YOU THINK IT'S **CUTE** THE WAY H TRIED TO KIDNAP PLUE?
LET ME SPELL IT OUT FOR YOU ANOTHER WAY-- WE ARE SERIOUSLY LOW ON FUNDS RIGHT NOW.
WE CAN'T AFFORD TO GIVE ANY-ONE ELSE A FREE RIDE.
COME ON...
WHAT? DID I HEAR YOU SAY YOU NEED MONEY, POYO?
WHAT?

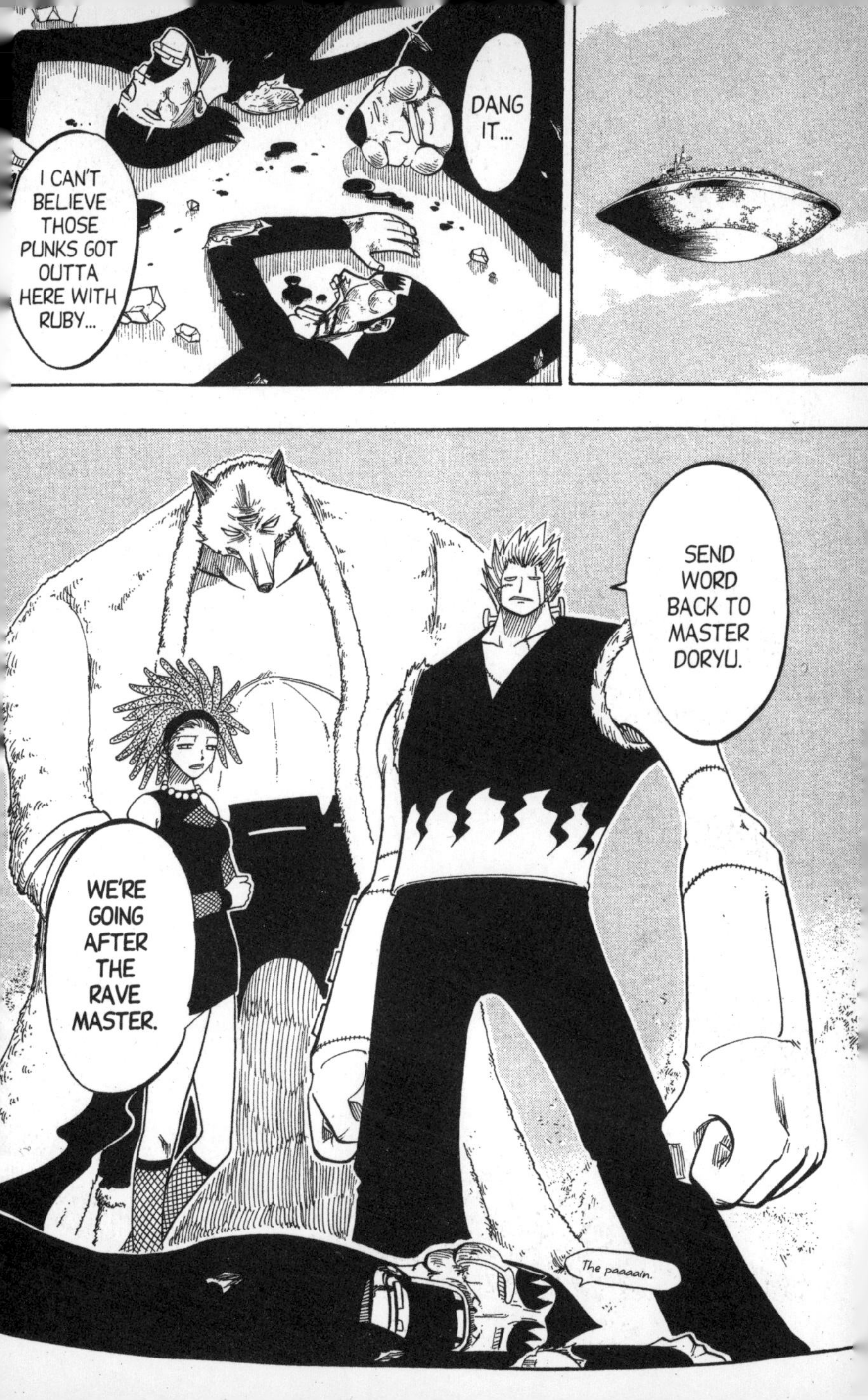
DANG IT...
I CAN'T BELIEVE THOSE PUNKS GOT OUTTA HERE WITH RUBY...
SEND WORD BACK TO MASTER DORYU.
WE'RE GOING AFTER THE RAVE MASTER.
The paaaain.

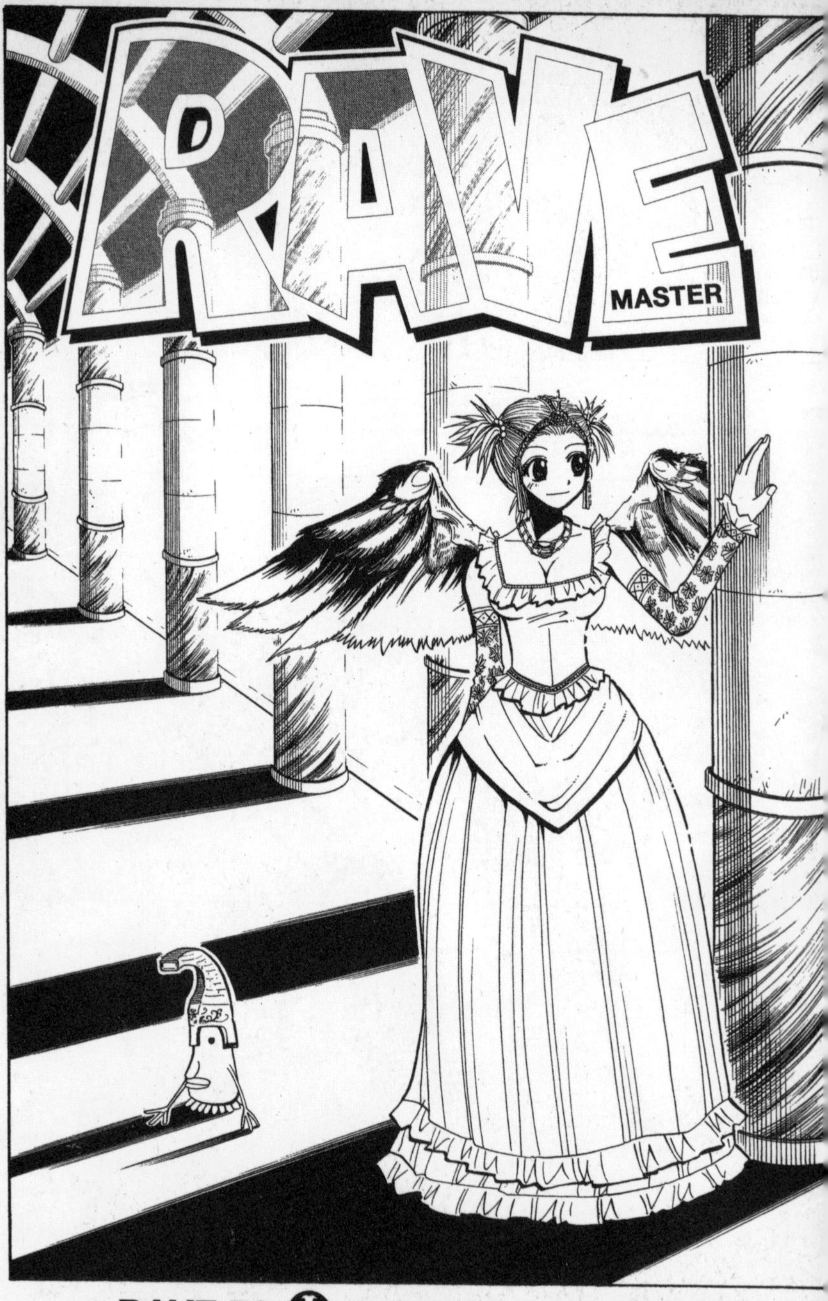
RAVE
MASTER

RAVE:79 ✠ BUSTING THROUGH!!

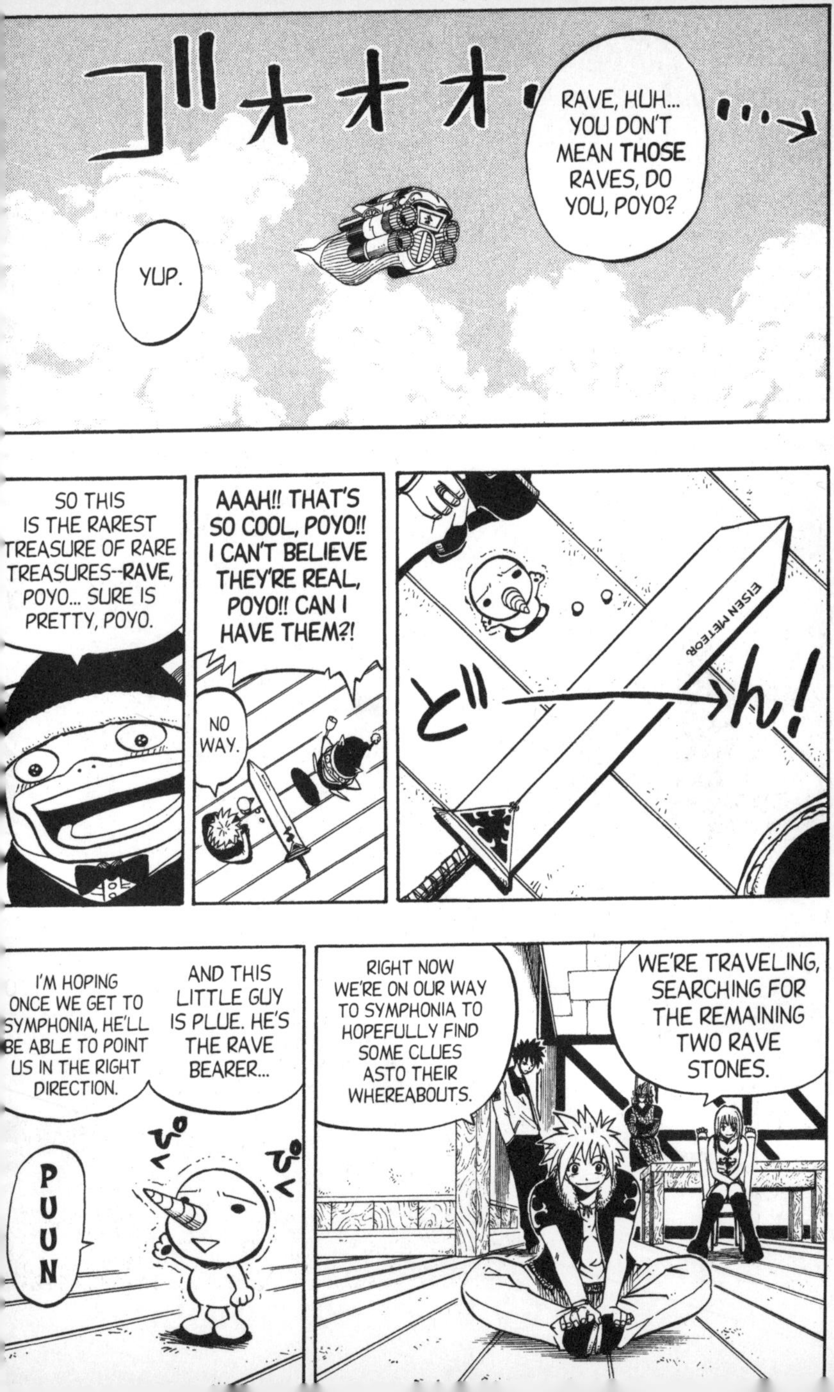
ゴォォォ…
RAVE, HUH... YOU DON'T MEAN **THOSE** RAVES, DO YOU, POYO?
YUP.
EISEN METEOR
どーーん!
AAAH!! THAT'S SO COOL, POYO!! I CAN'T BELIEVE THEY'RE REAL, POYO!! CAN I HAVE THEM?!
NO WAY.
SO THIS IS THE RAREST TREASURE OF RARE TREASURES--**RAVE**, POYO... SURE IS PRETTY, POYO.
WE'RE TRAVELING, SEARCHING FOR THE REMAINING TWO RAVE STONES.
RIGHT NOW WE'RE ON OUR WAY TO SYMPHONIA TO HOPEFULLY FIND SOME CLUES ASTO THEIR WHEREABOUTS.
AND THIS LITTLE GUY IS PLUE. HE'S THE RAVE BEARER...
I'M HOPING ONCE WE GET TO SYMPHONIA, HE'LL BE ABLE TO POINT US IN THE RIGHT DIRECTION.
ぴく
ぴく
PUUN

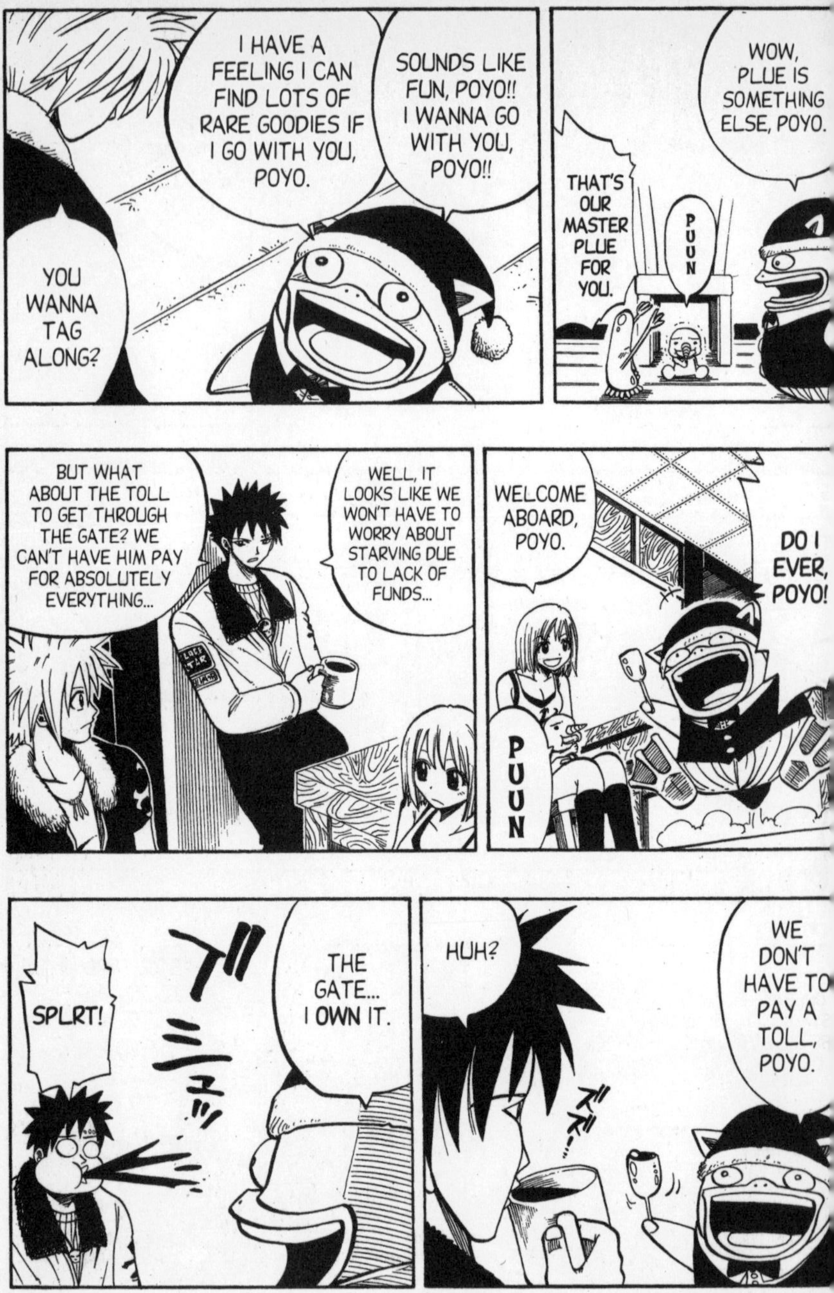
WOW, PLUE IS SOMETHING ELSE, POYO.
THAT'S OUR MASTER PLUE FOR YOU.
PUUN
SOUNDS LIKE FUN, POYO!! I WANNA GO WITH YOU, POYO!!
I HAVE A FEELING I CAN FIND LOTS OF RARE GOODIES IF I GO WITH YOU, POYO.
YOU WANNA TAG ALONG?
DO I EVER, POYO!
WELCOME ABOARD, POYO.
PUUN
WELL, IT LOOKS LIKE WE WON'T HAVE TO WORRY ABOUT STARVING DUE TO LACK OF FUNDS...
BUT WHAT ABOUT THE TOLL TO GET THROUGH THE GATE? WE CAN'T HAVE HIM PAY FOR ABSOLUTELY EVERYTHING...
WE DON'T HAVE TO PAY A TOLL, POYO.
HUH?
THE GATE... I OWN IT.
SPLRT!

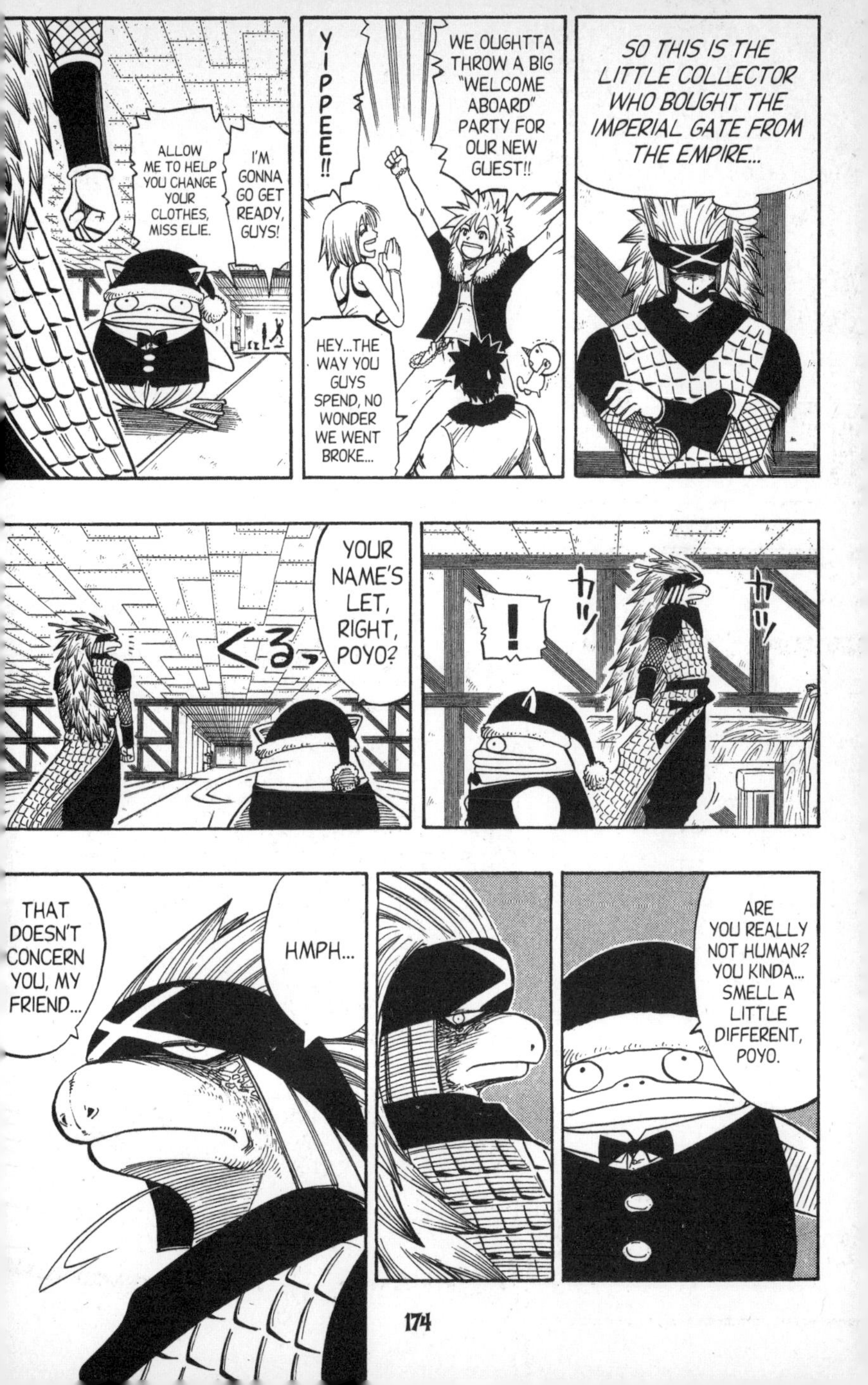
SO THIS IS THE LITTLE COLLECTOR WHO BOUGHT THE IMPERIAL GATE FROM THE EMPIRE...
WE OUGHTTA THROW A BIG "WELCOME ABOARD" PARTY FOR OUR NEW GUEST!!
YIPPEE!!
HEY...THE WAY YOU GUYS SPEND, NO WONDER WE WENT BROKE...
I'M GONNA GO GET READY, GUYS!
ALLOW ME TO HELP YOU CHANGE YOUR CLOTHES, MISS ELIE.
カッ
!
カッ
YOUR NAME'S LET, RIGHT, POYO?
くる
ARE YOU REALLY NOT HUMAN? YOU KINDA... SMELL A LITTLE DIFFERENT, POYO.
HMPH...
THAT DOESN'T CONCERN YOU, MY FRIEND...

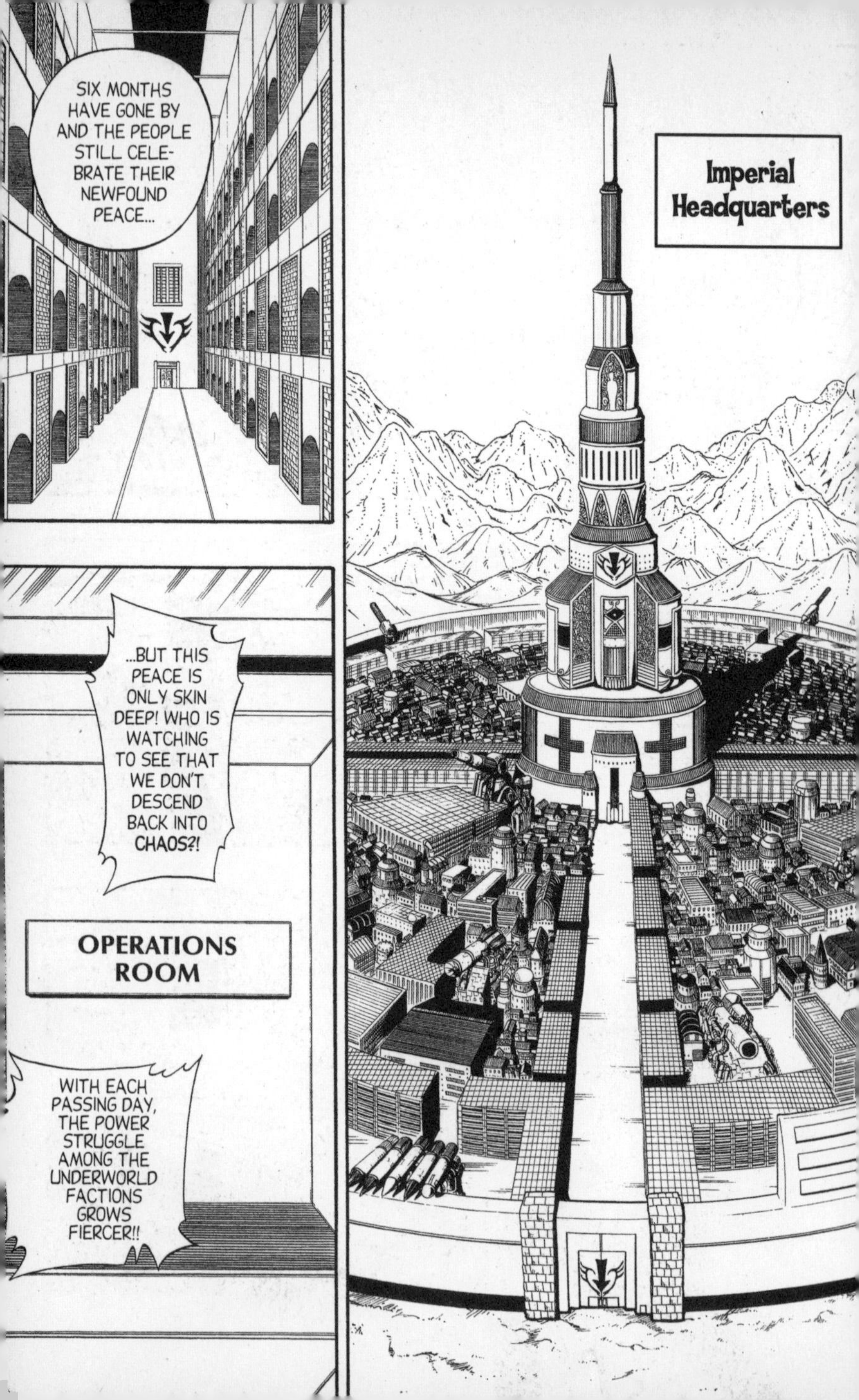
Imperial Headquarters
SIX MONTHS HAVE GONE BY AND THE PEOPLE STILL CELE-BRATE THEIR NEWFOUND PEACE...
...BUT THIS PEACE IS ONLY SKIN DEEP! WHO IS WATCHING TO SEE THAT WE DON'T DESCEND BACK INTO CHAOS?!
OPERATIONS ROOM
WITH EACH PASSING DAY, THE POWER STRUGGLE AMONG THE UNDERWORLD FACTIONS GROWS FIERCER!!

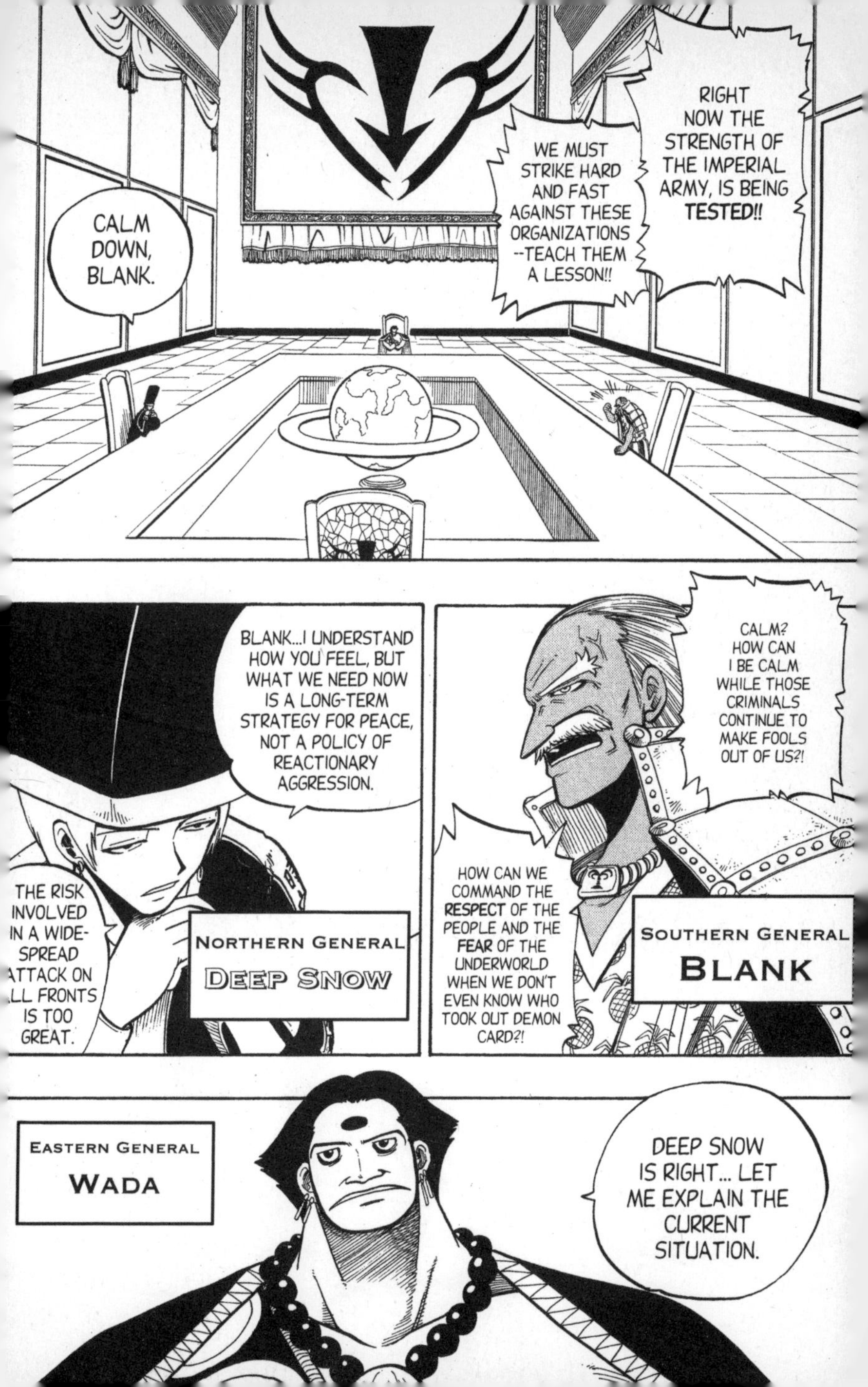
RIGHT NOW THE STRENGTH OF THE IMPERIAL ARMY, IS BEING TESTED!!
WE MUST STRIKE HARD AND FAST AGAINST THESE ORGANIZATIONS --TEACH THEM A LESSON!!
CALM DOWN, BLANK.
CALM? HOW CAN I BE CALM WHILE THOSE CRIMINALS CONTINUE TO MAKE FOOLS OUT OF US?!
SOUTHERN GENERAL
BLANK
HOW CAN WE COMMAND THE RESPECT OF THE PEOPLE AND THE FEAR OF THE UNDERWORLD WHEN WE DON'T EVEN KNOW WHO TOOK OUT DEMON CARD?!
BLANK...I UNDERSTAND HOW YOU FEEL, BUT WHAT WE NEED NOW IS A LONG-TERM STRATEGY FOR PEACE, NOT A POLICY OF REACTIONARY AGGRESSION.
NORTHERN GENERAL
DEEP SNOW
THE RISK INVOLVED IN A WIDE-SPREAD ATTACK ON ALL FRONTS IS TOO GREAT.
DEEP SNOW IS RIGHT... LET ME EXPLAIN THE CURRENT SITUATION.
EASTERN GENERAL
WADA

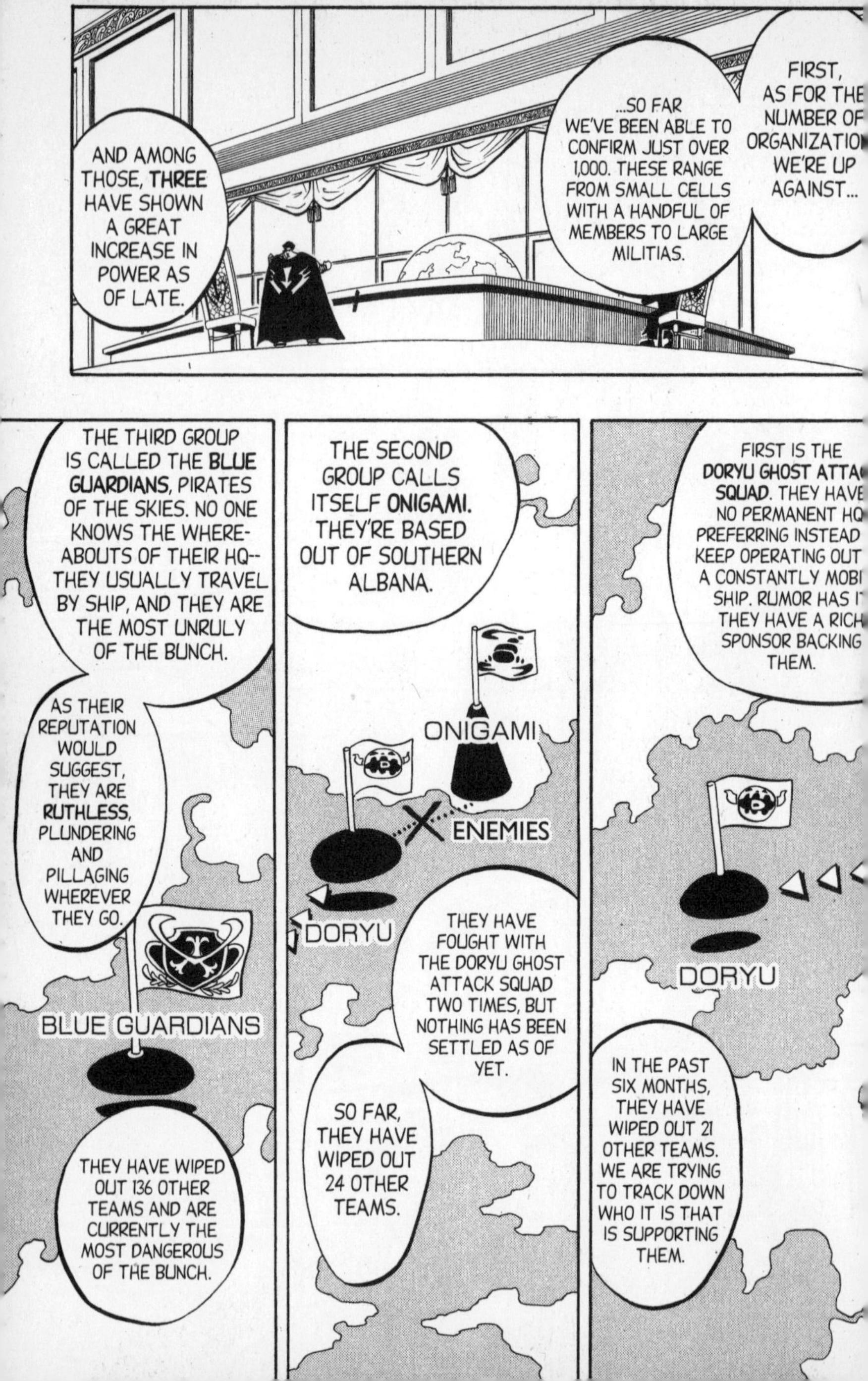
FIRST, AS FOR THE NUMBER OF ORGANIZATIO WE'RE UP AGAINST...
...SO FAR WE'VE BEEN ABLE TO CONFIRM JUST OVER 1,000. THESE RANGE FROM SMALL CELLS WITH A HANDFUL OF MEMBERS TO LARGE MILITIAS.
AND AMONG THOSE, THREE HAVE SHOWN A GREAT INCREASE IN POWER AS OF LATE.
FIRST IS THE DORYU GHOST ATTA SQUAD. THEY HAVE NO PERMANENT HQ PREFERRING INSTEAD KEEP OPERATING OUT A CONSTANTLY MOBI SHIP. RUMOR HAS IT THEY HAVE A RICH SPONSOR BACKING THEM.
DORYU
IN THE PAST SIX MONTHS, THEY HAVE WIPED OUT 21 OTHER TEAMS. WE ARE TRYING TO TRACK DOWN WHO IT IS THAT IS SUPPORTING THEM.
THE SECOND GROUP CALLS ITSELF ONIGAMI. THEY'RE BASED OUT OF SOUTHERN ALBANA.
ONIGAMI
ENEMIES
DORYU
THEY HAVE FOUGHT WITH THE DORYU GHOST ATTACK SQUAD TWO TIMES, BUT NOTHING HAS BEEN SETTLED AS OF YET.
SO FAR, THEY HAVE WIPED OUT 24 OTHER TEAMS.
THE THIRD GROUP IS CALLED THE BLUE GUARDIANS, PIRATES OF THE SKIES. NO ONE KNOWS THE WHERE-ABOUTS OF THEIR HQ-- THEY USUALLY TRAVEL BY SHIP, AND THEY ARE THE MOST UNRULY OF THE BUNCH.
AS THEIR REPUTATION WOULD SUGGEST, THEY ARE RUTHLESS, PLUNDERING AND PILLAGING WHEREVER THEY GO.
BLUE GUARDIANS
THEY HAVE WIPED OUT 136 OTHER TEAMS AND ARE CURRENTLY THE MOST DANGEROUS OF THE BUNCH.

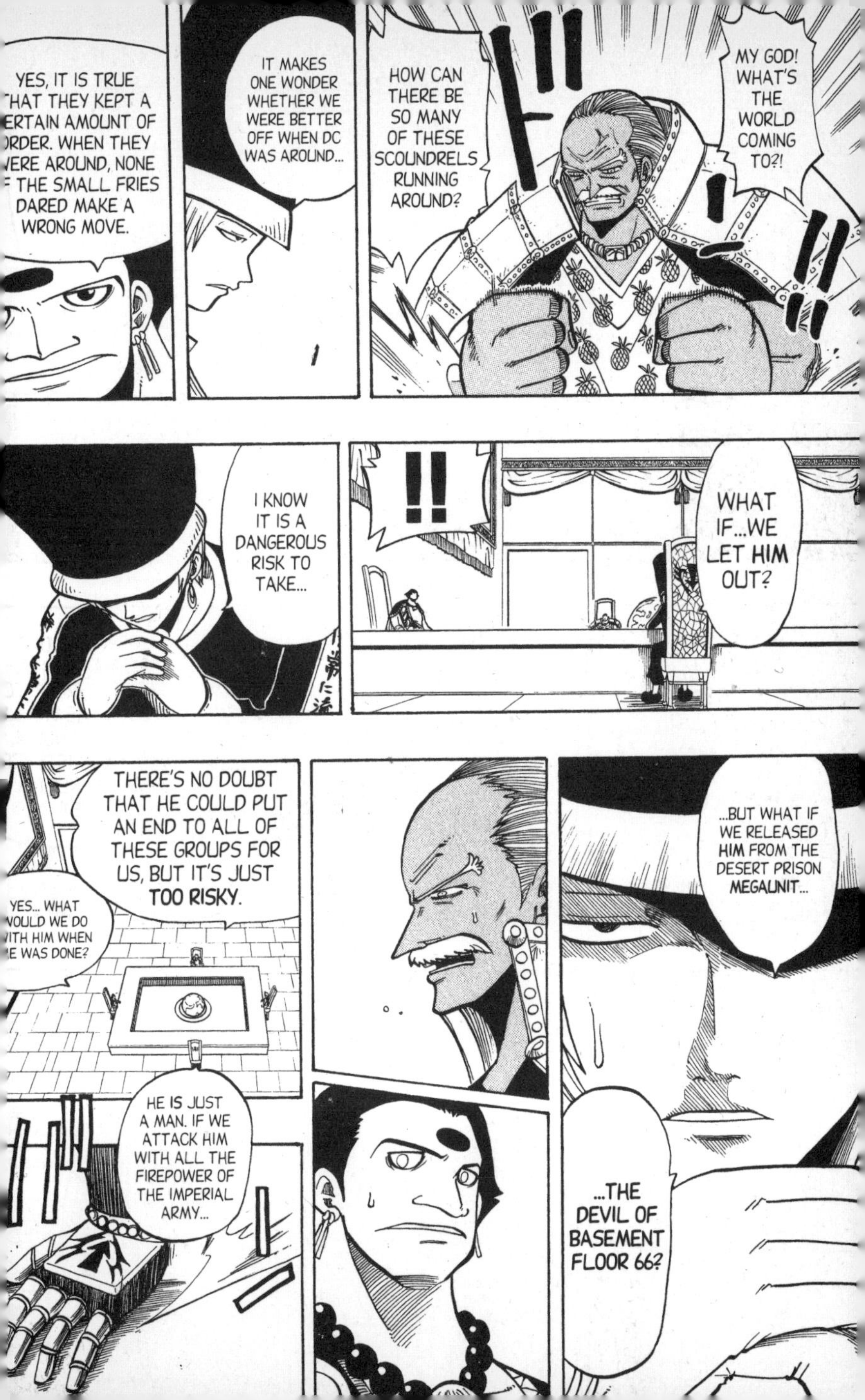
MY GOD! WHAT'S THE WORLD COMING TO?!
HOW CAN THERE BE SO MANY OF THESE SCOUNDRELS RUNNING AROUND?
IT MAKES ONE WONDER WHETHER WE WERE BETTER OFF WHEN DC WAS AROUND...
YES, IT IS TRUE HAT THEY KEPT A ERTAIN AMOUNT OF RDER. WHEN THEY VERE AROUND, NONE F THE SMALL FRIES DARED MAKE A WRONG MOVE.
WHAT IF...WE LET **HIM** OUT?
I KNOW IT IS A DANGEROUS RISK TO TAKE...
...BUT WHAT IF WE RELEASED **HIM** FROM THE DESERT PRISON **MEGAUNIT**...
...THE DEVIL OF BASEMENT FLOOR 66?
THERE'S NO DOUBT THAT HE COULD PUT AN END TO ALL OF THESE GROUPS FOR US, BUT IT'S JUST **TOO RISKY**.
YES... WHAT VOULD WE DO VITH HIM WHEN E WAS DONE?
HE **IS** JUST A MAN. IF WE ATTACK HIM WITH ALL THE FIREPOWER OF THE IMPERIAL ARMY...

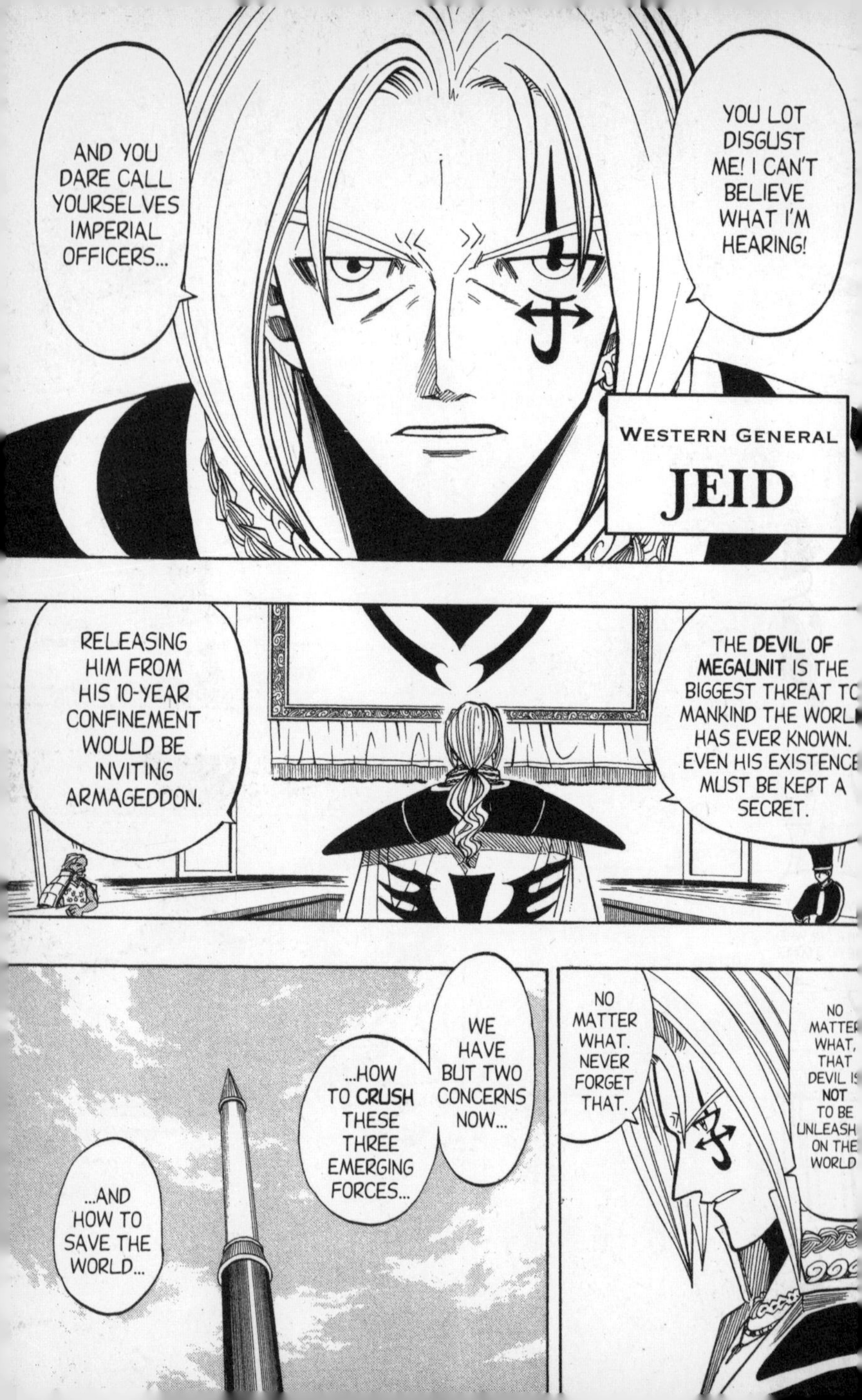
YOU LOT DISGUST ME! I CAN'T BELIEVE WHAT I'M HEARING!
AND YOU DARE CALL YOURSELVES IMPERIAL OFFICERS...
WESTERN GENERAL
JEID
THE **DEVIL OF MEGAUNIT** IS THE BIGGEST THREAT TO MANKIND THE WORLD HAS EVER KNOWN. EVEN HIS EXISTENCE MUST BE KEPT A SECRET.
RELEASING HIM FROM HIS 10-YEAR CONFINEMENT WOULD BE INVITING ARMAGEDDON.
NO MATTER WHAT, THAT DEVIL IS **NOT** TO BE UNLEASH ON THE WORLD
NO MATTER WHAT. NEVER FORGET THAT.
WE HAVE BUT TWO CONCERNS NOW...
...HOW TO **CRUSH** THESE THREE EMERGING FORCES...
...AND HOW TO SAVE THE WORLD...

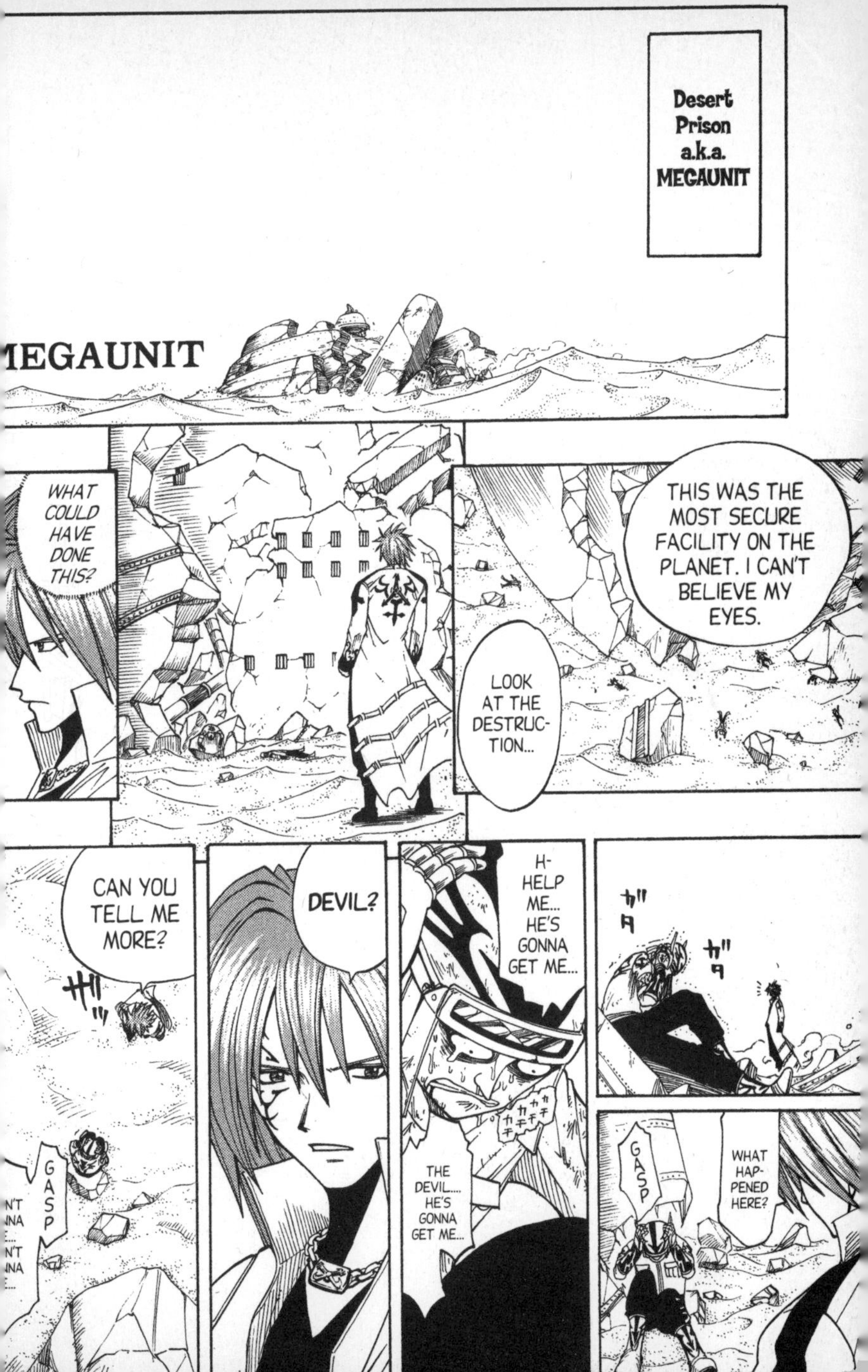
Desert Prison a.k.a. MEGAUNIT
IEGAUNIT
THIS WAS THE MOST SECURE FACILITY ON THE PLANET. I CAN'T BELIEVE MY EYES.
LOOK AT THE DESTRUCTION...
WHAT COULD HAVE DONE THIS?
ガタ
ガタ
WHAT HAPPENED HERE?
GASP
H-HELP ME... HE'S GONNA GET ME...
THE DEVIL... HE'S GONNA GET ME...
DEVIL?
CAN YOU TELL ME MORE?
GASP

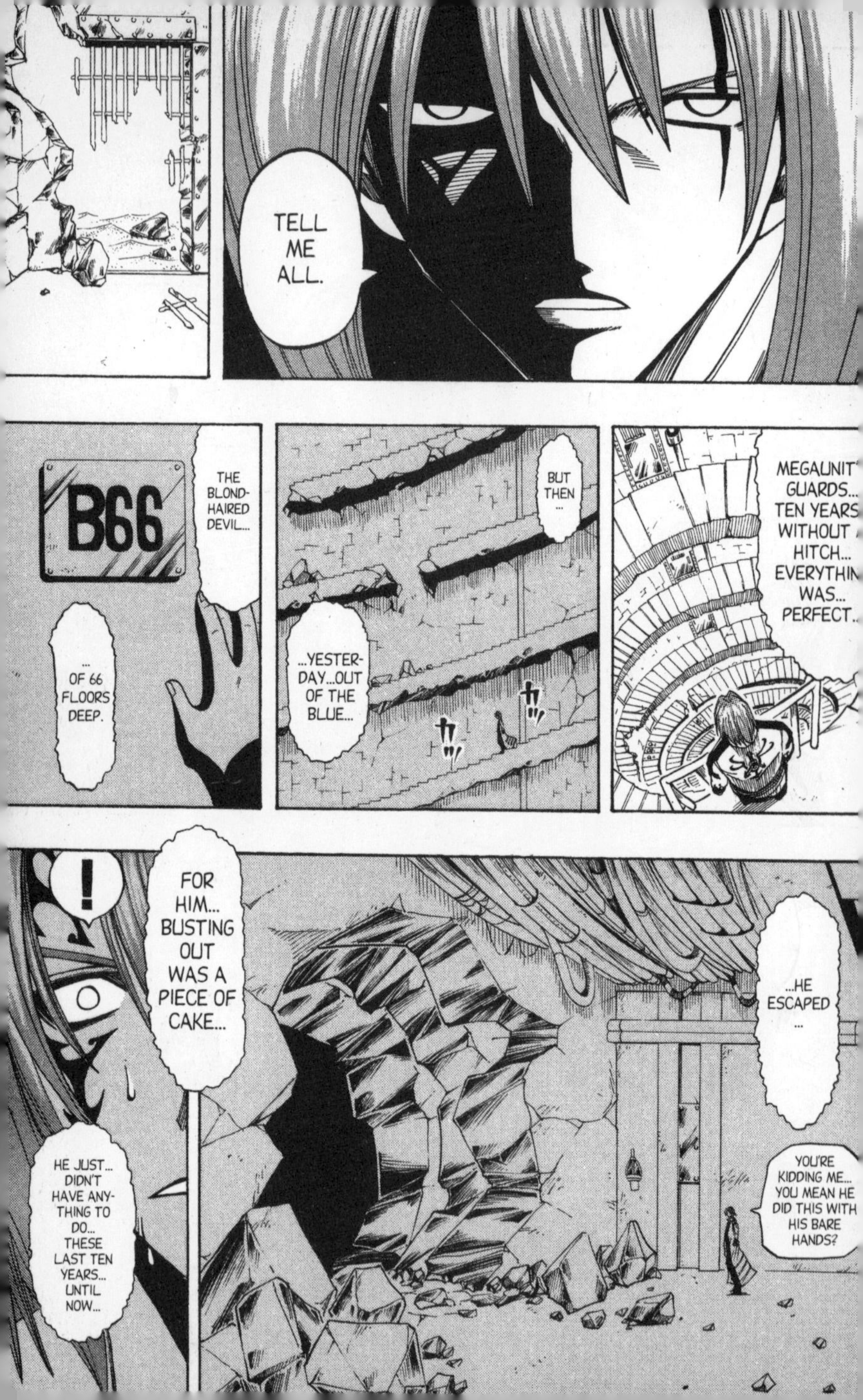
TELL ME ALL.
MEGAUNIT GUARDS... TEN YEARS WITHOUT HITCH... EVERYTHIN WAS... PERFECT...
BUT THEN...
...YESTERDAY...OUT OF THE BLUE...
THE BLOND-HAIRED DEVIL...
B66
...OF 66 FLOORS DEEP.
...HE ESCAPED...
YOU'RE KIDDING ME... YOU MEAN HE DID THIS WITH HIS BARE HANDS?
FOR HIM... BUSTING OUT WAS A PIECE OF CAKE...
!
HE JUST... DIDN'T HAVE ANYTHING TO DO... THESE LAST TEN YEARS... UNTIL NOW...

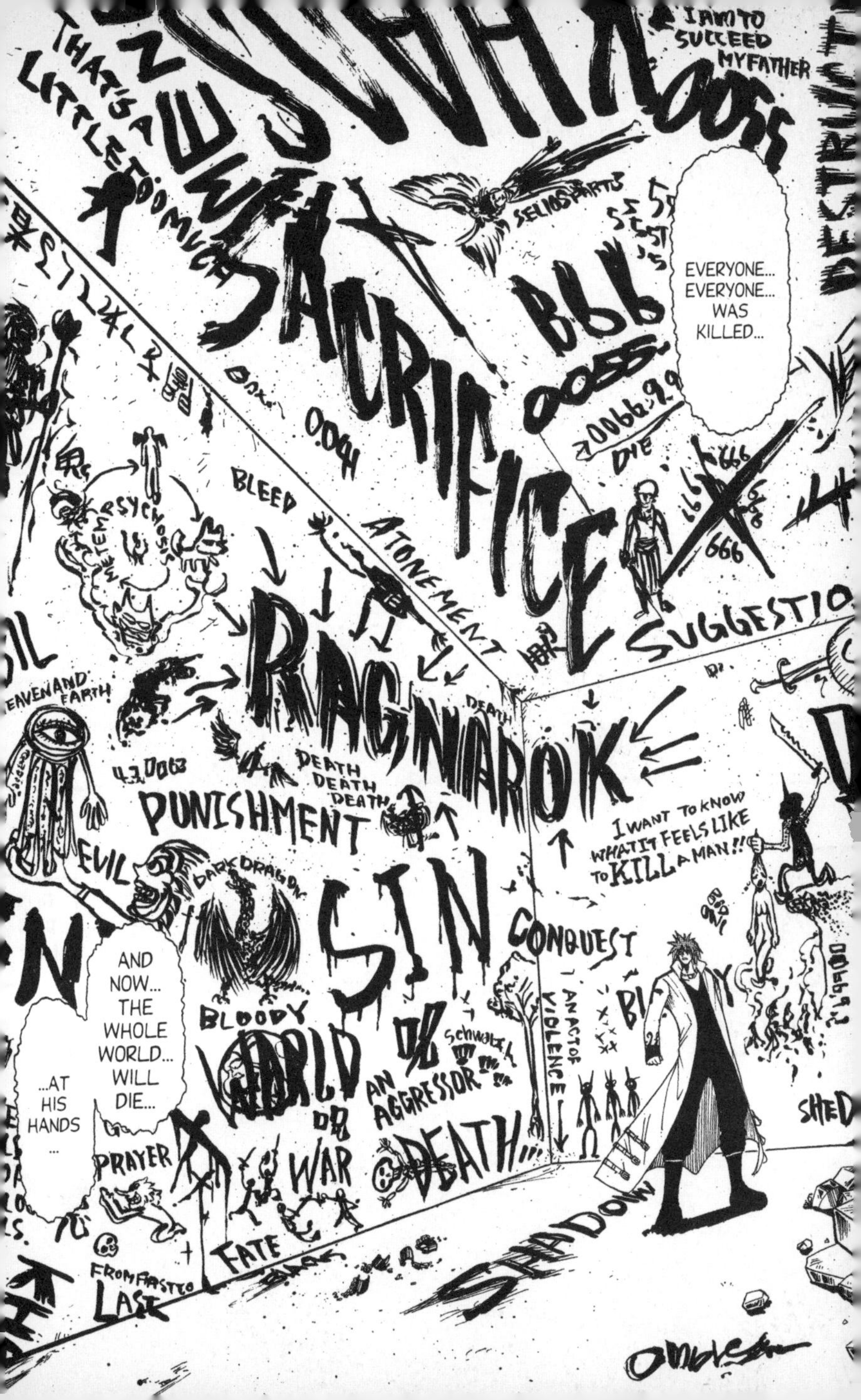
I AM TO SUCCEED MY FATHER
EVERYONE... EVERYONE... WAS KILLED...
SACRIFICE
DESTRU
SUGGESTIO
DIE
666
ATONEMENT
BLEED
METEMPSYCHOSIS
THAT'S A LITTLE TOO MUCH
RAGNAROK
DEATH
DEATH DEATH DEATH
PUNISHMENT
HEAVEN AND EARTH
EVIL
DARK DRAGON
SIN
I WANT TO KNOW WHAT IT FEELS LIKE TO KILL A MAN!!
CONQUEST
AN ACT OF VIOLENCE
BLOODY
WORLD
AN AGGRESSOR
WAR
DEATH!!!
SHED
AND NOW... THE WHOLE WORLD... WILL DIE...
...AT HIS HANDS ...
PRAYER
FATE
FROM FIRST TO LAST
SHADOW

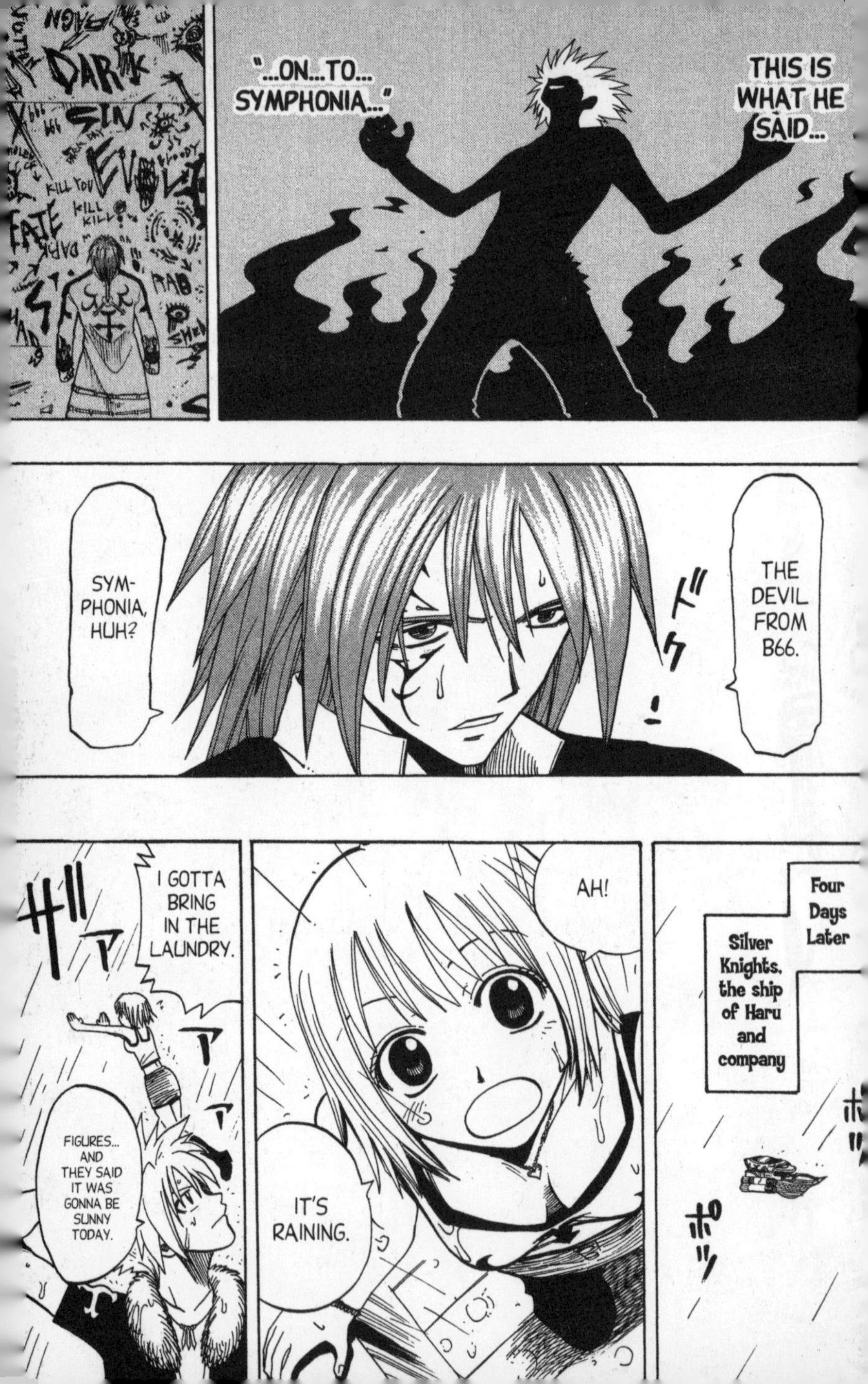
THIS IS WHAT HE SAID...
"...ON...TO... SYMPHONIA..."
DARK
SIN
KILL YOU
KILL KILL
FATE
THE DEVIL FROM B66.
SYM-PHONIA, HUH?
Four Days Later
Silver Knights, the ship of Haru and company
AH!
IT'S RAINING.
I GOTTA BRING IN THE LAUNDRY.
FIGURES... AND THEY SAID IT WAS GONNA BE SUNNY TODAY.

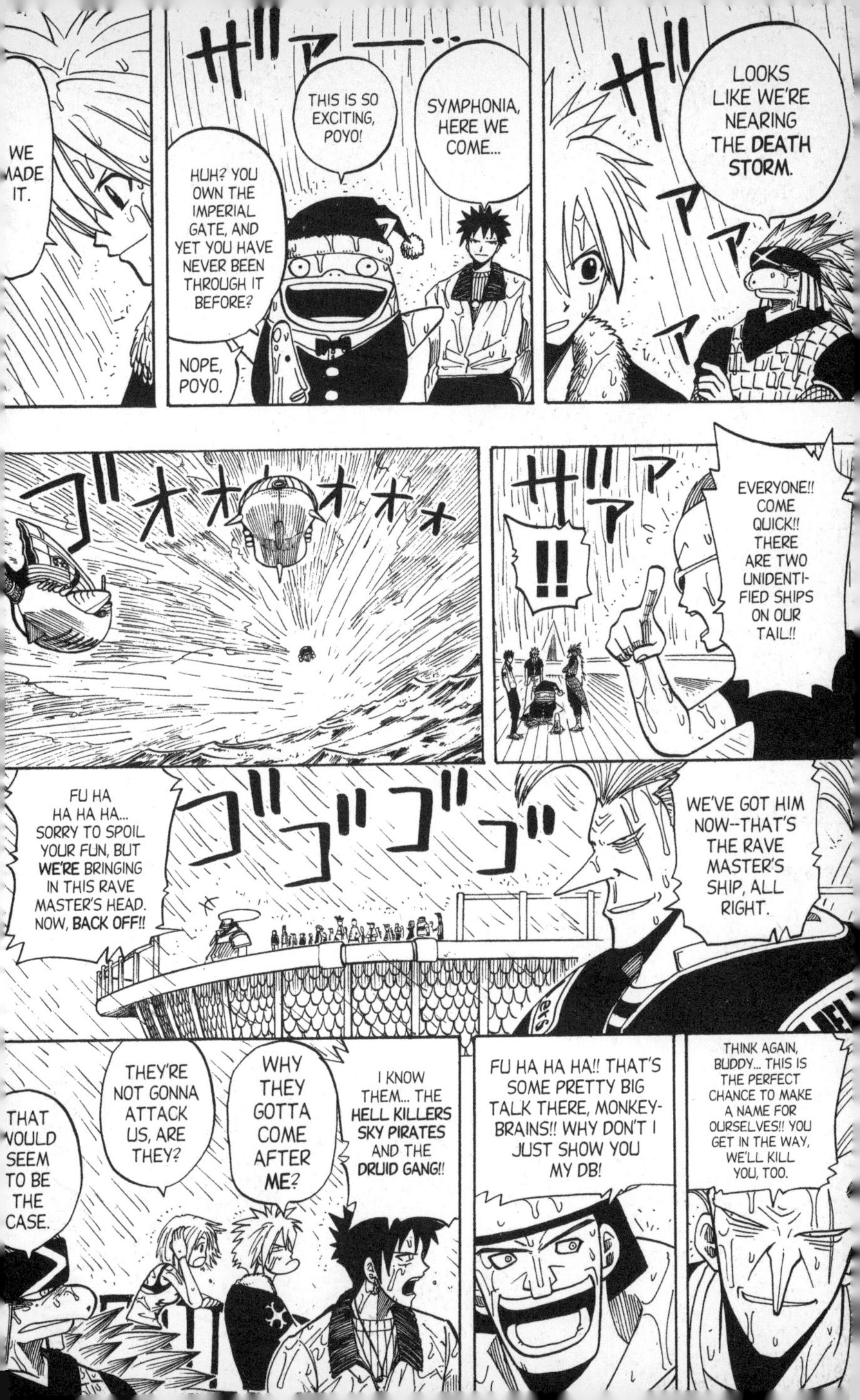

ザァ
LOOKS LIKE WE'RE NEARING THE DEATH STORM.
ザァー‥
SYMPHONIA, HERE WE COME...
THIS IS SO EXCITING, POYO!
HUH? YOU OWN THE IMPERIAL GATE, AND YET YOU HAVE NEVER BEEN THROUGH IT BEFORE?
NOPE, POYO.
WE MADE IT.
ザァ
!!
EVERYONE!! COME QUICK!! THERE ARE TWO UNIDENTI-FIED SHIPS ON OUR TAIL!!
ゴオオオオオオ
WE'VE GOT HIM NOW--THAT'S THE RAVE MASTER'S SHIP, ALL RIGHT.
ゴゴゴゴ
FU HA HA HA HA... SORRY TO SPOIL YOUR FUN, BUT WE'RE BRINGING IN THIS RAVE MASTER'S HEAD. NOW, BACK OFF!!
THINK AGAIN, BUDDY... THIS IS THE PERFECT CHANCE TO MAKE A NAME FOR OURSELVES!! YOU GET IN THE WAY, WE'LL KILL YOU, TOO.
FU HA HA HA!! THAT'S SOME PRETTY BIG TALK THERE, MONKEY-BRAINS!! WHY DON'T I JUST SHOW YOU MY DB!
I KNOW THEM... THE HELL KILLERS SKY PIRATES AND THE DRUID GANG!!
WHY THEY GOTTA COME AFTER ME?
THEY'RE NOT GONNA ATTACK US, ARE THEY?
THAT WOULD SEEM TO BE THE CASE.

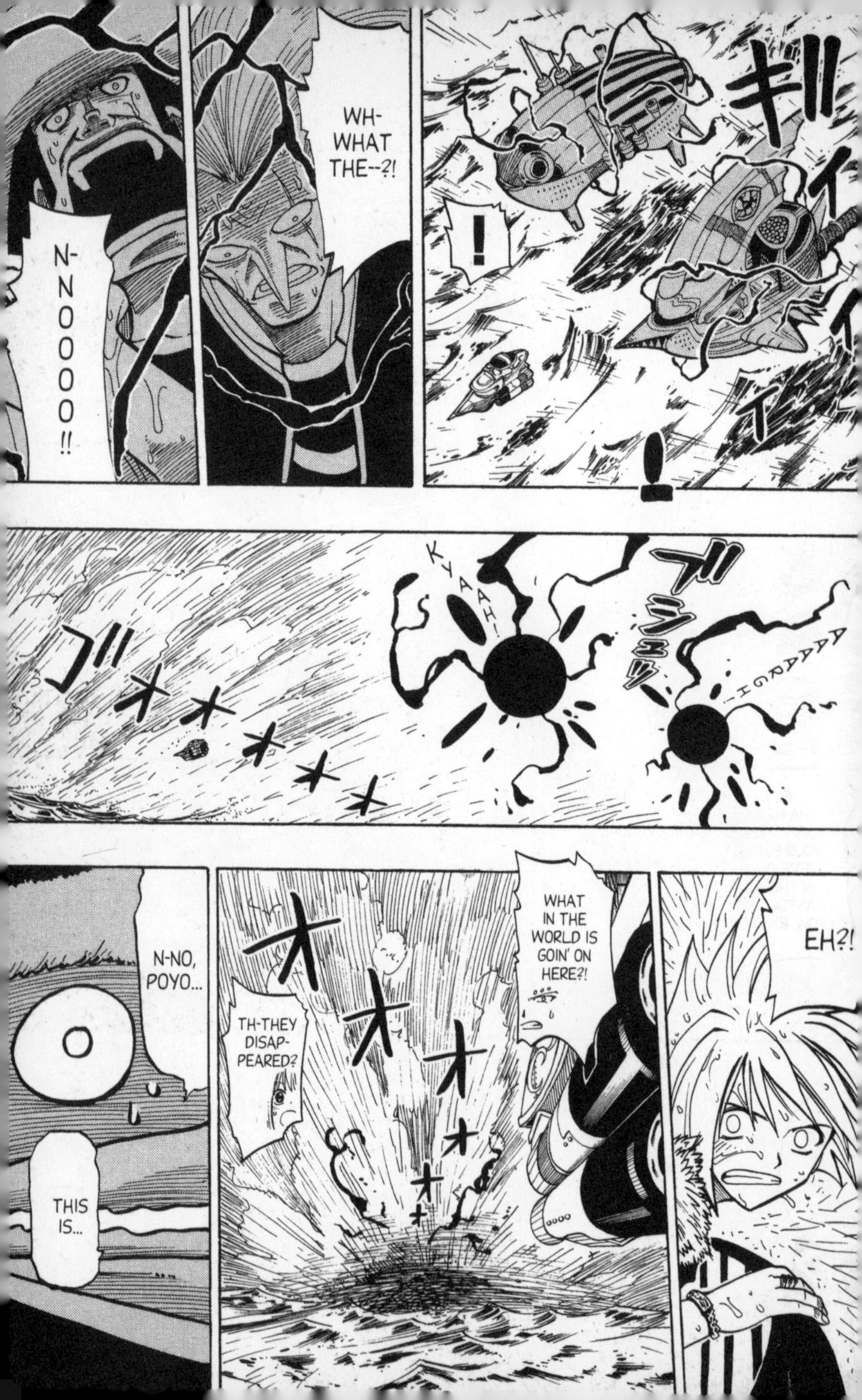
!
WH- WHAT THE--?!
N-NOOOOO!!
KYAAAH!
IGRAAAAA
EH?!
WHAT IN THE WORLD IS GOIN' ON HERE?!
TH-THEY DISAP-PEARED?
N-NO, POYO...
THIS IS...

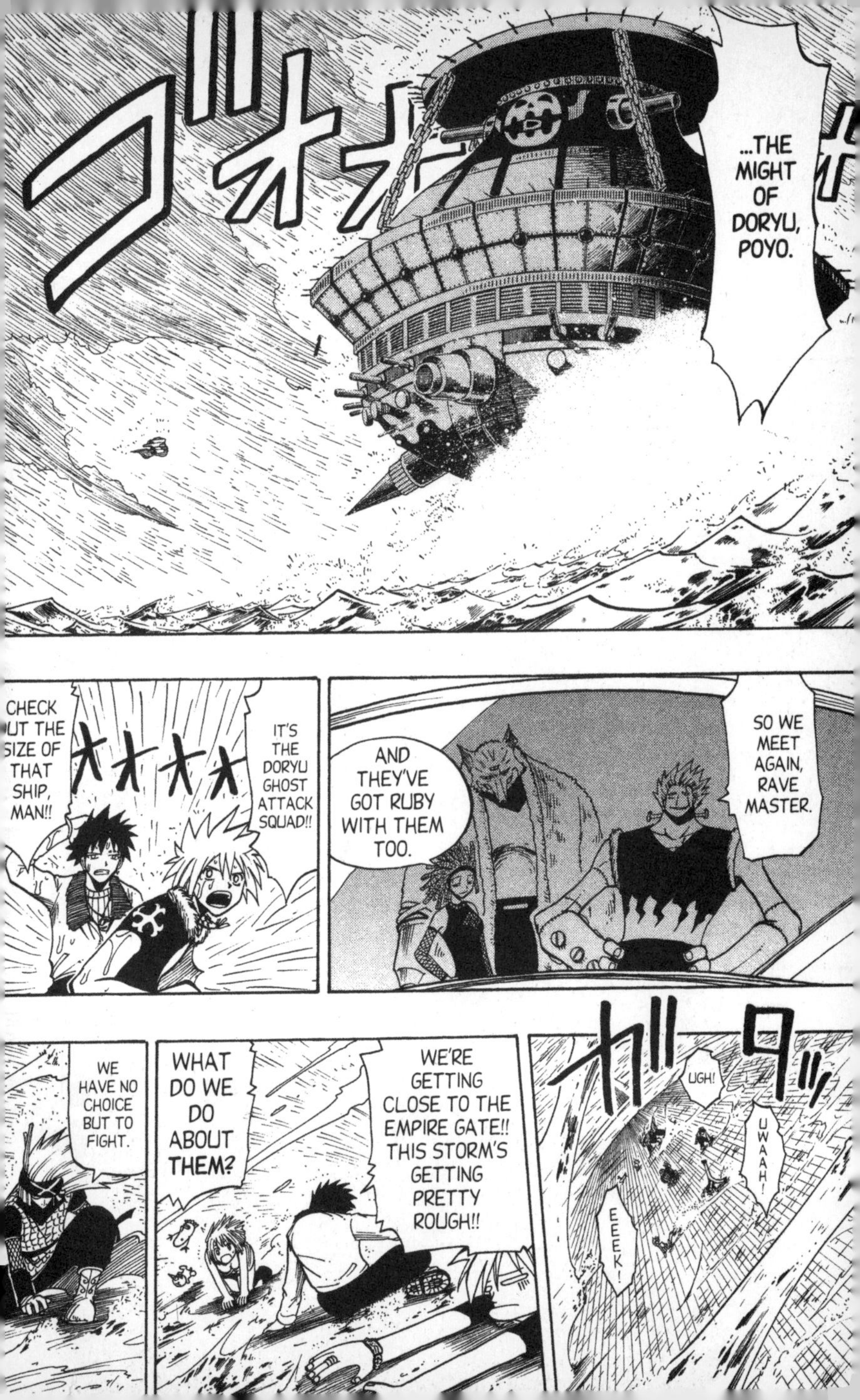
...THE MIGHT OF DORYU, POYO.
SO WE MEET AGAIN, RAVE MASTER.
AND THEY'VE GOT RUBY WITH THEM TOO.
IT'S THE DORYU GHOST ATTACK SQUAD!!
CHECK UT THE SIZE OF THAT SHIP, MAN!!
UGH!
UWAAH!
EEEK!
WE'RE GETTING CLOSE TO THE EMPIRE GATE!! THIS STORM'S GETTING PRETTY ROUGH!!
WHAT DO WE DO ABOUT THEM?
WE HAVE NO CHOICE BUT TO FIGHT.

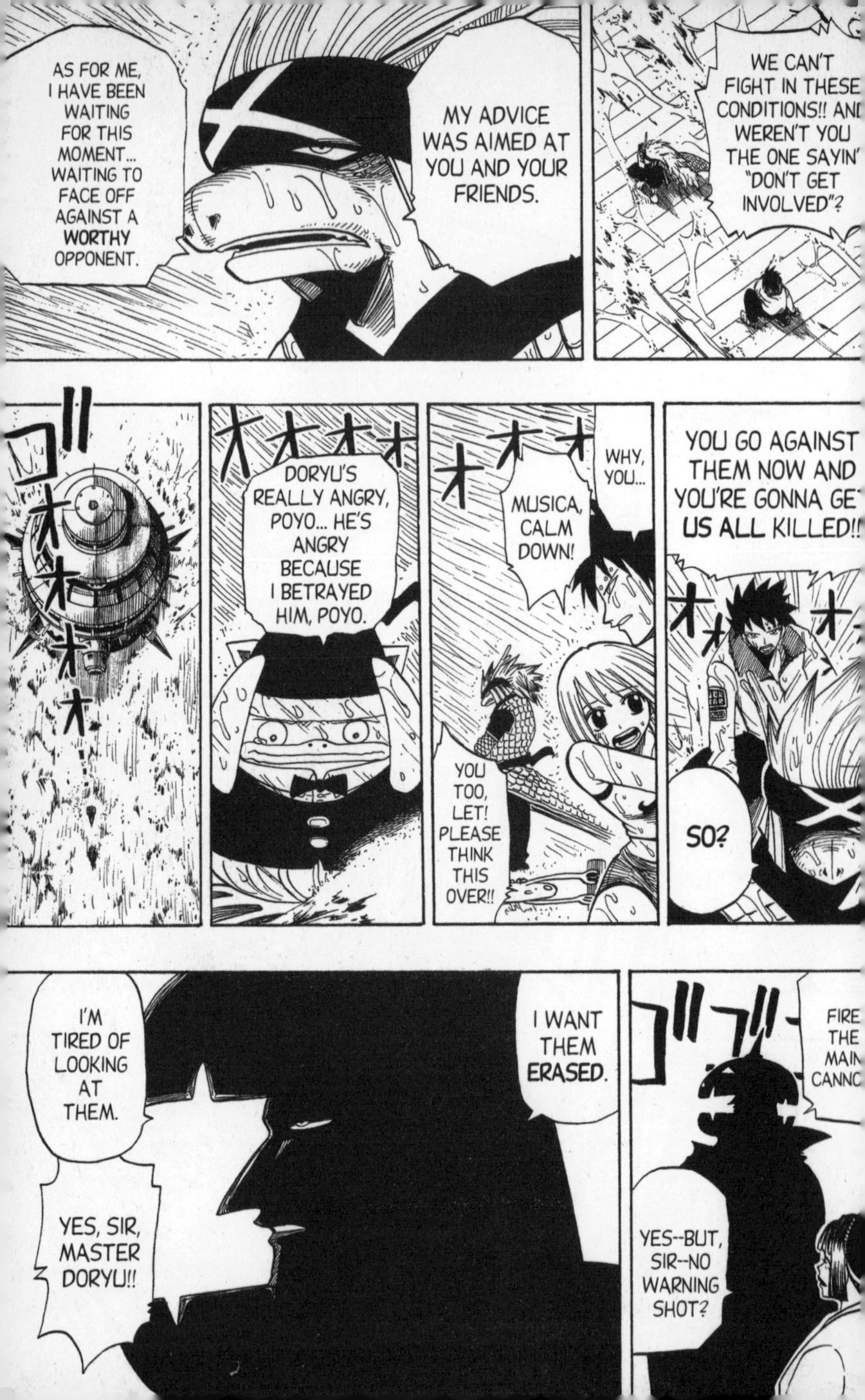
WE CAN'T FIGHT IN THESE CONDITIONS!! AN WEREN'T YOU THE ONE SAYIN' "DON'T GET INVOLVED"?
MY ADVICE WAS AIMED AT YOU AND YOUR FRIENDS.
AS FOR ME, I HAVE BEEN WAITING FOR THIS MOMENT... WAITING TO FACE OFF AGAINST A **WORTHY** OPPONENT.
YOU GO AGAINST THEM NOW AND YOU'RE GONNA GE **US ALL** KILLED!!
SO?
WHY, YOU...
MUSICA, CALM DOWN!
YOU TOO, LET! PLEASE THINK THIS OVER!!
DORYU'S REALLY ANGRY, POYO... HE'S ANGRY BECAUSE I BETRAYED HIM, POYO.
FIRE THE MAIN CANNO
YES--BUT, SIR--NO WARNING SHOT?
I WANT THEM **ERASED**.
I'M TIRED OF LOOKING AT THEM.
YES, SIR, MASTER DORYU!!

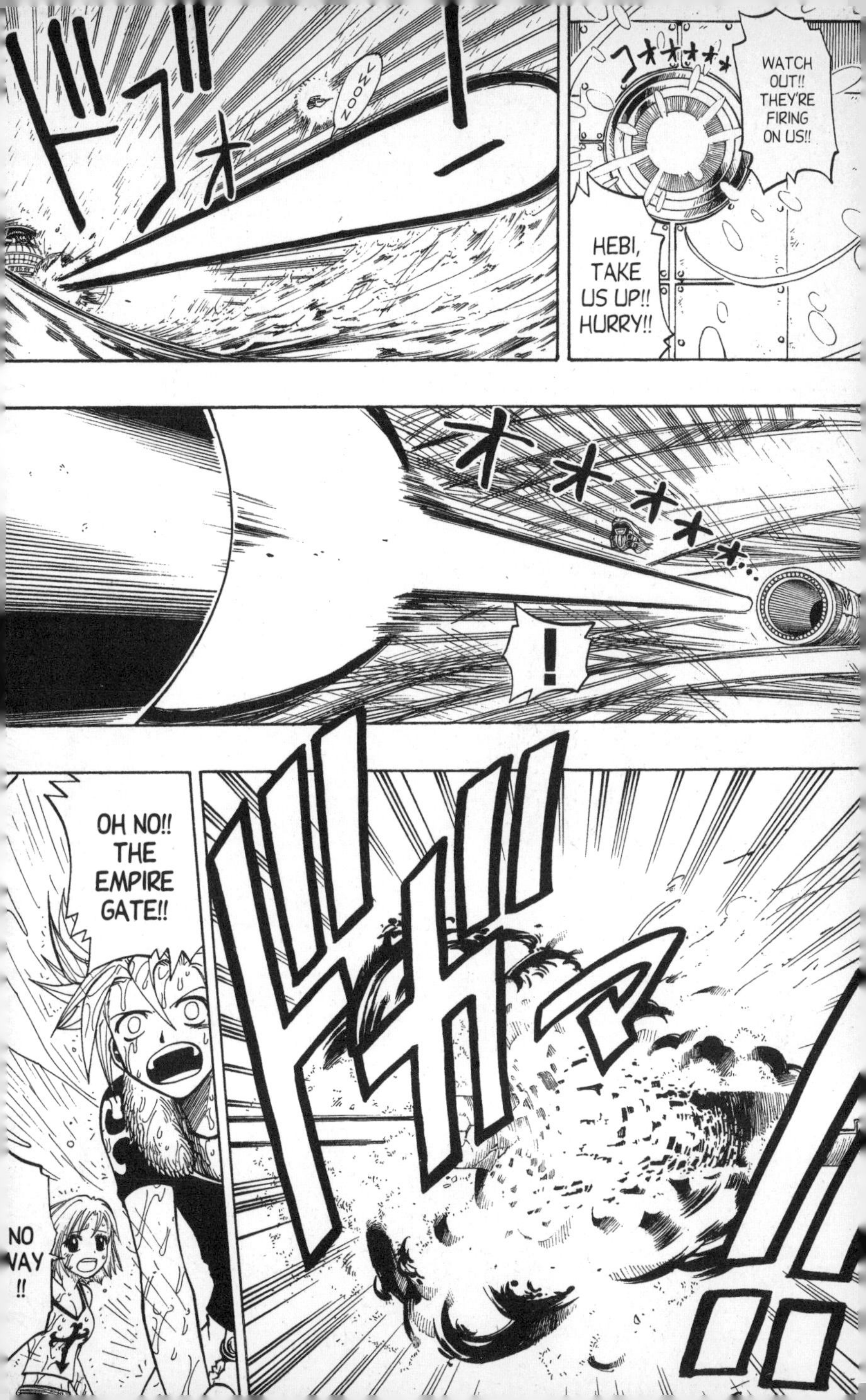

WATCH OUT!! THEY'RE FIRING ON US!!
HEBI, TAKE US UP!! HURRY!!
VZOOM
!
OH NO!! THE EMPIRE GATE!!
NO WAY !!

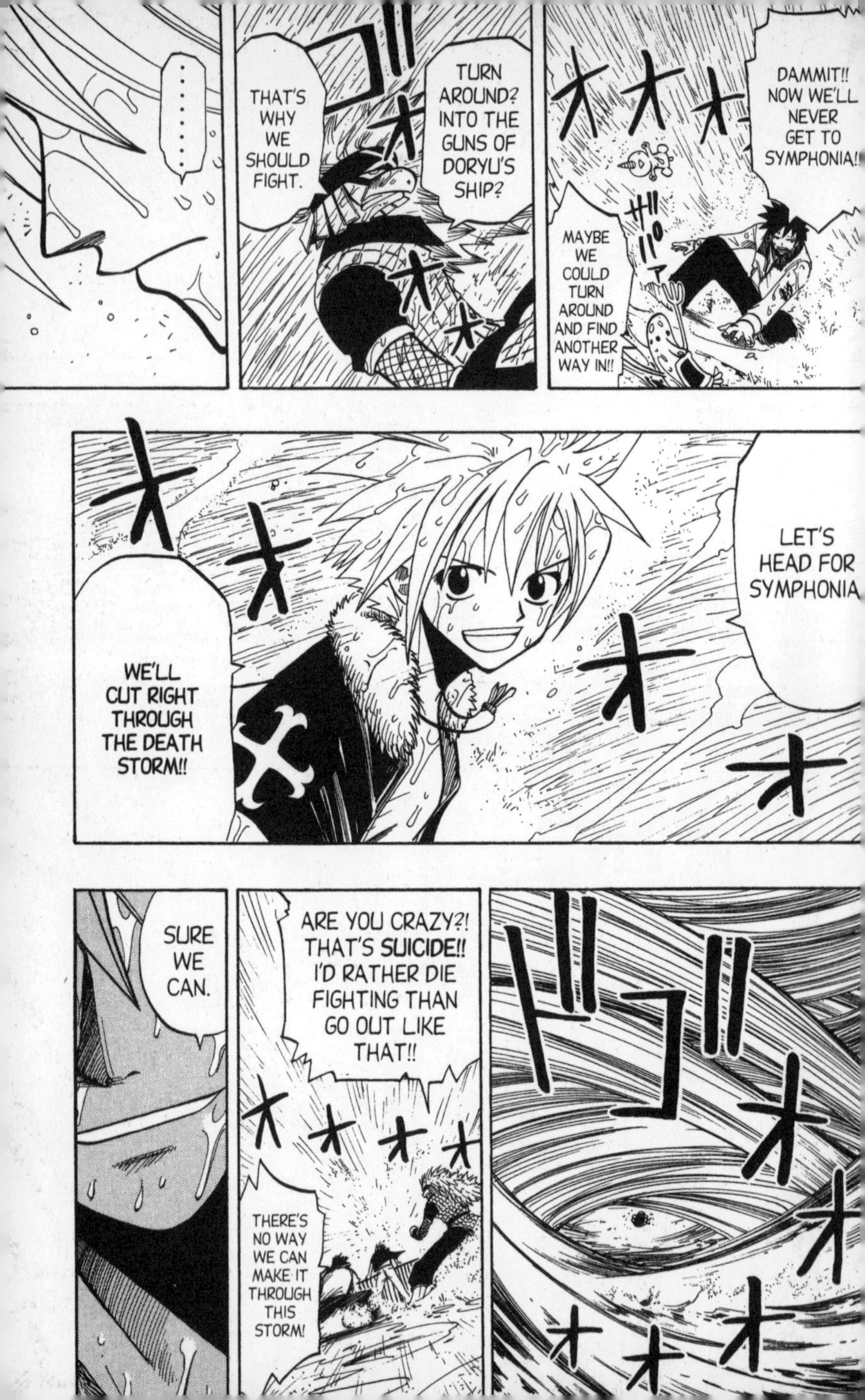
DAMMIT!! NOW WE'LL NEVER GET TO SYMPHONIA!!
MAYBE WE COULD TURN AROUND AND FIND ANOTHER WAY IN!!
TURN AROUND? INTO THE GUNS OF DORYU'S SHIP?
THAT'S WHY WE SHOULD FIGHT.
......
LET'S HEAD FOR SYMPHONIA
WE'LL CUT RIGHT THROUGH THE DEATH STORM!!
ARE YOU CRAZY?! THAT'S **SUICIDE!!** I'D RATHER DIE FIGHTING THAN GO OUT LIKE THAT!!
THERE'S NO WAY WE CAN MAKE IT THROUGH THIS STORM!
SURE WE CAN.

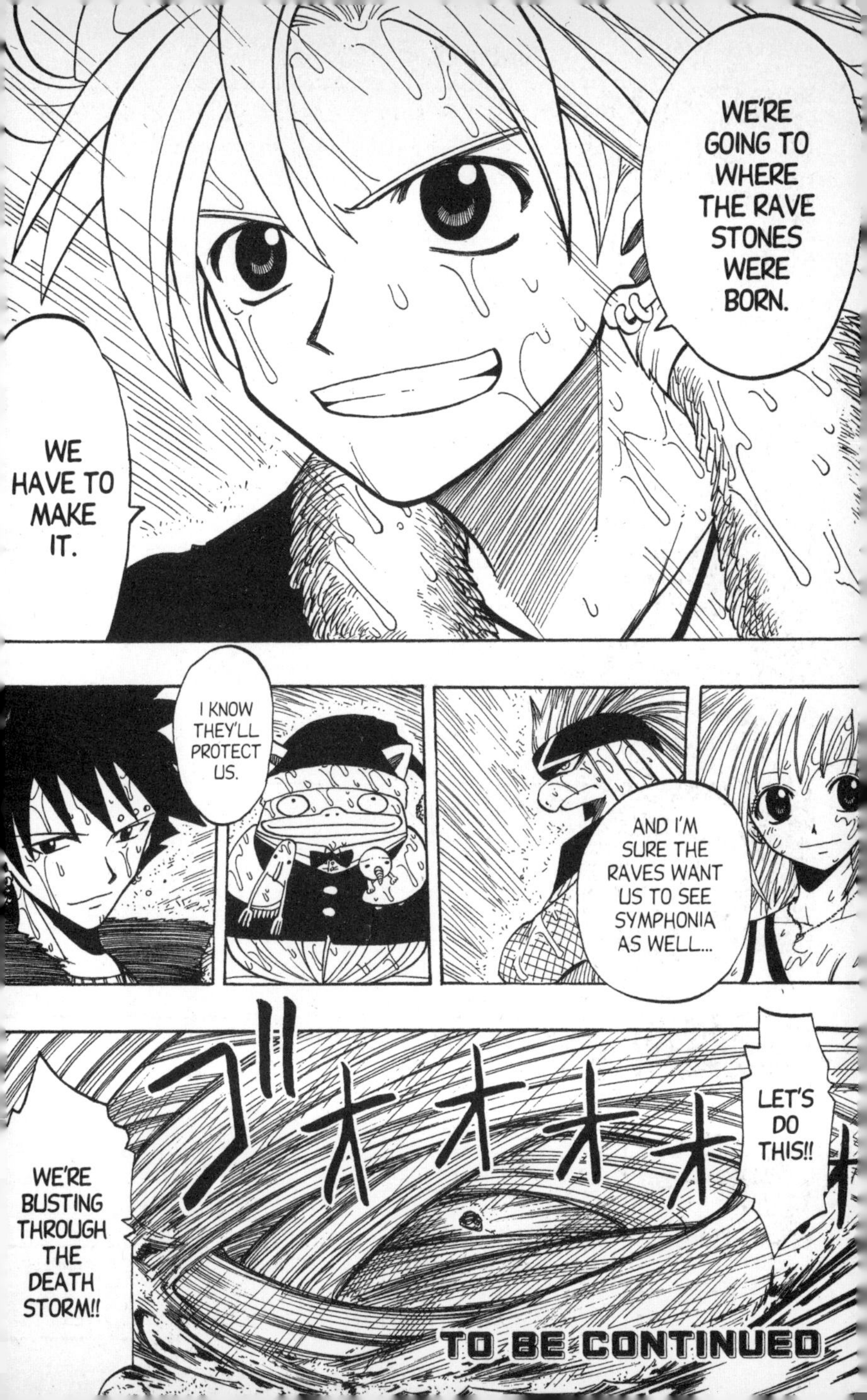

WE'RE GOING TO WHERE THE RAVE STONES WERE BORN.
WE HAVE TO MAKE IT.
AND I'M SURE THE RAVES WANT US TO SEE SYMPHONIA AS WELL...
I KNOW THEY'LL PROTECT US.
ゴオオオオ
LET'S DO THIS!!
WE'RE BUSTING THROUGH THE DEATH STORM!!
TO BE CONTINUED

Character Profiles

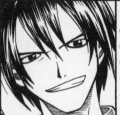

FIRST GENERATION RAVE MASTER: KENSEI SWORD SAINT SHIBA

① RAVE AND SWORD (TEN COMMANDMENTS)
② 11/18/9992 / 23YR
③ 173CM / 61KG / AB
④ GARAGE ISLAND
⑤ PRACTICING SWORDSMANSHIP
⑥ CAN CRY ANYPLACE, ANYTIME
⑦ HOMETOWN (GARAGE ISLAND)
⑧ FOUR KNIGHTS OF THE BLUE SKY

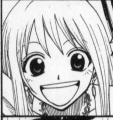

MASTER OF ETHERION: RESHA VALENTINE, THE DANCER

① NONE
② 1/1/0000 / 15YR
③ 159CM / 45KG / O
④ KINGDOM OF SYMPHONIA
⑤ DANCING
⑥ DANCING; WIELDING POWER OF ETHERION
⑦ FREEDOM
⑧ WAR

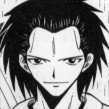

THE BEST BLACKSMITH ON SONG: GALEIN MUSICA

① HAMMER
② 10/4/9998 / 17YR
③ 178CM / 65KG / B
④ PUNK STREET
⑤ BOOZE AND WOMEN
⑥ NOBODY ON THE CONTINENT CAN MAKE A BETTER SWORD
⑦ SWORDS AND HAMMERS
⑧ WEIRD APPRENTICES

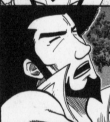

ORIGINAL OWNER OF CAFE TSUBOMI: BOTON

① SWORD
② 8/22/9992 / 23YR
③ 177CM / 72KG / A
④ GARAGE ISLAND
⑤ PRACTICING SWORDSMANSHIP
⑥ MAKING COFFEE
⑦ SHIBA, YURI
⑧ THE CURRENT GENERATION (0015)

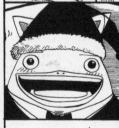

OWNER OF EDEL LAKE, THE FLYING CASINO: RUBY

① BELL? IT'S A MYSTERY
② 4/1/0057 / 10YR
③ 75CM / 30KG / ?
④ UNKNOWN
⑤ COLLECTING RARE ITEMS
⑥ APPRAISING VALUABLE ITEMS
⑦ ANYTHING AND EVERYTHING RARE, LATELY PLUE
⑧ DORYU GHOST ATTACK SQUAD

KEY ▷

① WEAPON ② BIRTHDAY/AGE ③ HEIGHT / WEIGHT BLOOD TYPE ④ BIRTHPLACE
⑤ HOBBIES ⑥ SPECIAL ABILITY ⑦ LIKES ⑧ HATES

ABOUT THE CHARACTERS

THERE WERE LOTS OF NEW FACES THIS TIME AROUND, BUT THE ONLY ONE FROM THIS ISSUE I'M GOING TO INTRODUCE HERE IS RUBY!! I AIN'T LETTING THE CAT OUT OF THE BAG ABOUT THE REST OF THEM JUST YET! BUT BEFORE WE GET TO HIM, LET'S TAKE A LOOK AT SOME OF THE OLD-TIMERS.

FIRST UP, SHIBA. OVER THE COURSE OF THE STORY, HE TURNS OUT TO BE QUITE THE COOL DUDE. YOU KNOW, I REALLY WANTED TO MAKE HIM INTO MORE OF A SISSY, CRYING LIKE "MMGAWW" ALL THE TIME, BUT YOU KNOW... GUESS THAT JUST WOULDN'T DO, THOUGH, HUH? (HA HA)

TRIED MY BEST TO DRAW RESHA AS CUTE AS POSSIBLE. YOU LIKE? I TOOK SPECIAL CARE WITH HER. SHE IS THE PERSON RAVE WAS NAMED FOR, AFTER ALL. I GET ASKED A LOT "HOW ARE ELIE AND RESHA RELATED?" C'MON--CUT ME SOME SLACK! I CAN'T GIVE THAT AWAY! (HA HA)

NOT MUCH ABOUT GALEIN MUSICA CAME OUT IN THE STORY, BUT THE SWORD OF THE WORLD HE WAS TALKING ABOUT TURNS OUT TO BE THE TEN POWERS. HIS APPRENTICE IS CREEPY.

BOTON IS GENMA'S OLD MAN. I TRIED MAKING HIM HAVE THE EXACT OPPOSITE PERSONALITY AS GENMA. INCIDENTALLY, "BOTON" MEANS "TSUBOMI" ("BUD" - NAME OF HIS CAFE) IN SOME LANGUAGE SOMEWHERE IN THE WORLD.

AND LAST BUT NOT LEAST, OUR NEWBIE, RUBY. WHY IN THE WORLD IS THIS GUY WITH HARU AND THEM, ANYWAY? (HA HA) I GUESS SINCE THIS WAS A NEW STORY ARC AND ALL, I WANTED TO BOOST UP THE NUMBER OF WEIRD CHARACTERS, LIKE PLUE AND GRIFF, SO I MADE UP RUBY AND KIND OF FORCED HIM ON HARU AND THE GANG. "WHAT'S 'POYO', ANYWAY?" I GET THAT A LOT... I'M NOT REALLY SURE, MYSELF. (HA HA) GUESS IT'S LIKE THE SOUND OF BOUNCING...POYO, POYO.

"AFTERWORDS"

THIS IS VOLUME 10. I'VE MET MY GOAL (SEE THE AFTERWORD IN VOLUME 2). THANK YOU--THANK YOU VERY MUCH! NO, THANK YOU. AND THANK YOU, TOO, OVER THERE IN THE CORNER. I COULDN'T HAVE DONE IT WITHOUT ALL OF YOUR WARM SUPPORT AND ENCOURAGEMENT. FROM THE BOTTOM OF MY HEART, THANKS A MILLION! I PRAY FOR YOUR CONTINUED SUPPORT, POYO!!

ALL RIGHT. I GUESS I SHOULD PROBABLY WRITE ABOUT THE KNIGHTS OF KINGDOM A BIT. WITH THE FIRST AND SECOND HALF, THAT WAS THE FIRST TIME I HAD WRITTEN A COMPLETE "SHORT STORY." IT WAS A LOT TOUGHER THAN I IMAGINED. THIS PIECE STARTED AS SOME VAGUE IDEAS I'VE HAD SINCE RAVE MASTER STARTED, SOMETHING I THOUGHT ALL ALONG I'D LIKE TO DO AS A SORT OF SPINOFF. SO HERE YOU HAVE IT, FOLKS. I'M VERY SATISFIED WITH IT AND I HOPE YOU ARE, TOO. ACTUALLY, I WISH I COULD HAVE HAD SOME MORE PAGES TO WORK WITH. THERE WERE SEVERAL SCENES I HAD TO CUT OUT, AS PAINFUL AS IT WAS. STUFF LIKE SHIBA WORKING ON HIS SWORDSMANSHIP BY HIM-SELF ON GARAGE ISLAND, OR ONE WHERE RESHA'S WRITING GRAFFITI ON THE SYMPHONIA FLAG AND A FASHION DESIGNER HAPPENS TO WALK BY AND SEE THIS, TAKING IT AS INSPIRATION FOR THE BRAND HEART KREUSS (THE CLOTHING BRAND ELIE ALWAYS WEARS). I CRIED AS I CUT OUT THESE PRECIOUS SCENES FROM THE STORY. WELL, EVEN SO, I THINK IT TURNED OUT WELL. ALSO, HERE'S ANOTHER SECRET. THERE ARE STILL SOME MYSTERIES HIDDEN INSIDE THE K.O.K.--UNFORTUNATELY, I CANNOT UNRAVEL THOSE MYSTERIES AT THIS TIME. ACTUALLY, I WAS TRYING TO WRITE IT SO AS TO HIDE THESE LITTLE MYSTERIES ANYWAY. CONSIDER IT A PRESENT FROM ME TO YOU. A NICE BUNDLE OF MYSTERIES, TO COM-MEMORATE THE TENTH VOLUME. HIDDEN AMONG THEM IS PART OF WHAT COULD BE CONSIDERED THE ULTIMATE RAVE MYSTERY. AND SOMEWHERE, SOMETIME, IT WILL CONNECT WITH THAT MYSTERY. I DESIGNED IT SO THAT WHEN THAT HAPPENS, YOU CAN COME BACK AND READ THE K.O.K. SIDE STORY AND YOU CAN SAY TO YOURSELF, "AH, NOW I GET IT!" BUT YOU'LL HAVE TO BE PATIENT. SO, THIS ABOUT WRAPS IT UP FOR ME... SEE YOU AGAIN IN VOLUME 11, POYO!!

PS. THE NUMBERMEN (1-8) ARE HIDING INSIDE K.O.K. THIS TIME THEY'RE PRETTY HIGH-CLASS! ESPECIALLY NUMBER 8! CAN YOU FIND THEM?

HIRO MASHIMA

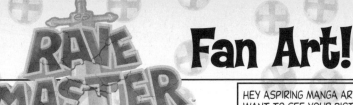

RAVE MASTER Fan Art!

GOGLORYGLORYGLORYGLORYGLO

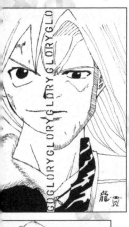

FATHER AND SON, TOGETHER AGAIN, ONE LAST TIME. VOLUME 9 STILL BRINGS A TEAR TO MY EYES. GREAT WORK, WILLIAM.

WILLIAM L.
AGE 25
CASCADE, VA

ELIE'S LOOKING PRETTY! WILL SHE EVER FIND HER MEMORIES?

MEGAN D.
AGE 14
OVERLAND PARKS, KS

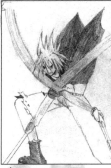

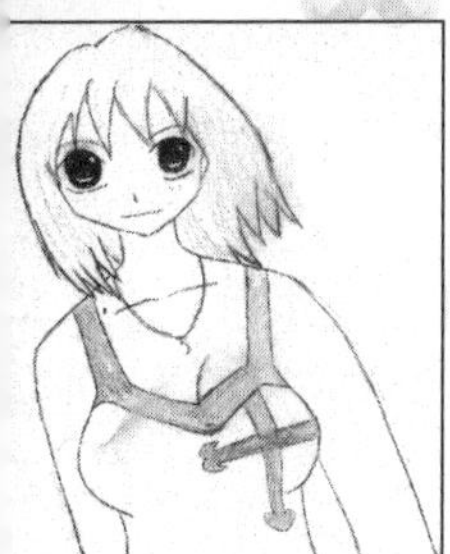

THE DOUBLE DRAGON SWORD, BLUE CRIMSON—WASN'T THAT A GREAT FIGHT? HOPEFULLY HARU WILL BUST OUT THIS MOVE AGAIN.

THOMAS MCGUIRE
AGE 10
INDIANAPOLIS, IN

COOL IDEA, ASHLEY. MASHIMA-SENSEI, ARE YOU LOOKING AT THIS? IF YOU NEED ANY MORE SIDE IDEAS, CALL UP ASHLEY!

ASHLEY T.
ALBUQUERQUE, NM

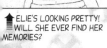

HERE IS MY FANTASY VERSION OF THE TEN POWERS SWORD'S ELEVENTH FORM: TOUGH LOVE.

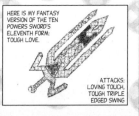

ATTACKS:
LOVING TOUCH,
TOUGH TRIPLE EDGED SWING

HEY ASPIRING MANGA ARTISTS! WANT TO SEE YOUR PICTURES IN PRINT? WELL, IF YOU THINK YOU CAN DRAW A COOL-LOOKING HARU, A SEXY ELIE OR A FUNNY PLUE, SEND 'EM THIS WAY! WE'LL PICK ONE LUCKY WINNER FROM EACH ROUND AND SEND THEM A SPECIAL PRIZE! WHAT DO HAVE TO LOSE? NOTHING!

HOW TO SUBMIT:

1) SEND YOUR WORK VIA REGULAR MAIL (NOT E-MAIL) TO:

RAVE MASTER FAN ART
C/O TOKYOPOP
5900 WILSHIRE BLVD.
SUITE 2000
LOS ANGELES, CA 90036

2) ALL WORK SUBMITTED SHOULD BE IN BLACK-AND-WHITE AND NO LARGER THAN 8.5" X 11". (AND TRY NOT TO FOLD IT TOO MANY TIMES!)

3) ANYTHING YOU SEND WILL NOT BE RETURNED. IF YOU WANT TO KEEP YOUR ORIGINAL, IT'S FINE TO SEND US A COPY.

4) PLEASE INCLUDE YOUR FULL NAME, AGE, CITY AND STATE FOR US TO PRINT WITH YOUR WORK. IF YOU'D RATHER US USE A PEN NAME, PLEASE INCLUDE THAT TOO.

5) IMPORTANT: IF YOU'RE UNDER THE AGE OF 18, YOU MUST HAVE YOUR PARENT'S PERMISSION IN ORDER FOR US TO PRINT YOUR WORK. ANY SUBMISSIONS WITHOUT A SIGNED NOTE OF PARENTAL CONSENT CANNOT BE USED.

6) FOR FULL DETAILS, PLEASE CHECK OUT HTTP://WWW.TOKYOPOP.COM/ABOUTUS/FANART.PHP

DRAW US! PUUN!

DISCLAIMER: ANYTHING YOU SEND TO US BECOMES THE PROPERTY OF TOKYOPOP INC. AND, AS WE SAID BEFORE, WILL NOT BE RETURNED TO YOU. WE WILL HAVE THE RIGHT TO PRINT, REPRODUCE, DISTRIBUTE OR MODIFY THE ARTWORK FOR USE IN FUTURE VOLUMES OF RAVE MASTER OR ON THE WEB WITHOUT PAYMENT TO YOU.

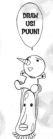

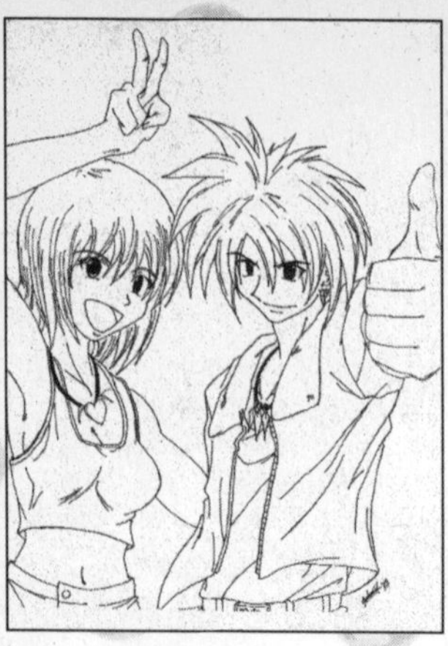

YOUR DRAWING HAS A LOT OF STYLE. I LOVE IT!

JOE S.
AGE 18
GAINESVILLE, VA

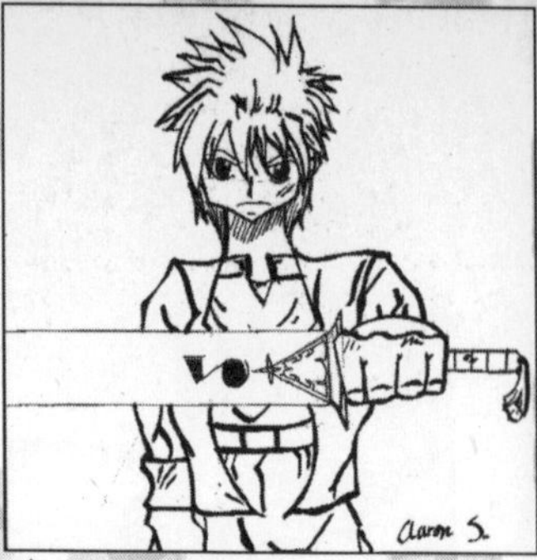
Aaron S.

COOL POSE OF A COOL GUY. THANK YOU SO MUCH FOR SENDING YOUR WORK!

AARON S.
AGE 11
CAROL STREAM, IL

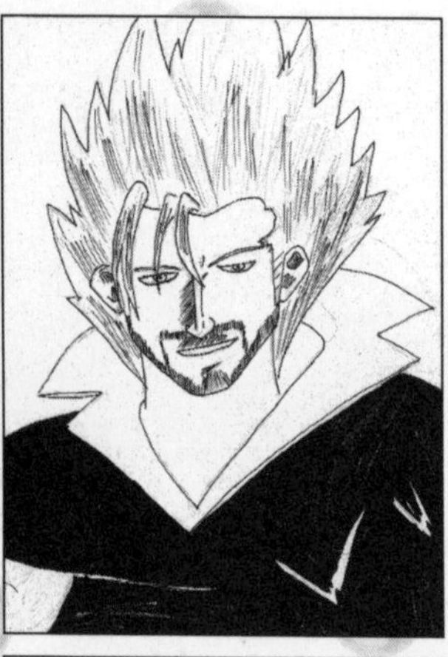

A PORTRAIT OF EVIL? ISN'T IT AMAZING HOW KING WENT FROM BEING SUCH A TOTAL BADDIE TO BEING A TRAGIC HERO? NOW **THAT'S** THE POWER OF RAVE—MASHIMA-SENSEI'S GREAT STORYTELLING. THANKS FOR THE COOL PIC, JARED.

JARED H.
CLARKSVILLE, OH

GREAT SHOT OF HARU. HE LOOKS LIKE HE COULD TAKE ON ANYBODY!

HEATH B
AGE 12
JACKSONVILLE, TX

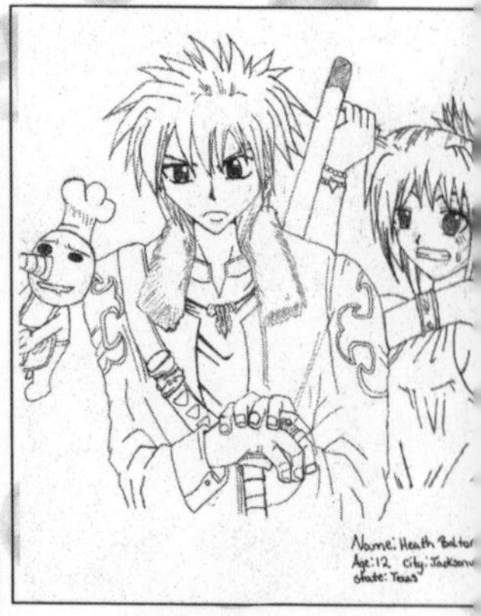

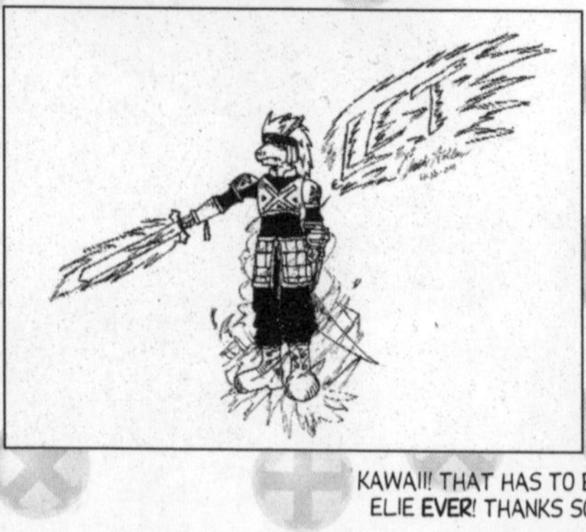

LET, THE ENEMY-TURNED-HERO. DON'T YOU JUST LOVE THE SAMURAI ARMOR? I'M GLAD HE'S HERE TO STAY!

JOSIAH A.
AGE 14
CLEARSPRING, MD

KAWAII! THAT HAS TO BE THE CUTEST ELIE **EVER**! THANKS SO MUCH, GENNA.

GENNA B.
AGE 15
STROUDSBURG, PA

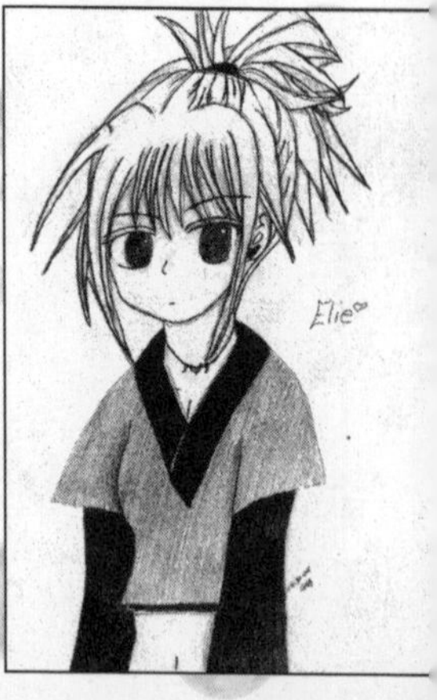
Elie

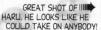

Ch-ch-ch-changes!

A RAVE MASTER MUST HAVE PATIENCE, DETERMINATION AND A KEEN EYE, AND YOU'LL NEED ALL OF THOSE TO SOLVE THIS PUZZLE. THERE ARE 12 DIFFERENCES BETWEEN THESE TWO PICTURES. CAN YOU SPOT THEM ALL?

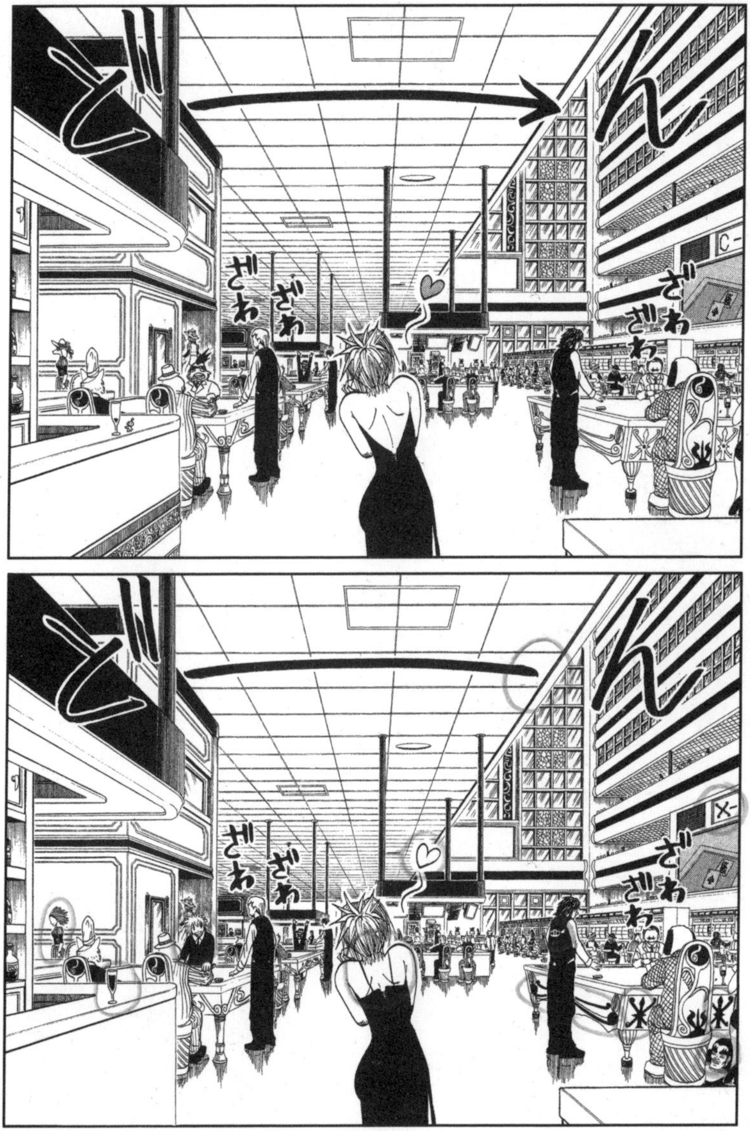

どん
ざわ
ざわ
ざわ
ざわ
C-
どん
ざわ
ざわ
ざわ
ざわ
X-

View the True Plue!

SOMEHOW PLUE GOT MIXED UP WITH A BUNCH OF OTHER DOG...BUG...THINGS.
CAN YOU IDENTIFY WHICH IS THE TRUE PLUE?

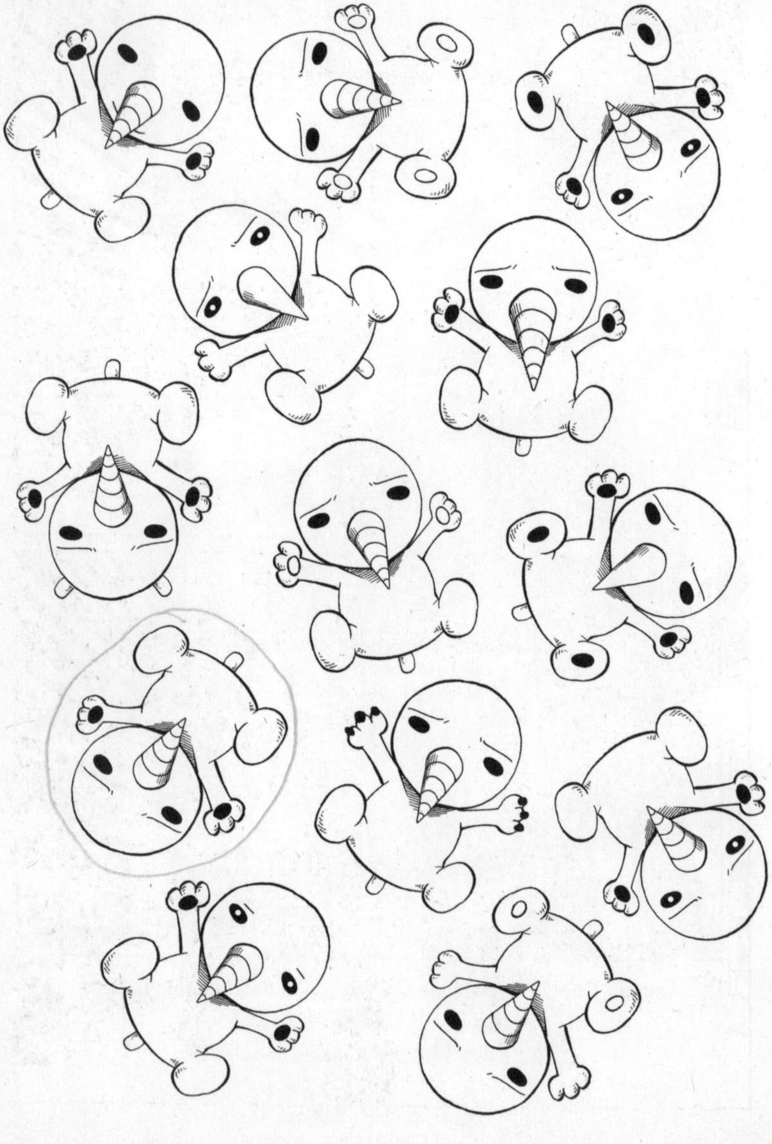

The Oracion Six are alive?!

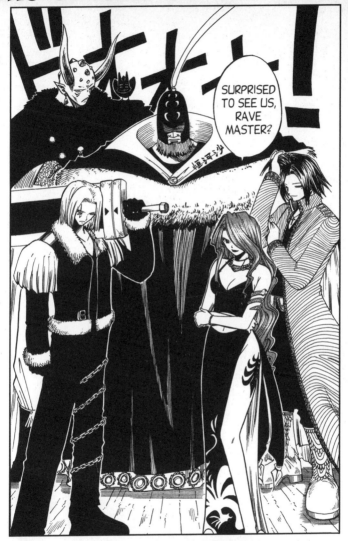

Demon Card's top generals are BACK with a new leader...
the DARK BRING MASTER!
The Rave Master meets his match!

Rave Master Volume 11
Available October 2004

ATTENTION ALL ACTION FANS!

BEFORE RAVE MASTER TOOK JAPAN BY STORM, ET CETERA WAS ONE OF THE MOST POPULAR MANGA IN KODANSHA'S GEKKAN SHONEN MAGAZINE. NOW TOKYOPOP IS EXCITED TO BRING THIS WACKY WILD WEST ADVENTURE TO ENGLISH-LANGUAGE READERS. HERE'S A SPECIAL SNEAK PREVIEW OF THE FIRST CHAPTER.

THE WILD WEST... A DANGEROUS FRONTIER WHERE THE ONLY LAW IS THE GUN. MINGCHAO ISN'T ABOUT TO LET A FEW OUTLAWS KEEP HER FROM HER HOLLYWOOD DREAMS! SHE HAS THE ETO GUN, A MYSTERIOUS WEAPON THAT USES THE SPIRITS OF THE ZODIAC ANIMALS TO FIRE UNSTOPPABLE BULLETS. TOGETHER WITH HER UNLIKELY TRAVELING COMPANION BASKERVILLE, A PRIEST ON A SECRET MISSION, MINGCHAO IS HEADING WEST TO BECOME A STAR!

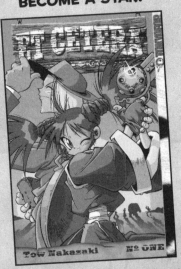

VOL. 1 AVAILABLE NOW!

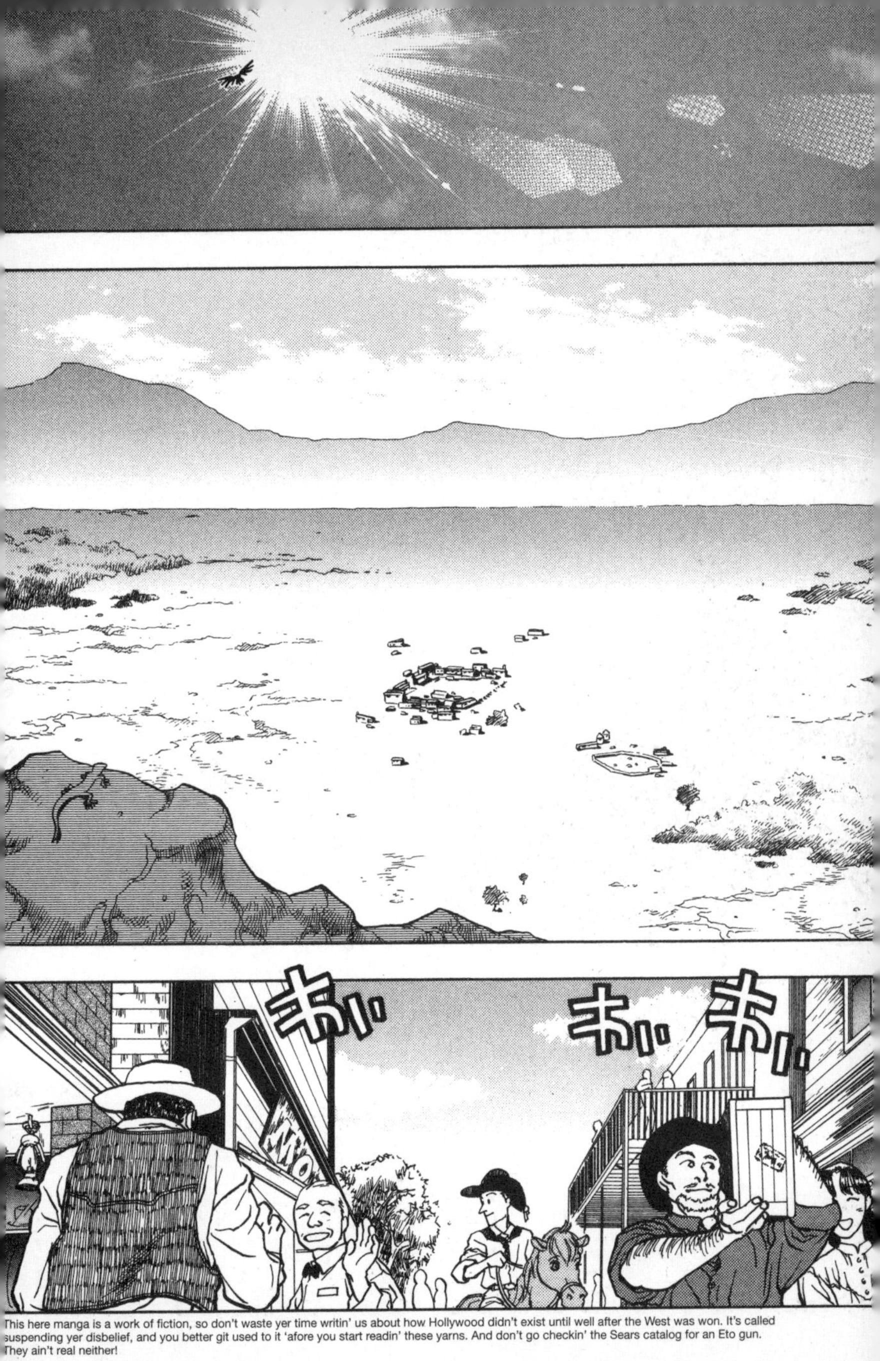
おい
おい
おい

This here manga is a work of fiction, so don't waste yer time writin' us about how Hollywood didn't exist until well after the West was won. It's called suspending yer disbelief, and you better git used to it 'afore you start readin' these yarns. And don't go checkin' the Sears catalog for an Eto gun. They ain't real neither!

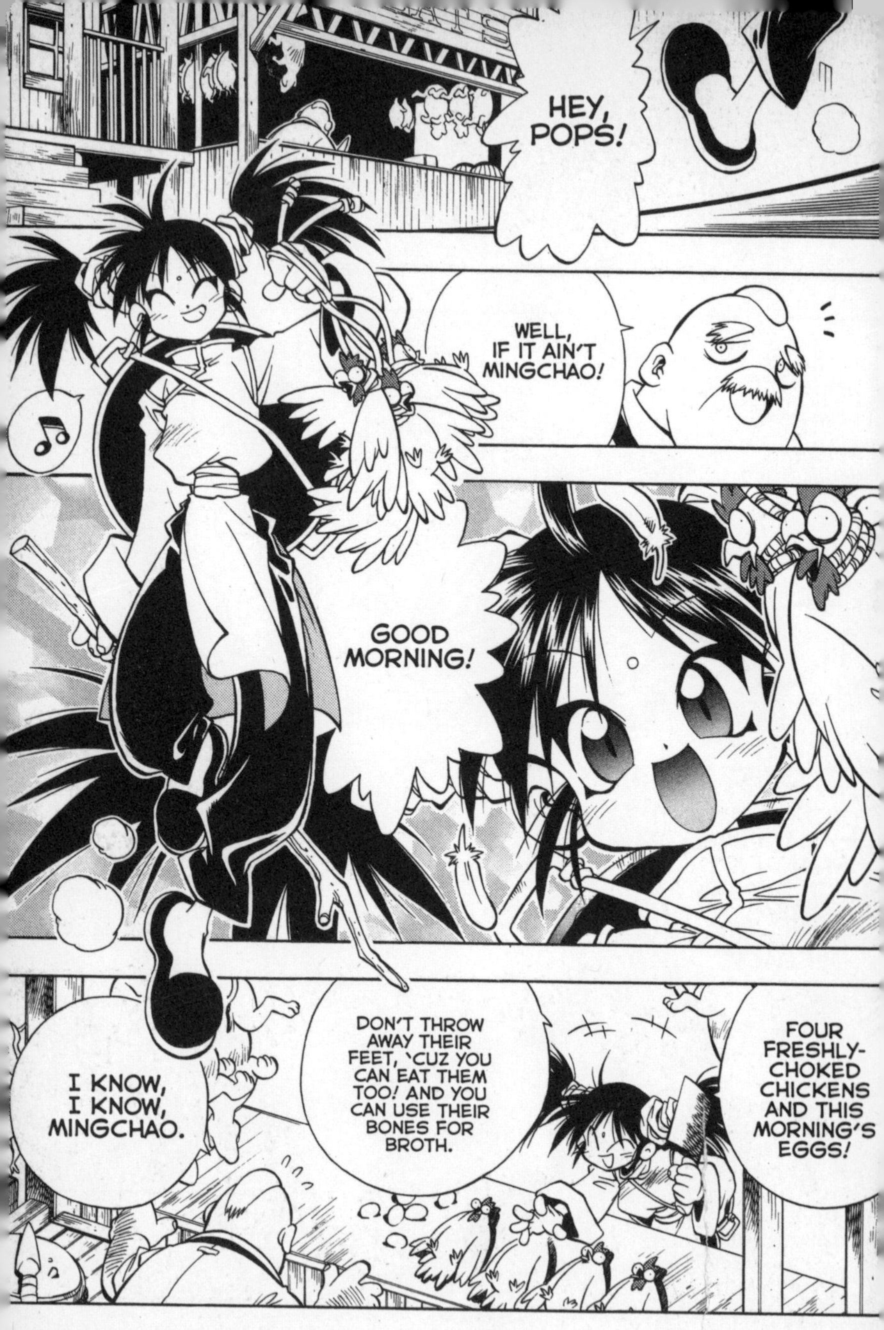
HEY, POPS!
WELL, IF IT AIN'T MINGCHAO!
GOOD MORNING!
FOUR FRESHLY-CHOKED CHICKENS AND THIS MORNING'S EGGS!
DON'T THROW AWAY THEIR FEET, 'CUZ YOU CAN EAT THEM TOO! AND YOU CAN USE THEIR BONES FOR BROTH.
I KNOW, I KNOW, MINGCHAO.

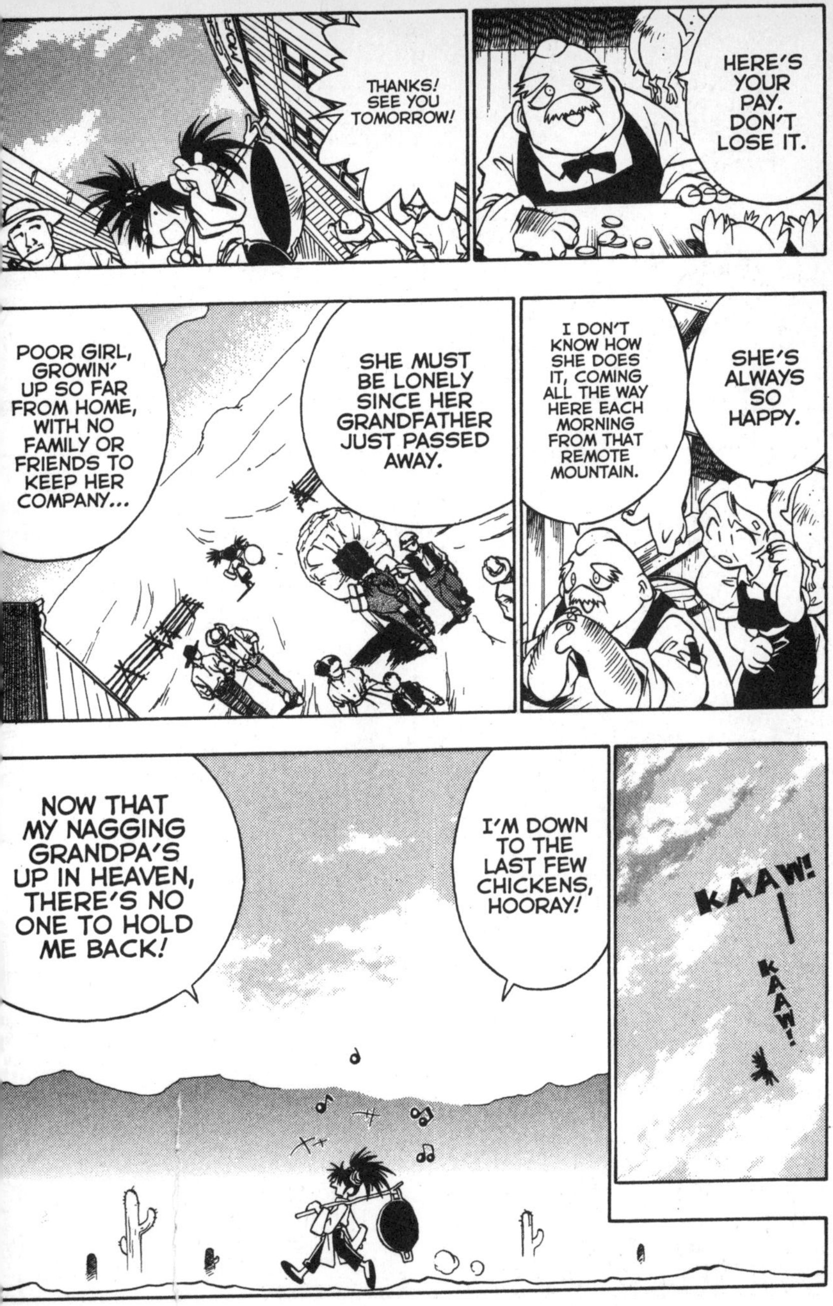
HERE'S YOUR PAY. DON'T LOSE IT.
THANKS! SEE YOU TOMORROW!
SHE'S ALWAYS SO HAPPY.
I DON'T KNOW HOW SHE DOES IT, COMING ALL THE WAY HERE EACH MORNING FROM THAT REMOTE MOUNTAIN.
SHE MUST BE LONELY SINCE HER GRANDFATHER JUST PASSED AWAY.
POOR GIRL, GROWIN' UP SO FAR FROM HOME, WITH NO FAMILY OR FRIENDS TO KEEP HER COMPANY...
KAAW!
KAAAW!
I'M DOWN TO THE LAST FEW CHICKENS, HOORAY!
NOW THAT MY NAGGING GRANDPA'S UP IN HEAVEN, THERE'S NO ONE TO HOLD ME BACK!

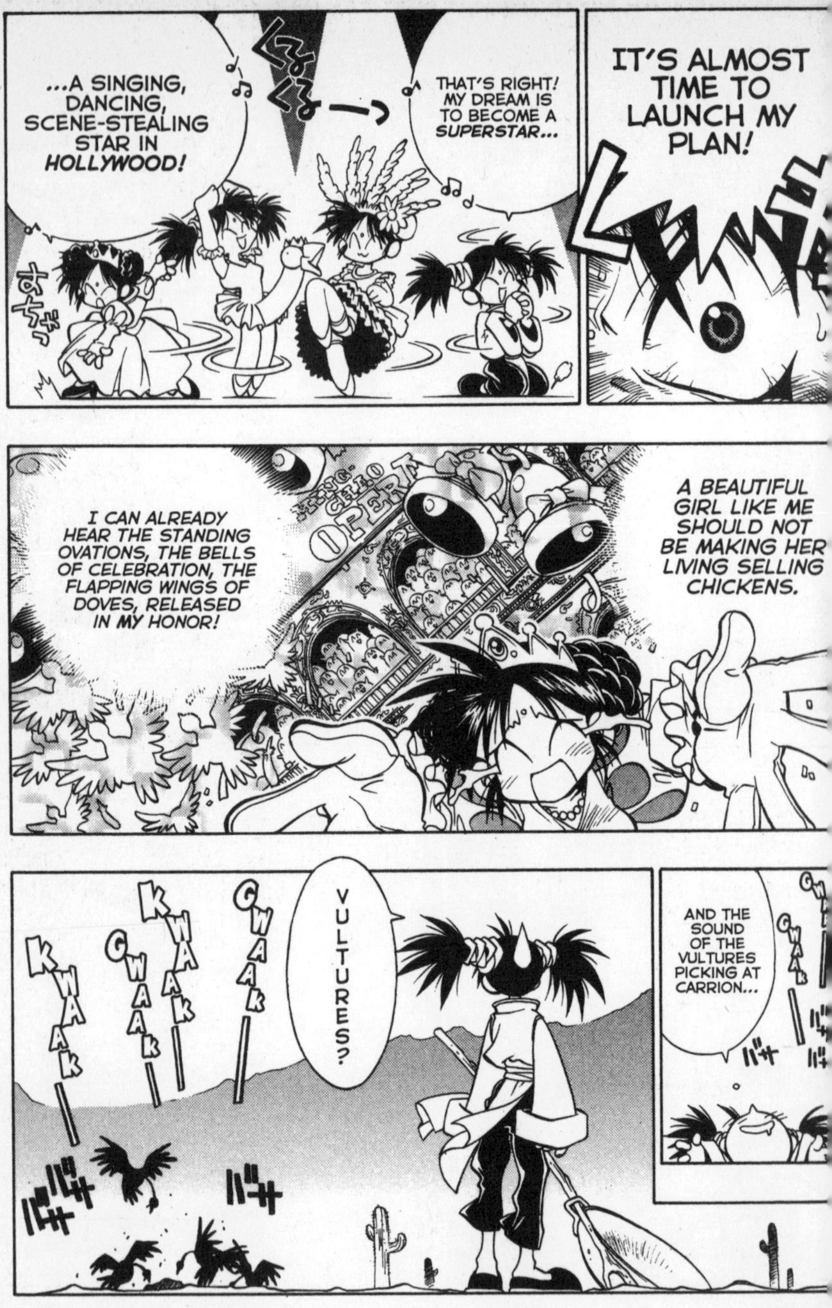
IT'S ALMOST TIME TO LAUNCH MY PLAN!
THAT'S RIGHT! MY DREAM IS TO BECOME A *SUPERSTAR*...
...A SINGING, DANCING, SCENE-STEALING STAR IN *HOLLYWOOD!*
A BEAUTIFUL GIRL LIKE ME SHOULD NOT BE MAKING HER LIVING SELLING CHICKENS.
I CAN ALREADY HEAR THE STANDING OVATIONS, THE BELLS OF CELEBRATION, THE FLAPPING WINGS OF DOVES, RELEASED IN MY HONOR!
AND THE SOUND OF THE VULTURES PICKING AT CARRION...
GWAAK
VULTURES?
GWAAK—
KWAAK—
GWAAK—
KWAAK—

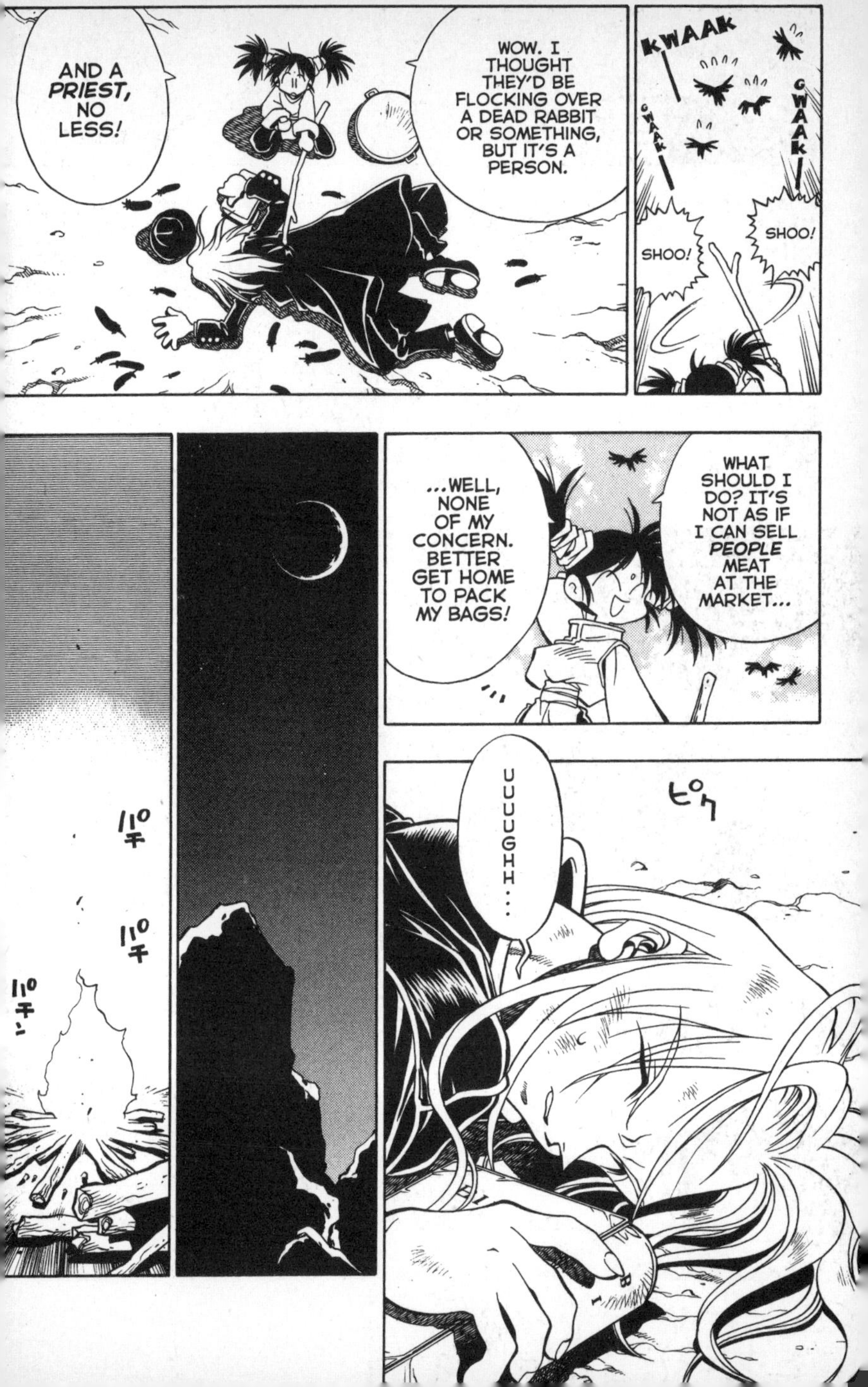
KWAAK
GWAAK
GWAAK
SHOO!
SHOO!
WOW. I THOUGHT THEY'D BE FLOCKING OVER A DEAD RABBIT OR SOMETHING, BUT IT'S A PERSON.
AND A *PRIEST*, NO LESS!
WHAT SHOULD I DO? IT'S NOT AS IF I CAN SELL *PEOPLE* MEAT AT THE MARKET...
...WELL, NONE OF MY CONCERN. BETTER GET HOME TO PACK MY BAGS!
ピク
UUUUGHH...
パチ
パチ
パチン

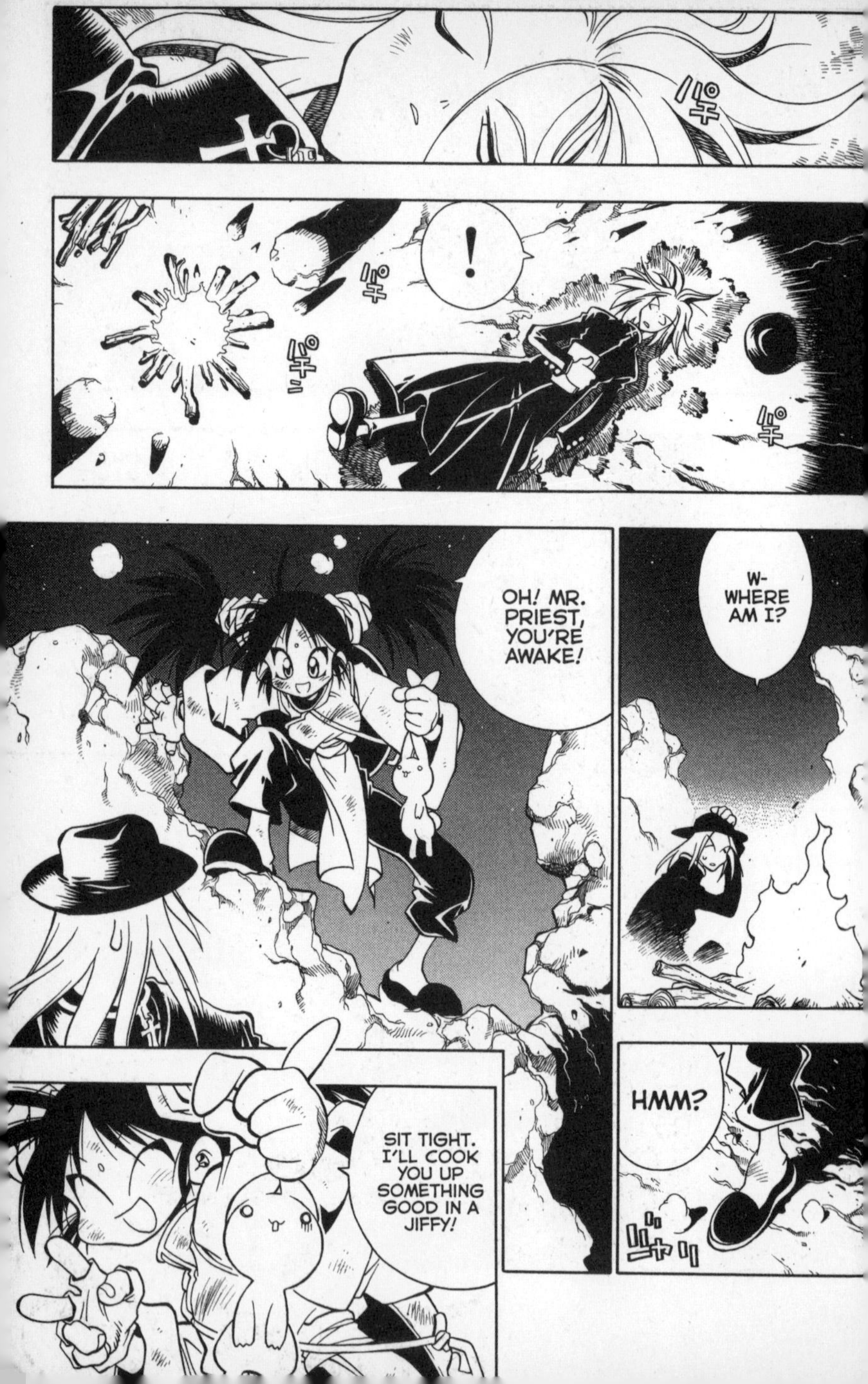
パキ
!
パキ
パキッ
パキ
W-
WHERE
AM I?
OH! MR.
PRIEST,
YOU'RE
AWAKE!
HMM?
ジャリ
SIT TIGHT.
I'LL COOK
YOU UP
SOMETHING
GOOD IN A
JIFFY!

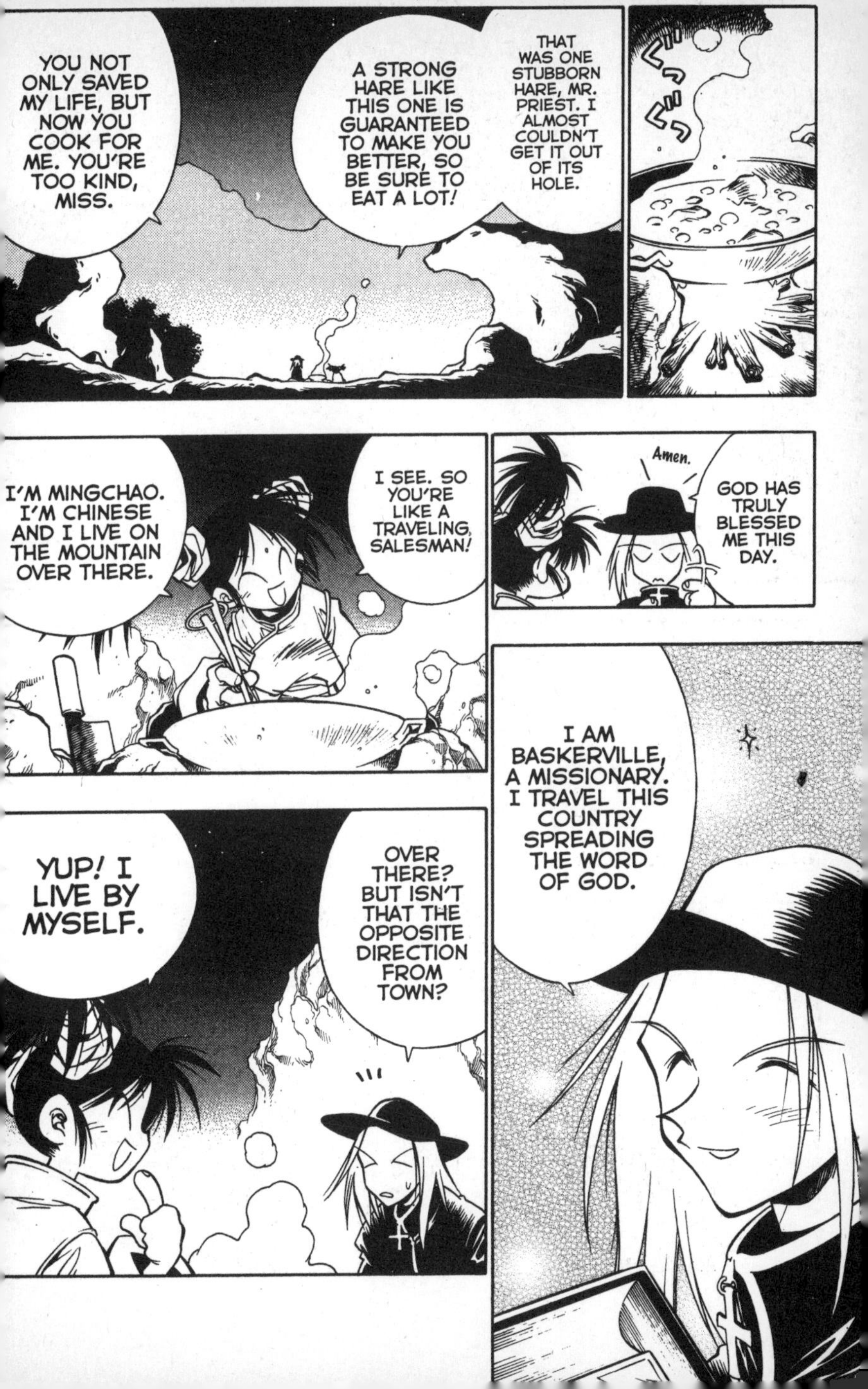
THAT WAS ONE STUBBORN HARE, MR. PRIEST. I ALMOST COULDN'T GET IT OUT OF ITS HOLE.
A STRONG HARE LIKE THIS ONE IS GUARANTEED TO MAKE YOU BETTER, SO BE SURE TO EAT A LOT!
YOU NOT ONLY SAVED MY LIFE, BUT NOW YOU COOK FOR ME. YOU'RE TOO KIND, MISS.
GOD HAS TRULY BLESSED ME THIS DAY.
Amen.
I AM BASKERVILLE, A MISSIONARY. I TRAVEL THIS COUNTRY SPREADING THE WORD OF GOD.
I SEE. SO YOU'RE LIKE A TRAVELING SALESMAN!
I'M MINGCHAO. I'M CHINESE AND I LIVE ON THE MOUNTAIN OVER THERE.
OVER THERE? BUT ISN'T THAT THE OPPOSITE DIRECTION FROM TOWN?
YUP! I LIVE BY MYSELF.

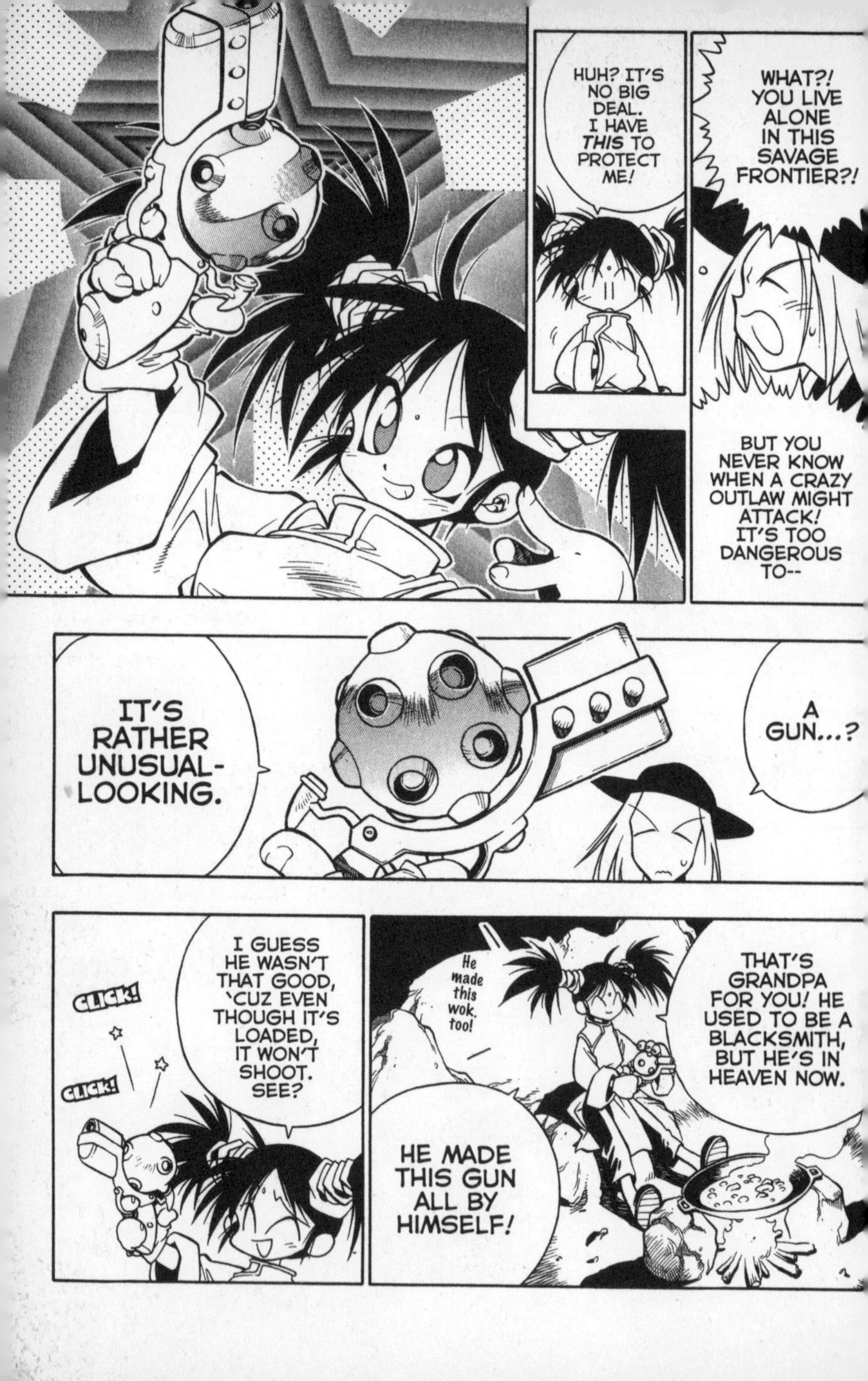
WHAT?! YOU LIVE ALONE IN THIS SAVAGE FRONTIER?!
BUT YOU NEVER KNOW WHEN A CRAZY OUTLAW MIGHT ATTACK! IT'S TOO DANGEROUS TO--
HUH? IT'S NO BIG DEAL. I HAVE *THIS* TO PROTECT ME!
A GUN...?
IT'S RATHER UNUSUAL-LOOKING.
THAT'S GRANDPA FOR YOU! HE USED TO BE A BLACKSMITH, BUT HE'S IN HEAVEN NOW.
He made this wok, too!
HE MADE THIS GUN ALL BY HIMSELF!
I GUESS HE WASN'T THAT GOOD, 'CUZ EVEN THOUGH IT'S LOADED, IT WON'T SHOOT. SEE?
CLICK!
CLICK!

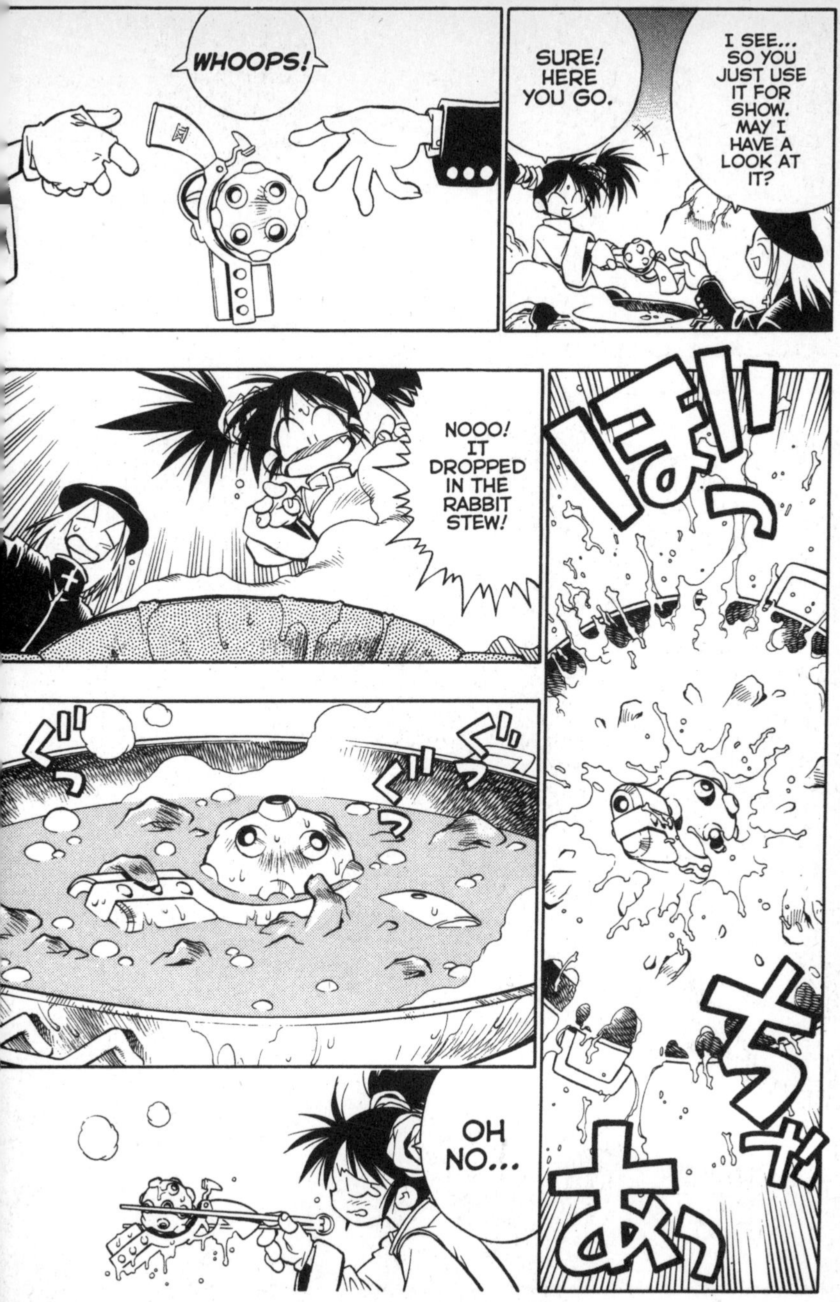
I SEE... SO YOU JUST USE IT FOR SHOW. MAY I HAVE A LOOK AT IT?
SURE! HERE YOU GO.
WHOOPS!
ぼっ
ぢあっ
NOOO! IT DROPPED IN THE RABBIT STEW!
ぐつ
ぐつぐつ
OH NO...

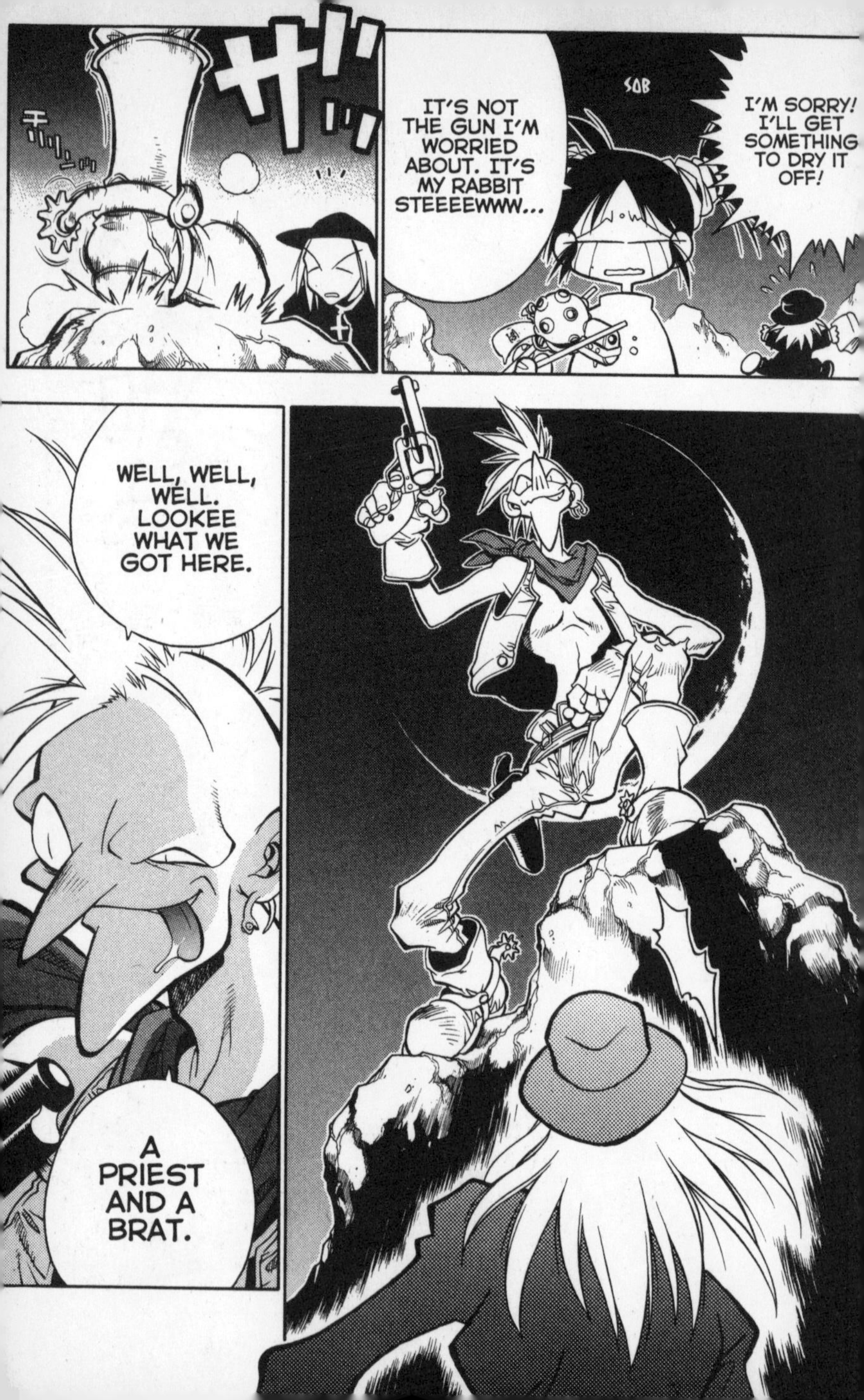
I'M SORRY! I'LL GET SOMETHING TO DRY IT OFF!
SOB
IT'S NOT THE GUN I'M WORRIED ABOUT. IT'S MY RABBIT STEEEEWWW...
WELL, WELL, WELL. LOOKEE WHAT WE GOT HERE.
A PRIEST AND A BRAT.

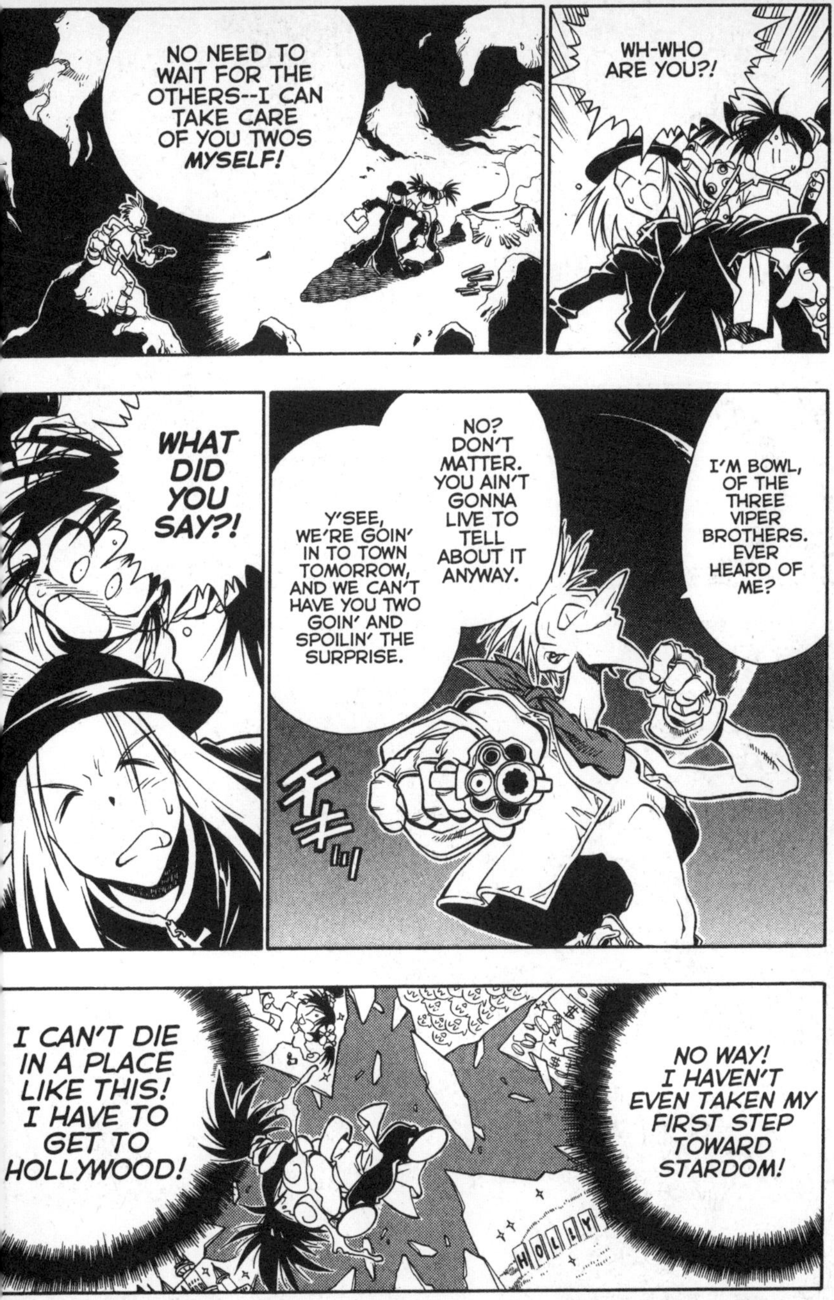
WH-WHO ARE YOU?!
NO NEED TO WAIT FOR THE OTHERS--I CAN TAKE CARE OF YOU TWOS *MYSELF!*
I'M BOWL, OF THE THREE VIPER BROTHERS. EVER HEARD OF ME?
NO? DON'T MATTER. YOU AIN'T GONNA LIVE TO TELL ABOUT IT ANYWAY.
Y'SEE, WE'RE GOIN' IN TO TOWN TOMORROW, AND WE CAN'T HAVE YOU TWO GOIN' AND SPOILIN' THE SURPRISE.
WHAT DID YOU SAY?!
NO WAY! I HAVEN'T EVEN TAKEN MY FIRST STEP TOWARD STARDOM!
HOLLY
I CAN'T DIE IN A PLACE LIKE THIS! I HAVE TO GET TO HOLLYWOOD!

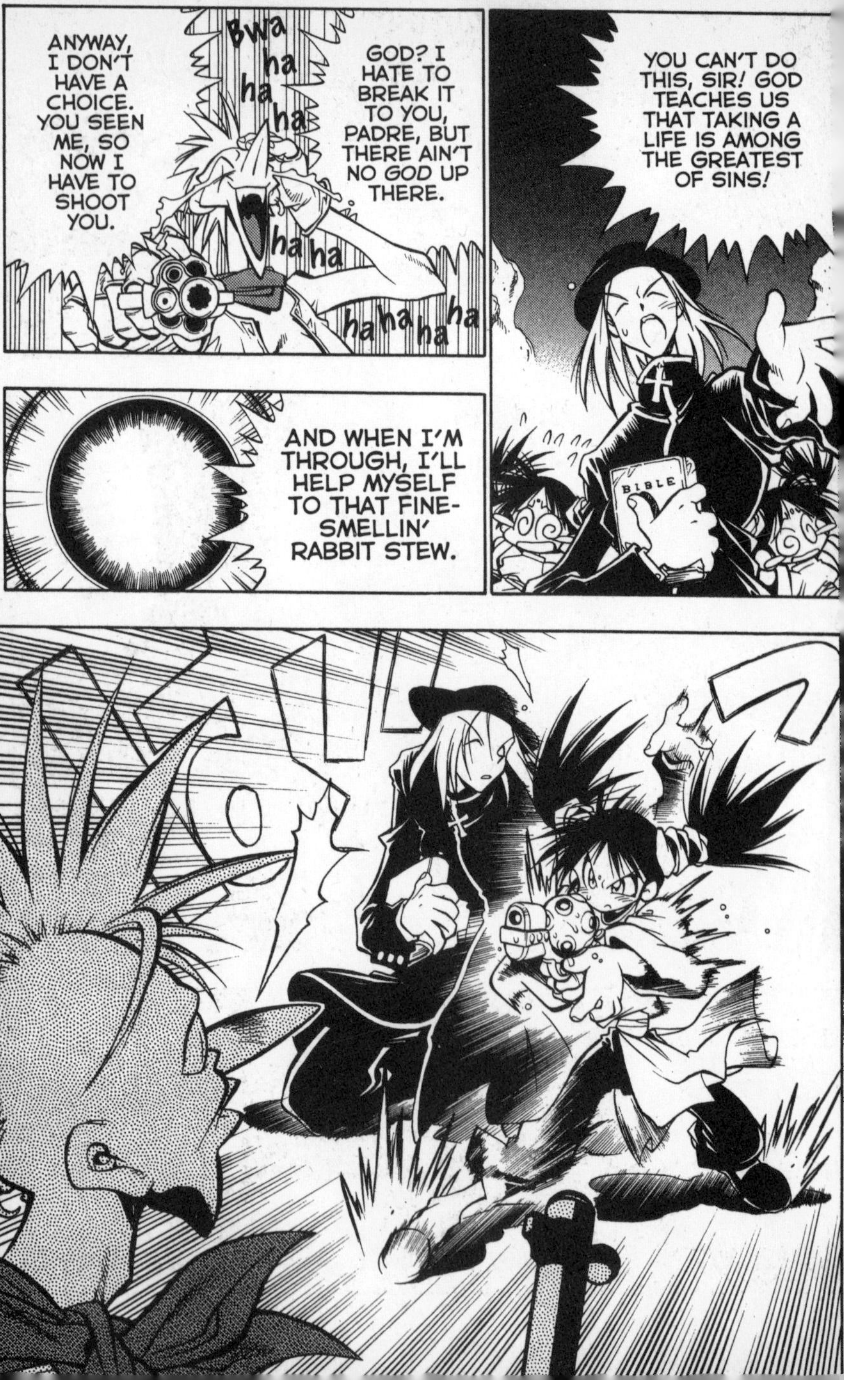
YOU CAN'T DO THIS, SIR! GOD TEACHES US THAT TAKING A LIFE IS AMONG THE GREATEST OF SINS!
BIBLE
GOD? I HATE TO BREAK IT TO YOU, PADRE, BUT THERE AIN'T NO GOD UP THERE.
Bwa ha ha ha ha ha ha ha ha ha ha ha
ANYWAY, I DON'T HAVE A CHOICE. YOU SEEN ME, SO NOW I HAVE TO SHOOT YOU.
AND WHEN I'M THROUGH, I'LL HELP MYSELF TO THAT FINE-SMELLIN' RABBIT STEW.

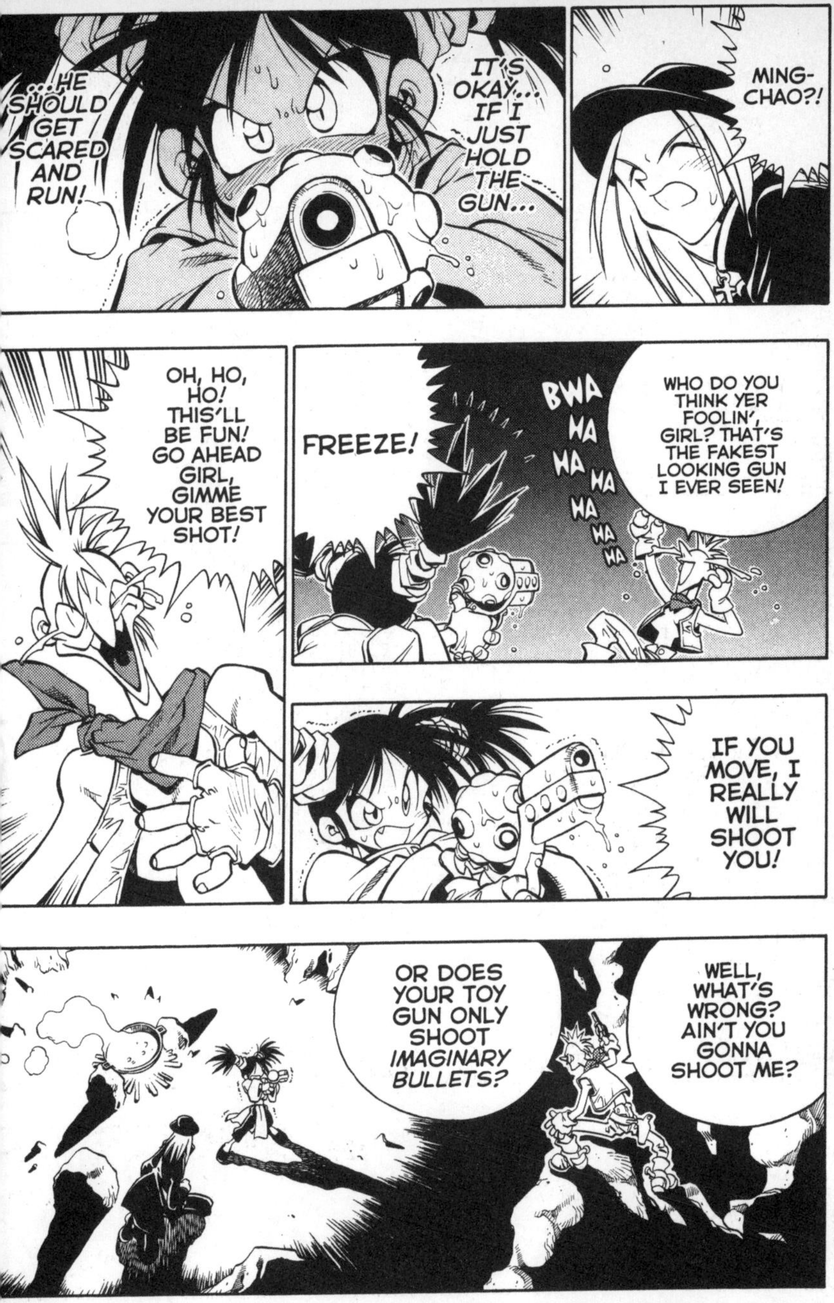
MING-CHAO?!
IT'S OKAY... IF I JUST HOLD THE GUN...
...HE SHOULD GET SCARED AND RUN!
WHO DO YOU THINK YER FOOLIN', GIRL? THAT'S THE FAKEST LOOKING GUN I EVER SEEN!
BWA HA HA HA HA HA HA
FREEZE!
IF YOU MOVE, I REALLY WILL SHOOT YOU!
OH, HO, HO! THIS'LL BE FUN! GO AHEAD GIRL, GIMME YOUR BEST SHOT!
WELL, WHAT'S WRONG? AIN'T YOU GONNA SHOOT ME?
OR DOES YOUR TOY GUN ONLY SHOOT *IMAGINARY* BULLETS?

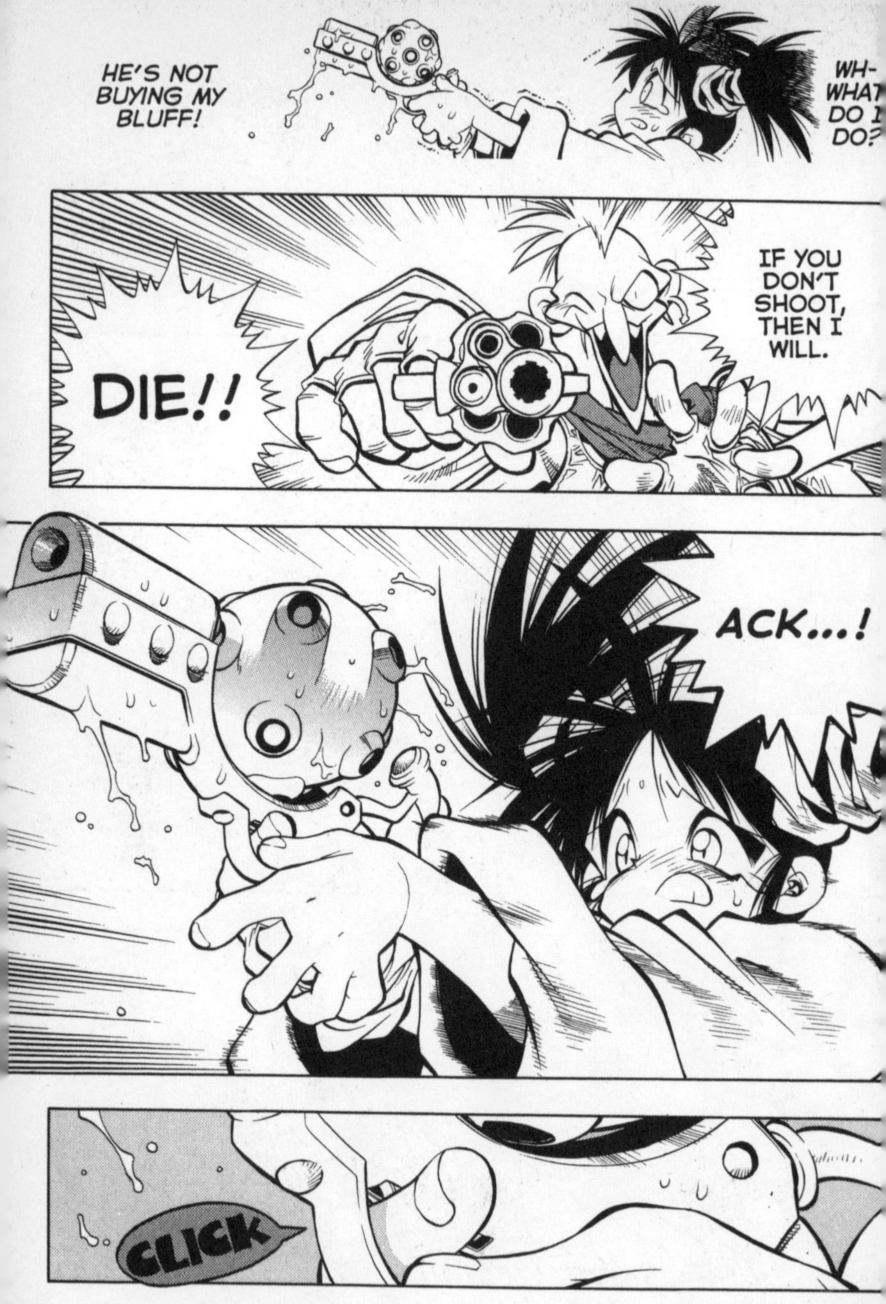
WH- WHAT DO I DO?
HE'S NOT BUYING MY BLUFF!
IF YOU DON'T SHOOT, THEN I WILL.
DIE!!
ACK...!
CLICK

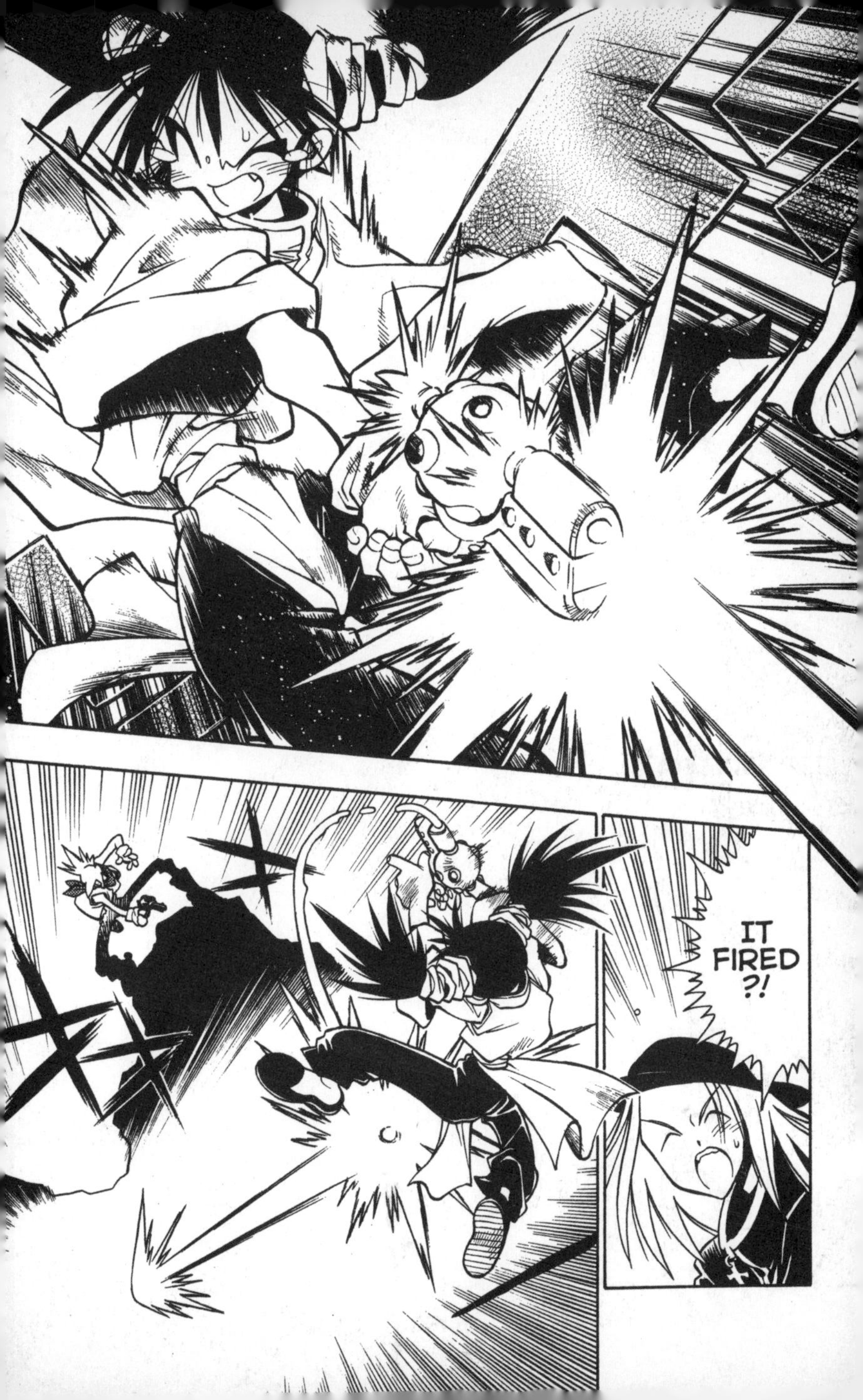
IT FIRED ?!

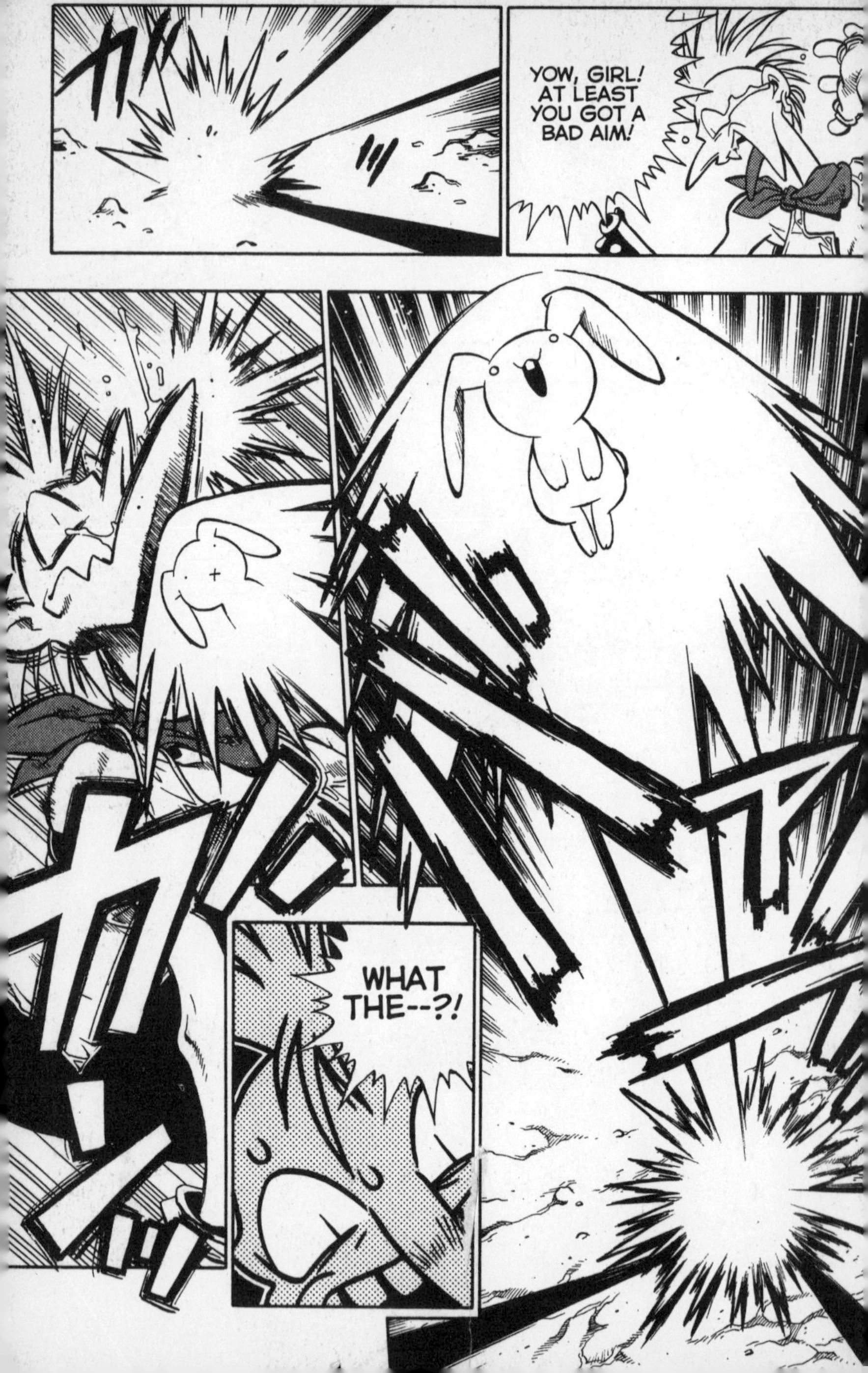
YOW, GIRL! AT LEAST YOU GOT A BAD AIM!
WHAT THE--?!

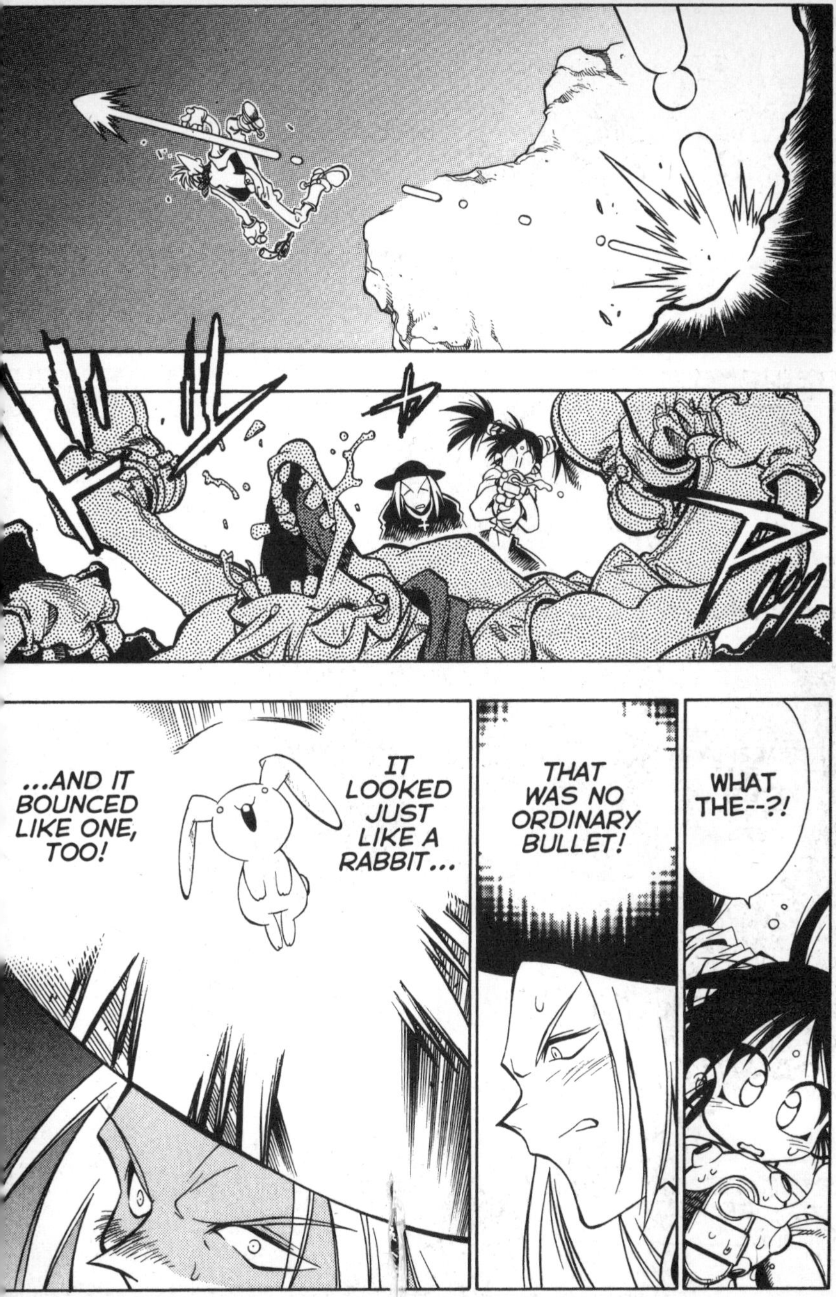
WHAT THE--?!
THAT WAS NO ORDINARY BULLET!
IT LOOKED JUST LIKE A RABBIT...
...AND IT BOUNCED LIKE ONE, TOO!

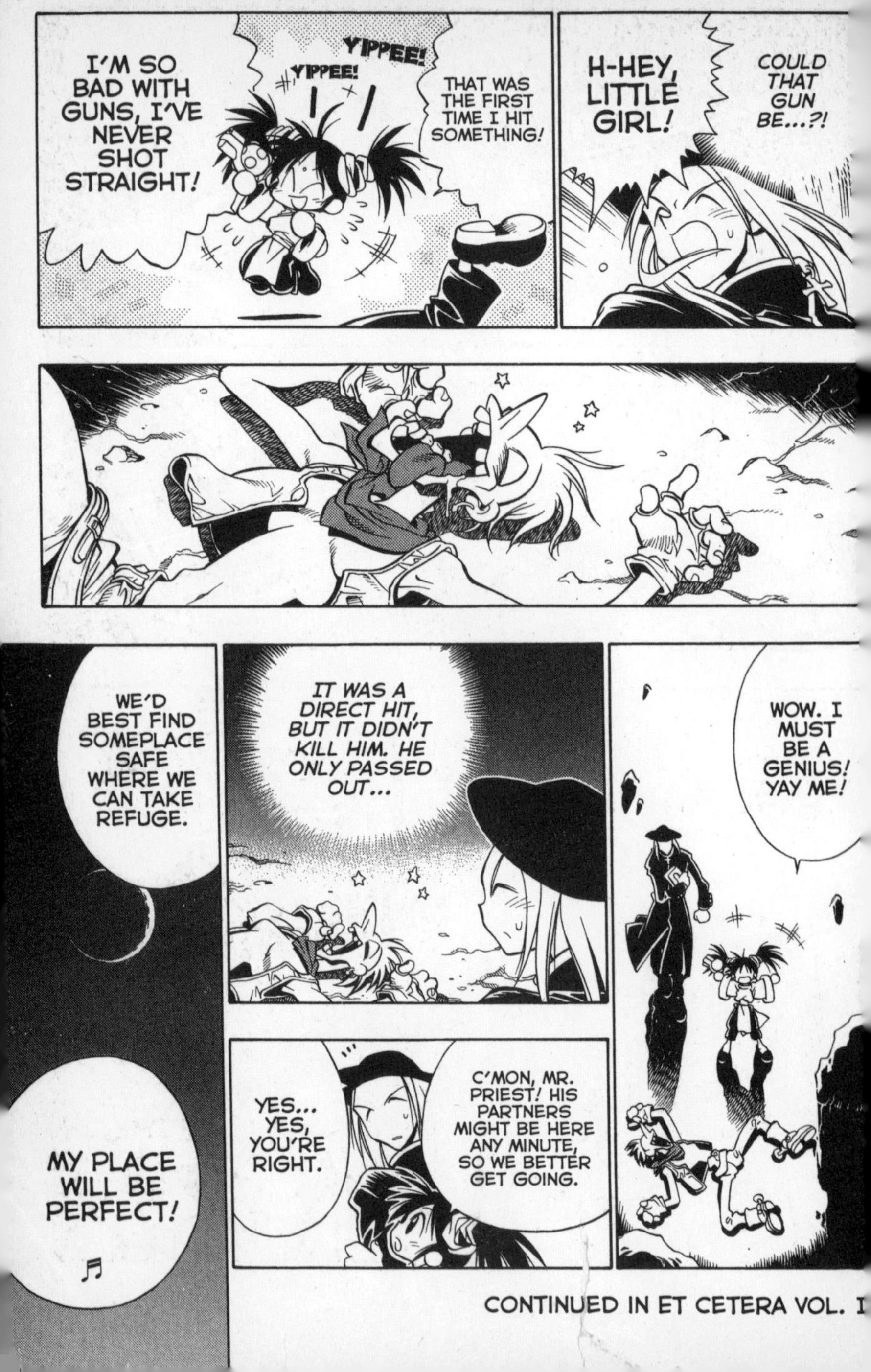
COULD THAT GUN BE...?!
H-HEY, LITTLE GIRL!
YIPPEE!
YIPPEE!
THAT WAS THE FIRST TIME I HIT SOMETHING!
I'M SO BAD WITH GUNS, I'VE NEVER SHOT STRAIGHT!
WOW. I MUST BE A GENIUS! YAY ME!
IT WAS A DIRECT HIT, BUT IT DIDN'T KILL HIM. HE ONLY PASSED OUT...
C'MON, MR. PRIEST! HIS PARTNERS MIGHT BE HERE ANY MINUTE, SO WE BETTER GET GOING.
YES... YES, YOU'RE RIGHT.
WE'D BEST FIND SOMEPLACE SAFE WHERE WE CAN TAKE REFUGE.
MY PLACE WILL BE PERFECT! ♫

CONTINUED IN ET CETERA VOL. 1

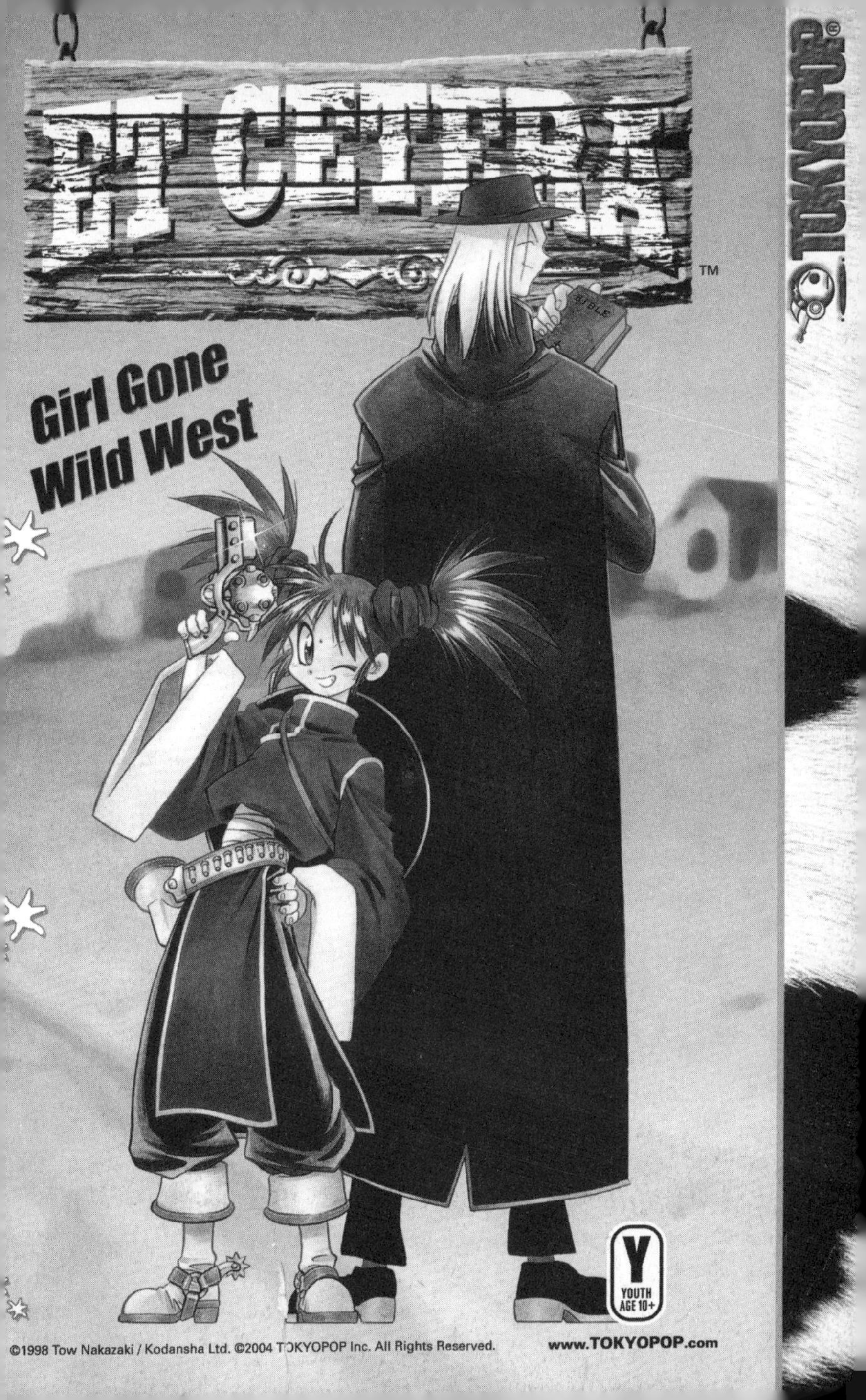
TOKYOPOP
TM
BIBLE
Girl Gone
Wild West
Y
YOUTH
AGE 10+
©1998 Tow Nakazaki / Kodansha Ltd. ©2004 TOKYOPOP Inc. All Rights Reserved.
www.TOKYOPOP.com

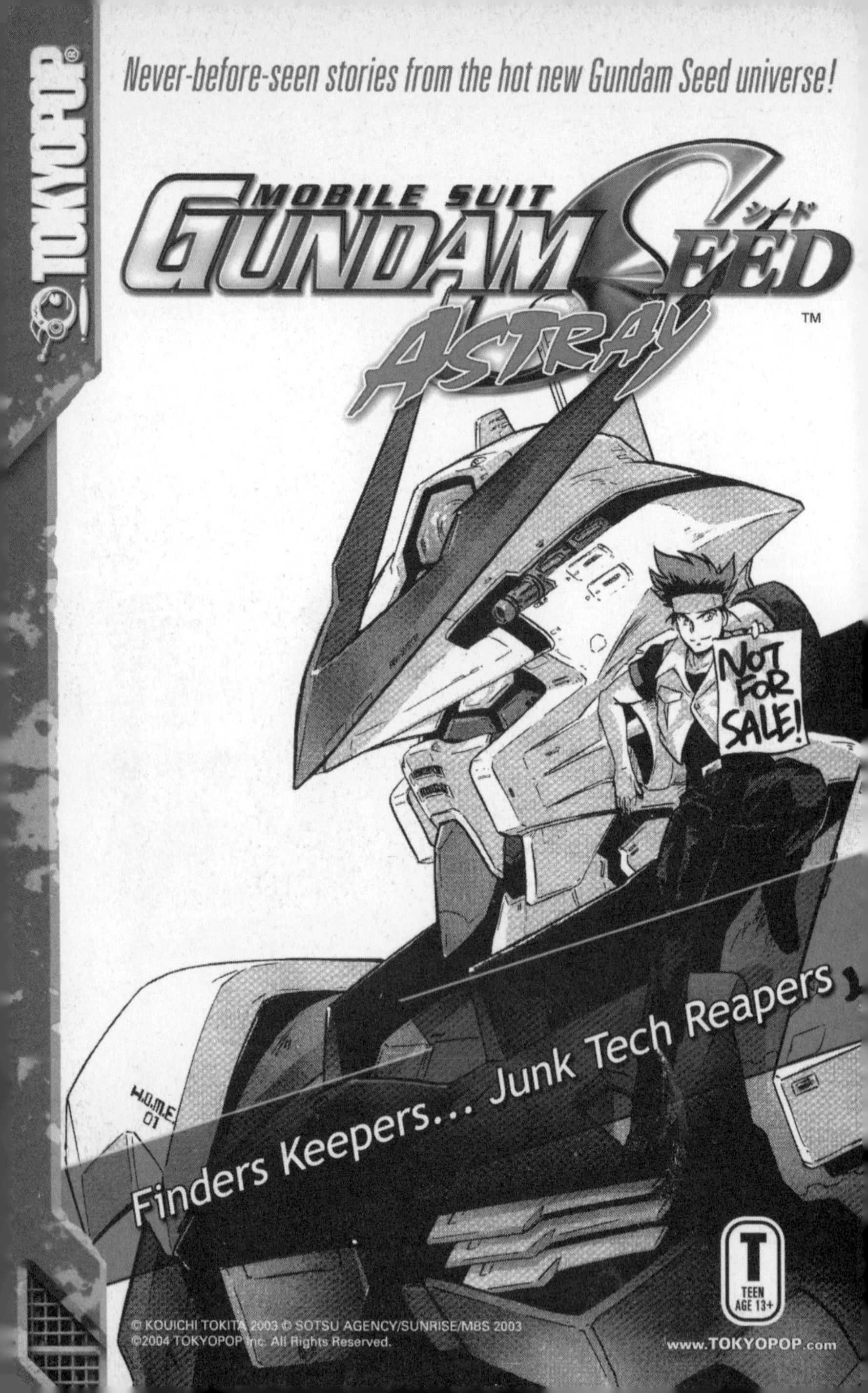
TOKYOPOP
Never-before-seen stories from the hot new Gundam Seed universe!
MOBILE SUIT
GUNDAM SEED
シード
ASTRAY
TM
NOT FOR SALE!
H.O.M.E.
01
Finders Keepers... Junk Tech Reapers
T
TEEN
AGE 13+
© KOUICHI TOKITA 2003 © SOTSU AGENCY/SUNRISE/MBS 2003
©2004 TOKYOPOP Inc. All Rights Reserved.
www.TOKYOPOP.com

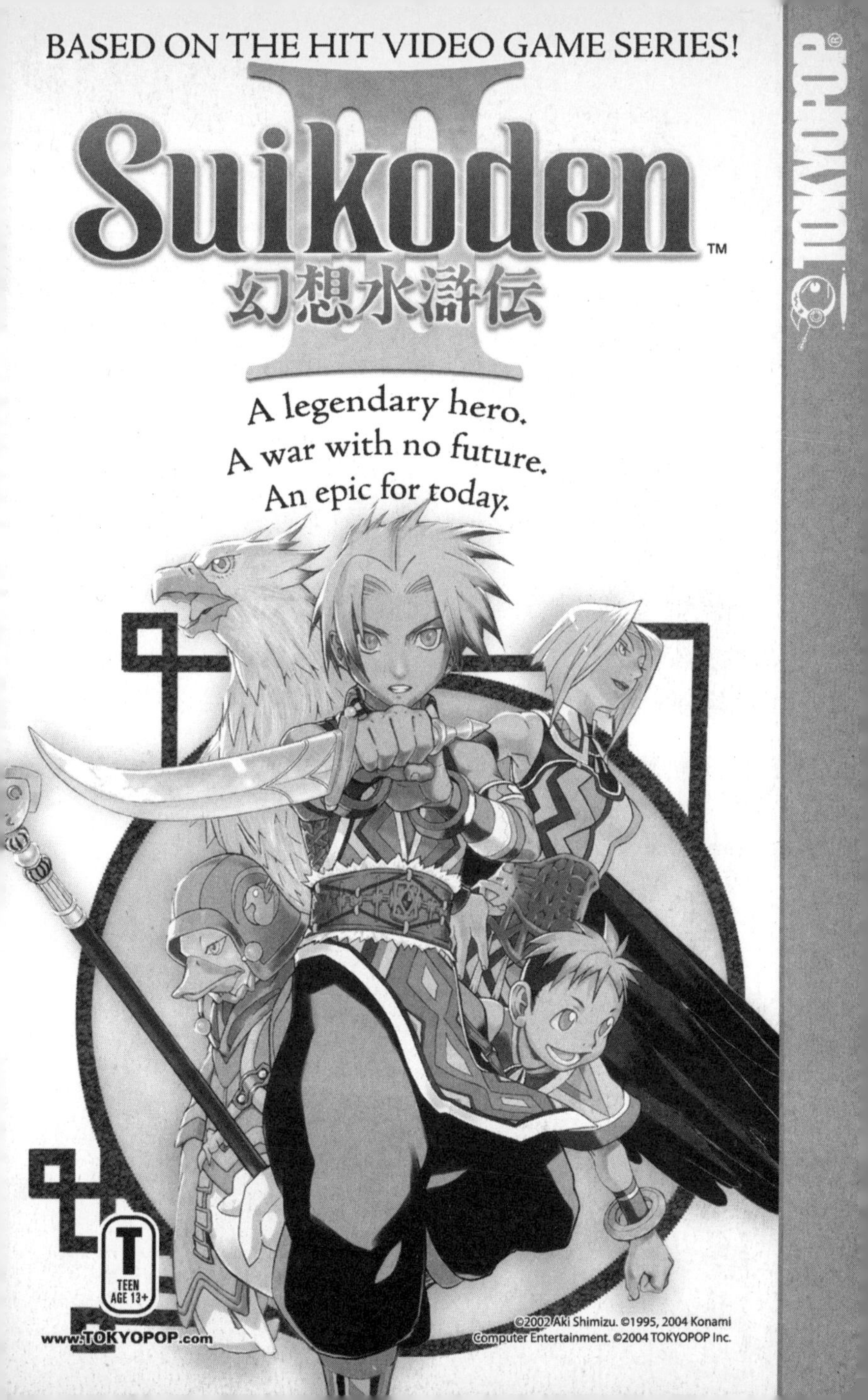
BASED ON THE HIT VIDEO GAME SERIES!
Suikoden III™
幻想水滸伝
A legendary hero.
A war with no future.
An epic for today.
T
TEEN
AGE 13+
www.TOKYOPOP.com
©2002 Aki Shimizu. ©1995, 2004 Konami Computer Entertainment. ©2004 TOKYOPOP Inc.
TOKYOPOP

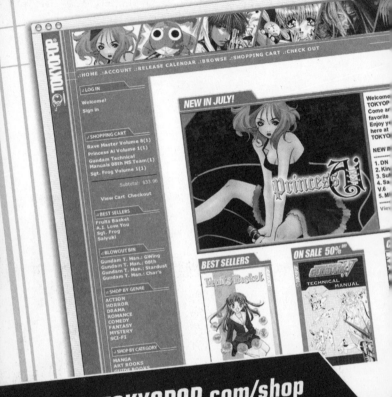
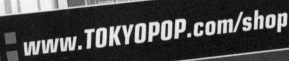

ALSO AVAILABLE FROM ⟦TOKYOPOP⟧®

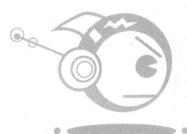

You want it? We got it!
A full range of TOKYOPOP
products are available now at:
www.TOKYOPOP.com/shop

04.23.04T

MANGA

.HACK//LEGEND OF THE TWILIGHT
@LARGE
ABENOBASHI: MAGICAL SHOPPING ARCADE
A.I. LOVE YOU
AI YORI AOSHI
ANGELIC LAYER
ARM OF KANNON
BABY BIRTH
BATTLE ROYALE
BATTLE VIXENS
BRAIN POWERED
BRIGADOON
B'TX
CANDIDATE FOR GODDESS, THE
CARDCAPTOR SAKURA
CARDCAPTOR SAKURA - MASTER OF THE CLOW
CHOBITS
CHRONICLES OF THE CURSED SWORD
CLAMP SCHOOL DETECTIVES
CLOVER
COMIC PARTY
CONFIDENTIAL CONFESSIONS
CORRECTOR YUI
COWBOY BEBOP
COWBOY BEBOP: SHOOTING STAR
CRAZY LOVE STORY
CRESCENT MOON
CROSS
CULDCEPT
CYBORG 009
D•N•ANGEL
DEMON DIARY
DEMON ORORON, THE
DEUS VITAE
DIABOLO
DIGIMON
DIGIMON TAMERS
DIGIMON ZERO TWO
DOLL
DRAGON HUNTER
DRAGON KNIGHTS
DRAGON VOICE
DREAM SAGA
DUKLYON: CLAMP SCHOOL DEFENDERS
EERIE QUEERIE!
ERICA SAKURAZAWA: COLLECTED WORKS
ET CETERA
ETERNITY
EVIL'S RETURN
FAERIES' LANDING
FAKE
FLCL
FLOWER OF THE DEEP SLEEP
FORBIDDEN DANCE
FRUITS BASKET
G GUNDAM

GATEKEEPERS
GETBACKERS
GIRL GOT GAME
GIRLS' EDUCATIONAL CHARTER
GRAVITATION
GTO
GUNDAM BLUE DESTINY
GUNDAM SEED ASTRAY
GUNDAM WING
GUNDAM WING: BATTLEFIELD OF PACIFISTS
GUNDAM WING: ENDLESS WALTZ
GUNDAM WING: THE LAST OUTPOST (G-UNIT)
GUYS' GUIDE TO GIRLS
HANDS OFF!
HAPPY MANIA
HARLEM BEAT
I.N.V.U.
IMMORTAL RAIN
INITIAL D
INSTANT TEEN: JUST ADD NUTS
ISLAND
JING: KING OF BANDITS
JING: KING OF BANDITS - TWILIGHT TALES
JULINE
KARE KANO
KILL ME, KISS ME
KINDAICHI CASE FILES, THE
KING OF HELL
KODOCHA: SANA'S STAGE
LAMENT OF THE LAMB
LEGAL DRUG
LEGEND OF CHUN HYANG, THE
LES BIJOUX
LOVE HINA
LUPIN III
LUPIN III: WORLD'S MOST WANTED
MAGIC KNIGHT RAYEARTH I
MAGIC KNIGHT RAYEARTH II
MAHOROMATIC: AUTOMATIC MAIDEN
MAN OF MANY FACES
MARMALADE BOY
MARS
MARS: HORSE WITH NO NAME
MINK
MIRACLE GIRLS
MIYUKI-CHAN IN WONDERLAND
MODEL
MY LOVE
NECK AND NECK
ONE
ONE I LOVE, THE
PARADISE KISS
PARASYTE
PASSION FRUIT
PEACH GIRL
PEACH GIRL: CHANGE OF HEART
PET SHOP OF HORRORS
PITA-TEN

STOP!

This is the back of the book.
You wouldn't want to spoil a great ending!

This book is printed "manga-style," in the authentic Japanese right-to-left format. Since none of the artwork has been flipped or altered, readers get to experience the story just as the creator intended. You've been asking for it, so TOKYOPOP® delivered: authentic, hot-off-the-press, and far more fun!

DIRECTIONS

If this is your first time reading manga-style, here's a quick guide to help you understand how it works.

It's easy... just start in the top right panel and follow the numbers. Have fun, and look for more 100% authentic manga from TOKYOPOP®!

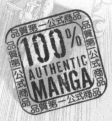

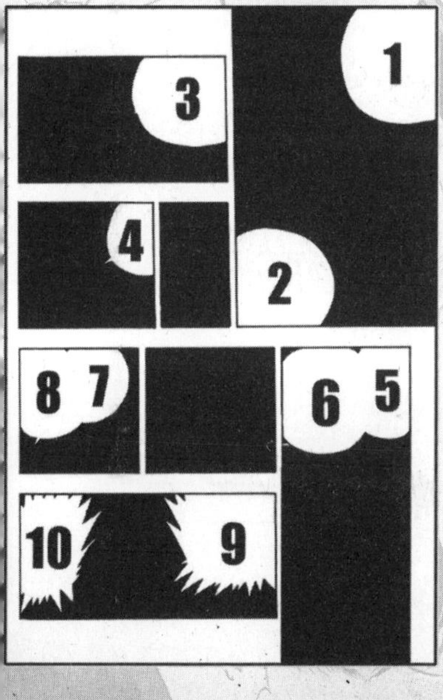